FRENCH
FOR ORAL AND WRITTEN REVIEW

Fifth Edition

FRENCH
FOR ORAL AND WRITTEN REVIEW
Fifth Edition

Charles Carlut   Walter Meiden

THE OHIO STATE UNIVERSITY

THOMSON
™
HEINLE

Australia Canada Mexico Singapore Spain United Kingdom United States

French for Oral and Written Review
Fifth Edition
Carlut/Meiden

Art and Design Supervisor: *Brian Salisbury*
Text and Cover Design: *Brian Salisbury*
Copy Editor: *Melissa M. Gruzs*

Cover photo by Charlie Waite. Courtesy of Tony Stone Worldwide.

Text Printer: *The Maple-Vail Book Manufacturing Group/Binghamton*
Cover Printer: *Coral Graphic Services, Inc.*

Thomson Higher Education
25 Thomson Place
Boston, MA 02210-1202
USA

Printed in the United States of America
17 18 19 20 09 08 07

Library of Congress Catalog Card Number: 92-81578

ISBN-13: 978-0-03-075899-7
ISBN-10: 0-03-075899-8

For more information about our products, contact us at:

Thomson Learning
Academic Resource Center
1-800-423-0563

For permission to use material from this text or product, submit a request online at
http://www.thomsonrights.com

Any additional questions about permissions can be submitted by e-mail to
thomsonrights@thomson.com

Contents

Chapter 9

Demonstratives   119

Chapter 10

Relatives   134

Chapter 11

The Subjunctive   146

Chapter 12

The Article   167

Chapter 13

Indefinite Nouns   184

Exercices d'ensemble 271

To the Teacher

This text is designed to review all the common elements of French grammar, both orally and in written French. To that end it is provided with numerous all-French exercises and English-to-French translations on various phases of the French language and with a set of tapes containing numerous structure drills.

The organization of the chapters

Each chapter deals with a specific grammatical topic. The chapters are divided into short sections, each one of which takes up a particular aspect of the subject under consideration. After one or several sections treating related topics there are written exercises that afford practice on the material of the preceding paragraphs. At the end of the grammatical parts of the chapter are review exercises that give additional practice on the topics taken up in chapter. Each chapter ends with three or four problem words and a verb review.

This type of organization allows for great flexibility : it permits teachers who so desire to assign a limited amount of grammar each day with reading from other texts; it permits those using the book in a pure grammar review course to adjust the number of sections and exercises to the needs of the class; topics can easily be omitted without disturbing the unity of the whole. For those wishing exercises that offer practice on all aspects of a grammatical topic, there are *Exercices d'ensemble* at the end of the book which may be torn out and handed in if the teacher so desires.

The grammar is presented in a sequence designed to make its study graduated in difficulty. The first three chapters take up relatively uncomplicated topics : interrogatives, adjectives, and adverbs. In Chapter 4 the use of most tenses is studied; other aspects of the verb are presented in Chapters 6, 8, 11, and 14, so that not too much material on verbs is taken up consecutively. Since no chapter depends on any preceding one, however, the chapters may be taken up in any order the instructor prefers.

An Answer Key to the text exercises is available to the instructor upon request to the publisher.

The "textes"

Each chapter except the sixth begins with a selection from some twentieth-century author with italicized examples of the grammar presented in the chapter. The sixth includes a number of selections from well-known nineteenth- and twentieth-century authors. Most texts have been slightly modified to make them more readable at the intermediate level and to permit the presentation of the grammatical topics taken up in the chapter. Attention is called to grammatical points by italics. For those who wish, these selections may be used for class discussion in French or for grammatical analysis of the examples they contain.

A list of six questions follows the reading selections. Five of these are based directly on the text. The last question is usually more general.

In the Exercise Manual there are two questions based on each text that suggest a topic of composition or conversation for the students.

The structure drills

Along with the grammar is a set of tapes with a complete set of structure drills dealing with each aspect of the chapter except those that do not lend themselves to oral drill. These drills consist of simple rather than complex sentences so that the students can remember them long enough to repeat them and to internalize the structure. For maximum benefit students should hear these drills but not see them. They should go to the laboratory and listen to and repeat each drill until they can do it automatically and without any hesitation.

A complete tapescript of the structure drills is available to the instructor upon request to the publisher.

The Exercise Manual

A newly formatted Exercise Manual supplements the text. It consists of two parts : 1) written exercises on all phases of French grammar; 2) an outline of the taped structure drills, which gives the directions to each drill and the model sentence preceding each drill. These directions and model sentences are also heard on the tapes.

The written exercises in the Manual are different from those in the text. Many of them encourage the students to show their understanding of grammatical points by completing a statement or answering a question. In certain exercises choices of several possible answers must be made. These all-French exercises provide additional drill on grammatical topics in a somewhat more imaginative form than those in the text. They are designed to add a further dimension to the study of French—an opportunity for personalized work and self-expression.

New vocabulary for the exercises is found in footnotes or in the vocabulary of the text.

Ways in which the book may be adjusted to fit the needs of different types of courses

Where the number of recitations in a course is limited, parts of the book or parts of a chapter may be omitted without affecting the study of the parts that are assigned, for each chapter and each section (with the exception of certain sections in Chapter 11) are independent units.

For the shorter grammar course, the *Problem Words*, the **Exercices d'ensemble** at the end of the book, and Chapter 17 dealing with Problem Prepositions could be omitted at the discretion of the instructor.

Some schools that are on the shorter quarter system take up the majority of the chapters of FRENCH FOR ORAL AND WRITTEN REVIEW in their grammar review course and use the rest of them as the grammatical portion of one or more conversation-composition courses.

For the course where an emphasis on the proper use of words is paramount, the core of the study could be built around the *Problem Words* and, where necessary, certain grammatical sections might be omitted.

Innovations in the fifth edition

1. Texts

All texts have been simplified so that more common words have been substituted in many cases and footnotes have been added. New texts are included for Chapters 5 and 17.

2. Exercises

Certain exercises have been modified.

3. *Exercices Oraux*

After the grammar explanations and written exercises of each chapter there follows an **exercice oral** which the users of the book may do orally. This important feature justifies even more the word "oral" in the title of the book.

4. *Exercices d'Ensemble*

These exercises have been placed on perforated pages at the end of the book. The placement and perforation will enable the students to write out the answers on the pages and to hand them in to the teacher for correction.

To the Student

Grammar is an organized study of the usages of the various aspects of a language. This study usually consists of a series of principles or rules. A rule is simply a statement of usage in a generalized form.

To formulate a rule to govern any French grammatical construction, one looks for as many examples as possible of this construction in both written and spoken French, and, after carefully examining how the construction is expressed, one tells how it is expressed in generalized form.

In a small way, you should try to make your own rules by studying the examples of the constructions found in this book.

To that end, each section of a chapter begins with a question on some type of French construction. There follow examples of the construction. Study these examples carefully in light of the question that precedes them. From what you observe, try to derive a generalization that will answer the question and will then constitute your own rule for that construction. To permit you to check the accuracy of your generalization, the answer to the question follows the examples. This answer is likewise in form of a generalization and constitutes a rule.

It is not necessary to learn these rules verbatim, but it is valuable to understand the principle at hand and to be able to state it accurately and clearly as a generalization.

Naturally, a knowledge of French grammar will not be of much use to you unless you can apply it in speaking and writing. For that reason, each grammatical unit is followed by exercises that will give you the opportunity to apply what you have learned in the unit, and for each chapter there are oral structure drills to be listened to in the laboratory. Practice the oral exercises and work out the written exercises in the Exercise Manual as your teacher directs. If you have access to a laboratory, listen carefully to the tapes and repeat with the indicated changes during the intervals of silence until you can say the pattern in question without hesitation.

But a knowledge of grammatical principles and the ability to apply them will not alone give you a mastery of French, even if you learn to say the patterns automatically. In addition, you must know how to use the common words of the language properly.

In English and French, there are a certain number of common words and ideas that are expressed in several ways in each language, but their usages do not correspond. Let us consider two examples:

Example 1 : The French word temps

Je n'ai pas beaucoup de *temps*.	I don't have much *time*.
Le *temps* est splendide aujourd'hui.	The *weather* is marvelous today.

In each sentence, we find the French word **temps**. But English expresses *temps* of the first sentence by *time*, of the second sentence by *weather*.

Example 2 : The English word time

Je n'ai pas beaucoup de *temps*.	I don't have much *time*.
Je vous ai appelé trois *fois*.	I called you three *times*.
Quelle *heure* est-il ?	What *time* is it ?
Que faites-vous en ce *moment* ?	What are you doing at this *time* ?
A cette *époque*-là, j'étais très jeune.	At that *time* I was very young.
Vous êtes-vous *amusé* à cette soirée ?	*Did you have a good time* at that party ?

In each sentence, English has used the same word—*time*. But French has used successively **temps**, **fois**, **heure**, **moment**, and **époque** to express the English word *time*, and in the last sentence it uses the verb *s'amuser* to convey the idea of *having a good time*.

It is very important to know when French uses one word and when another to express a given English word, for often the various French words that express the same English word cannot be interchanged. To teach you how to deal with such words, there is at the end of each lesson a group of some three or four "problem words." Through the examples, explanations, and exercises, familiarize yourself with all aspects of the words given.

A thorough knowledge of the forms of the most used tenses of regular and irregular verbs is essential if you wish to speak and write French correctly. For that reason, two verbs are reviewed at the end of each lesson. On pages 316–317 you are shown how you can organize your knowledge of the verb by deriving its tenses from the five principal parts.

Permissions

Marcel Aymé : « Le petit coq noir », excerpt from *Les Contes du chat perché*, by permission of Éditions Gallimard.

Simone de Beauvoir : « Pourquoi j'ai choisi d'écrire », excerpt from *Mémoires d'une jeune fille rangée*, by permission of Éditions Gallimard.

Yves Berger : « Christophe Colomb », excerpt from *Le fou d'Amérique*, by permission of Éditions Grasset.

Georges Brassens : « Moi, le plus heureux des Français ? », by permission of *The New York Times*.

Jacques Chessex : « Manifestation au lycée de Lausanne », excerpt from *L'Ogre*, by permission of Éditions Bernard Grasset.

Romain Gary : « Pages blanches », excerpt from *Les Enchanteurs*, by permission of Éditions Gallimard.

René Goscinny : « Une soirée perdue », excerpt from *Interludes*, © by Editions Denoël.

Jacques Lacarrière : « Les chiens », excerpt from *Chemin faisant*, by permission of Librairie Arthème Fayard.

Françoise Mallet-Joris : « Le souterrain », excerpt from *Cordelia*, by permission of Éditions Julliard.

André Maurois : « La maison », excerpt from *Toujours l'inattendu arrive*, © Héritiers Maurois.

Jules Romains : « L'espace d'Amérique », excerpt from *Visite aux Américains*, by permission of Flammarion.

Gabrielle Roy : « Souvenirs du Canada », excerpt from *La Route d'Altamont* (Montréal, Editions H. M. H.; Paris, Éditions Flammarion), © Gabrielle Roy, 1966.

Françoise Sagan : « Émancipation », excerpt from *Bonjour tristesse*, by permission of Éditions Julliard.

Antoine de Saint-Exupéry, « Miracle dans le désert », excerpt from *Terre des hommes*, by permission of Éditions Gallimard.

Jean-Paul Sartre : « Villes d'Amérique », excerpt from *Situations III*, by permission of Éditions Gallimard.

Georges Simenon : Excerpt from *De la Cave au Grenier*, by permission of the author.

Claude Spaak : « Le tableau soluble », excerpt from *Le Pays des miroirs*, by permission of Éditions Julliard.

Acknowledgments

We are very indebted to the many teachers who have made suggestions which have led to the changes in this fifth edition. We are especially grateful to the following, who have made detailed suggestions :

Rose Y. Bugnet, St. George's School, Newport, Rhode Island
Richard J. Bourcier, University of Scranton
Patrice Caux, University of Houston
Weber D. Donaldson, Jr., Tulane University
Bernadette Ernould, The American University
James D. Eakin, Canada College, Redwood City, California
André Gabriel, University of Minnesota, Twin Cities
Dominique Pena-Albinet, University of Kansas

In addition, we wish to thank :

Diane Birckbichler, Ohio State University
Thérèse Bonin, Ohio State University
Andrée Carlut, Columbus, Ohio
Robert Kreiter, University of the Pacific
Jean Perrot, Moulincourt, France
Paul Socken, Waterloo University

We are also indebted to our developmental editor at Harcourt Brace Jovanovich, Mary K. Bridges, and to our project editors, Bill Hardey, Cindy Hannah, and Erica Lazerow; additional thanks are due to Melissa M. Gruzs for copyediting the text.

Charles Carlut
Walter Meiden

Interrogatives

L'auteur, un journaliste, ne se rappelle pas qu'il y a une grève[1] de la télévision et est tout surpris par le silence en rentrant chez lui. Il se demande ce qui arrive. Il devra passer la soirée le mieux possible.

Une soirée perdue

Avant même d'ouvrir la porte de mon appartement, ce soir-là, j'avais été surpris par un grand silence. D'ordinaire, dans l'ascenseur[2], j'entends déjà des bruits de la télévision, paroles ou musiquette[3]. Mais là, rien. *Qu'est-ce que*
5 cela signifiait ? Inquiet, je suis entré chez moi et je suis resté sidéré[4] par l'étrange spectacle qui m'attendait : les lumières étaient allumées dans la salle à manger; c'était pourtant l'heure du dîner. *Qu'est-ce qui* pouvait bien se passer ? J'ai ouvert la porte et ai demandé, angoissé :

—*Qui* est malade ?

10 —Eh bien *quoi*, c'est la grève de la télévision. Tu ne lis pas les journaux ?

C'est vrai, à force[5] d'y collaborer, je les lis de moins en moins. Je ne lis que ce que j'y écris, pour y corriger, trop tard, le passé simple de mes verbes, que je n'ai jamais su utiliser correctement.

—Et alors, ai-je demandé, *qu'*allons-nous faire ?

15 —Nous allons manger, m'a-t-on répondu.

Je n'avais pas faim. L'angoisse obstruait ma gorge, et la lumière crue[6] qui tombait sur les aliments me les rendait étranges, hostiles et peu appétissants. Nous avons commencé le dîner dans un silence inhabituel, troublé seulement par le bruit des fourchettes et des couteaux, qui prenait alors une
20 importance considérable. De temps en temps nous tournions la tête vers le petit écran[7], sombre et muet, témoin mort de notre triste repas...

Nous avons essayé d'engager une conversation. Mais de *quoi* parler ? N'étant pas téléspectateurs passifs, c'est le petit écran, encore, qui nous fournissait des sujets de discussion. Nous étions tous nerveux, comme des
25 intoxiqués privés de drogue...

---

[1]*strike* [2]*elevator* [3]*light music* [4]*flabbergasted* [5]**à force de** *by dint of* [6]*glaring*
[7]*screen* (Examples of the grammar points discussed in the chapters are italicized in the readings.)

Après le dîner, nous sommes allés nous asseoir dans le « living », dans les
30 fauteuils placés autour de la table basse[8] où tout le monde se cogne les ge-
noux[9]. Et justement, ils étaient là, les fauteuils, à leur place, autour de la table
basse, alors que, tous les soirs, ils sont disposés en rang, face au récepteur.
Lequel d'entre nous aurait pensé à autre chose qu'à regarder les programmes ?
Nous nous sommes trouvés mal assis, mal à l'aise, gênés d'être face à face,
35 bêtement...
   —*Qu'est-ce que* nous pourrions bien faire ?
   —On pourrait jouer aux cartes, à n'importe quoi.
   Mais le seul jeu que nous possédons a un défaut. Il manque un coin au valet
de cœur[10]. Or, il n'existe aucun jeu qui puisse se passer de[11] valet de cœur. Nous
40 n'avons donc pas pu jouer aux cartes.
   J'ai essayé de faire des mots croisés, mais j'ai abandonné bien vite devant
un petit champignon de douze lettres. J'ai tourné en rond[12], je me suis cogné
le genou contre la table basse, j'ai allumé et j'ai éteint plusieurs fois le
récepteur; *quel* fol espoir[13] m'animait, vite déçu, évidemment ?
45   —*Qui* veut aller au cinéma ? ai-je demandé. Mais il pleuvait si fort que
ç'aurait été de la folie de sortir.
   Il fallait faire quelque chose, je ne pouvais pas rester comme ça... Mais *que*
faire ?
   Alors, tant pis[14], j'ai pris un livre, et j'ai commencé à lire.

D'après René Goscinny, humoriste, auteur, avec Albert Uderzo, de la
célèbre série *Astérix*, qui raconte l'histoire de France à leur manière.
(« Grève », dans *Interludes*, Denoël, 1966)

Questions

1. Qu'est-ce qui a étonné l'auteur avant même d'entrer dans son appartement ? **2.** Quel étrange spectacle l'y attendait ? **3.** Comment s'est
passé le dîner avec sa famille ? **4.** Quelles distractions aurait-il pu avoir
pour finir la soirée ? **5.** Pourquoi les membres de cette famille—et de tant
d'autres—en sont-ils arrivés à mettre la télévision même pendant les repas ?
6. Comment est-il possible de se défendre contre l'envahissement de la
télévision « obligatoire » ?

NOTE: Voir aussi les deux sujets de composition dans le *Manuel d'exercices.*

---

[8]*coffee table* [9]**tout... genoux** *everybody's knees hit (the table)* [10]**Il manque... cœur.**
A corner is missing from the Jack of Hearts. [11]*do without* [12]*turn around in*
circles [13]*what a foolish hope (that the strike was over)* [14]*so much the worse*

I. INTERROGATIVE ADJECTIVES

An interrogative adjective is one that modifies a noun and asks a question. In English the interrogative adjectives are *which ?* and *what ?*

1. What are the French interrogative adjectives and how are they used before a noun ?

Quel livre lisez-vous ?	*Which* book are you reading ?
Quelles leçons préparent-ils ?	*Which* lessons are they preparing ?
Quel homme ! *Quels* beaux enfants !	*What* a man ! *What* good-looking children !

The interrogative adjectives are:

	Masculine	**Feminine**
Singular	quel	quelle
Plural	quels	quelles

Interrogative adjectives precede their noun and its modifiers directly and agree with it in gender and number.

The interrogative *quel* is also used in an exclamation and is then the equivalent of the English *what... !* or *what a... !*

> **Note:** The interrogative adjective *Whose... ?* is usually expressed by *De qui... ?* Ex.: *De qui* fera-t-il le portrait ? (*Whose* portrait will he do ?)
> In sentences in which the French equivalent of *Whose... ?* is used with a form of *être* it is expressed by *De qui... ?* except when *Whose... ?* indicates ownership. Ex.: *De qui* est-il le fils ? (*Whose* son is he ?) *De qui* est ce livre ? (*Whose* book is that ? = Who is the author of *that book ?*)
> But when *Whose... + être...* indicates possession, *A qui... ?* is used. Ex.: *A qui* est cette radio ? (*Whose* radio is that ?)

2. Under what circumstances is the interrogative *quel* used before some form of the verb *être* ?

Quelle est la route la plus directe ?	*Which* is the shortest route ?
Quels sont ces hommes en noir ?	*Who* are these men in black ?

NOTE: It is also possible to say: **Qui sont ces hommes en noir ?** But by using **Quels** the nature of the question is changed slightly to mean: *What sort of... ?*

The interrogative adjective is used before a form of the verb *être* to ask *which ?* or *which one ?* when there are a number of possible answers and to ask about the nature of a person or thing.

A. Un étudiant de Paris visite une classe de français aux États-Unis. Voici quelques questions que les étudiants de la classe lui ont posées.

1. De ___ ville venez-vous ?   **2.** ___ heure est-il maintenant à Paris ?   **3.** A ___ profession vous préparez-vous ?   **4.** ___ sont vos opinions sur la situation politique actuelle ?   **5.** ___ est votre impression des États-Unis ?   **6.** ___ sport pratiquez-vous ?   **7.** ___ sont les chanteurs de rock américains les plus connus en France ?   **8.** C'est déjà l'heure ? ___ malchance !

B. Traduisez en français.

1. (tu) What dress do you want to buy ?   **2.** Which is the best car this year[1] ?   **3.** What are the real reasons for[2] his departure ?   **4.** (tu) What programs interest you the most ?   **5.** What a catastrophe !   **6.** What is that girl's telephone number[3] ?   **7.** What animals do you prefer, dogs[4] or cats[4] ?

II. INTERROGATIVE PRONOUNS

An interrogative pronoun is one that asks a question. In English, the interrogative pronouns are *who ? whose ? whom ? which ? what ? which one ?*

3. What interrogative pronoun is used in French to refer to persons ?

Qui a ouvert la porte ?	*Who* opened the door ?
Qui avez-vous vu ?	*Whom* did you see ?
Avec qui êtes-vous sorti ?	With *whom* did you go out ?

In French, **qui** is the interrogative pronoun which refers to persons.

NOTE: For **qui** as the subject, the longer form **qui est-ce qui** may be used; for **qui** as the object, the longer form **qui est-ce que** may be used. But

---

[1] **de cette année** [2] **de** [3] **numéro de téléphone** [4] *Use the proper form of the definite article with these nouns.*

since the longer forms sometimes entail a change in word order, students are advised to use the shorter forms for the present.

4. When *qui* is the object of the sentence, what word order is used when the subject of the sentence is a pronoun ? a noun ?

Qui voyez-vous là-bas ?	*Whom* do you see over there ?
Qui Jacques voit-il là-bas ?	*Whom* does Jack see over there ?

When *qui* is the direct object of the sentence, note the word order :

Qui + Verb + Pronoun Subject
Qui + Noun Subject + Verb + Pronoun Subject

5. Which interrogative pronouns are used to refer to things in French ?

Qu'est-ce qui est sur la table ?	*What* is on the table ?
Que faites-vous ?	
Qu'est-ce que vous faites ?	*What* are you doing ?
Avec *quoi* avez-vous ouvert la boîte ?	With *what* did you open the box ?

The four French interrogative pronouns referring to things are ***qu'est-ce qui*, *que*, *qu'est-ce que*,** and ***quoi*.** Their use depends on their function in the sentence.

6. When is *que* and when is *qu'est-ce que* used as the object of the sentence to refer to a thing ?

Que voyez-vous ?	
Qu'est-ce que vous voyez ?	*What* do you see ?
Que fait Françoise ?	
Qu'est-ce que Françoise fait ?	*What* does Frances do ?

When the direct object is a thing, either ***que*** or ***qu'est-ce que*** may be used, but notice the difference in word order:

Que + verb + subject	and	**Qu'est-ce que** + subject + verb

After *que* the verb and subject are inverted; after *qu'est-ce que* there is no inversion.

> NOTE: In a question such as *What is John doing ?*, where the subject of the sentence is a noun and the interrogative object is *what ?*, the above word order must be used. Incorrect is "*Que* + noun subject + verb." WRONG: « Que Jean fait-il là-bas ? » RIGHT: *Que fait Jean là-bas ?* (or) *Qu'est-ce que Jean fait là-bas ?*

7. What are the various uses of the word *quoi* ?

De *quoi* parlez-vous ?	Of *what* are you speaking ?
— Ah ! je vois quelque chose.	"Oh, I see something."
— Quoi ?	"What ?"
Je ne sais pas *quoi* faire.	I don't know *what* to do.
Quoi ! ⎫ **Vous partez ?**	*What !* You're leaving ?
Comment ! ⎭	

The word *quoi* is used to refer to a thing after a preposition, it is used when asking "*What ?*" alone, it is often used instead of *que* before an infinitive, especially in a negative sentence, and it is used to express the exclamatory *What !* The word **Comment !** may also be used to express *What !*

— Allez chercher le dossier du candidat.	"Go and get the candidate's file."
— Comment ?	"What ?"

In English, when we do not hear or do not understand what someone has said, we normally ask: "*What ?*" The French normally ask « **Comment ?** » rather than « **Quoi ?** » under such circumstances. However, « **Quoi ?** » is often used by children who have not yet learned the amenities and by certain uneducated people.

8. How can the interrogative pronouns be presented in graphic tabular form ?

FUNCTION	PERSONS	THINGS
SUBJECT	qui	qu'est-ce qui
OBJECT	qui	⎰que ⎱qu'est-ce que
AFTER PREPOSITION	qui	quoi

C. Brigitte rentre tard le soir. Sa jeune sœur qui partage sa chambre lui pose quelques questions.

1. Avec (whom) es-tu sortie ?   **2.** (Who) te l'a présenté ?   **3.** (What) il fait dans l'affaire de son père ?   **4.** (What) avez-vous fait après le dîner ?   **5.** (What) t'a décidé d'aller voir ce film ?   **6.** (Whom) as-tu vu au café après le cinéma ?   **7.** Tu dis qu'il t'a donné quelque chose. (What) ? **8.** (What) te fait rire ?   **9.** (What) je donnerais pour être à ta place !

D. Traduisez en français.

1. Who took my ballpoint pen ?   **2.** (vous) We don't have any[1] vases. In[2] what do you want to put these flowers ?   **3.** (tu) What makes you smile ?   **4.** (tu) With whom are you going to the party ?   **5.** (vous) What are you going to read ?   **6.** (tu) Whom did your brother meet[3] at the station ? **7.** (vous) He seems[4] angry. What did you say to him ?   **8.** Whom will Maurice and Marie see ?   **9.** (tu) "I'd like to tell you something." "What ?" **10.** (tu) What ! You're crying ?

9. When is a form of *lequel* used to ask *which one* in French ? What are the forms of *lequel* ?

J'ai trois stylos. *Lequel* voulez-vouz ?	I have three pens. *Which one* do you want ?
***Laquelle* de ces personnes parle français ?**	*Which one* of these people speaks French ?

The interrogative *which one*, referring to a definite object already mentioned or mentioned immediately after *which one of*, is expressed by the following:

	MASCULINE	FEMININE
SINGULAR	lequel	laquelle
PLURAL	lesquels	lesquelles

These pronouns contract with *à* and *de* forming : *auquel, auxquels, auxquelles; duquel, desquels, desquelles*.

***Auxquels* de nos amis allons-nous rendre visite ?**	To *which* of our friends are we going to pay a visit ?

---

[1]de   [2]dans   [3]Use a form of **aller chercher**.   [4]Use a form of **avoir l'air**.

> **Duquel de ces romans le
> professeur va-t-il parler
> aujourd'hui ?**

Of which one of these novels
is the professor going to
speak today ?

10. When must *qui, que,* or *qu'est-ce que* be used to express *which one* ?

> **Que préférez-vous, le français
> ou l'italien ?**
> **Qu'est-ce que vous préférez,
> le français ou l'italien ?**

Which one do you prefer,
French or Italian ?

When asking a question about something which as not yet been mentioned, *which one* must be expressed by **qui... ?** (referring to persons), or **que... ?** or **qu'est-ce que... ?** (referring to things) except that *which one of* + THE OBJECT is expressed by a form of **lequel de** + THE OBJECT.

E. *Remplacez les tirets par la forme convenable de* lequel. *Faites les contractions nécessaires.*

1. ___ de vous deux veut bien me prêter sa voiture ?   **2.** —Votre ami est très original. —De ___ parlez-vous ?   **3.** —Voyez-vous ces deux dames ? —___ ?   **4.** ___ de ses filles va épouser Henri ?   **5.** Tous ces exercices sont bons, mais ___ sont les plus utiles ?

F. *Traduisez en français.*

1. These watches are expensive[1]; I do not know which one to buy. **2.** "There will be many difficulties." "Which ones ?"   **3.** Which of the two roads[2] must we take ?   **4.** (*vous*) Which do you prefer, some tea or some coffee ?   **5.** (*tu*) I like Italian films a great deal[3]. Which ones do you prefer ? **6.** (*vous*) There are several programs this afternoon. Which one do you wish to see ?

11. When does French use a variation of *quel est...* to express *what is...* or *what are...* ?

> **Quelle est la capitale de la
> Belgique ?**
> **Quels sont les produits les plus
> importants de ce pays ?**

What is the capital of
Belgium ?
What are the most important
products of that country ?

When *what is... ?* or *what are... ?* asks "*which of a number of possibilities... ?*" French uses *quel est... ?* or some variation of it.

---

[1]*Use a form of* **coûter cher**.   [2]**routes**   [3]*The adverb comes immediately after the verb.*

12. How does French express *what is... ?* or *what are... ?* when asking for a definition ?

Qu'est-ce que la philosophie ?	*What is* philosophy ?
Qu'est-ce que c'est que le marxisme ?	*What is* Marxism ?
Qu'est-ce que c'est que les mathématiques ?	*What is* mathematics ?

When *what is... ?* or *what are... ?* asks for a definition of a word, French uses either *qu'est-ce que... ?* or *qu'est-ce que c'est que... ?* + ARTICLE + *that word*.

G. *Remplacez les tirets par l'équivalent de* what is *ou* what are *selon le cas.*

1. ___ un programmateur ? **2.** ___ les présidents des États-Unis les plus connus ? **3.** ___ la biologie ? **4.** ___ votre fleur favorite ? **5.** ___ le meilleur système de gouvernement ?

H. *Traduisez en français.*

1. What is the longest river in[1] the United States ? **2.** What is the Louvre ? **3.** What are the qualities of a good teacher ? **4.** What is democracy ? **5.** (*vous*) What is the aim of your work ?

EXERCICE ORAL[2]

Vous êtes dans un restaurant avec des amis. L'orchestre joue si fort que la conversation est presque impossible. L'ami qui vous a invité vous parle et vous êtes obligé de lui demander de répéter une partie de la phrase.

Chacune des phrases données dans cet exercice est suivie par un mot ou par quelques mots que vous n'avez pas compris. Posez une question basée sur ces mots en employant l'interrogatif convenable. Employez la forme tu dans vos questions.

EXEMPLE: Juliette vient d'arriver. (Juliette) **Qui vient d'arriver ?**

1. Jean Lacroix doit nous retrouver ici. (Jean Lacroix)

. . . . . .

---

[1]Not « **dans** » [2]For information on this type of exercise, see page xii.

2. L'orage a dû causer son retard. (l'orage)

3. Tiens ! Je vois mon avocat à la table près de l'orchestre. (mon avocat)

4. Il a la réputation d'être très habile. (d'être très habile)

5. Il parle avec une journaliste bien connue. (avec une journaliste bien connue)

6. Nous pourrions commander un apéritif ou un cocktail. (un apéritif ou un cocktail)

7. Ce restaurant est connu pour sa cuisine provinciale. (pour sa cuisine provinciale)

8. Il a d'excellents vins. Moi, je préfère le vin blanc. (le vin blanc)

9. J'aime les pâtisseries, mais les desserts me sont défendus. (les desserts)

10. Je n'ai jamais entendu des musiciens aussi bruyants. (des musiciens aussi bruyants)

11. Excusez-moi. Je vais parler au patron du restaurant. (au patron du restaurant)

See pages 271-314 for the *Exercices d'ensemble*.

· · · · · ·

PROBLEM WORDS

1. actually

(a) When *actually* = *really*

Avez-vous *réellement* vu l'accident ?	} Did you *actually* see the
Avez-vous *vraiment* vu l'accident ?	accident ?

When *actually* means *really*, it may be expressed by **vraiment**, **véritablement**, or **réellement**, depending on the sentence.

(b) When *actually* = *as a matter of fact*

Il caresse vos chats, mais *en fait* il en a peur.	} He pets your cats, but *actually* he is afraid of them.
Il caresse vos chats, mais *à vrai dire*, il en a peur.	

When *actually* means *as a matter of fact* and contradicts what seems to be the case, it may be expressed by **en fait** or **à vrai dire**.

> CAUTION: DO NOT use « actuellement » for *actually*. It means *at present*.

2. advice

(a) How to say *a piece of advice*

Donnez-moi un conseil.	Give me *a piece of advice.*

The singular **un conseil** means *some advice* or *a piece of advice*.

(b) How to say *advice*

J'ai toujours écouté *les conseils* de mon vieux maître.	I always listened to *the advice* of my old teacher.

The word *advice* is expressed by the plural form, **les conseils**.

> CAUTION: The French word **avis** means *opinion*. DO NOT use it for *advice*.

3. again

(a) The prefix **re-** + VERB = *again*

Voulez-vous *relire* cette phrase ?	Will you *read* that sentence *again* ?
Je te *retéléphonerai* tout de suite.	I'll *telephone* you *again* right away.

(b) *encore*, *encore une fois*, *de nouveau*, and *à nouveau* = *again*

Mon avocat m'a parlé *de nouveau* à ce sujet.	My lawyer talked to me about that matter *again*.
Est-ce que nous allons *encore* avoir la guerre ?	Are we going to have war *again* ?
Faites cela *encore une fois*.	Do that *again*.

In affirmative sentences, *again* is expressed by **encore une fois**, and **de nouveau** and only occasionally by **à nouveau** and **encore**.

> NOTE: The word **encore** usually means *still*, although it occasionally means *again*. Ex. : **Je regrette d'être en retard. Je ne croyais pas que vous seriez encore ici.**

(c) In negative sentences **ne... plus** = *not... again*

Je *ne* le ferai *plus*.	I will *not* do it *again*.

In negative sentences, *not... again* is often expressed by **ne... plus**, but it may also be expressed by **ne... re-** + VERB when **re-** + VERB exists.

4. agree

(a) When *agree to* = *consent to*

> **Monsieur Pommier *a consenti à***
>   **venir parler devant notre groupe.** ⎫ Mr. Pommier *has agreed to*
> **Monsieur Pommier *a accepté de*** ⎬ come and speak to our group.
>   **venir parler devant notre groupe.** ⎭

When *agree to* means *consent to*, it may be expressed by **consentir à** or by **accepter de**.

(b) When *agree* = *be in agreement*

> **Ma femme et moi *sommes d'accord*** My wife and I *agree* on the
>   **sur l'éducation de nos enfants.**   upbringing of our children.

When *agree* means *be in agreement*, it may be expressed by **être d'accord**.

(c) When **agreed** = OK

> **— Voulez-vous venir à six heures ?** "Do you want to come at
>   six o'clock ?"
> **— *C'est entendu.***   "Agreed."

The English *agreed*, indicating assent, may be rendered by : **c'est entendu** or : **entendu**, or : **d'accord**, or : **OK**.

(d) When *agree* is a grammatical term

> **L'adjectif *s'accorde* avec le nom** The adjective *agrees* with the
>   **qu'il modifie.**   noun it modifies.

Grammatical agreement is expressed by forms of the verb ***s'accorder***.

> CAUTION: DO NOT use « agréer » for *agree*. French uses **agréer** only in special situations, and it normally means *accept*.

I. Remplacez les mots anglais par leur équivalent français.

1. Jacques est (*again*) en retard.   **2.** Est-ce que le participe passé (*agrees*) avec le sujet ?   **3.** Vos (*advice*) sont toujours très utiles.   **4.** Il paraît que Marcel est (*actually*) très malade.   **5.** Le patron (*agreed to*) vous voir ce soir après cinq heures.   **6.** Je vous répète (*again*) que vous regretterez cette action.   **7.** (*Actually*), j'aimerais mieux ne pas aller voir cet opéra. **8.** (*Advice*) ne servent à rien à la plupart des gens.   **9.** Il faut (*begin the lesson again*).   **10.** —Voulez-vous venir me chercher à midi ? —(*Agreed*). **11.** Je (*agree*) avec vous sur la politique actuelle.

J. Traduisez en français. Attention aux mots en italique.

   1. (*vous*) Copy that exercise *again*.   **2.** He *agreed* to write a letter of recommendation for me.   **3.** (*tu*) Do you want me to give you a good piece of *advice* ?   **4.** John says he works hard, but *actually* he wastes a great deal of time.   **5.** (*vous*) You should follow my *advice*.   **6.** Jack told me that he would *not* smoke *again*.   **7.** (*vous*) We all *agree* that you must leave immediately.   **8.** (*tu*) Did you *actually* go to the movies yesterday evening ?   **9.** (*tu*) Tell me *again* what you want.   **10.** Does the present participle *agree* with the noun it modifies ?   **11.** (*vous*) You don't see them ? Look *again*.

Verb Review

Review the verbs **parler** and **finir** according to the outline on pages 318–319.

Adjectives

L'auteur, un pilote à l'époque héroïque de l'aviation commerciale, est tombé avec son avion dans le désert de Libye. Il raconte ses souffrances physiques et morales. Épuisé[1] par une marche inutile, par la faim, par la soif, par les hallucinations, il va succomber avec son camarade Prévot quand il a soudain le sentiment que quelque chose vient de changer et il reprend espoir.

Miracle dans le désert

Et cependant, qu'ai-je aperçu ? Un souffle d'espoir a passé sur moi comme une risée[2] sur la mer. Quel est le signe qui vient d'alerter mon instinct avant de frapper ma conscience ?

Cette étendue de sable, ces collines et ces *légères* plaques de verdure[3] ne
5 composent plus un paysage mais une scène[4]. Une scène *vide* encore, mais toute *préparée*... Le désert s'est animé. Cette absence, ce silence sont tout à coup plus *émouvants* qu'un tumulte de place *publique*... Que se passe-t-il ?

Nous sommes *sauvés*, il y a des traces dans le sable !... Ah ! nous avions perdu la piste de l'espèce *humaine*, nous étions *seuls* au monde, et voici que
10 nous découvrons, *imprimés* dans le sable, les pieds *miraculeux* de l'homme...

Un Bédouin sur son chameau passe là-bas ! Nous lui tendons les bras, nous appelons mais nos cordes *vocales* sont *sèches*. Il s'éloigne. Peut-être cet homme est-il *seul*. Un démon *cruel* nous l'a montré et le retire[5]... Et nous ne pouvons plus courir...

15 Un *autre* Arabe apparaît de profil sur la dune. Nous hurlons mais tout bas[6]. Alors nous agitons les bras et nous avons l'impression de remplir le ciel de signaux *immenses*. Mais ce Bédouin regarde toujours vers la droite.

Et voici que, sans hâte, il a amorcé un quart de tour[7]. A la seconde *même* où il se présentera de face, tout sera *accompli*. A la seconde *même* où il regardera
20 vers nous il aura déjà effacé[8] en nous la soif, la mort et les mirages. Il a amorcé

---

[1]*exhausted* [2]*light squall* [3]**légères... verdure** *sparse patches of greenery* [4]*(here) stage*
[5]*takes it away* [6]*in a whisper (because of their exhaustion)* [7]**a amorcé... tour** *began a right angle turn toward us* [8]**aura déjà effacé** *will have caused to disappear*

un quart de tour qui, déjà, change le monde. Par un mouvement de son *seul* buste, par la promenade de son *seul* regard[9], il crée la vie, et il me paraît *semblable* à un dieu...

C'est un miracle... Il marche vers nous sur le sable *blond*, comme un dieu 25 sur la mer...

L'Arabe nous a simplement regardés. Il a pressé de ses mains *nos* épaules, et nous lui avons obéi. Nous nous sommes étendus. Il n'y a plus ici ni races ni langages ni divisions... Il y a ce nomade *pauvre* qui a posé sur nos épaules ses mains d'archange[10].

30 Nous avons attendu, le front dans le sable *chaud*. Et maintenant, nous buvons à *plat* ventre[11], la tête *plongée* dans la bassine, comme des veaux[12]...

Toi qui nous sauves, Bédouin de Libye, tu t'effaceras cependant à jamais de ma mémoire. Je ne me souviendrai jamais de ton visage. Tu es l'Homme et tu m'apparais avec le visage de *tous* les hommes à la fois. Tu ne nous as jamais 35 dévisagés[13] et déjà tu nous as reconnus. Tu es le frère *bien-aimé*. Et, à mon tour, je te reconnaîtrai dans tous les hommes.

D'après Antoine de Saint-Exupéry, pilote pionnier de l'aviation civile, pilote de guerre, homme d'action et l'un des écrivains les plus importants de sa génération. (*Terre des hommes*, Gallimard, 1939)

Questions

1. Quelles sont les souffrances de ces hommes tombés depuis trois jours dans le désert ?   **2.** Dans ce paysage inchangé, comment l'aviateur se sent-il soudain rendu à la vie ?   **3.** Qu'est-ce qu'il découvre qui lui rend l'espoir ?   **4.** Qu'est-ce qu'il pense quand le Bédouin qu'il a vu s'éloigne sur son chameau ?   **5.** Pourquoi compare-t-il à un dieu l'Arabe qui se dirige vers lui ?   **6.** On dit parfois que l'homme est un loup pour l'homme. Commentez plutôt ce que dit Saint-Exupéry de ce Bédouin inconnu qui le sauve : « un frère bien-aimé ».

NOTE: Voir aussi les deux sujets de composition dans le *Manuel d'exercices*

An adjective is a word that modifies a noun or pronoun. Ex. : the *green* house; the *tall* tree; the *interesting* letter. The house is *green*. The trees were *tall*. The letter will be *interesting*.

---

[9]**par... regard** *by simply looking toward us*   [10]**archange** [arkāz] *archangel*   [11]**à plat ventre** *lying on our bellies*   [12]**la tête... veaux** *our heads in the pan like calves*   [13]**Tu... dévisagés** *You never looked at us straight in the face*

I. THE FORMATION AND AGREEMENT OF ADJECTIVES

In English, adjectives have one form only. In French, they usually have four forms : masculine singular, feminine singular, masculine plural, feminine plural.

Plural of Adjectives

1. How do most French adjectives form their masculine plural ?

    petit   *petit**s***

Most French adjectives form their masculine plural by adding **-s** to the masculine singular.

2. What about the masculine plural of adjectives whose masculine singular ends in -*s*, -*x*, or -*z* ?

    gris   *gris*
    heureux   *heureux*

Adjectives whose masculine singular ends in **-s**, **-x**, or **-z** do not change in the masculine plural.

3. What about the masculine plural of adjectives whose masculine singular ends in -*eau* ?

    *nouv**eau***   *nouv**eaux***

Adjectives whose masculine singular ends in **-*eau*** add **-x** to form the masculine plural.

4. What about the masculine plural of adjectives whose masculine singular ends in -*al* ?

    *nation**al***   *nation**aux***

Most adjectives whose masculine singular ends in **-*al*** change the **-*al*** to **-*aux*** in the masculine plural.

5. How is the feminine plural of adjectives formed ?

petite	*petites*
grise	*grises*
nouvelle	*nouvelles*
nationale	*nationales*

Feminine adjectives normally form their plural by adding *-s* to the feminine singular form.

A. *Écrivez le pluriel de l'adjectif indiqué.*

1. des chats (gris)　**2.** de (nouveau) livres　**3.** de (grand) événements **4.** des enfants très (gentil)　**5.** deux (gros) garçons　**6.** des personnes (distingué)　**7.** de (riche) touristes　**8.** de (mauvais) livres　**9.** des hôtels (élégant)　**10.** de (vieux) amis　**11.** des amis (loyal)　**12.** de (beau) musées

Feminine of Adjectives

English adjectives have no feminine form. French adjectives have a special feminine form (with few exceptions). The forms of the examples that follow are given in this order : masculine singular; feminine singular; masculine plural; feminine plural.

6. How do most adjectives form their feminine singular and plural ?

petit	*petite*	*petits*	*petites*
fermé	*fermée*	*fermés*	*fermées*

Most adjectives form their feminine singular by adding *-e* to the masculine singular form, and their feminine plural by adding *-s* to the feminine singular form.

7. What about adjectives whose masculine form ends in unaccented *-e* ?

difficile	*difficile*	*difficiles*	*difficiles*

Adjectives whose masculine form ends in unaccented *-e* do not change in the feminine.

8. What about certain adjectives whose masculine form ends in *-e* + CONSONANT ?

prémier	*première*	*premiers*	*premières*
étranger	*étrangère*	*étrangers*	*étrangères*
complet	*complète*	*complets*	*complètes*

Certain adjectives whose masculine form ends in *-e-* + CONSONANT place a grave accent (`) over this *e-* as well as adding the regular *-e* to form the feminine.

9. What about adjectives whose masculine form ends in *-f* ?

actif	*active*	*actifs*	*actives*
neuf	*neuve*	*neufs*	*neuves*

Adjectives whose masculine form ends in *-f* change the *-f* to *-ve* in the feminine.

10. What about adjectives whose masculine form ends in -x ?

nombreux	*nombreuse*	*nombreux*	*nombreuses*
heureux	*heureuse*	*heureux*	*heureuses*

Adjectives whose masculine form ends in *-x* change the *-x* to *-se* in the feminine.

11. What about adjectives whose masculine form ends in *-el, -eil, -ien, -as,* and *-os* ?

quel	*quelle*	*quels*	*quelles*
pareil	*pareille*	*pareils*	*pareilles*
ancien	*ancienne*	*anciens*	*anciennes*
bas	*basse*	*bas*	*basses*
gros	*grosse*	*gros*	*grosses*

Adjectives whose masculine form ends in *-el, -eil, -ien, -as,* and *-os* double the final consonant before adding *-e*.

12. What are the irregular feminine forms of the adjectives *blanc, bon, doux, épais, faux, frais, gentil, grec, long, public,* and *sec* ?

blanc	**blanche**	**blancs**	**blanches**	white
bon	**bonne**	**bons**	**bonnes**	good
doux	**douce**	**doux**	**douces**	soft, sweet
épais	***épaisse***	**épais**	***épaisses***	thick
faux	***fausse***	**faux**	***fausses***	false

frais	*fraîche*	frais	*fraîches*	*fresh*
gentil	*gentille*	gentils	*gentilles*	*nice*
grec	*grecque*	grecs	*grecques*	*Greek*
long	*longue*	longs	*longues*	*long*
public	*publique*	publics	*publiques*	*public*
sec	*sèche*	secs	*sèches*	*dry*

B. *Écrivez la forme féminine de l'adjectif indiqué.*

1. une leçon (difficile)   2. des femmes (actif)   3. la semaine (dernier)
4. deux robes (pareil)   5. une (long) histoire   6. les familles (nombreux)
7. des chaussures (usé)   8. la maison (blanc)   9. des chansons (italien)
10. des années (heureux)   11. une armoire (massif)   12. une nuit (frais)

13. **What are the masculine and feminine singular and plural forms of the adjectives *beau, fou, mou, nouveau*, and when is the second masculine form used ?**

SINGULAR			PLURAL		
MASCULINE					
(BEFORE CONSONANT)	(BEFORE VOWEL)	FEMININE	MASCULINE	FEMININE	
beau	*bel*	*belle*	*beaux*	*belles*	*beautiful*
fou	*fol*	*folle*	*fous*	*folles*	*foolish*
mou	*mol*	*molle*	*mous*	*molles*	*soft*
nouveau	*nouvel*	*nouvelle*	*nouveaux*	*nouvelles*	*new*
vieux	*vieil*	*vieille*	*vieux*	*vieilles*	*old*

Some adjectives have two masculine singular forms, one of which is used when the word it directly precedes begins with a consonant, the other when the word it directly precedes begins with a vowel or a mute *h*. In the plural, they have only one form for the masculine and one for the feminine.

Agreement of Adjectives

14. **How does a French adjective agree with its noun ?**

Je voudrais une petite **voiture. Ces enfants sont vraiment** bruyants.
Avez-vous lu des livres   **Ces chaussures sont** usées.
   intéressants **récemment ?**

In French the adjective agrees in gender and number with the noun it modifies. This is true whether the adjective precedes or follows its noun and also when it is used in the predicate after a form of the verb *être*.

C. Écrivez la forme convenable de l'adjectif indiqué.

1. de (vieux) rues   **2.** la (nouveau) mode   **3.** un très (beau) homme
4. le (nouveau) an   **5.** une vitesse (fou)   **6.** une personne un peu (mou)
7. de (vieux) souvenirs   **8.** les (beau) quartiers   **9.** un (vieux) oncle
10. de (vieux) dames   **11.** un (beau) arbre

II. COMPARISON OF ADJECTIVES

In English, adjectives are compared with *more* or *less* (comparative degree) and *most* and *least* (superlative degree) if they have more than two syllables.

POSITIVE	COMPARATIVE	SUPERLATIVE
beautiful	*more* beautiful	*most* beautiful
interesting	*less* interesting	*least* interesting

French adjectives are compared in somewhat the same way.

15. How are French adjectives compared ?

POSITIVE	COMPARATIVE	SUPERLATIVE
cher	***plus* cher**	***le plus* cher**
difficile	***moins* difficile**	***le moins* difficile**

The comparative form of the French adjective is formed by placing **plus** (*more*) or **moins** (*less*) before the positive form. The superlative form is reached by placing the definite article (**le, la, les**) before the comparative form.

16. How are the adjectives *bon, mauvais,* and *petit* compared ?

POSITIVE	COMPARATIVE	SUPERLATIVE
bon	**meilleur**	**le meilleur**
mauvais	{ **plus mauvais** { **pire**	{ **le plus mauvais** { **le pire**
petit	{ **plus petit** { **moindre**	{ **le plus petit** { **le moindre**

The adjective **bon** is always compared irregularly except with **moins**, the adjectives **mauvais** and **petit** have a regular and irregular comparative form. The form **moindre** is ordinarily used in the superlative and means *slightest*.

17. How is *than* expressed in French ?

Les hivers sont plus froids *que* les autres saisons.

After a comparative, *than* is expressed by **que**.

BUT

Nous avons <u>*plus de*</u> vingt pages à lire.
Vous avez <u>*moins de*</u> dix minutes pour y arriver.

After **plus** and **moins** before a numeral *than* is expressed by **de**.

18. When the superlative form of an adjective follows its noun, what is the sign of the superlative ?

Pour moi le russe est la langue <u>*la* plus *difficile*</u> à apprendre.

When the superlative form of an adjective follows its noun, the definite article must always directly precede **plus** or **moins**.

19. What preposition regularly follows the French superlative ?

La France et l'Allemagne sont les plus grands pays <u>*d'* </u>Europe.	France and Germany are the largest countries *in* Europe.
Quel est le meilleur élève <u>*de*</u> la classe ?	Who is the best pupil *in* the class ?

In English, the superlative is usually followed by *in*. But in French, **de** is regularly used after the superlative.

20. How is the *as... as* comparative expressed in French ?

Jacques est *aussi* consciencieux *que* Paul.	Jacques is *as* conscientious *as* Paul.
Le français n'est *pas aussi* difficile *que* le latin.	French is *not as* hard *as* Latin.

The comparison with *as... as* is called the comparative of equality. In French this comparative is formed with **aussi... que**. In present-day French, the negative is expressed by **pas aussi... que**.

D. *Remplacez les adjectifs indiqués entre parenthèses par le comparatif ou le superlatif de l'adjectif, selon le cas. Faites l'accord de l'adjectif avec le nom.*

1. Robert est l'élève (vif) de la classe.   2. Est-ce que les hommes sont (curieux) que les femmes ?   3. L'étoile du Berger est (brillant) des étoiles. 4. Les automobiles françaises sont (petit) que les américaines.   5. Quels sont les livres (récent) de votre bibliothèque ?   6. Je trouve les poires (savoureux) que les pommes.   7. Mon chien est mon (bon) ami.   8. Le tennis est bien (fatigant) que le ping-pong.   9. Les (beau) années sont souvent celles de la jeunesse.   10. Il travaille plus et pourtant ses résultats sont (mauvais) que l'année dernière.

E. Remplacez les mots anglais par leur équivalent français.

1. Il habite dans la plus belle maison (in) la ville.   2. Je vais vous montrer le timbre le plus rare (in) ma collection.   3. Nous avons moins (than) cent dollars pour faire ce voyage.   4. Qui est plus chargé de responsabilités (than) le président ?   5. Ce chien est (as) dangereux (as) un loup.   6. Les routes sont (as) bonnes en France (as) en Angleterre.   7. Les prix des repas ne sont pas (as) élevés en Espagne (as) en Italie.

F. Traduisez en français.

1. What is the largest city in Canada ?   2. He refuses to read even the most interesting books.   3. I never have more than five dollars with[1] me. 4. He has nothing, but he is as happy as a king.   5. His closest friends do not understand his attitude.   6. A conversation class[2] is too large if there are more than twelve students.   7. (vous) I waited for you more than half an hour.   8. Motorcycles are more dangerous than cars.   9. The shortest answers are sometimes the best.   10. He allows himself to be stopped[3] by the slightest difficulty.   11. The richest people are often the least generous.

III. POSITION OF ADJECTIVES

In English, adjectives precede their nouns. Ex. : *bad* weather, *disagreeable* work.

21. What is the normal position of a descriptive adjective in French ?

Il m'a fait une proposition *intéressante*.
C'est une maison *blanche*.
Quelles sont les couleurs du drapeau *français* ?
Voulez-vous du pain *grillé* ?

---

[1]sur   [2]**classe de conversation**   [3]Use a form of **se laisser arrêter**.

In French, descriptive adjectives normally follow their nouns. They distinguish the object under consideration from others of its kind. Adjectives of color, nationality, and religion and past participles almost always follow their noun.

22. Why are descriptive adjectives sometimes placed before their noun ?

Il a été victime d'un *terrible* accident.
M. Garet est un *excellent* professeur.
Chenonceaux est un *magnifique* château de la Renaissance.
Elle oubliait la *triste* soirée de la veille.

Many descriptive adjectives may precede their noun for stylistic effect. In such cases, the adjective, which usually indicates a quality inherent in the noun, adorns its noun rather than distinguishing it from other objects of its kind.

23. When an adjective has both a literal and a figurative meaning, where is the adjective usually placed to denote its figurative meaning ?

une *porte étroite*   un *lac profond*
une *étroite amitié*   un *profond sentiment*

une *boisson amère*   un *chat maigre*
un *amer reproche*   un *maigre salaire*

Certain adjectives are sometimes placed before and sometimes after their noun. They usually have a literal meaning when they follow their noun and take on a figurative meaning when they precede the noun.

24. What is the meaning of the following adjectives when they precede and when they follow their noun ?

MEANING WHEN PRECEDING NOUN	ADJECTIVE	MEANING WHEN FOLLOWING NOUN
former	**ancien**	*old, ancient*
fine, good (referring to a person)	**brave**	*brave* (but usually the word **courageux** is used instead)
certain (one of many)	**certain**	*certain (sure)*
dear, beloved	**cher**	*dear, expensive*
last (of a series)	**dernier**	*last* (used with time element to indicate the one just passed)

MEANING WHEN PRECEDING NOUN	ADJECTIVE	MEANING WHEN FOLLOWING NOUN
different, various	***différent***	*different (unlike)*
great	***grand***	*tall*[1]
slight	***léger***	*light*
same	***même***	*very*
many different kinds	***nombreux***	*many of the same kind*
poor (unfortunate)	***pauvre***	*poor (not rich) (often used with **très**)*
next (in a series)	***prochain***	*next (used with time element to indicate one about to come)*
own	***propre***	*clean*
darned, confounded	***sacré***[2]	*sacred*
ugly, bad	***sale***	*dirty*
only	***seul***	*alone*
mere	***simple***	*simple in character*
real	***vrai***	*true*

25. What is the position of limiting adjectives in French ?

deux leçons *ces* journaux *son* père
quelles difficultés *plusieurs* personnes *quelques* amis

Numerals, both cardinal and ordinal, as well as demonstrative, interrogative, possessive, and indefinite adjectives regularly precede their noun. These are called LIMITING ADJECTIVES, for they limit the meaning of the noun.

26. What about the position of the short, common descriptive adjectives ?

une *autre* femme un *beau* rêve une *bonne* solution
une *grande* ville un *jeune* enfant une *jolie* maison
une *longue* histoire un *mauvais* tour une *petite* bouche

A number of commonly used short adjectives regularly precede their noun. The most common of these are : ***autre, beau, bon, gentil, grand, gros, haut, jeune, long, mauvais, méchant, meilleur, moindre, nouveau, petit, vieux,*** and ***vilain.***

> NOTE: The superlative of most of these short adjectives is formed by ***le (la, les) + plus +*** ADJECTIVE. The superlative forms of these particular adjectives only may either precede or follow the noun. Ex. : **C'est *la plus longue* rue de la ville.** (or) **C'est la rue *la plus longue* de la ville.**

---

[1]*When* **grand** *follows its noun, it is usually preceded by* **très**. [2]*In the expression* **le sacré cœur,** *the word* **sacré** *means* sacred *even though it precedes its noun.*

G. Mettez l'adjectif à la position convenable, en faisant l'accord de l'adjectif.

1. (rouge) une fleur   **2.** (inestimable) des trésors   **3.** (difficile) une leçon   **4.** (mauvais) une route   **5.** (anglican) l'église   **6.** (gentil) un garçon   **7.** (social) les conflits   **8.** (bruyant) une salle   **9.** (insupportable) des enfants   **10.** (noir) le drapeau   **11.** (usé) des chaussures **12.** (profond) un puits   **13.** (vert) des volets   **14.** (secondaire) les écoles **15.** (indien) des étoffes

H. Traduisez en français. Faites attention à l'accord et à la position de l'adjectif.

1. We saw a terrible[1] accident.   **2.** There are American tourists in every country in[2] the world.   **3.** There is a real hero.   **4.** There are still certain[3] difficulties.   **5.** We want a free country.   **6.** Those fine people don't have any luck.   **7.** It was a somber story.   **8.** High[4] mountains separate those two countries.   **9.** (tu) You always make the same mistakes. **10.** There is a slight difference between those two words.   **11.** (vous) Take[5] a course with that excellent professor.   **12.** Paul has a bad cold.   **13.** I like illustrated magazines.   **14.** (vous) Have you seen those elegant models ?   **15.** I would like a good warm meal.   **16.** That book made a deep impression on the students.   **17.** (vous) Next week you will write your last résumé.

EXERCICE ORAL

Vous racontez votre jeunesse dans le village où vous habitiez.
Répétez chaque phrase en remplaçant l'adjectif donné par celui qui est entre parenthèses. Attention à la forme et à la place de l'adjectif.

EXEMPLE: Les enfants s'amusent dans le bois voisin. (petit)
Les enfants s'amusent dans le *petit* bois.

1. Je suis né dans le petit village de Saint-Martin. (joli)

2. J'y ai passé une enfance agréable. (heureux)

3. Mon père dirigeait une grosse usine. (important)

4. Ma mère s'occupait de l'école maternelle. (enfantin)

---

[1]Consider this as an adjective used to adorn its noun for stylistic effect, as described in §22.   [2]du   [3]Do not use the partitive or any substitute for it here.   [4]Use a form of **haut**. Place de in front of **haut**.   [5]Use a form of **suivre**.

5. Nous habitions dans une grande maison. (ancien)

6. Une rivière tranquille passait près du village. (profond)

7. J'y ai souvent fait des pêches extraordinaires. (sensationnel)

8. Avec mes camarades nous faisions de longues courses dans la campagne. (fatigant)

9. Nous marchions très loin jusqu'à un énorme chêne. (centenaire)

10. Je suis venu plus tard à la ville pour faire des études avancées à la faculté. (supérieur)

11. Quand je peux, je retourne à Saint-Martin pour une bonne réunion avec ma famille. (joyeux)

See pages 271–314 for the *Exercices d'ensemble.*

. . . . . .

PROBLEM WORDS

5. become

(a) When *become* is followed by a NOUN

Jacques *est devenu* <u>officer</u>.   Jack *became* <u>an officer</u>.

The verb *become* is **devenir**, and when a noun follows *become*, the French usually employ a form of **devenir**.

(b) However, when *become* is followed by an ADJECTIVE

Ne *vous fâchez* pas si je vous dis cela.   Don't *become* angry if I tell you that.

Le patron *s'est impatienté* en vous attendant.   The boss *became impatient* while waiting for you.

French often uses the reflexive form of a verb where English uses *become* + ADJECTIVE.

(c) How to express *became* in certain idiomatic expressions

Tout à coup *il a fait* très *chaud*.   Suddenly it *became* very *warm*.

Vers onze heures *j'ai eu* très *sommeil*.   About eleven o'clock I *became* very *sleepy*.

The English *became* + ADJECTIVE is often expressed in French by using the simple past or the compound past of the verb. This is especially true in the case of idiomatic expressions with *avoir* and *faire*.

> CAUTION: Avoid using *devenir* + ADJECTIVE. To express *become* + ADJECTIVE, French occasionally does use *devenir* + ADJECTIVE, but far more often it uses a reflexive verb or a past tense of *avoir* or *être*.

6. better

(a) When *better* is an adjective

Je cherche une *meilleure* solution.   I am looking for a *better* solution.

As an adjective, *better* is normally expressed by *meilleur*.

Ces peintures sont que les autres. } *mieux* / *meilleures*   These paintings are *better* than the others.

However, when the English adjective *better* is to be expressed after a form of *être*, French sometimes uses *mieux*. In such cases, a form of *meilleur* could also be used.

(b) When *better* is an adverb

Jacques lit *mieux* que Jean.   Jack reads *better* than John.

The adverb *better* is expressed by *mieux*.

(c) How to say *much better*

Le livre est *bien meilleur* que le film.
Le livre est *beaucoup mieux* que le film. }   The book is *much better* than the film.

After forms of *être*, *much better* may be expressed by *bien meilleur*, *bien mieux*, and *beaucoup mieux*. But the French do not say « beaucoup meilleur ».

Cet élève comprend { *bien* / *beaucoup* } **mieux l'algèbre maintenant.**   This pupil understands algebra *much better* now.

As an adverb, *much better* is either *beaucoup mieux* or *bien mieux*.

> CAUTION: When expressing *better* in French, determine whether it is used as an adjective or an adverb. Do NOT use « meilleur » as an adverb.

CAUTION: DO NOT use « beaucoup meilleur » for *much better*. This combination does not exist in French.

7. bring

(a) How to say *bring a thing*

Apportez-moi ce livre.   *Bring* me that book.

When it is a question of *bringing a thing,* French usually employs a form of **apporter**.

(b) How to say *bring a person*

Est-ce que je pourrais *amener*   Could I *bring* my husband ?
mon mari ?

When it is a question of *bringing a person,* a form of **amener** is used. But **amener** is also used for taking a person somewhere.

CAUTION: DO NOT use « apporter » when it is a question of bringing a *person*.

8. can

(a) When *can = be able*

Vous ne *pouvez* pas porter cela   You *cannot* carry that all
tout seul. Laissez-moi vous aider.   alone. Let me help you.

The English *can* (= *be able*) is ordinarily expressed by **pouvoir**.

(b) When *can = may*

Vous *pouvez* partir si vous voulez.   You $\begin{cases} can \\ may \end{cases}$ leave if you wish.

Careful speakers of English distinguish between *can* and *may*. In French, the verb **pouvoir** is used for both ideas.

(c) When to use *je peux* and when *je puis*

***Je peux* vous accompagner demain.**   *I can* go with you tomorrow.
***Puis-je* vous voir à huit heures ?**   *Can I* see you at eight o'clock ?

The *je* form of the present tense of **pouvoir** is both **peux** and **puis**. In non-interrogative sentences *je peux* is normally used. When an interrogative sentence has inverted word order, **puis-je** is used, but this form is mainly literary.

(d) When *can* = *know how to*

 Est-ce que Thérèse *sait* conduire?   *Can* Theresa drive ?

When *can* = *know how to*, French often uses a form of ***savoir*** rather than of ***pouvoir***.

I. *Remplacez les mots anglais par leur équivalent français.*

 1. Il a fallu à Georges plusieurs années d'études pour (*become*) pharmacien. **2.** N'hésitez pas à (*bring*) votre frère; nous serons très heureux de faire sa connaissance.   **3.** Les programmes du dimanche sont (*much better*) que ceux de la semaine.   **4.** (*Can*)-vous me dire l'heure ?   **5.** Quand la lumière s'est éteinte, tout le monde (*became frightened*[1]).   **6.** Les résultats de cet étudiant sont (*better*) ce trimestre.   **7.** Finis tes études avant de te marier, ce serait (*much better*).   **8.** (*Can*) -on traverser l'Atlantique en moins de trois heures ?   **9.** On (*becomes tired*) à faire toujours la même chose.   **10.** Claude nous (*brings*) toujours des chocolats quand il vient nous voir.   **11.** François a beaucoup souffert ces derniers jours, mais maintenant il se sent (*better*).   **12.** Les repas dans ce petit bistrot sont (*much better*) que dans les autres restaurants du quartier.

J. *Traduisez en français. Attention aux mots en italique.*

 1. The climate of the Riviera would be *much better* for them.   **2.** (*vous*) *Could* you explain this problem to me ?   **3.** Henry *became* interested in that writer after hearing his lecture[2].   **4.** (*tu*) If these stamps interest you, I'll *bring* you my collection next week.   **5.** The day[3] was warm, but it *became* cold as soon as the sun set.   **6.** (*vous*) *Can* your fiancée play the[4] piano ?   **7.** (*vous*) It is in Paris that you will find the *best* perfumes. **8.** Mr. Borel *became* one of the directors of the company[5].   **9.** *Can* I *bring* my friend Roger to the next meeting of our club ?   **10.** (*vous*) *Bring* me what you have just written.   **11.** (*tu*) *Can* you type on my word processor ?

Verb Review

Review the verbs ***dormir*** and ***perdre*** according to the outline on pages 318–321.

---

[1]Use a form of **avoir peur**.   [2]Not « **lecture** »   [3]**journée**   [4]Not « **le** »   [5]**société**

Adverbs

L'auteur, ayant couché dans la grange de fermiers dans un village au cen-
tre de la France, repart de bon matin pour continuer sa marche de mille
kilomètres à travers le pays. Il parle ici de ses rencontres avec les chiens.

Les chiens

Dès l'entrée du village, le sentier monte au flanc[1] d'une colline en longeant
une longue forêt. Dans un grand pré, juste à côté, une femme garde *tranquille-*
ment ses vaches. Près d'elle un chien au museau[2] noir hésite, hargneux[3] :
qui est cet intrus, ce vagabond, cet homme bon à mordre avec ses mollets[4]
5 bien dodus[5] ? Des chiens, j'en ai vu des centaines au cours de ce voyage. A
l'exception de quelques cas, ces rencontres se placèrent toutes sous le signe
d'une incompréhension totale—et sans doute réciproque. Est-ce le bâton que
je prends *parfois* (*pas toujours d'ailleurs* car il est souvent gênant[6]) ou la seule
vue d'un inconnu qui provoque les chiens? *Généralement,* ils se contentaient
10 de me suivre à distance respectueuse et sans *trop* se mettre sur ma route.
Moi, j'avançais *négligemment* comme si je n'avais *rien* remarqué. Les gens
malins[7]—et ceux qui savent *toujours* tout—vous diront qu'un chien n'attaque
jamais un passant hors de son propre territoire. Erreur. J'en ai fait l'expérience
maintes fois... D'autres vous expliqueront qu'il suffit de *ne pas* avoir peur
15 (*personnellement,* je n'ai *jamais* eu peur, j'ai éprouvé *seulement* des in-
quiétudes pour mes mollets), de les approcher *gentiment,* de leur parler, de les
flatter, d'attendre qu'ils vous flairent[8] et se calment. Erreur *aussi.* Ce n'est *pas*
toujours vrai. Non. Quiconque considère une marche à pied à travers la France
doit savoir que son problème numéro un *ne* sera *ni* la faim, *ni* la soif, *ni* la
20 fatigue, *ni* les entorses[9], *ni* les marécages[10]... mais LES CHIENS. On *n'*imagine
pas le nombre de chiens qu'il peut y avoir en France. J'en ai recontré *partout...*
Il y a quelques jours, je me trouvai sur une route de montagne sur le chemin
d'un chien errant[11] qui décida que je *ne* ferais *pas* un pas *de plus*—et cela dans

---

[1]**monte au flanc** *goes up the side* [2]*snout* [3]*snarling* [4]*calves (of the legs)* [5]*plump*
[6]*bothersome* [7]**les gens malins** *the wise guys* [8]*sniff* [9]*sprains* [10]*marshes* [11]*roaming wild*

un paysage *entièrement* dépourvu de[12] trace d'habitation et d'être humain. Je
25 *ne* sus *que* faire. Impossible d'avancer d'un pas : le fauve l'emboîtait[13]. *De plus*,
c'était un chien-loup, de belle taille, à l'œil rouge et aux aux crocs[14] bien
visibles, si furieux, si hurlant contre moi que je le crus un moment enragé[15].
Il se tenait à un mètre, gueule[16] ouverte, prêt à bondir. *Stoïquement*, je lui
tournai le dos, essayant de continuer ma route. Mais je dus m'arrêter. Je le
30 sentais sur mes mollets, prêt à me mordre. Impossible de continuer *ainsi*... Je
restai au milieu de la route, indécis, dans l'espoir que quelqu'un passerait et
qu'ensemble on trouverait sans doute une solution. Mais *personne ne* se
montra, *aussi* adoptai-je une nouvelle tactique. Je posai mon sac sur la route
lentement, et je m'assis *dessus*. *Puis*, je tendis ma main à l'animal, en lui
35 prodiguant[17] les noms les plus flatteurs (et les moins mérités). Il cessa d'aboyer
un instant, m'observa, *puis* aboya encore plus *fort*. J'insistai. *Alors*, toujours
grognant[18], il s'approcha *lentement*, flaira *longtemps* ma main tendue *puis*
d'un coup partit *droit*[19] dans la direction opposée.

D'après Jacques Lacarrière, grand voyageur, à travers la France comme ici,
et dans le monde méditerranéen, la Grèce notamment, sur laquelle il a
écrit les plus beaux livres. (*Chemin faisant*, Fayard, 1974)

Questions

1. Quels sont les principaux problèmes auxquels l'auteur a dû faire face
dans ses marches à travers le pays ?   **2.** D'après « les gens malins », comment peut-on se débarrasser des chiens qui vous suivent, menaçants ?
3. Racontez la rencontre de l'auteur avec le chien-loup décidé à lui barrer la
route.   **4.** A quelles sortes d'activités physiques se livrent les Américains
qui ne font pas beaucoup de marche ?   **5.** Quelles sont les caractéristiques
des différentes sortes de chiens que vous connaissez ?   **6.** Parlez d'un animal qui vous a intéressé ou amusé dans les dessins animés ou dans les bandes
dessinées.

NOTE: Voir aussi les deux sujets de composition dans le *Manuel d'exercices*.

An adverb is a word that modifies a verb, an adjective, or another adverb.
Ex. : He writes *clearly*. They have a *very* difficult lesson. He speaks *somewhat*
slowly.

---

[12]**dépourvu de** *without*   [13]**le fauve l'emboîtait** *the beast followed step by step*   [14]**crocs**
[kro] *fangs*   [15]*mad, rabid*   [16]*mouth (of an animal)*   [17]**lui prodiguant** *lavishing on him*
[18]*growling*   [19]*straight*

I. FORMATION OF ADVERBS

1. How are adverbs usually formed from adjectives ?

rapide	rapide*ment*	sérieux	sérieuse*ment*
vrai	vrai*ment*	naturel	naturelle*ment*

Many French adverbs are formed by adding **-ment** to the masculine form of adjectives that end in a vowel and to the feminine form of adjectives whose masculine form ends in a consonant.

> NOTE: A certain number of adverbs have an **-é-** before **-ment**. The most common of these are: ***aveuglément, commodément, conformément, énormément, obscurément, précisément, profondément.***
>
> To the adjective **gentil** corresponds the adverb **gentiment**, to **bref** the adverb **brièvement**. The adjective **bon** has not only the very common adverb **bien** (meaning *well*) but also **bonnement** (meaning *simply*), which is normally preceded by **tout**.

A certain number of adjectives do not have a corresponding adverbial form. Such adjectives may be used adverbially in a phrase. For instance, **charmant** and **amusant** have no adverbial form. But one can say : **Elle a agi *d'une façon charmante*. Il a parlé *d'une façon amusante.***

2. How are adverbs formed from adjectives ending in -ant and -ent ?

suffisant	suffis*amment*	récent	réc*emment*

Adjectives in **-ant** and **-ent** usually have adverbial forms in **-amment** and **-emment**. These suffixes are both pronounced [amã].
But the adjective **lent** has the corresponding adverb **lentement**.

3. Which adjectives have irregular adverbial forms ?

bon	*bien*	meilleur	*mieux*	petit	*peu*	mauvais	*mal*

> NOTE 1: The adjective *quick* is most often expressed in French by **rapide**, whereas the adverb *quickly* is rendered in French by **rapidement** and **vite** (« vitement » does not exist) or in certain cases by the popular expression **en vitesse**. The French equivalent of the exclamatory *Quick !* is **Vite !**
>
> NOTE 2: The verb **sentir** (meaning *smell*) is followed by the masculine singular form of an adjective.

Ces fleurs sentent *bon*.	These flowers smell *good*.
Cette potion sent *mauvais*.	This potion smells *bad*.

The verb *se sentir* (meaning *feel*) is modified by an adverb.

Marie se sent *bien*.	Marie feels *good*.
Paul se sent très *mal*.	Paul feels very *bad*.

A. *Écrivez les adverbes qui correspondent aux adjectifs suivants.*

1. clair	**2.** heureux	**3.** rare	**4.** évident	**5.** faux
6. constant	**7.** discret	**8.** patient	**9.** profond	**10.** ardent
11. bruyant	**12.** mauvais	**13.** bon	**14.** tendre	**15.** violent
16. élégant				

II. POSITION OF ADVERBS

4. What is the usual position of the adverb in a sentence with a simple verb ?

Jean sait *aussi* le russe.	John *also* knows Russian.

The adverb usually follows a simple verb directly.

5. What is the position of most common adverbs in sentences with compound tenses ?

Nous avons *beaucoup* travaillé.	We worked *a great deal*.
Il a *bien* compris la phrase.	He understood the sentence *well*.
Vous n'avez pas *encore* remis votre devoir.	You have not *yet* handed in your homework.

In sentences with compound tenses, most common adverbs not ending in **-ment** are placed between the auxiliary verb and the past participle and after **pas**. But sometimes the position of these adverbs is changed because the speaker wishes to stress a certain word. Also, see §7.

> NOTE: When an adverb modifies an infinitive it normally precedes that infinitive. Ex. : **Il faudrait venir sans _trop_ tarder.** You should come without waiting *too long*.) **Alice a pu _beaucoup_ travailler quand il n'y avait personne.** (Alice could work *a great deal* when no one was around.)

6. Where are adverbs ending in -*ment* placed ?

Nous avons soulevé ce piano *facilement*.	We lifted this piano *easily*.
Il a *complètement* oublié mon nom.	He *completely* forgot my name.
Vous avez *probablement* négligé d'envoyer cette lettre.	You *probably* neglected to send this letter.
Évidemment vos amis se sont trompés de route.	*Obviously* your friends took the wrong road.
Nous avons marché *lentement* jusqu'à la poste.	We walked *slowly* up to the post office.

Some adverbs in **-*ment*** come between the auxiliary verb and the past participle, some follow the past participle directly and some follow the noun object of the sentence. Certain adverbs in **-*ment*** may also begin a sentence. The length of the adverb in **-*ment*** does not determine its position in sentences with compound tenses. The position of each adverb in **-*ment*** must be learned.

7. What is the position of adverbs of place and time ?

Paul est venu me voir *hier*.	Paul came to see me *yesterday*.
Aujourd'hui, nous avons parlé avec votre avocat.	*Today* we spoke with your lawyer.
M. Dupont est arrivé *ici* après un long voyage.	Mr. Dupont arrived *here* after a long trip.

The adverbs of time and place **aujourd'hui, hier, demain, autrefois, tôt, tard, ici, là, ailleurs**, and **partout** never come between the auxiliary verb and the past participle. They normally follow the past participle, but not always directly. The adverbs of time **aujourd'hui, hier, demain**, and **autrefois** often begin or end the sentence.

8. When a sentence begins with *peut-être* or *à peine*, what word order follows ?

Peut-être est-il déjà parti. *Peut-être* qu'il est déjà parti. Il est *peut-être* déjà parti.	*Perhaps* he has already left.
A *peine* était-il parti que les autres ont commencé à parler. Il était *à peine* parti que les autres ont commencé à parler.	*Scarcely* had he left when the others began to speak.

After **peut-être** and *à peine* when placed at the beginning of the sentence, the subject and the verb are inverted. After **peut-être** this construction is normally found only in written literary style. In conversational French, the usual word order is **peut-être que** + SUBJECT + VERB.

However, **peut-être** and *à peine* do not have to come at the beginning of the sentence. They often come immediately after a simple verb or after the auxiliary of a compound verb, and in that case the word order is not inverted.

9. What does *aussi* mean when it begins a sentence, and what kind of word order is used in that case ?

Marc est jaloux. *Aussi* a-t-il perdu ses amis.	Mark is jealous. *Therefore* he lost his friends.
Noël approche. *Aussi* Michel est-il très occupé.	Christmas is getting near. *So* Michael is very busy.

When **aussi** has the meaning of *therefore,* it must come first in its clause, and it is usually followed by inverted word order. For that reason, **aussi** meaning *also* must NEVER come first in a sentence.

However, **Aussi...** = *So / Therefore* is literary. To express this idea in conversation, a word such as **Alors** or **Et alors** would be used. Ex. : **Alors il a perdu ses amis**. (So he lost his friends.)

B. *Introduisez les adverbes indiqués pour qu'ils modifient le verbe en italique.*

EXEMPLE: (vite) Il *a fermé* la porte. **Il a <u>vite</u> fermé la porte.**

1. (trop) Il *travaille*; il se rendra malade. **2.** (toujours) Le vice *est* puni et la vertu aussi. (*Flaubert*) **3.** (attentivement) *Avez*-vous *lu* cette page ? **4.** (immédiatement) Pourquoi *est*-il *parti* après la conférence ? **5.** (peut-être) Vous *devriez* voir un docteur. **6.** (déjà) Il *a raconté* cette histoire aux enfants. **7.** (follement) Elle l'*a aimé* dans sa jeunesse. **8.** (continuellement) Le pauvre *se plaint* de ses douleurs. **9.** (à peine) Je *dois* m'en aller; j'*ai* le temps de manger. **10.** (lentement) Ils *se sont promenés* le long de la rivière. **11.** (demain) Je vous *enverrai* la lettre. **12.** (tôt) Marie *est rentrée* à la maison.

C. *Traduisez en français.*

1. (vous) You received him well at your house. **2.** (tu) Have you read a good book recently ? **3.** I often wonder what John was writing. **4.** (vous) You have scarcely arrived, and you already wish to leave. **5.** It

rained so much[1] that I could[2] not come.   **6.** Man always seeks happiness.
7. John is persistent, so[3] he often gets what he wants.   **8.** We haven't
received any news from him[4]; perhaps he is dead.

III. NEGATIVE CONSTRUCTIONS

**10. What is the normal position of *ne... pas* in a negative statement with a
simple verb ?**

Je *ne* parle *pas* allemand.   Paul *ne* le lui montrera *pas*.
Il *ne* me donnera *pas* ce livre.   Ce jeune homme *ne* me
                                          salue *pas*.

The word order is:

$$\text{S\scriptsize UBJECT}^* + \textbf{ne} + \begin{matrix}\text{P\scriptsize RONOUN}\\ \text{O\scriptsize BJECT}^{**}\end{matrix} + \text{V\scriptsize ERB} + \textbf{pas}$$

**11. What is the position of *ne... pas* in interrogative sentences with a
simple verb ?**

Ne parle-t-il *pas* allemand ?   **Paul *ne* le lui montrera-
                                          t-il *pas* ?**

Ne me donnera-t-il *pas* ce livre ?   **Pourquoi ce jeune homme *ne*
                                          vous salue-t-il *pas* ?**

In sentences with a pronoun-subject, negative interrogative order is :

$$\textbf{Ne} + \begin{matrix}\text{P\scriptsize RONOUN}\\ \text{O\scriptsize BJECT}^*\end{matrix} + \text{V\scriptsize ERB} + \begin{matrix}\text{P\scriptsize RONOUN}\\ \text{S\scriptsize UBJECT}\end{matrix} + \textbf{pas} + \text{following words}$$

In questions with a noun-subject, negative interrogative word order is:

$$\begin{matrix}\text{N\scriptsize OUN}\\ \text{S\scriptsize UBJECT}^*\end{matrix} + \textbf{ne} + \begin{matrix}\text{P\scriptsize RONOUN}\\ \text{O\scriptsize BJECT}^{**}\end{matrix} + \text{V\scriptsize ERB} + \begin{matrix}\text{P\scriptsize RONOUN}\\ \text{S\scriptsize UBJECT}\end{matrix} + \textbf{pas} + \text{following words}$$

---

[1]**tellement** [2]Use a form of the passé composé. [3]Write first in conversational, then in
literary, French. [4]*any news from him* **de ses nouvelles** *that is, the subject with all
its modifiers **The pronoun-object comes here if there is one. Many sentences do not
have a pronoun-object.

12. What is the position of *ne... pas* in sentences with compound verbs ?

Je *n'*ai *pas* parlé allemand.

*N'*avez-vous *pas* parlé allemand ?

Il *ne* m'a *pas* donné ce livre.

Paul *ne* le lui a-t-il *pas* montré ?

In sentences with verbs in compound tenses, the auxiliary verb is regarded as the only verb as far as the position of negative words is concerned. In other words, the word order in §§10–11 is followed, but ***pas*** comes directly after the auxiliary verb.

D. Mettez les phrases suivantes au négatif.

1. Je partirai avant son retour.   **2.** Claude lui a donné beaucoup d'argent.   **3.** Êtes-vous allé en Europe l'année dernière ?   **4.** Pourquoi venez-vous me voir ?   **5.** Se décidera-t-il à venir ?   **6.** Les questions politiques m'intéressent.

E. Traduisez en français.

1. This news[1] did not surprise me a great deal.   **2.** Isn't it difficult to learn Arabic ?   **3.** He doesn't go to[2] Florida every winter.   **4.** These events do not worry me.   **5.** (*tu*) Didn't this painter do your portrait ?   **6.** He didn't continue his work.   **7.** (*vous*) Didn't you buy that car last year ?

13. What other negative combinations are there ?

ne...aucun	no, not any	*ne...plus*	no longer, no more
ne...guère	scarcely	*ne...point*	not at all
ne...jamais	never	*ne...que*	only
ne...personne	no one	*ne...rien*	nothing
ne...ni...ni		neither...nor	
ne...pas...non plus		neither, not either	

In addition to ***ne... pas*** these are the negative combinations often used in French.

14. What word order is used with *ne... guère, ne... jamais, ne... plus,* and *ne... point* ?

Je *ne* le vois *jamais.*

*N'*avez-vous *jamais* visité la Suisse ?

---

[1]Use the singular to indicate *piece of news.*   [2]**en**

Il *ne* vient *plus* ici.   **Paul *n'*a-t-il *jamais* vu son**
oncle ?

In all negative sentences, ***ne*** comes exactly where it would if used with ***pas***. (See §§10–12 in this chapter.)

The negatives ***guère***, ***jamais***, ***plus***, and ***point*** follow the same rules for position as ***pas***. (See §§10–12 in this chapter.)

15. What is the word order of *personne* and *rien* in sentences with a simple tense ?

Personne ne viendra.   *Rien ne* le sauvera.
Je *ne* connais *personne* dans   Ces élèves *ne* font *rien*.
  ce quartier.

In sentences with a simple tense, ***personne*** and ***rien*** come where they would in the corresponding English sentence.

> NOTE: The two forms of the negative, **ne... pas**, **ne... jamais**, etc., come to- gether before a present infinitive. Ex : **Nous avons peur de *ne pas* réussir.**

16. Where are *personne* and *rien* placed when they are used as the direct object in sentences with compound tenses ?

Je *n'*ai vu *personne*.   **Ils *n'*ont *rien* compris.**

In sentences with compound tenses, ***personne*** as the direct object follows the past participle; ***rien*** as the direct object comes between the auxiliary verb and the past participle.

17. What is the position of *que* in the *ne... que* (*only*) construction ?

Il *n'*a vu *que* trois élèves.   **Nous *n'*avons écrit *que* dix**
pages.

The ***que*** of the ***ne... que*** construction follows the entire verb, and ***que*** immediately precedes the word or words that it restricts.

18. Where does the negative adjective *aucun* come in a sentence ?

Nous *n'*avons trouvé *aucune* trace   **Aucun étudiant *ne* travaille**
de lui.   **suffisamment.**

The negative ***aucun*** is an adjective and comes directly before its noun. The ***ne*** comes before the verb and before the preceding pronoun-objects if there are any.

19. How is *neither... nor* expressed in French, and what is the position of *ni* ?

Ni **mon chat *ni* mon chien *ne* sont revenus à la maison ce matin.**
Nous *n'*avons trouvé *ni* le journal *ni* la revue dont vous avez parlé.
***N'*avez-vous apporté *ni* papier *ni* stylo pour votre travail ?**

The negative adverbs *ni... ni* precede their nouns immediately. If these nouns are indefinite, they follow *ni... ni* without any article. (See page 189, §9.)

20. When it refers to the subject of the sentence, how is *neither* (*not... either*) expressed in French ?

Je partirai *aussi*.	Je *ne* partirai *pas non plus*.
—Georges travaille beaucoup.	—Georges ne travaille pas beaucoup.
—Nous *aussi*.	—Nous *non plus*.

When the English *neither* (*not...either*) refers to the subject of the sentence and has a negative implication, it is expressed in French by *non plus* and comes at the end of the sentence. In such cases it is the negative of *aussi* (= *too*). When *non plus* ends a sentence with a verb, both *ne* and *pas* are used to make the sentence negative.

21. When negative words are used in a sentence without a verb, what happens to *ne* ?

—Qui a-t-il trouvé ?	—*Personne.*
—Quand le ferez-vous ?	—*Jamais.*
—Puis-je boire du café, docteur ?	—*Non, plus de café.*
—Combien de fautes avez-vous trouvées ?	—*Aucune.*

When negative words are used in a sentence without a verb, the *ne* disappears.

F. *Mettez au négatif le mot en italique. Faites les changements nécessaires dans la phrase.*

Exemple: Je vais au cinéma *quelquefois*. Je **ne** vais ja**mais** au cinéma.

1. —Y allez-vous souvent ? —*Quelquefois*.   **2.** J'ai vu *quelqu'un* dans le jardin.   **3.** —Je *partirai* demain[1]. —Moi *aussi*.   **4.** Il y avait *quelques* indications[2] dans la lettre.   **5.** Laurent a trouvé *quelque chose* sur la

---

[1]Make this sentence negative also.   [2]Put in the singular with the negative.

plage.   **6.** Nous connaissons Mme Dufour *aussi*.   **7.** Jean-Jacques arrive *toujours* en retard.   **8.** *Quelqu'un* est entré dans la chambre de Marguerite.   **9.** Il y avait *quelqu'un* dans mon bureau.   **10.** Ces jeunes garçons ont *des*[1] disques et *des*[1] cassettes.   **11.** *Quelque chose* est arrivé aux voyageurs du vol 907.   **12.** —Qu'est-ce que vous avez fait ce matin ? —*Quelque chose* d'intéressant.

G. Traduisez en français.

1. I like movies[2] very much, but I no longer have the time to[3] go[4].
2. Edward has neither money nor friends.   **3.** "Who knocked at the door ?" "No one."   **4.** In any case, I didn't hear anything.   **5.** —I don't like tea[2], and I don't like coffee[2] either. —Then what do you want ?   **6.** No gift gave[5] me so much pleasure.   **7.** I won't stay in this town any longer. —And I won't either.

EXERCICE ORAL

Un homme vient d'entrer dans un bar quand se produit une bagarre. Coups de poing, chaises et bouteilles cassées. La police arrive sans tarder. Un policier interroge cet homme.

Répondez négativement aux questions par une phrase complète en variant les adverbes négatifs.

EXEMPLE: Qu'est-ce que vous avez fait ? **Je n'ai rien fait.**

1. Avez-vous une pièce d'identité ?

2. Avez-vous déjà été arrêté par la police ?

3. Est-ce que vous venez souvent dans ce bar ?

4. Cela vous amuse de venir dans ces cafés ?

5. Avec qui étiez-vous dans ce bar ?

6. Avez-vous vu un de ces hommes dans le bar commencer la bataille ?

7. Avez-vous un pistolet ou un couteau sur vous ?

8. Qu'est-ce que vous avez bu ?

9. Est-ce que vous avez des parents dans cette ville ?

---

[1]Since **disques** and **cassettes** are indefinite nouns, see page 187, §4.   [2]Use the singular definite article.   [3]*d'*   [4]French says *to go there*.   [5]Use a form of *faire*.

10. Habitez-vous dans cette ville ?

11. Avez-vous du travail ?

See pages 271–314 for the *Exercices d'ensemble.*

. . . . . .

PROBLEM WORDS

9. change

(a) How to say *a change*

Avez-vous remarqué *un changement* en entrant ?	Did you notice *a change* when you came in ?
Ces dernières années il y a eu de grands *changements* dans le monde.	In these last few years there have been great *changes* in the world.

The ordinary French word for *change* is **le changement**.

> CAUTION: Do NOT use « le change » for *change*. The French **le change** is used for financial transactions in expressions such as **le cours du change** (*the rate of exchange*), **l'office des changes** (*office dealing with foreign exchange*), **agent de change** (*stockbroker*), etc.

(b) How to say *small change*

Je n'aime pas avoir toute cette *monnaie* dans ma poche.	I don't like to have all this *change* in my pocket.

When *change* = *small change*, French uses **la monnaie**.

(c) How to say that *someone* or *something changes*

Cécile *a* beaucoup *changé* depuis l'année dernière.	Cecilia *has changed* a great deal since last year.

The English *to change* is expressed by **changer**.

(d) When **changer** has a direct object

J'ai changé mes projets de voyage au dernier moment.	I *changed my travel plans* at the last minute.

The verb **changer** + OBJECT means *to alter something*.

(e) When *changer de* is used

Tous les combien *change*-t-on *de* How often do they *change*
serviettes dans cet hôtel ? *towels* in this hotel ?

The expression *changer de quelque chose* means *to replace things of the same kind.*

(f) When *se changer* is used

Vous êtes tout mouillé; allez vite You're all wet; quick, go and
vous changer. *change your clothes.*

The reflexive *se changer* = *change one's clothes.*

(g) When to use *échanger*

Je voudrais *échanger* ma moto I'd like *to exchange* my motor-
contre une voiture. cycle for a car.

The verb *échanger* means *exchange,* and to *exchange one thing for another* is *échanger une chose contre une autre.*

10. character

(a) How to say *a character* (in a literary work)

Combien de *personnages* y a-t-il How many *characters* are
dans cette pièce ? there in that play ?

A *character* in a literary work is *un personnage.*

(b) How to speak of *a person's character*

Georges est intelligent, mais je George is intelligent, but I
n'aime pas beaucoup son don't care much for his
caractère. *character.*

One's personal attributes or one's *character* is *le caractère.*

> NOTE: The French equivalent of *character* as used in the sentence "He's a
> *character*" is **numéro**, referring to either men or women, and *type* or
> *drôle de type*, referring only to men. Ex. : **C'est un *numéro* ! C'est un**
> *type* ! C'est un *drôle de type* !

> CAUTION: Do NOT use « le caractère » to indicate *a character* in a novel
> or play.

11. day (morning, evening)

(a) The ordinary way of saying *day*

Nous avons passé trois *jours* **à Rome.**	We spent three *days* in Rome.

The common word for *day* is **jour**, for *morning* is **matin**, for *evening* is **soir**.

(b) When the **-ée** forms are used

***Toute la journée* nous avons visité des églises et des musées.**	*The whole day* we visited churches and museums.

The word *la journée* is used to indicate *day* when the speaker wishes to emphasize the duration of the time during the day and what happened during that time. The same distinction applies to *la matinée* and *la soirée*, but *la soirée* has the additional meaning of *evening gathering* or *evening party*.

(c) When *tous les jours* and when *toute la journée* are used

Note the following:

toute la journée = *the whole day*	*tous les jours* = *every day*
toute la matinée = *the whole morning*	*tous les matins* = *every morning*
toute la soirée = *the whole evening*	*tous les soirs* = *every evening*

H. *Remplacez les mots anglais par leur équivalent français dans H et I.*

1. Pierre a cessé de fumer, mais cela influe sur son (*character*). **2.** Il faut comprendre que les gens (*change*). **3.** J'ai peu dormi cette nuit et j'ai eu sommeil (*the whole day*). **4.** Avec quelques (*changes*), notre salle de séjour serait beaucoup mieux. **5.** Pour réussir, une pièce ne doit pas avoir trop de (*characters*). **6.** C'est ennuyeux de (*change clothes*) juste pour leur dire bonjour et au revoir. **7.** En hiver il fait sombre à six heures (*in the*[1] *evening*). **8.** Il serait bon de (*exchange*) nos vues sur la question. **9.** J'ai toujours (*change*) sur moi quand je prends l'autobus.

I.

1. J'ai passé (*the whole evening*) à rédiger cette composition. **2.** Suzanne a la manie de tout (*change*) au dernier moment. **3.** Jean a si mauvais (*character*) qu'on ne peut rien lui dire sans qu'il se fâche. **4.** La traversée en bateau a duré cinq (*days*). **5.** Qu'est-ce qui a pu (*change*) Paul comme

---

[1]*in the* (here) **du**

cela ?   **6.** A midi je prends mon repas au restaurant, (*in the*[1] *evening*) je dîne chez moi.   **7.** Va (*change*) chaussures si tu veux aller à la pêche. **8.** Roland organise (*an evening party*) la semaine prochaine.

J. Traduisez en français. Attention aux mots en italique.

1. I spoke of it to Daniel two *days* ago.   **2.** That author had to make many *changes* in his book in order to have it published[2].   **3.** At Christmas everyone *exchanges* gifts.   **4.** Who are the main *characters* in[3] that play ?   **5.** (*tu*) Where did you spend the *day* ?   **6.** (*vous*) Do you have any *change* to buy a newspaper ?   **7.** Which of Molière's *characters* has become the most famous ?   **8.** The Carrels[4] will come to play bridge tomorrow *evening*.   **9.** Mrs. Doré has *changed* chauffeurs[5] again. **10.** How can a person *change* in that way ?   **11.** I must *change clothes* in order to go out this *evening*.

Verb Review

Review the verbs **recevoir** and **avoir** according to the outline on pages 320–323.

---

[1]*in the* (here) **le**   [2]**le faire publier**   [3]*in* **de**   [4]French proper names do not take an -s in the plural.   [5]Use the singular form.

Use of Tenses

Le petit coq noir est à la recherche du renard[1] qui vient trop souvent rôder autour du poulailler[2] et auquel il veut « donner une leçon ». Pour mieux observer la forêt, il est monté sur un arbre. Le renard l'a vu et arrive au pied de cet arbre.

Le petit coq noir

Le renard regardait le coq perché sur une haute branche et il voulait le manger. Il ne s'en cachait pas[3] du tout.

—Tu ne *sais* pas, dit-il au coq, ce que j'ai appris hier soir en passant sous les fenêtres de la ferme ? J'ai appris que les maîtres allaient te faire cuire[4] dans une
5 sauce au vin pour te servir dimanche prochain au repas de midi. Tu n'*imagines* pas combien l'annonce de cette nouvelle m'a fait de la peine.

—Mon Dieu ! Ils me *feraient* cuire dans une sauce au vin !

—Je ne l'*aurais* pas *cru* si je ne les *avais* pas *entendus* moi-même ! Mais, *sais*-tu ce que tu *feras*, si tu *veux* leur jouer un bon tour[5] ? Tu *descendras* de
10 ton arbre, et moi je te *mangerai*. Alors, eux, ils *seront* bien attrapés[6].

Mais le coq ne voulait pas descendre. Il disait qu'il *aimerait* mieux être mangé par ses maîtres que par le renard.

—Tu en *penseras* ce que tu *voudras*, mais je *préfère* mourir de ma mort naturelle, être mangé par mes maîtres.

15 —Que tu *es* bête ! Mais la mort naturelle, ce n'*est* pas ça du tout !

—Tu ne *sais* pas ce que tu *dis*, renard. Il *faut* bien que les maîtres nous tuent[7] un jour ou l'autre. C'*est* la loi commune. Il n'y *a* personne qui puisse y échapper...

—Mais, coq, suppose que les maîtres ne vous mangent pas... tu *vivrais*
20 toujours, sans inquiétude. C'*est* ce que je voulais te faire comprendre. Tu n'*aurais* pas le souci, au réveil, de te demander si tu ne *serais* pas saigné[8] dans le courant de la journée. Oui, je *sais*, tu *vas* encore me *parler* de tes maîtres. Et si tu n'*avais* pas de maîtres[9] ?

---

[1]*fox* [2]**rôder... poulailler** *prowl around the chicken coop* [3]**ne s'en cachait pas** *made no secret of it* [4]*cook you* [5]**leur... tour** *play a good trick on them* [6]**Ils... attrapés** *that will fix them* [7]**Il faut... tuent** *The masters will have to kill us* [8]*bled* [9]**Et si tu... maîtres ?** *What if you didn't have any masters ?*

—Pas de maîtres ? dit le coq. Et, d'étonnement, il resta le bec ouvert[10].

25   —On *peut* très bien vivre sans maîtres... Moi, je n'ai jamais regretté une seule fois d'être libre ! Et comment le *regretterais*-je ? Si *j'avais accepté* comme toi d'avoir des maîtres, il y a longtemps que je *serais* mangé.

Le coq l'écoutait, et il était perplexe. Il se demandait s'il *serait* vraiment fait pour mener cette vie-là.

30   —Je *vais* y *réfléchir*, dit-il; car, me *vois*-tu errant[11] par les bois à la recherche de ma nourriture ? Je n'*aurais* pas ce beau jabot[12] plein avec lequel tu me *vois* aujourd'hui et je m'*ennuierais* dans cette grande forêt, tout seul de mon espèce[13].

—Mon Dieu, que le souci de la nourriture ne t'occupe pas[14] ! Il *suffit* de se
35   baisser pour trouver les plus délicieux vers de terre[15], et je *connais* des coins d'avoines folles[16] où tu *seras* très heureux. Je *craindrais* plutôt pour toi le désagrément[17] de la solitude. Mais je vois à cela un remède bien simple : décider tous les coqs, toutes les poules du village à suivre ton exemple. La cause *est* si belle qu'elle *intéressera* d'abord, et ton éloquence *fera* le
40   reste. Alors quelle satisfaction pour toi d'avoir guidé ta race vers une existence meilleure. Quelle gloire tu en *auras* ! Et quelle délivrance aussi pour vous tous de mener une vie sans fin, exempte de soucis, dans la verdure[18] et le soleil !

D'après Marcel Aymé. Avec humour et sévérité il a mis dans ses romans et ses pièces ses observations des gens et des mœurs. Conteur, il était le meilleur « fabuliste » moderne. (« Le petit coq noir », dans *Les Contes du chat perché*, Gallimard, 1939)

Questions

1. Qu'est-ce que le renard prétend avoir entendu en passant sous les fenêtres de la ferme ?   **2.** Pourquoi le coq considère-t-il comme la mort naturelle d'être mangé par ses maîtres ?   **3.** Décrivez la vie idyllique que le renard peint au coq si celui-ci veut bien l'écouter et mener une vie libre.   **4.** Quelles autres objections le coq pourrait-il faire au renard sur les dangers de cette vie nouvelle ?   **5.** Quelle est la morale de cette histoire touchant le problème de la liberté et de la destinée ?   **6.** On compare quelquefois les gens à des animaux pour leurs caractéristiques physiques ou morales (un renard, un mouton, etc.). Donnez d'autres exemples.

NOTE: Voir aussi les deux sujets de composition dans le *Manuel d'exercices*.

---

[10]**d'étonnement... ouvert** *in surprise, he stood with his bill open*   [11]*wandering*   [12]*crop (of a bird)*   [13]**tout... espèce** *the only one of my kind*   [14]**que... pas** *don't worry about food*   [15]**vers de terre** *earthworms*   [16]**coins... folles** *patches of wild oats*   [17]*unpleasantness*   [18]**dans la verdure** *in the green meadows*

I. THE PRESENT

1. What use of the simple present tense is exactly the same in French and English ?

Jean *travaille* beaucoup.	John *works* a great deal.
Hélène *lit* un peu tous les jours.	Helen *reads* a little every day.

In both French and English, the SIMPLE PRESENT tense is used to state a general truth.

2. How does French express the English progressive present, that is, the present in -*ing* ?

Jean *travaille* maintenant.	John *is working* now.
Hélène *lit* le journal en ce moment.	Helen *is reading* the newspaper right now.
Je *suis en train de corriger* mes fautes.	I *am correcting* my mistakes.

In general, French expresses the English progressive present by a simple present. But if French wishes to insist on the progressive nature of an action, it then uses a form of *être en train de* + INFINITIVE.

3. When may the French present tense express a future idea ?

Demain nous *partons* pour Paris.	*Tomorrow* we *leave* for Paris.

The present is occasionally used to express an action in the immediate future when some other word in the sentence indicates futurity.

> NOTE: The student should recognize this use of the present for the future but use it very sparingly, for it can be used only in certain cases.

4. When is the present tense used in French to express an action that would be expressed in the present perfect in English ?

Nous *apprenons* le français *depuis* deux ans.	We *have been learning* French *for* two years.
Il y a trois jours *qu'il pleut.*	It *has been raining for* three days.
Voilà un an *que* Marc *habite* ici.	Mark *has been living* here *for* a year.

When an action which began in the past is still continuing in the present, French uses the *present tense* with *depuis, il y a... que, voici... que*, and *voilà... que*. English generally uses the progressive form of the present perfect with *for* to express the same concept.

In this type of sentence, *Il y a... que*, *Voici... que*, and *Voilà... que* normally come at the beginning of the sentence, whereas *depuis* + TIME EXPRESSION usually come at the end of the sentence.

> NOTE 1: But in a negative sentence with *depuis, voici... que, voilà... que*, and *il y a...que*, the passé composé is used because the action does not continue up to the present. Ex. : *Je n'ai pas vu* Guy *depuis* trois jours. (I *haven't seen* Guy *for* three days.) *Voilà* deux mois que Mme Simon *n'a pas payé* son loyer. (Mrs. Simon *hasn't paid* her rent *for* two months.)

> NOTE 2: If an action that is finished took place over a definite period of time in the past, the verb is in the **passé composé** and *for* is expressed by *pendant*. Ex. : **Nous *avons appris* le français *pendant* deux ans. Il *a plu pendant* trois jours.**

A. *Dans cet exercice vous imaginez que vous avez une correspondante en France. Dans cette lettre vous lui parlez de votre maison et de votre famille. Traduisez en français les phrases suivantes, qui sont dans votre lettre.*

1. Our house has several large windows which look out on[1] a beautiful garden.   **2.** We have been living here for[2] many years.   **3.** My grandmother often comes to spend two weeks with us.   **4.** But we haven't seen our grandfather for several months.   **5.** Right now[3] we are painting the house.   **6.** In fact, we have been painting it for[4] a month.   **7.** Unfortunately, it has been raining for[5] several days.   **8.** Because[6] of the rain, we have been shut up[7] in the house since yesterday.   **9.** (*vous*) I am sending you a picture of my family with me on the right.   **10.** This evening, my sister and I will probably go[8] to the movies.

II. THE FUTURE

5. In what two ways does French usually express the future?

Un de ces jours j'*achèterai* un chien.	One of these days *I'll buy* a dog.
Je *vais partir* bientôt pour Rome.	Soon *I'll leave* for Rome.

---

[1]Use a form of **donner sur**.   [2]Use **il y a... que**.   [3]**en ce moment**   [4]Use **voilà... que**.   [5]Use **depuis**.   [6]Not **parce que**.   [7]**enfermés**   [8]Use the present tense here.

French usually expresses the future with the FUTURE TENSE or with the present of ***aller*** + INFINITIVE. This normally parallels English usage, but in certain cases of an immediate future French tends to use ***aller*** + INFINITIVE where English might use the future.

6. When do the French use the future tense where the present would be used in English?

Quand vous *saurez* le français, nous irons en France ensemble.	*When* you *know* French, we'll go to France together.
Dès que je *recevrai* sa lettre, je vous l'enverrai.	*As soon as* I *receive* his letter, I'll send it to you.
Tant que vous *parlerez* ainsi, vous aurez des ennuis.	*As long as* you *speak* this way, you'll have trouble.

In French, the future is used after *quand, lorsque, dès que, aussitôt que,* and *tant que* if the action will take place at some future time. English uses the present in such constructions.

B. *Marc rencontre un ami dans la rue. Il lui parle d'un voyage que lui et un autre ami vont faire en Europe.*

1. (*tu*) I'll tell you about our plans right now. **2.** Soon we'll take[1] a trip abroad. **3.** We'll leave as soon as our passports arrive. **4.** We'll stay in Europe as long as we have money. **5.** (*tu*) When we are in Paris, I'll send you a postcard. **6.** As soon as I have time, I'll visit the Louvre. **7.** As long as there are so many well-known museums in Paris, it will always attract many tourists.

III. THE CONDITIONAL

7. When is the conditional used to indicate a future action ?

Richard croyait que Georges le *ferait*.	Richard thought that George *would do* it.
Je lui ai demandé s'il *partirait* bientôt.	I asked him if he *would leave* soon.

When the main clause of a sentence is in a past tense, the CONDITIONAL is often used in the dependent clause to indicate a future action.

NOTE: English uses the same sort of construction. Compare :

---

[1]Not **prendre**.

| He says he <u>will</u> leave. | He said he <u>would</u> leave. |
| I think it <u>will</u> rain. | I thought it <u>would</u> rain. |

8. How is the conditional used in polite requests or questions ?

| Je **voudrais** un verre d'eau. | I *would like* a glass of water. |
| **Aimeriez**-vous sortir avec moi ? | *Would* you *like* to go out with me ? |

The conditional is sometimes used to soften a statement or question that would be somewhat direct and blunt if stated in the present tense.

> NOTE: Compare the politeness of the above examples with the bluntness of the same sentences stated in the present, e.g., *I want a glass of water. Do you want to go out with me ?*

C. Un jeune homme considère les invitations qu'il a eues et qu'il aura pour la fin de la semaine. Mettez en français les mots entre parenthèses.

1. Monsieur et Madame Payot pensaient que je (*would spend*) la journée chez eux, mais je n'ai pas pu.   **2.** Leur fils Paul m'a dit que je (*would be*) invité à leur soirée samedi.   **3.** J'ai entendu dire qu'ils (*would have*) un orchestre connu.   **4.** Cependant, je (*would have preferred*) aller chez les Rochemont ce jour-là.   **5.** J'ai quand même demandé à Claudine si elle (*would go*) avec moi chez les Payot.   **6.** (*vous*) Si elle ne peut pas, (*would you like*) y aller à ma place ?

IV. THE PLUPERFECT AND RELATED TENSES[1]

9. What is the basic use of the pluperfect ?

| J'*avais fini* mon travail quand Pierre est arrivé. | I *had finished* my work when Peter arrived. |
| Colette *était* déjà *sortie* quand il a commencé à pleuvoir. | Colette *had* already *left* when it began to rain. |

The PLUPERFECT indicates a past action that took place before the beginning of another past action. In most cases, French uses the pluperfect in the same places that English does, but there are two important exceptions, explained below.

---

[1]The uses of the imperfect and the **passé composé** will be taken up in Chapter 6 (pp. 77–82).

Two Cases When the French Pluperfect Is Not Equivalent to the English

10. What tense does French use in cases when an action begins at a certain time in the past and continues until another time in the past ?

Monsieur Lenoir *travaillait depuis* dix ans quand il a découvert ce nouveau procédé.	Mr. Lenoir *had been working for* ten years when he discovered that new process.
Il y avait un an *qu'il apprenait* le français quand il est parti pour l'Afrique.	*He had been learning* French *for* one year when he left for Africa.

When an action that begins in the past and continues up to a certain point in the past is interrupted by another action, stated or implied, the French express the first action by the IMPERFECT with *depuis* or *il y avait... que.* In such cases, English uses the pluperfect and usually the progressive form of the pluperfect.

D. *Remplacez les mots anglais entre parenthèses par l'équivalent français.*

1. Quand nous avons voulu l'acheter, nos voisins (*had sold*) leur auto.   **2.** (*He had been trying*[1] *for a year*) à s'évader quand l'occasion s'est enfin présentée.   **3.** Vous a-t-il demandé où vous (*had found*) le porte-feuille ?   **4.** Nous (*had been reading*) depuis une heure quand quelqu'un a frappé à la porte.   **5.** Il y avait une heure que Julie (*had been*) chez Nicole quand son ami est venu la chercher.   **6.** Jean-Paul (*had found*) une bonne place quand il a dû faire son service militaire.   **7.** Jacques et Paulette (*had been going out*) ensemble depuis trois semaines quand ils ont décidé de se marier.   **8.** Il y avait longtemps qu'il nous (*had been calling*) quand nous l'avons enfin entendu.

11. In French, the pluperfect cannot be used to express the underlined *had finished* in a sentence such as *When I had finished my work yesterday, we went out.* How can such an English pluperfect be expressed in French ?

(a) by the **passé composé** in conversation

Quand j'*ai fini* mon travail hier soir, nous *sommes sortis*.
Dès que Louis *a écrit* la lettre, je l'*ai mise* à la poste.

When a past action introduced by *quand, lorsque, dès que, aussitôt que*, or *après que* immediately precedes a second past action that is in the

---

[1]Use a form of **chercher**.

compound past, the first action may also be expressed by the compound past. The use of the compound past here is not elegant but it is heard. In any case, the first action cannot be in the pluperfect.

(b) by the **passé surcomposé** in conversation

> Quand j'*ai eu fini* mon travail hier soir, nous *sommes sortis*.
> Dès que Louis *a eu écrit* la lettre, il l'*a mise* à la poste.

When a past action introduced by *quand, lorsque, dès que, aussitôt que*, or *après que* immediately precedes a second past action that is in the compound past, the first action is usually in the **passé surcomposé**. It cannot be in the pluperfect.

> NOTE: The **passé surcomposé**, which is relatively infrequent, is formed as follows:

> **Passé surcomposé** = COMPOUND PAST OF AUXILIARY + PAST PARTICIPLE

Reflexive verbs are not used in the **passé surcomposé**.

(c) by the **passé antérieur** in literary French

> Quand j'*eus fini* mon travail, nous *sortîmes*.
> Dès que Louis *eut écrit* la lettre, je la *mis* à la poste.

When a past action introduced by *quand, lorsque, dès que, aussitôt que*, or *après que* immediately precedes a second past action that is in the simple past, the first action must be in the **passé antérieur**. It cannot be in the pluperfect. The **passé antérieur**, which is used only in literary French and generally with *quand, lorsque, dès que, aussitôt que*, and *après que*, is formed as follows:

> **Passé antérieur** = SIMPLE PAST OF AUXILIARY + PAST PARTICIPLE

(d) by *après* + PAST INFINITIVE under certain conditions

> *Quand j'ai eu fini* mon travail hier,   *Après avoir fini* mon travail
> *je suis sorti.*   hier, *je suis sorti.*
> *Après qu'il a eu écrit* la lettre,   *Après avoir écrit* la lettre,
> *Louis l'a mise* à la poste.   *Louis l'a mise* à la poste.

When the subject of a clause beginning with *quand, lorsque*, or *après que* refers to the same person as the subject of the main clause, and when the main clause is in the **passé composé**, then *après* + PAST INFINITIVE may be used instead of a *quand*, *lorsque*, or *après que* clause.

> NOTE: The past infinitive = infinitive of auxiliary verb + past participle
> Ex. : *finir*—avoir fini; *sortir*—être sorti; *se laver*—s'être lavé

E. Remplacez les mots anglais entre parenthèses par l'équivalent français, en employant une des méthodes indiquées ci-dessus pour éviter le plus-que-parfait français dans la proposition subordonnée.

1. Dès que (*I had begun my work*), le téléphone a sonné.   **2.** Quand Michel (*had visited*) le musée, il nous a rejoints au restaurant.   **3.** Dès que nous (*had eaten*), le garçon a débarrassé la table.   **4.** Après que nos nouveaux voisins (*had seen*) notre maison, nous les avons menés au jardin. **5.** Jean a prévenu Marc dès que nous (*had arrived*).

F. Traduisez en français en employant une des méthodes indiquées ci-dessus pour éviter le plus-que-parfait français dans la proposition subordonnée.

1. After I had lost my job, I had[1] to move.   **2.** When I had signed the letter, Maurice mailed it.   **3.** Jack left after he had watched television with us.   **4.** After I had gone to bed, I read for[2] an hour.   **5.** As soon as we heard the news, we telephoned Mr. Lesage[3].

V. THE FUTURE PERFECT

— Things you have to do before a future action

12. What French use of the future perfect corresponds to the English use ?

J'*aurai vu* ton professeur quand tu rentreras.	I *will have seen* your teacher when you get back.

In French, as in English, the FUTURE PERFECT describes an action that will have taken place before another future action.

> NOTE: The FUTURE PERFECT (**futur antérieur**) is made up of the future of the
> AUXILIARY + THE PAST PARTICIPLE of the verb. Ex. : **J'*aurai parlé*, Je *serai*
> *sorti*.**

13. When is the future perfect used in French where the English might use the present perfect ?

Quand Albert *aura écrit* la lettre, je vous la montrerai.	*When* Albert *has written* the letter, I'll show it to you.

---

[1]Use a form of **être obligé de**.   [2]**pendant**   [3]This is an indirect object in French.

The FUTURE PERFECT is used in French with adverbial conjunctions of time such as **quand, lorsque, dès que, aussitôt que**, and **après que** to express an action that will have taken place before another future action. English generally uses the present perfect in such cases.

G. Traduisez en français.

1. (*vous*) That family will have already left when you arrive in Tours. **2.** (*tu*) When you have finished that report, send it to me. **3.** As soon as the children have arrived, we'll go for a walk. **4.** Jack will learn to play[1] the violin after his brother has learned to play[1] the piano. **5.** When I have received my check, I'll cash it immediately. **6.** (*tu*) Come back as soon as you get out of the meeting.

VI. CONDITIONAL SENTENCES

14. What are the most common types of French conditional sentences ?

(a) Si nous *travaillons*, nous *gagnerons* de l'argent.	If we *work*, we *will earn* some money.
(b) Si nous *étions* riches, nous *irions* en France.	If we *were* rich, we *would go* to France.
(c) Si vous *aviez parlé* français, Marie-Claire vous *aurait compris*.	If you *had spoken* French, Marie-Claire *would have understood* you.

Semantically about the present [handwritten annotation]

The three most common tense sequences in conditional sentences are :

SI-(*IF*)-CLAUSE	CONCLUSION
present	future
imperfect	conditional
pluperfect	past conditional

Future impending [handwritten annotation]

H. Remplacez les infinitifs par la forme convenable du verbe.

1. Si Philippe partait, il (falloir) lui demander pourquoi. **2.** Si vous me (poser) la question, je vous aurais répondu. **3.** S'il le faut, nous (se battre). **4.** Je (être) très content si mon frère réussissait. **5.** Si je (savoir)

---

[1]Omit *to play* in translation.

cela, je n'y serais pas allé.   **6.** Je (partir) si vous continuez à me regarder comme cela.   **7.** Si l'auto ne marche pas, nous (prendre) l'autobus. **8.** S'il avait fait beau, nous (aller) vous voir.

I. Traduisez en français.

1. (*tu*) If you do what I tell you, everything will come out all right[1].   **2.** I would be glad if my father could retire[2] next year.   **3.** If I were free, I'd accept their invitation.   **4.** If the professor would speak louder, one could hear what he is saying.   **5.** (*vous*) You would have seen our slides if you had come sooner.   **6.** If I earned more[3], I'd look for a larger apartment. **7.** If I go to Paris now, I will not come back until[4] Easter.   **8.** I would have answered him[5] if I had heard him call.

15. What other tense sequences exist in conditional sentences ?

PRESENT + PRESENT

S'il *pleut*, je *reste* à la maison.   If it *rains*, I *stay* home.

PLUPERFECT + CONDITIONAL

Si nous *avions pris* des précautions,   If we *had taken* precautions,
nous n'*aurions* pas ces ennuis   we *wouldn't have* this
maintenant.   trouble now.

PASSÉ COMPOSÉ + FUTURE

S'ils *ont pris* l'avion, ils *seront*   If they *have taken* the air-
bientôt ici.   plane, they *will* soon
                                             be here.

Almost any tense sequence that is possible in English conditional sentences is also possible in French conditional sentences. However :

Si vous *faites* votre travail, vous   *If* you *will do* your work, you
gagnerez beaucoup d'argent.   *will earn* a lot of money.
Si elle *écoutait* ses parents, elle ne *If* she *would obey* her parents,
sortirait jamais.   she *would* never *go out*.

In French, neither the future nor the conditional can ever be used after *si* when *si* means *if*.

Je ne sais pas si Jean *viendra*.   I don't know *whether* John
                                             will come.

---

[1]come out all right **s'arranger** [2]Use a form of **prendre sa retraite**. [3]**davantage**
[4]**avant** [5]This is an indirect object in French.

When **si** means *whether*, the French future and conditional may follow it.

J. *Traduisez en français.*

1. (*vous*) If you had left earlier, you would already be in Cannes.   **2.** If the children have gone to bed, they must be asleep[1] now.   **3.** If the students spent a lot of money, they always managed to get more[2].   **4.** (*vous*) If you listen carefully, you will be able to follow his thought.   **5.** If he would paint his car, he could keep it another year[3].   **6.** (*vous*) You mustn't hesitate to tell me if you are bored.   **7.** If he has found[4] that out, he must be furious.

EXERCICE ORAL

Voici quelques questions. Répondez à chaque question par une phrase complète. Commencez votre réponse par la proposition qui se trouve après la question. Attention au temps du verbe de votre réponse.

EXEMPLE: Si vous n'aviez pas beaucoup travaillé avant un examen, qu'est-ce qui serait arrivé ? (Si je n'avais pas beaucoup travaillé avant un examen,...)
Si je n'avais pas beaucoup travaillé avant un examen, j'aurais été collé(e).

1. Si vous avez très sommeil, que faites-vous ? (Si j'ai très sommeil,...)

2. Quelle langue auriez-vous parlé si vous aviez passé votre vie à Paris ? (Si j'avais passé ma vie à Paris,...)

3. Si vous tombiez malade, qui consulteriez-vous ? (Si je tombais malade,...)

4. Si le ciel est couvert, quel temps fera-t-il probablement bientôt ? (Si le ciel est couvert,...)

5. S'il se mettait à pleuvoir, qu'est-ce que vous feriez pour ne pas être mouillé ? (S'il se mettait à pleuvoir,...)

6. Si vous n'avez pas d'argent chez vous, où allez-vous en chercher ? (Si je n'ai pas d'argent chez moi,...)

7. Si quelqu'un frappe à la porte, que faites-vous ? (Si quelqu'un frappe à la porte,...)

8. Si vous étiez sorti sans manteau quand il faisait très froid, qu'est-ce que vous auriez attrapé ? (Si j'étais sorti(e) sans manteau quand il faisait très froid,...)

---

[1] *be asleep* **dormir**   [2] *to get more* **pour en avoir davantage**   [3] **encore un an**   [4] Use a form of **apprendre**.

9. Que feriez-vous si vous entendiez quelqu'un qui essayait d'entrer chez vous au milieu de la nuit ? (Si j'entendais quelqu'un qui essayait d'entrer chez moi au milieu de la nuit,...)

10. Si un inconnu vous avait aidé(e) après un accident, qu'est-ce que vous lui auriez dit ? (Si un inconnu m'avait aidé(e) après un accident,...)

See pages 271–314 for the *Exercices d'ensemble*.

. . . . . .

PROBLEM WORDS

12. early

(a) When *early* means *early in a certain period of time.*

Est-ce que vous vous couchez *tôt* ?
Est-ce que vous vous couchez *de bonne heure* ? } Do you go to bed *early* ?
Ne venez pas trop *tôt*. Don't come too *early*.

Both ***tôt*** and ***de bonne heure*** mean *early* in a given period of time.

(b) When *early = ahead of time*

Il y aura beaucoup de monde; il vaut mieux arriver *en avance*. There will be a lot of people there; it is better to arrive *early*.

Early, meaning *ahead of time*, is expressed by ***en avance***, which is the opposite of ***en retard***.

Sometimes ***d'avance*** and ***à l'avance*** are also used to express *early = ahead of time*, but it is rather difficult to indicate just when one of these expressions is used rather than the other.

Prenez vos billets { ***d'avance*** / ***à l'avance*** } **si vous ne voulez pas faire la queue au guichet.** Get your tickets *in advance* if you don't want to stand in line at the ticket window.

13. end

(a) When *end* is the opposite of *beginning*

C'est *la fin* de la leçon. It is *the end* of the lesson.

The word *la fin* means *end* when it implies the opposite of *beginning*.

(b) When *end* means *tip* or *extremity*

Ne touchez pas *le bout* de ce fil.	Don't touch *the end* of this wire.
Il y a un cinéma au *bout* de la rue.	There is a movie theater at *the end* of the street.

French uses *le bout* to express *end* meaning *tip* or *extremity*.

(c) How to say *at the end of* + PERIOD OF TIME

***A la fin du mois* il ne me reste jamais rien.**	*At the end of the month* I don't ever have anything left.
***Au bout de trois mois* M. Roux a donné sa démission.**	*At the end of three months* Mr. Roux resigned.
***Au bout de quelques semaines* j'en ai eu assez.**	*At the end of a few weeks* I had enough (of it).

French expresses *at the end of the* + PERIOD OF TIME by *à la fin de* + DEFINITE ARTICLE + PERIOD OF TIME. On the other hand, when the period of time is accompanied by a numeral or by some other adjective indicating quantity, *au bout de...* is used.

14. escape

(a) When *escape* means *avoid*

La criminel a réussi à *èchapper à* la police.	The criminal succeeded in *escaping* the police.

The non-reflexive form *échapper à* is used to indicate that one has avoided or escaped someone or something that one has not yet confronted.

(b) When *escape* means *get out of*

Ce voleur réussit toujours à *s'échapper de* prison.	That thief always succeeds in *escaping from* prison.

The reflexive form *s'échapper de* is used to indicate that one has succeeded in getting away from a person or thing that one has confronted.

In the first example, the thief evaded the police, therefore, never came in contact with them, whereas in the second he was in prison and got out of it.

15. every

(a) How to express *every* by **chaque**

Chaque fois que je vois Paul, il me parle de ses ennuis.	*Every* time I see Paul, he talks to me of his troubles.

The adjective **chaque** means *every* or *each*.

(b) How to express *every* by **tous les...**

Tous les matins nous sortons de bonne heure et tous les soirs nous rentrons tard.	*Every morning* we leave early and *every evening* we return home late.

The English *every* is frequently expressed by **tous les** + UNIT OF TIME (**toutes les** + UNIT OF TIME). This formula is more common with units of time than **chaque**, although **chaque** is not incorrect.

(c) How to say *everyone*

Tout le monde est parti.	*Everyone* has left.

The pronoun *everyone* is expressed by **tout le monde**, which is singular and which must be followed by a singular verb.

CAUTION: DO NOT use a plural verb after **tout le monde**.

(d) How to say *everything*

Tout est perdu.	*Everything* is lost.
J'ai tout oublié.	I've forgotten *everything*.

The pronoun *everything* is expressed by **tout**. In the compound tenses, **tout** comes between the auxiliary and the past participle.

(e) How to say *everything that*

Tout ce qui est sur la table est à Jean.	*Everything that* is on the table is John's.
Donnez-moi tout ce que vous pouvez.	Give me *everything that* you can.

In French, *everything* used as the subject of its clause = **tout ce qui**; *everything* used as the object of its clause = **tout ce que**.

CAUTION: The indefinite *ce* must come between **tout** and the relative pronoun. DO NOT write « tout qui » or « tout que ».

K. Remplacez les mots anglais par leur équivalent français.

1. Sauve qui peut ! Un lion (*has escaped from*) sa cage.   **2.** Il me reste tant de travail à faire que je n'en vois pas (*the end*).   **3.** Je préfère travailler le soir; je n'aime pas me lever (*early*).   **6.** Voilà la carte; commande (*everything that*) tu veux.   **5.** (*Everyone laughed*) quand Pierre a raconté ses aventures.   **6.** (*At the end*) du deuxième acte, la situation semblait inextricable.   **7.** Jacques fait une période militaire (*every summer*). **8.** Nous avons eu de la chance de (*escape*) cette épidémie.

L. Remplacez les mots anglais par leur équivalent français.

1. (*Everything that*) vous dites est très juste.   **2.** Vous arrivez trop (*early*), Jacques n'est pas encore rentré.   **3.** —Où se trouve le bureau de tabac ? —(*At the end*) de la rue, à droite.   **4.** Il y aura un cadeau pour (*every*) invité.   **5.** Saluez (*everyone*) de ma part.   **6.** Il vaudrait mieux arriver (*early*) au théâtre; sinon, nous ne trouverons plus de places.   **7.** Leurs enfants aiment (*everything that*) fait du bruit.

M. Traduisez en français. Attention aux mots en italique.

1. Nicole likes *everything that* is beautiful.   **2.** The airplane will not wait for us; it is better to arrive *early* than to be[1] late.   **3.** At the *end* of the book I finally understood what the author meant.   **4.** *Every* time that he gets angry, he regrets it.   **5.** We are invited for seven o'clock; we must not arrive too *early*.   **6.** If I am caught[2], I'll do *everything* to[3] *escape*.   **7.** At the *end* of two weeks at the university, Jack dropped two courses.   **8.** Paul and Anne-Marie see each other *every* day.   **9.** She is hurt[4] because they put her at the *end* of the table.   **10.** *Everyone* knows that.   **11.** That teacher is remarkable; he knows absolutely *everything*.   **12.** Is *everyone* there ? **13.** (*vous*) I don't know how you can *escape* his anger.   **14.** I heard *everything*[5].

Verb Review

Review the verbs *être* and *aller* according to the outline on pages 322–325.

---

[1]**que d'être** [2]**pris** [3]**pour** [4]**vexée** [5]In French, this word does not come at the end of the sentence.

Personal Pronouns

Un Français vient en Amérique et tombe amoureux de Luronne, une belle Indienne, qui évoque pour lui l'histoire de son pays.

Christophe Colomb

—*Vous m*'avez raconté l'arrivée des Indiens en Amérique. Mais, pour *moi*, le destin du monde ne commence pas avec *eux* mais avec Christophe Colomb. *Vous me* comprenez, n'est-ce pas ? Parlons de *lui*.

—Comme beaucoup d'explorateurs, *il* veut trouver, pour toucher aux Indes,
5 au Japon, à la Chine une route par "l'Océan de l'Ouest", plus courte que celle que prennent les Portugais qui longent[1] de près la côte de l'Afrique. Le 17 avril 1492 le roi et la reine d'Espagne, Ferdinand et Isabelle, *lui* accordent leur aide. *Il* part de Palos, au Portugal, pour changer la forme et le destin du monde.

Pouvez-*vous* imaginer, comme *moi*, les trois navires avec leurs quatre-
10 vingt-cinq matelots[2] ? *Ils* sont violents, superstitieux, toujours prêts à *se* mutiner. Colomb tient deux comptabilités[3] des distances parcourues, l'une pour *lui-même* et, pour ses marins l'autre, pour qu'*ils* ne s'effraient[4] pas de naviguer si loin des terres. *Il* a dû *leur* promettre, une fois, de s'en retourner si après trois jours la terre n'apparaissait pas. Mais enfin, la nuit du 9 octobre
15 est pleine de cris d'oiseaux migrateurs !... Et le 12 Colomb découvre la terre. C'est un grand enthousiasme. Quant à *lui*, désormais[5] immortel, *il nous* dit que Dieu *l*'a choisi pour découvrir ce passage.

Il cherche tout de suite à reconnaître le Japon avec ses palais à toits d'or[6] et la Chine décrite par Marco Polo qui a passé seize ans dans ce pays. Mais *il* est
20 arrivé dans une île des Bahamas qui ne *leur* ressemble pas !

Colomb voit pour la première fois des "Indiens". Ne *vous* étonnez pas de ce nom puisqu'*il* croit avoir touché aux Indes. C'est une tribu de Taïnos. D'abord effrayés, *ils* reviennent sur la plage et crient leur joie. Colomb et ses hommes descendent à terre, chargés de mille choses qu'*ils* vont donner aux Indiens ou
25 échanger avec *eux*. Ce qui *le* frappe est leur beauté et leur gentillesse[7]. *Il*

---

[1]*hug* [2]*sailors* [3]*ways of measuring* [4]*become frightened* [5]*from now on* [6]**palais...**
d'or *palaces with golden roofs* [7]*graciousness*

écrit : « Ces hommes et ces femmes sont nus, jeunes, bien faits, avec des yeux très beaux et très grands. » Et encore : « *Ils* sont doux, *nous* invitent à partager tout ce qu'*ils* ont et montrent autant d'amour que s'*ils* donnaient en même temps leur coeur. » *Il* admire aussi la belle nature. A Haïti, à Cuba, *il* croit avoir
30 trouvé quelques régions "du paradis". Pourtant, *il* ne rêve que de découvrir des mines d'or.

    —Cela n'est pas bon signe. *Nous* devrions *nous* arrêter sur ces images idylliques, *vous* et *moi*.

    —*Il* faut pourtant bien continuer. Après avoir construit un petit fort avec les
35 débris[8] de la Santa Maria, convaincu qu'*il* avait découvert les Indes, *il* rentre en Espagne où *il* sera reçu avec de grands honneurs. Mais voici ce qu'*il* écrit aux souverains : « *Je* ramènerai[9] plus tard des Indiens... Ces gens sont bons à être commandés, à ce qu'on *leur* apprenne à se vêtir[10] et à adopter nos coutumes... *Il* serait facile de *les* convertir et de *les* faire travailler pour nous. »
40 Toute l'histoire des rapports entre les peuples, les hommes, est là, dès 1492, dont on peut souffrir, mourir aussi bien encore aujourd'hui.

    Christophe Colomb reviendra en effet, mais hélas, le héros que nous avons tant aimé dans son premier voyage est devenu un chercheur d'or, un chasseur d'esclaves[11], un administrateur tyrannique des pays où *il* aborde[12]...

    D'après Yves Berger, éminent essayiste, romancier, auteur notamment de livres enthousiastes sur l'Amérique. (*Le Fou d'Amérique*, Grasset, 1976)

Questions

    1. Que cherchaient avec passion les nombreux navigateurs à l'époque de Christophe Colomb ?   **2.** Quels étaient les dangers de l'expédition de Colomb ?   **3.** Quels sont les signes annonciateurs de la terre pour les marins ?   **4.** Comment décrit-il les Indiens d'une part, les îles où il a abordé d'autre part ?   **5.** Pourquoi les choses changent-elles si vite après des débuts idylliques ?   **6.** Que veut dire l'auteur à propos de la lettre aux souverains sur les Indiens : « Toute l'histoire des rapports entre les peuples, les hommes, est là, dès 1492 » ?

    Note: Voir aussi les deux sujets de composition dans le *Manuel d'exercices*.

    A pronoun is a word that takes the place of a noun. The subject pronouns are : *I, you, he, she, it, we,* and *they*; the object pronouns are : *me, you, him, her, it, us,* and *them*.

---

[8]*remnants*   [9]*bring back*   [10]*put on clothes*   [11]**chasseur d'esclaves** *hunter of slaves*
[12]*lands*

I. OBJECT PRONOUNS AND THEIR USES

1. What are the direct object pronouns ?

Jean *me* voit.
Jacques *la* vend.
Je *l'*achète.

Louise *nous* appelle.
Mes amis *vous* connaissent.
Nous *les* trouverons.

The direct object pronouns are :

me	*me*	**nous**	*us*
te	*you*	**vous**	*you*
le	{ *him, it*	**les**	*them*
la	*her, it*		

NOTE: When the forms *me, te, se, le,* or *la* precede a verb beginning with a vowel or a mute *h*, they elide, becoming *m', t', s',* or *l'*.

2. What are the indirect object pronouns ?

Gilbert *me* montre sa voiture.
Jacques *te* parlera demain.
Anne *lui* explique la leçon.

Brigitte *nous* téléphonera.
Gérard *vous* indiquera la route.
Vous *leur* obéirez.

The indirect object pronouns are :

me	*to me*	**nous**	*to us*
te	*to you*	**vous**	*to you*
lui	{ *to him*	**leur**	*to them*
	to her		

The reflexive pronoun *se* may be either a direct or an indirect object and means : (to) *himself, herself, itself, themselves, oneself.* As a reciprocal pronoun, *se* means (to) *each other.*

A. *Un directeur de journal intervient dans les relations difficiles de deux de ses amis, Paul et Henri. Remplacez les tirets par un pronom qui convient au sens.*

1. Entrez donc, Henri, vous ne _____ dérangez pas.   **2.** En fait, je voulais _____ voir.   **3.** Dites-moi ce que Paul _____ a fait.
4. Vous ne cessez pas de _____ provoquer.   **5.** Qu'est-ce qui s'est passé

de si grave entre _____ deux ? **6.** Est-ce la critique que vous avez faite de son livre *Premier amour* qui _____ a fâché ? **7.** Paul était ici tout à l'heure mais il est parti avant que j'aie pu _____ parler. **8.** J'aurais voulu _____ dire de se joindre à _____. **9.** Mais je vais _____ inviter ensemble chez moi et vous pourriez _____ expliquer votre point de vue, à _____ et à _____. **10.** Nous dînerons et vous pourriez _____ réconcilier. **11.** Cela _____ ferait très plaisir car j'ai beaucoup d'estime pour _____ deux.

B. Traduisez en français.

1. (*tu*) Do you like spring ? Yes, I prefer it to the other seasons. **2.** (*vous*) My sons have arrived. I will ask them if they know your children and if they saw them on the way. **3.** We'll tell them to[1] write him at once. **4.** (*vous*) I will give you that magazine.

3. When is *y* used as the place pronoun *there*, and when is the adverb *là* used ?

—Allez-vous à Paris ? —J'y vais demain.
—Je vais en classe. —Y serez-vous à neuf heures ?
—Où est Georges ? —Il est *là*, derrière vous.

The pronoun *y* is used to express *there* when the place has been previously mentioned. The adverb *là* points out *where*, usually when the place has not been previously mentioned.

4. When is *en* used as a pronoun object instead of *le, la,* and *les* ?

Il **voit** *sa soeur* souvent.	He sees *his sister* often.
Il *la* **voit** souvent.	He sees *her* often.
Il **achète** *des fleurs* chaque semaine.	He buys *some flowers* every week.
Il *en* **achète** chaque semaine.	He buys *some* every week.
Il a **retrouvé** *trois amis* au café.	He found *three friends* in the café.
Il *en* **a retrouvé** trois au café.	He found three *of them* in the café.

The pronoun *en* replaces a noun object when that object is indefinite in nature. A noun object is indefinite when it is modified by a partitive construction, by a numeral, by adverbs of quantity, etc.

For practical purposes, one can say that *en* is used whenever in the English sentence the pronoun object is rendered by *some*, by *of it*, or by *of them*.

---

[1] de

C. *Remplacez les tirets par* le, la, les, y, *ou* en, *selon le cas.*

1. —Comment trouvez-vous sa maison ?   —Je _____ trouve superbe.
2. —Voyez-vous des taxis dans la rue ? —Oui, nous _____ voyons deux.
3. —Combien d'enfants ont-ils ? —Ils _____ ont cinq.   **4.** —Il est parti pour Bordeaux. —Qu'est-ce qu'il va _____ faire ?   **5.** —Combien de courses avez-vous à faire ? —Nous _____ avons beaucoup.   **6.** — Georges a-t-il un but dans la vie ? —Oui, il _____ a même plusieurs.   **7.** —Vous me dites que vous allez en France. _____ allez-vous bientôt ?   **8.** —Connaissez-vous cette pauvre femme ? —Oui, et je _____ plains.

D. *Traduisez en français.*

1. I have many friends and I see them every week.   **2.** (*vous*) I would like to spend a few days in the country. Do you want to go there with me ? **3.** (*tu*) Do you want some tea ? Yes, I'll take some.   **4.** When will he arrive in Paris ? He has already arrived there.   **5.** (*vous*) How many brothers do you have ? I have two[1].   **6.** (*tu*) Are there many students in your class ? Yes, there are many[2].   **7.** The telephone book is there on the desk.

II. POSITION OF OBJECT PRONOUNS

5. Where do object pronouns come in relation to the verb ?

Je *le* donne à Jean.	**Je ne *la* vois pas.**	**Donnez-*le* à Marc.**
Il *en* a trouvé.	**Ne *me le* dites pas.**	**Allez-*y*.**

Pronoun objects come immediately before the verb except in the affirmative imperative, in which case they follow the verb and are appended to it by a hyphen.

6. Where do object pronouns come when the sentence contains an auxiliary verb followed by an infinitive ?

Jacques veut *vous* voir.	**Qui peut *me le* dire ?**
Vous devez *en* chercher.	**Nous commencerons à *le* faire.**
Qui a refusé de *lui* parler ?	**Ils vont *y* aller.**

When there is a pronoun object in a sentence that has a verb followed by an infinitive, the pronoun object normally precedes the infinitive. This is because, in most cases, it is the infinitive that governs the pronoun object.

---

[1]In French, one must say *two of them*.   [2]In French, one must say *many of them*.

NOTE: When the auxiliary verb governs a pronoun object, that pronoun object precedes it. Ex. : **Je *l'*ai laissé partir. *Vous* a-t-il vu sortir ?**

7. Where do *y* and *en* come in relation to other pronoun objects ?

**Je *lui en* ai donné.   Donnez-*lui-en*.   Il *y en* a dans le couloir.
Il *vous en* a montré.   Montrez-*m'en* trois.   Donnez-*leur-en*.**

The pronouns *y* and *en* follow all other object pronouns and *y* always precedes *en*.

8. What is the order of pronoun objects other than *y* and *en* ?

**Georges *me le* montre.   Montrez-*le-moi*.
Ils *nous les* expliquent.   Expliquez-*les-nous*.**

When there are two object pronouns other than *y* or *en*, the *l*-form comes nearest the verb.

Je *le lui* indique.   Indiquez-*la-leur*.

When there are two *l*-forms, they come in alphabetical order, that is, **le, la,** and **les** always precede **lui** and **leur**.

E. Remplacez les expressions en italique par des pronoms compléments.

1. —Expliquera-t-il aux élèves la théorie de l'évolution ? —Non, il n'expliquera pas *aux élèves la théorie de l'évolution.*   **2.** —Portez ce paquet à mon cousin. —Je porterai *ce paquet à votre cousin* quand j'aurai le temps.   **3.** —Êtes-vous allé voir ce film ? —Oui, je suis allé voir *ce film.*   **4.** —Voulez-vous montrer vos tableaux à notre ami ? —Oui, je veux bien montrer *mes tableaux à notre ami.*   **5.** —Prêtez-moi les notes de votre cours. —Je vous rendrai *les notes* la semaine prochaine.   **6.** —Donnez ce dossier au directeur. —Je donnerai *ce dossier au directeur.*   **7.** —Puis-je demander des renseignements à cet agent ? —Oui, bien sûr, vous pouvez demander *des renseignements à cet agent.*   **8.** —Ne voulez-vous pas raconter votre accident à ces journalistes ? —Non, je ne veux pas raconter *cet accident aux journalistes.*   **9.** —Voulez-vous m'acheter un magazine ? —Oui, je vous achèterai un magazine.   **10.** Les enfants aiment les jouets à Noël, mais il ne faut pas donner *aux enfants* trop *de jouets.*

F. Traduisez en français.

1. (*tu*) Here are some oranges. If you see your brother, give him some.
2. (*vous*) Your first French class[1] must have been[2] interesting. Describe it

---

[1] **classe de français**   [2] **a dû être**

to us.   **3.** (*tu*) I have two dictionaries. I will bring them to you tomorrow.
4. (*vous*) Where are your magazines ? Show them to him at once.   **5.** (*vous*)
Did you hear the news[1] ? Do not tell it to them.   **6.** She spoke of it to
him.   **7.** (*tu*) Those rules are difficult. The teacher will explain them to you
tomorrow.   **8.** (*vous*) You have grapefruit[2] ? Send me some this afternoon.
9. (*vous*) Do you have that article ? Do you want to read it to me ?
10. (*vous*) Give it to us tomorrow.   **11.** (*tu*) Do you know[3] any good jokes ?
Tell us some.

III. DISJUNCTIVE PRONOUNS

9. What are the disjunctive pronouns ?

moi	*me*	**nous**	*us*
toi	*you*	**vous**	*you*
lui	*him*	**eux**	*them (m.)*
elle	*her*	**elles**	*them (f.)*
	soi	*oneself*	

10. What are the seven most common uses of the disjunctive pronouns ?

The disjunctive pronoun is always used in an emphatic position.

(a) **Nous sommes allés en France avec *eux*.**

The disjunctive pronoun is used after prepositions.

(b) **Jean et *lui* sont partis ce matin.**
   ***Eux* et *moi* avons l'intention de la voir.**
   Vous les avez vus les deux, Maurice et *lui* ?

The disjunctive pronoun is used as part of a compound subject or object.

(c) ***Moi*, je vais y aller.**
   ***Lui*, il n'en sait rien.**
   ***Eux* seuls peuvent le faire.**

The disjunctive pronoun is used to emphasize the subject of the sentence
or when the subject is separated from the verb.

---

[1] Use the singular form.   [2] The French word for *grapefruit* is plural as used here.   [3] Use a
form of **connaître**.

(d) **Mes frères sont plus grands**   Je suis aussi intelligent qu'*eux*.
    que *moi*.

    Vous parlez mieux que *lui*.   Vous êtes aussi riche qu'*elle*.

The disjunctive pronoun is used after ***que*** meaning *as* or *than* in comparisons.

(e) **C'est *moi*.**   **C'est *lui*.**   ~~C'est~~   } *eux*.
                                 Ce sont

The disjunctive is used after ***ce*** + a form of the verb ***être***.

(f) —**Qui est là ?**   —**Qui partira le premier ?**
    —***Lui*.**   —***Toi*.**

The disjunctive is used alone in answer to questions.

(g) ***moi*-même**   ***lui*-même**   ***eux*-mêmes**   ***soi*-même**

The disjunctive is used when compounded with ***-même*** (*self*).

11. When is *soi* ordinarily used as a disjunctive ?

    Là, on ne pense qu'à *soi*.   **Il est si bon de rester chez *soi*.**
    Chacun travaille pour *soi*.   **Il ne faut pas être trop content**
    La télévision en *soi* n'est pas   **de *soi*.**
    mauvaise.   **Ça va de *soi*.**

The disjunctive ***soi*** is most often used after a preposition in a sentence where an indefinite subject such as *on* or ***chacun*,** or one introduced by an impersonal expression, is its antecedent and in the fixed expressions ***en soi*** and ***de soi*.**

G. *Remplacez le mot anglais par le pronom disjoint convenable.*

1. Je crois qu'ils finiront par se marier, (*she*) et Pierre.   **2.** Regardez ce que cet enfant a fabriqué (*himself*).   **3.** Pierre va aller avec (*me*) au bureau.   **4.** (*As for me*), maintenant, je m'en moque[1].   **5.** Ah ! qu'on est bien chez (*oneself*[2]).   **6.** —Les voilà. —Qui ? —(*They*).   **7.** Tu es ingrat après tout ce qu'ils ont fait pour (*you*).   **8.** Chacun parle pour (*himself*). **9.** (*You*), tu as toujours eu de la chance !   **10.** Vous pouvez continuer sans

---

[1]In this sense, the expression means : *I don't care.* [2]French tends not to use the **-même** form unless it is absolutely needed for clarity.

(*me*).   **11.** C'est (*he*) qui m'a raconté votre aventure.   **12.** —Qui a cassé le vase ? —Ce n'est pas (*I*).   **13.** Est-ce qu'elle est aussi amusante que (*he*) ?   **14.** Dans un moment de danger, pense-t-on à (*oneself*) ?

H. Traduisez en français.

1. (*vous*) Would you like to work for him ?   **2.** He and his friend can go to the movies this evening.   **3.** I found out[1] this news[2] through them. **4.** (*tu*) You must do your exercises yourself.   **5.** They[3] are the ones who are happy at[4] his return.   **6.** (*vous*) You have a better car than he.   **7.** Who will go to that meeting ? She and I.   **8.** He is much more patient than they.

12. What pronoun construction replaces *de* + NOUN ?

(a) when the noun is a person

Je parle *de ma sœur.*	**Je parle *d'elle.***
Il se souvient *de son grand-père.*	**Il se souvient *de lui.***
J'ai besoin *d'amis.*	**J'*en* ai besoin.**

In general, one may say that *de* + NOUN (person) is replaced by *de* + DISJUNC-TIVE PRONOUN. However, *en* sometimes replaces this construction, especially when the person in question is indefinite.

(b) when the noun is a thing

Je parle *de mon travail.*	**J'*en* parle.**
Il se souvient *de ses voyages.*	**Il s'*en* souvient.**
Ils ont besoin *d'argent.*	**Ils *en* ont besoin.**

The construction *de* + NOUN (thing) is regularly replaced by *en*.

13. What pronoun construction replaces *à* + NOUN ?

(a) when the noun is a person after verbs that take an indirect object

Jacques a raconté son accident à *l'agent.*	**Jacques *lui* a raconté son accident.**
Vous ressemblez *à vos frères.*	**Vous *leur* ressemblez.**
Ils obéissent *à leur mère.*	**Ils *lui* obéissent.**

When *à* + NOUN (person) follows a non-reflexive verb that takes an indirect object, the construction is replaced by the indirect object pronouns. In French, in addition to the common verbs such as **dire, raconter, demander**, etc., a

---

[1]Use a form of **apprendre**.   [2]Use the singular noun.   [3]lit. : *It is they who*   [4]**contents de**

number of other verbs such as **obéir à, ressembler à**, and **plaire à** take an indirect object.

(b) When the noun is a person after reflexive verbs and after certain non-reflexive verbs that are followed by *à* but do not take an indirect object

Je m'intéresse *à cet enfant.*	**Je m'intéresse** *à lui.*
Nous pensons *à Marie.*	**Nous pensons** *à elle.*
Faites attention *aux pickpockets.*	**Faites attention** *à eux.*

When *à* + NOUN (person) follows any reflexive verb and certain other verbs, the most common of which are **penser à** and **faire attention à**, the construction is replaced by *à* + DISJUNCTIVE PRONOUN.

(c) when the noun is a thing

Je réponds *à la lettre.*	**J'y réponds.**
Nous pensons *à nos problèmes.*	**Nous y pensons.**
Qui s'intéresse *aux sports* ?	**Qui s'y intéresse** ?

When *à* + NOUN (thing) follows a verb, it is generally replaced by **y**.

I. Remplacez l'expression en italique par le pronom convenable.

1. La police s'est emparée *de ces terroristes.*   **2.** Nous ressemblons *à nos parents.*   **3.** Je me chargerai *de ce problème.*   **4.** Croyez-vous *à cette histoire* ?   **5.** Essayez de ne plus penser *à ces imbéciles.*   **6.** Je m'intéresse beaucoup *à la politique.*   **7.** A-t-on besoin *d'argent* pour s'amuser ?
8. Ne vous adressez pas *à cet homme.*   **9.** Il a dit *à sa mère* ce qu'il voulait.   **10.** Obéissez *aux agents.*   **11.** Nous avons parlé *de vos camarades.*   **12.** Vous souvenez-vous *de ce monsieur* ?   **13.** Je me souviens bien *de ma première moto.*   **14.** Ne vous fiez pas *à ces statistiques.*
15. Faites attention *au signal.*   **16.** Faites attention *à ces gens.*

J. Un jeune homme parle à un ami de la rencontre qu'il a faite d'une connaissance commune ancienne. Traduisez en français, employant tu *pour* vous.

1. This morning I met Claude Delame in[1] the Latin Quarter. Do you remember him ?   **2.** We had lunch at Dupont's with a girlfriend who was with him and we talked about you.   **3.** He asked why you hadn't written him since we left the university.   **4.** He had the luck to find a position as a teacher.   **5.** He had been a candidate at several schools, but this school answered him right away.   **6.** He has many pupils but he takes an interest in[2] each one of them.   **7.** He spoke to me of his parents, of his father in

---

[1]**au**   [2]a form of **s'intéresser à**

particular, whom Claude must obey even today. **8.** His girlfriend is a pretty redhead, a little strange, but one quickly gets used to her. **9.** Would you like to invite them with us some evening ?

EXERCICE ORAL

Michel rentre à la maison. Sa sœur lui pose des questions sur sa matinée.

Vous êtes Michel. Répondez affirmativement aux questions de votre sœur avec une phrase complète en employant des pronoms personnels.

1. Es-tu allé à la bibliothèque ce matin ?

2. Y avait-il beaucoup de monde ?

3. As-tu retrouvé des amis ?

4. As-tu vu notre ami Jacques ?

5. As-tu parlé à Jacques ?

6. As-tu rendu à Jacques l'argent que tu lui avais emprunté ?

7. T'a-t-il remercié ?

8. As-tu trouvé de nouveaux livres à la bibliothèque ?

9. Es-tu sorti de la bibliothèque avec tes amis ?

10. Es-tu allé à la poste avec Pierre ?

11. Après, es-tu allé à la cafétéria avec Louise ?

See pages 271–314 for the *Exercices d'ensemble.*

. . . .

PROBLEM WORDS

16. expect

(a) How to say *expect a person* or *a material thing*

J'*attends* **ma femme demain.**	I *expect* my wife tomorrow.
Nous *attendons* **une augmentation le mois prochain.**	We *expect* a raise next month.

The non-reflexive *attendre* may mean *expect* when it is followed by a direct object that is either *a person* or *a material thing*.

(b) How to say *expect an event* or *some other immaterial thing*

Nous *nous attendons* à une belle surprise.	We *are expecting* a great surprise.
Je ne m'attendais pas à **vous voir.**	I *did not expect* to see you.

The reflexive *s'attendre à* is often the equivalent of *to expect* followed by an event or some other immaterial thing.

(c) How to say *expect that* + CLAUSE

Jacques *s'attend à ce que nous venions*.	Jack *expects us to come*.

The expression *s'attendre à ce que* + SUBJUNCTIVE is the equivalent of *expect that* + CLAUSE.

(d) When *expect to* = *intend to*

Nous *comptons* le voir cet après-midi.	We *expect to* see him this afternoon.
J'ai l'intention de lire cet article.	I *expect to* read that article.

When *expect to* = *intend to*, French may express it by **compter** + INFINITIVE or **avoir l'intention de** + INFINITIVE.

(e) How to say : *What do you expect ? What do you expect me to... ?*

Que *voulez-vous*, il est si jeune !	*What do you expect*, he is so young !
Où *veut-il* que j'aille ?	*Where does he expect* me to go ?

When *expect* is used to ask a question with a shrug of the shoulders and implies inevitability, the French often use a form of **vouloir** as in the above examples.

17. fail

(a) How to say *to fail to do something*

Il *ne s'est pas arrêté* au feu rouge.	He *failed to stop* at the red light.

The French have no special way of expressing *to fail to do something*. They simply use the negative form of the main verb.

(b) How to say *not to fail to do something*

*Ne **manquez pas de** nous **écrire** dès votre arrivée.*	*Don't fail to write* us as soon as you arrive.

To express *not to fail to do something*, use the negative of **manquer de** + INFINITIVE.

Notice that the affirmative of **manquer de** has another meaning, as for example : *J'ai manqué de tomber* = *I almost fell*. One can equally well express this sentence by *J'ai manqué tomber* and *J'ai failli tomber*.

(c) How to say *fail an examination* or *a course*

Jean-Pierre *a échoué à* son examen de biologie. ⎫
Jean-Pierre *n'a pas réussi à* son examen de biologie. ⎬ Jean-Pierre *failed* his biology test.
Jean-Pierre *a raté* son examen de biologie. ⎭

The English *to fail an examination* is **échouer à un examen** or, familiarly, **rater un examen**; and *fail a course* is **échouer à un cours**. But one can also say **ne pas réussir, ne pas être reçu**, or **être collé à un examen**.

(d) How to say *to fail someone in a course*

Ce professeur *colle* rarement ses élèves.	That teacher rarely *fails his pupils.*

To express the English *to fail someone*, the expression **coller quelqu'un** is used colloquially. More formal but not so common are : **refuser quelqu'un, ne pas recevoir quelqu'un**, and **faire échouer quelqu'un**.

> CAUTION: DO NOT say « échouer quelqu'un ». Say either **refuser quelqu'un**, **faire échouer quelqu'un**, or **coller quelqu'un**.

18. feel

(a) When to use **sentir que**

Georges *a senti qu'*il valait mieux partir.	George *felt that* it was better to leave.

The English *to feel that* + CLAUSE = **sentir que** + CLAUSE.

(b) When to use **se sentir**

Je *me sens* vraiment mal.	I really *feel* bad.
***Vous sentez*-vous un peu mieux ?**	*Do* you *feel* a little better ?
Je *me sens* bien.	I *feel* well.

Forms of *se sentir* are used to express *feel* when it refers to the state of one's health; this verb is used with the adverbs **bien, mal, mieux,** etc. The verb *se trouver* is also used to express *feel.* Ex. : **Si ça continue, je vais *me trouver* mal.**

> CAUTION: The verb *sentir* sometimes means *to smell.* Do not confuse : **Il se sent bien.** (*He feels good.*) with : **Ça sent bon.** (*That smells good.*)

(c) How to express *How do you feel*?

Comment *allez*-vous ? ⎫	How *are* you ? How *do* you *feel* ?
Comment *ça va* ? ⎬	
Je *vais* bien, merci. ⎭	I'm well, thank you.

To ask a person how he feels in English, we normally say : *How are you*? although we sometimes say : *How do you feel*? To ask how a person is, French normally uses the verb **aller.** The familiar impersonal « **Comment ça va**? » and « **Ça va**? » are also very common.

19. get

(a) When *get* = *obtain*

J'ai pu *obtenir* un exemplaire de ce livre.	I was able *to get* a copy of that book.
Où est-ce que je peux *me procurer* un ordinateur ?	Where can I *get* a computer ?
Où *as*-tu *trouvé* cette machine à écrire ?	Where *did* you *get* that type writer ?

When *get* = *obtain*, it may be expressed by **obtenir** or **se procurer** and in certain contexts by **trouver.**

(b) When *get* = *receive*

Avez-vous *reçu* ma lettre ce matin ?	*Did* you *get* my letter this morning ?

The verb **recevoir** is used to express *get* in the sense of *receive.*

Louis *a eu* une augmentation de salaire.	Louis *got* a raise in pay.
Philippe *a eu* une bonne note.	Philip *got* a good grade.

The compound past and simple past of **avoir** are often used in the sense of *got.*

(c) When *get* = *go and get*

Veux-tu *chercher* le journal ?   Will you *get* the paper ?
Allez *chercher* le courrier.   *Get* the mail.

When *get* = *go and get*, it may be expressed by ***chercher*** or ***aller chercher***.

(d) When *get* = *catch* (a disease)

Jean a dû *attraper* la rougeole à   John must have *gotten* the
   l'école.   measles at school.

The verb ***attraper*** + DISEASE is used to mean *get a disease*.

(e) When *get* = *become*

Anne *se fatigue* facilement.   Anne *gets tired* easily.
Raymond *a* beaucoup *maigri*   Raymond *got* very *thin* this
   cette année.   year.

Some reflexive verbs and also certain non-reflexive verbs carry with them the sense of *get* + ADJECTIVE in all tenses, some only in past tenses.

Tout à coup *il a fait* très *froid*.   Suddenly *it got* very *cold*.
J'*ai eu* très *sommeil* après le dîner.   I *got* very *sleepy* after dinner.

The compound past and the simple past of idiomatic expressions with ***avoir*** and ***faire*** are often used to express *get*.

Elle *est devenue* furieuse.   She *got* furious.

Normally, ***devenir*** + ADJECTIVE is used in the sense of *get* only when there is no verb equivalent to express that idea.

K. Remplacez les mots anglais par leur équivalent français.

1. Arrêtez-vous de tourner en rond, je vais (*feel*) mal.   **2.** Comment fait-on pour (*get*) un passeport ?   **3.** (*vous*) Que (*do you expect*) qu'il fasse contre tous ces gens ?   **4.** Je (*won't fail*) lui transmettre votre message.   **5.** On (*gets*) facilement des rhumes dans l'autobus.   **6.** Georges a l'air très fatigué; est-ce qu'il (*feels*) bien ?   **7.** Je ne sais pas pourquoi il (*failed to come*). **8.** Je (*expected*) un mot d'excuse de sa part.   **9.** Dans ce milieu mondain Jules (*feels*) mal à l'aise.   **10.** Si Jean-Paul (*fails*) son examen, il sera obligé de suivre des cours de vacances.   **11.** Je (*expect*) faire le voyage de Paris à Marseille en six heures.   **12.** Éric était sûr de lui, mais les examinateurs le (*failed*).   **13.** Ma femme voudrait bien (*get*) cette recette.   **14.** Voudriez-vous (*get*) cette revue pour moi à la bibliothèque ?   **15.** Ma propriétaire (*is getting*) complètement sourde.

L. *Traduisez en français. Attention aux mots en italique.*

1. I *got* good results with that machine.   **2.** *(tu)* Do you want me to open the window ? You'll *feel better*.   **3.** *(vous)* Don't *fail* to telephone me tomorrow before noon.   **4.** *(vous)* What do you *expect* her to do for him now ?   **5.** The most intelligent pupils can *fail* an examination.   **6.** I *got* an immediate reply to my letter.   **7.** If Monique *feels* tired, she should go to see the doctor.   **8.** Alan *failed* to hand in his work.   **9.** I did not *expect* to go to Brussels before next week.   **10.** *(tu)* George, I left my purse in the car. Will you *get* it, please ?   **11.** Frances *expects* a letter from Paul.   **12.** I did not *expect* to be invited to the Dubois.   **13.** *(tu)* What did you *get* for Christmas ?   **14.** Odette *gets* angry when people don't do everything she wishes.   **15.** It *got* so warm that we were able to go out without a coat.

Verb Review

Review the verbs **boire** and **connaître** according to the outline on pages 324–327.

Chapter 6

Past Tenses in Narration

1. What sort of actions are expressed by the verbs in boldface type in the following passage ? What is the normal function of the compound past ?

Dans les deux passages suivants, Raymond, un homme sans éducation, a invité un voisin, « l'étranger », à partager son repas. Il lui demande d'écrire pour lui une lettre à son amie, une femme arabe. Ils restent ensuite un moment encore à boire et à fumer.

Il **s'est** alors **levé** après avoir bu un verre de vin. Il **a repoussé**[1] les assiettes et le peu de boudin[2] froid que nous avions laissé. Il **a** soigneusement **essuyé** la toile cirée[3] de la table. Il **a pris** dans un tiroir de sa table de nuit une feuille de papier quadrillé[4], une enveloppe jaune, un petit porte-plume de bois rouge et
5 un encrier carré[5] d'encre violette. Quand il m'**a dit** le nom de la femme, j'**ai vu** que c'était une Mauresque[6]. J'**ai fait** la lettre. Je l'**ai écrite** un peu au hasard, mais je **me suis appliqué**[7] à contenter Raymond parce que je n'avais pas de raison de ne pas le contenter. Puis j'**ai lu** la lettre à haute voix. Il m'**a demandé** de la relire. Il **a été** tout à fait content.

Camus : *L'Étranger*

The COMPOUND PAST expresses a series of successive actions in conversation or in an informal narrative. Each successive action serves to forward the plot of the narrative.

The COMPOUND PAST also expresses a change of mental state. Thus, the last sentence in the above passage : **Il a été tout à fait content** means : *He was* (in the sense of *became*) *quite satisfied.*

2. What sort of actions are expressed by the italicized verbs in the following passage ? What are the various functions of the imperfect ?

... Il m'a dit : « Je *savais* bien que tu *connaissais* la vie ». Je ne me suis pas aperçu d'abord qu'il me *tutoyait*[8]. C'est seulement quand il m'a déclaré :

---

[1]*pushed back* [2]*black pudding* [3]*oil cloth* [4]*paper ruled in squares* [5]*square-shaped inkwell* [6]*Moorish woman* [7]*did my best* [8]*used the familiar* **tu** *form*

« Maintenant, tu es un vrai copain », que cela m'a frappé. Il a répété sa phrase et j'ai dit : « oui ». Cela m'*était* égal d'être son copain et il *avait* vraiment l'air
5   d'en avoir envie. Il a cacheté[1] la lettre et nous avons fini le vin. Puis nous sommes restés un moment à fumer sans rien dire. Au dehors, tout *était* calme, et nous avons entendu le glissement[2] d'une auto qui *passait*. J'ai dit : « Il est tard ». Raymond le *pensait* aussi. Il a remarqué que le temps *passait* vite, et, dans un sens, c'*était* vrai. J'*avais* sommeil, mais j'*avais* de la peine à me lever.

   Camus : *L'Étranger*

The IMPERFECT describes a state or action that was going on when some other action took place. The imperfect often sets a background for the principal actions. Actions in the imperfect do not take place successively; they have no beginning or end in reference to the time of the main action. They simply go on.

Let us consider the various types of imperfects in the above passage.

(a) Cela m'*était* égal d'être son copain et il *avait* vraiment l'air d'en avoir envie... Au dehors, tout *était* calme... C'*était* vrai. J'*avais* sommeil, mais j'*avais* de la peine à me lever.

The IMPERFECT is used in past descriptions. Each of these verbs describes a state of being in the past. Note that these states have neither beginning nor end, nor are they successive actions which forward a narrative.

(b) Je ne **me suis** pas **aperçu** d'abord qu'il me *tutoyait*... Nous **avons entendu** le glissement d'une auto qui *passait*... Il **a remarqué** que le temps *passait* vite.

The IMPERFECT often describes what was going on when it was interrupted by some other action.

As a rule of thumb, we can say that most past actions in which the verb has an -*ing* ending in English are expressed by the imperfect in French.

The action of each of the italicized verbs in the above passage was going on when it was interrupted by the action of the verbs in boldface type.

(c) « Je *savais* bien que tu *connaissais* la vie ».... Raymond le *pensait* aussi.

The IMPERFECT is used to indicate a mental state in the past, for there is no beginning nor end to this state as far as the immediate actions are concerned.

Each of the above italicized verbs expresses a mental state.

---

[1]*sealed*   [2]*swishing*

3. The imperfect has still another important common function. What is the function of the imperfects in italics in the following passage ?

Chateaubriand, un grand écrivain du dix-neuvième siècle, évoque les soirées qu'il passait dans le vieux château de ses parents, isolé dans la campagne bretonne, où s'est développée sa sensibilité romantique.

A huit heures la cloche *annonçait* le souper. Après le souper, dans les beaux jours, on *s'asseyait* sur le perron[1]. Mon père, armé de son fusil, *tirait* les chouettes[2] qui *sortaient* des créneaux[3] à l'entrée de la nuit. Ma mère, Lucile et moi, nous *regardions* le ciel, les bois, les derniers rayons du soleil, les pre-
5 mières étoiles. A dix heures, on *rentrait* et l'on *se couchait.*

Les soirées d'automne et d'hiver *étaient* d'une autre nature. Le souper fini et les quatre convives revenus de la table à la cheminée, ma mère *se jetait*, en soupirant, sur un vieux lit de jour de siamoise[4] flambée; on *mettait* devant elle un guéridon[5] avec une bougie[6]. Je *m'asseyais* auprès du feu avec Lucile; les
10 domestiques *enlevaient* le couvert et *se retiraient.* Mon père *commençait* alors une promenade qui ne *cessait* qu'à l'heure de son coucher. Il *était* vêtu d'une robe de ratine[7] blanche, ou plutôt d'une espèce de manteau que je n'ai vu qu'à lui. Sa tête, demi-chauve, *était* couverte d'un grand bonnet blanc qui *se tenait* tout droit. Lorsqu'en se promenant il *s'éloignait* du foyer, la vaste
15 salle *était* si peu éclairée par une seule bougie qu'on ne le *voyait* plus; on l'*entendait* seulement encore marcher dans les ténèbres, puis il *revenait* lentement vers la lumière et *émergeait* peu à peu de l'obscurité comme un spectre, avec sa robe blanche, son bonnet blanc, sa figure longue et pâle...

Chateaubriand : *Mémoires d'outre-tombe*

Habitual or repeated past actions are expressed by the IMPERFECT. In English, such actions are usually expressed by $\left.\begin{array}{l} used\ to \\ would \end{array}\right\}$ + VERB.

4. How can an English-speaking person avoid overusing the French imperfect ?

English-speaking students tend to use the French imperfect where the French would use the compound past (**passé composé**). Before expressing an action or state in the imperfect, ask yourself some questions to test whether this is the proper tense.

Use of the Compound Past (Passé Composé)

(a) Does the action advance the narrative even in the slightest degree ? In that case, use the compound past rather than the imperfect.

---

[1]*porch* [2]*shot at the owls* [3]*indentures in the wall* [4]*bright colored Siamese cotton*
[5]*round table* [6]*candle* [7]*woolen cloth*

(b) Is the action limited in time in any way ? In that case, use the compound past rather than the imperfect. Even if the action takes place over twenty years or twenty centuries, if the time is limited, do not use the imperfect.
(c) Does the action state a past fact, one that does not set a background ? Then use the compound past rather than the imperfect.

> NOTE: The fact that the action is continued has nothing to do with whether it is imperfect or **passé composé**. All actions continue for some time—some much longer than others—but the mere fact that they continue is no criterion for the choice of tense.

Use of the Imperfect (Imparfait)

(a) Does the action merely form a background for the plot by describing a state ? Then use the imperfect.
(b) Is it a question of a continuing action interrupted by another action ? In this case, put the continuing action in the imperfect.
(c) Is it a question of a past action expressed in English by $\left.{was \atop were}\right\}$ + the *-ing* form of the verb ? Then use the imperfect.
(d) Is it a customary action, repeated regularly, which would be expressed in English by $\left.{would \atop used\ to}\right\}$ + verb ? Then use the imperfect.
(e) Is it a question of a state of mind rather than a change of state of mind ? Then use the imperfect.

There are a few other less common uses of the imperfect, but these are the principal ones.

5. What is the basic difference between actions expressed by the *passé composé* and those expressed by the *imparfait* ?

C'*était* le 31 décembre. Je me *trouvais* seul chez moi ce soir-là. Je *lisais* dans mon bureau. Un peu avant minuit j'**ai entendu** des gens qui *chantaient* dans la rue. Ils **ont vu** de la lumière et **ont frappé** à ma fenêtre. Je ne les *connaissais* pas, mais je leur **ai ouvert** la porte. Ils *étaient* drôles, et nous **avons fêté** le Nouvel an ensemble.

Graphically, the imperfect may be represented by a straight line that indicates the flow of time. Actions above this line are going on while something else takes place. The **passé composé** (and the **passé simple**) may be represented by points in time (X) indicating the interrupting actions which take place successively.

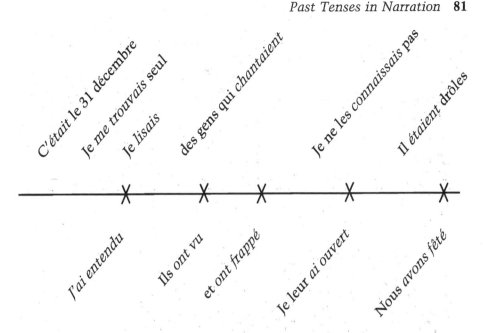

A. Remplacez l'infinitif par la forme convenable du passé composé ou de l'imparfait, selon le cas. Expliquez oralement chaque emploi de l'imparfait.

Il (faire) froid hier soir et nous n'(avoir) rien de spécial à faire. Je (vouloir) rester chez moi, mais Philippe (préférer) sortir. Nous (décider) d'aller voir Bernard, un de nos amis qui avait partagé notre appartement l'année dernière. Donc, nous y (aller), espérant le trouver chez lui. Nous (quitter)
5 la maison à huit heures du soir; quand nous (arriver) dans la rue, il (faire) déjà sombre[1] et il (neiger). Nous (prendre) ma voiture et nous (rouler) pendant une demi-heure. Bernard (habiter) maintenant une jolie maison de la banlieue. Quand il nous (ouvrir) la porte, nous (entendre) des gens qui (parler). Nous ne (savoir) pas qui (être) là et nous ne (vouloir) pas déranger
10 notre ami. Mais il nous (dire) d'entrer.

Philippe (s'excuser) de ne pas l'avoir prévenu, disant que notre téléphone ne (marcher) pas. Nous (enlever) nos manteaux et nous (entrer) dans la salle de séjour. Il y (avoir) là plusieurs personnes que nous (connaître) et qui (parler) avec animation. Nous (être) en pleine conversation sur le bestseller
15 de la semaine quand la sœur de notre hôte (proposer) de nous montrer des diapositives[2] de leurs vacances. Il (falloir) dire que oui et pendant une heure nous (regarder) les projections. Ensuite on nous (servir) une bonne collation[3]. Nous (rester) chez Bernard deux heures. A onze heures nous (rentrer) chez nous, ayant passé après tout une agréable soirée.

---

[1]**faire sombre** *to be dark* [2]*slides* [3]*snack*

B. *Traduisez en français en employant le passé composé et l'imparfait.*
Expliquez oralement chaque emploi de l'imparfait.

A curious thing happened[1] to me the other day. I was taking a walk[2] in the
country with my dog. I was walking[3] along a road when I saw a man who
wore an old coat. He was about[4] forty years old. When he caught[5] sight of
me, he became afraid and began to run. That surprised me, and I decided
5   to follow him. We walked rapidly[6] for[7] five minutes. Finally, he slowed[8]
down and I overtook him. I asked him why he was acting like that. He told
me that I resembled a policeman[9] he knew and said : "I was afraid[10] when
I saw you." The man spoke with an accent. I learned that he was a foreigner
and that he didn't know English well. He told me that he often used to go
10   walking in the country, where he would pick up fruit[11] and would eat at the
farmer's[12]. We chatted a bit, and I tried to reassure him. Finally, we shook
hands, and then we continued[13] on our way.

6. When is the simple past used ?

Alexandre Dumas, le célèbre auteur des Trois Mousquetaires, *raconte*
un souvenir de son voyage aux Indes.

LE TIGRE

Une femme *lavait* son linge dans une fontaine, à cent pas de la maison; elle
avait avec elle un enfant de quatorze à quinze mois.
    Elle **manqua** de savon, **retourna** chez elle pour en chercher, et, jugeant
inutile d'emmener son enfant, le **laissa** jouer sur le gazon, près de la fontaine.
5   Pendant qu'elle *cherchait* son savon, elle **jeta**[14] par la fenêtre ouverte les
yeux sur la fontaine pour s'assurer si l'enfant ne *s'aventurait* pas au bord de
l'eau; mais sa terreur **fut** grande lorsqu'elle **vit** un tigre sortir de la forêt,
traverser le chemin, aller droit à l'enfant et poser sur lui sa large patte.
    Elle **resta** immobile, haletante[15], pâle, presque morte.
10   Mais sans doute l'enfant **prit** l'animal féroce pour un gros chien; il lui
empoigna[16] les oreilles avec ses petites mains et **commença** de[17] jouer avec lui.
    Le tigre ne **fut** pas en reste[18]; c'*était* un tigre d'un caractère jovial, il **joua**
lui-même avec l'enfant.

---

[1]Use a form of **arriver**. [2]Use a form of **se promener**. [3]Use a form of **marcher**.
[4]**environ** [5]Use a form of **apercevoir**. [6]**à grand pas** [7]**pendant** [8]*slow down* **ralentir**
[9]**un policier** [10]This means that he became frightened. Use a form of **avoir peur**.
[11]**des fruits** [12]*farmer* **le fermier** [13]Use a form of **continuer notre route**. [14]**jeta les yeux**
glanced [15]*breathless* [16]*seized* [17]Most often one finds **commencer à** + INFINITIVE, but
sometimes **commencer de** + INFINITIVE is found in literary style. [18]*backward, reticent*

Ce jeu effroyable **dura** dix minutes, puis le tigre, laissant l'enfant, **retraversa**
15 la route et **rentra** dans le bois.

La mère **s'élança, courut** tout éperdue[19] à l'enfant, et le **trouva** riant et sans
une égratignure[20].

Alexandre Dumas : *Le Caucase*

The SIMPLE PAST is normally used in written French to express a series of
successive actions in a literary narrative. It also sometimes states a past fact.

The SIMPLE PAST is a written tense, not used in speaking except in very formal
lectures or orations. It is used in formal literary writing rather than in letters.

The SIMPLE PAST has the advantage over the COMPOUND PAST of being a single
form and thus producing a smoother effect.

Notice the exact use of the simple past (**passé simple**) in the following
sentences taken from the above passage :

Elle *manqua* de savon.
Mais sa terreur *fut* grande lorsqu'elle *vit* un tigre sortir de la forêt.
Elle *resta* immobile, haletante, pâle, presque morte.
Le tigre ne *fut* pas en reste; c'était un tigre d'un caractère jovial.
Ce jeu effroyable *dura* dix minutes.

The uses of the IMPERFECT are the same, whether the passage is written in the
passé simple or the **passé composé**.

C. *Remplacez les infinitifs entre parenthèses par la forme convenable du
passé composé ou de l'imparfait.*
*(Use the compound past for successive actions unless your instructor
tells you to use the simple past for such actions.)*

Monsieur Grinci (être) toujours de mauvaise humeur. Pour un rien il
(crier), il (gronder) et il (faire) peur à tous ceux qui l'(approcher). Il (avoir)
un domestique, Jean, qui (être) bien malheureux. Mais Jean (être) aussi
intelligent et (savoir) bien qu'il (falloir) obéir à son maître s'il (vouloir)
5 garder sa place.

Un jour, Monsieur Grinci (rentrer) chez lui en colère et (se préparer) à
dîner. La table (être) mise près d'une fenêtre qui (donner) sur[1] la cour. Tout
(être) joliment arrangé et il y (avoir) même un vase de fleurs au milieu.
Pendant que Jean (être) à la cuisine, Monsieur Grinci (goûter) la soupe et
10 la (trouver) trop chaude. Il (se mettre) encore plus en colère et la (jeter) dans
la cour par la fenêtre ouverte.

Ce jour-là, Jean (être) plus calme qu'à l'ordinaire. Quand il (voir) cela, il
(penser) que son maître (mériter) une leçon. Il (aller) vers la table, (prendre)

---

[19]*in a panic*   [20]*scratch*   [1]**donner sur** *overlook*

l'assiette de son maître et la (jeter) dans la cour. Puis, il (prendre) les ser-
15   vices, les verres et les fleurs et (jeter) le tout par la fenêtre.

Cela (mettre) monsieur Grinci hors de lui et il (ordonner) à Jean de lui
dire ce qu'il (faire).

Jean lui (répondre) tranquillement : « Monsieur, quand je vous (voir)
jeter la soupe par la fenêtre, je (penser) que vous (vouloir) dîner dans la cour
20   et c'est pour cela que je (jeter) tout le reste ».

Monsieur Grinci (comprendre) cette leçon. Il (sourire) quand même et,
depuis ce jour, s'il ne (changer) pas de caractère, du moins il (maîtriser) ses
colères.

**D. Traduisez en français, en employant le passé composé et l'imparfait
où il y a lieu.**
*(Use the compound past for successive actions unless your instructor
tells you to use formal literary style. In that case, use the simple past
for such actions.)*

Balzac, the great French writer of the nineteenth century, had the habit of
working late into the night. Most of the time he did not take the trouble
to lock the door of his house.

One night as Balzac was sleeping, a thief entered the house and opened
5   the door of the room of the writer. The latter seemed to be sleeping
soundly[1]. The thief, reassured, went to Balzac's desk and began to rummage[2] around in the drawers. Suddenly, he heard a loud laugh[3]. He turned
around[4] and caught sight[5] of the writer, who was laughing heartily. The
thief became frightened[6], but he was not able to keep from[7] asking Balzac
10   what was making him laugh. The latter answered him that it[8] amused him
a great deal to see that a thief was coming in the night without light to look
in a desk for money which he[9] had never been able to find even in plain
daylight[10].

EXERCICE ORAL

*Cécile rend visite à ses grands-parents dans une ville à trois cents
kilomètres de chez elle.*
*Mettez les phrases suivantes à un temps passé, soit à l'imparfait, soit
au passé composé, selon le sens de la phrase. Dans la première phrase, au
lieu de la semaine prochaine, dites il y a un mois.*

1. La semaine prochain Cécile ira voir ses grands-parents.

2. D'abord elle passera chez son agent de voyage.

---

[1]**profondément**   [2]Use a form of **fouiller**.   [3]Use a form of **entendre rire très fort**.   [4]Use a
form of **se retourner**.   [5]Use a form of **apercevoir**.   [6]Use a form of **avoir peur**.
[7]**s'empêcher de**   [8]**ça**   [9]**lui**   [10]**en plein jour**

3. Elle y prendra son billet d'avion.

4. Son frère l'amènera à l'aéroport.

5. A l'aéroport il y aura beaucoup de monde.

6. Le voyage en avion sera très intéressant.

7. Il durera deux heures.

8. Son grand-père ira la chercher à son arrivée.

9. Cécile rend souvent visite à ses grands-parents.

10. Elle passera huit jours chez eux.

11. Tous les jours elle fera une promenade dans les environs de leur maison.

12. Ces promenades seront très agréables.

13. Après sa visite elle rentrera chez elle.

See page 271–314 for the *Exercices d'ensemble.*

. . . . . .

PROBLEM WORDS

20. go

(a) How to say *I'm going, I went,* etc.

—**Il paraît qu'il y a bon film au Rex.** **Tu y es allé ?**	"It seems that there's a good film at the Rex. *Did you go ?*"
—**Oui, j'y suis allé hier soir.**	"Yes, *I went* last night."
—**Moi, j'irai demain.**	"*I'll go* tomorrow."

In English, we often say : *Are you going ? Yes, I'm going.* French rarely uses the verb **aller** without indicating a place to which one is going; and if the place has already been mentioned, it then uses the verb **y** to refer to it.

But **y** is not used with the forms of the future and conditional of **aller,** because then two *i*-sounds would come together.

> CAUTION: In French sentences such as the English *I'm going* and *Did you go ?,* do not use the verb **aller** without indicating the destination or without using the adverb **y.** Note that *I'm going* is often expressed by *Je m'en vais* which also means *I'm going away.*

Je m'en vais demain matin.	*I'm going (away)* tomorrow morning.

(b) How to express certain combinations of *go* + PREPOSITION and *go* +
ADVERB

go back	**retourner**	*go out*	**sortir**
go back home	**rentrer**	*go through, across*	**traverser**
go by	**passer**	*go toward*	**se diriger vers**
go down	**descendre**	*go up*	**monter**
go in	**entrer**	*go with*	**accompagner**

The English verb *go* is used with certain prepositions and adverbs in special
ways, and such combinations are expressed by separate verbs in French.

(c) When *go to* = *attend*

Avez-vous *assisté à la* **conférence ?**	*Did* you *go to the* lecture ?
Non, *j'ai assisté au* **match de basketball.**	No, I *went to the* basketball game.
En France il n'est pas obligatoire *d'assister aux* **cours de la faculté tous les jours.**	In France you don't have to *go to* university classes every day.

The verb **assister** means *go to* when *go to* is equivalent to *be present at* or
attend. However, **assister à** may be used only with certain places and specific
occasions and not with all places. For instance, *I go to the university* is
rendered in French by : *Je vais à l'université.*

The verb **assister** could not be used with **université**. Therefore, be careful
when using **assister à**. In general, one can safely use **aller à** to express the idea
of *being present at*.

21. happen

(a) When to use *se passer*

Qu'est-ce qui *s'est passé* **?**	What *happened* ?
Il *s'est passé* **beaucoup de choses.**	Many things *happened*.
Dites-moi ce qui *s'est passé* **chez les Monnier.**	Tell me what *happened* at the Monniers.

When *happen* = *take place*, when there is no personal indirect object, and
when the subject is impersonal and somewhat indefinite, **se passer** may be
used to express *to happen*.

> CAUTION: When there is a definite subject, avoid using « se passer » for
> *happen*.

> CAUTION: When something *happens to someone*, DO NOT use « se passer » for
> *happen*. See Section (b).

(b) When to use *arriver*

Qu'est-ce qui *est arrivé* ?	What *happened* ?
Dites-moi ce qui *est arrivé* chez vous.	Tell me what *happened* at your home.
Qu'est-ce qui *est arrivé à Simone* ?	What *happened to Simone* ?
Quand est-ce que *cet accident est arrivé* ?	When *did that accident happen* ?

Whenever *happen* may be expressed by **se passer**, it may also be expressed by **arriver**. But, in addition, **arriver** may be used when there is a personal indirect object (something *happens to someone*) and when the subject is neither impersonal nor indefinite.

(c) How to say that someone *happened to do something*

J'étais là *par hasard.*	I *happened to be* there.
Nous *avons rencontré* Jean dans la rue *tout à fait par hasard.*	We *happened to meet* John on the street.

When *happen to* + verb means *happen by chance*, French often uses **par hasard** or **tout à fait par hasard** with the verb.

(d) When *happen* = *it happens that...* (or *someone happens to...*)

*Il se trouvait que j'*habitais dans le même immeuble que Monsieur Martin.	I *happened to* live in the same building as Mr. Martin.
Il se trouve justement que Monsieur et Madame Drouet doivent venir ce soir.	It *(just) happens that* Mr. and Mrs. Drouet are to come over this evening.

When a sentence with *happen* can be begun *It happens that...*, the French often express this idea by placing the proper tense of : **Il se trouve...** or **Il se trouve justement que...** before the main part of the sentence.

(e) How to say *How does it happen that...* ?

Comment se fait-il que vous { avez / ayez } acheté une nouvelle voiture ?	How *does it happen that* you bought a new car ?
Comment se fait-il que Marc { est / soit } absent ?	How *does it happen that* Mark is absent ?

How does it happen that... ? is expressed by **Comment se fait-il que... ?**, which is sometimes followed by the indicative, sometimes by the subjunctive.

22. hear

(a) How to say *to hear* (someone or something)

J'ai entendu un bruit en bas.	I *heard* a noise downstairs.

To hear (someone or something) is expressed by the verb **entendre**. Here there is no problem, for English and French usage are the same.

(b) How to say *to hear of* (someone or something)

Avez-vous entendu parler de cette invention ?	*Have* you *heard of* that invention ?

In French *to hear of* must be expressed by **entendre parler de**.

(c) How to say *to hear from* (someone)

Nous avons { **eu** / **reçu** } **des nouvelles de notre fils ce matin.**	We *heard from* our son this morning.

French expresses *to hear from* by **avoir** (or **recevoir**) **des nouvelles de**.

(d) How to say *to hear that...*

Nous avons entendu dire que le premier ministre va démissionner.	We *heard that* the prime minister is going to resign.

In French *to hear that* must be expressed by **entendre dire que**.

> CAUTION: DO NOT use « entendre de » for *to hear of* nor « entendre que » for *to hear that*.

E. Remplacez les mots anglais par leur équivalent français.

1. Je (*heard*) de cette affaire, mais il y a déjà longtemps.   **2.** Je me demande ce qui (*happened*) pendant mon absence.   **3.** Georgette refuse absolument de (*go*) à un match de boxe.   **4.** Est-ce que ce sont les cloches de la cathédrale que nous (*hear*) ?   **5.** La chose (*happened*) comme je l'avais prévu.   **6.** J'aime bien (*hear*) tomber la pluie.   **7.** Vous les (*hear*) rire ? **8.** Je voudrais bien savoir ce qui (*is happening*).   **9.** C'est ennuyeux de (*hear*) la radio du voisin tous les soirs.   **10.** Il (*are happening*[1]) des choses

---

[1]In French this verb agrees with **Il**.

bizarres dans la maison d'en face.   **11.** Je (*hear*) sortir les employés. Est-ce qu'il est déjà cinq heures ?   **12.** Daniel (*heard from*) ses cousins hier.

F. Traduisez en français. Attention aux mots en italique.

1. (*vous*) Did you *hear* that we will have another meeting Thursday ?
2. (*tu*) There will be a football game Saturday. Do you want to *go* ?   **3.** (*tu*) How does it *happen* that you left[1] New York ?   **4.** (*vous*) Did you *hear* from your mother-in-law recently ?   **5.** (*vous*) To what lycée did you *go* ?
6. (*tu*) Did you *hear* of Raoul's marriage ?   **7.** Bernard broke his leg. How did that *happen* ?   **8.** (*vous*) If you don't *go* to the concert, I won't *go* either.   **9.** (*vous*) We *heard* that you *were going* to Greece this summer.
10. I *happened* to see the Benoîts[2] at the florist's.   **11.** It was raining, but I *went* all the same.   **12.** (*vous*) Come to dinner[3]; we *happen* to have a nice[4] roast duck.   **13.** (*tu*) If you *happen* to receive a letter from Nicolas, telephone me right away.   **14.** How does it *happen* that the children are not in school[5] today ?   **15.** (*tu*) There will be a parade tomorrow. Can you *go* ?

Verb Review

Review the verbs **courir** and **craindre** according to the outline on pages 326–327.

---

[1]Use a form of **quitter**. [2]French family names do not take **-s** in the plural. [3]French says : *come to dine*. [4]**beau** [5]*in school* **à l'école**

Possessives

Un ingénieur, Richard, a découvert une grotte[1] dans le domaine d'un château. Il a des raisons de croire qu'un trésor y est caché. On l'a autorisé à faire des fouilles. Ce jour il emmène avec lui une jeune femme, Fanny, qui s'attend à une aventure agréable.

Le souterrain

—Ce souterrain est très intéressant, dit Richard, en ressortant[2] *son* visage sali. Il y a une pente à droite, mais je ne peux pas voir si c'est profond. Il faudrait que je puisse passer *les* épaules, elles sont trop larges. *Les vôtres* sont plus étroites. Voulez-vous essayer ?

5   Devant l'obstacle Fanny hésitait. Elle pouvait imaginer *sa* photo en première page d'un journal... mais quand il s'agit de passer *la* tête dans un trou, cela devient très difficile. Elle s'approcha cependant, pencha[3] *la* tête vers le trou noir et étroit.

—Mais Richard, ce n'est pas possible ! dit-elle. Le trou est trop petit !

10   Il se mit à rire.

—Il faut mettre *la* tête de côté, voyons. *Ma*[4] tête, qui est plus grosse que *la* vôtre, y passe bien[5]...

Elle s'allongea sur *le* flanc[6], introduisit *la* tête dans la fente[7] rocheuse. Elle vit une petite caverne qui s'élargissait un peu au-dessus de *sa*[8] tête et dans

15 laquelle, accroupie[9], elle eût pu tenir tout entière[10].

Elle ressortit *la* tête avec un grand soulagement[11].

—Il faudrait tourner la lampe pour que je voie, dit-elle.

Quelle joie d'être enfin à l'air libre ! Richard *lui* essuya *le* front avec un grand mouchoir qu'il tira de *sa* poche.

20   —Alors ? Vous avez vu quelque chose ?

—Ça a l'air de descendre, mais c'est trop noir.

---

[1]*cave* [2]*bringing out* [3]*lowered* [4]For this use of the possessive adjective with a part of the body, see page 94, §5 (c). [5]**passe bien** *does go in indeed.* In this case, **bien** simply intensifies the meaning of the verb. [6]**s'allongea... flanc** *stretched out on her side* [7]*crevice* [8]For this use of the possessive adjective with a part of the body, see page 94, §5 (a). [9]*squatting* [10]**eût... entière** *could have gotten in completely* [11]*relief*

—Il faut que vous[12] entriez vos[13] épaules. En vous tenant sur le côté, vous pourriez arriver à y entrer tout entière.

Tout entière ! Tout entière dans ce trou ? Et si elle n'arrivait pas à en
25 ressortir[14] ?

—Oh non, ce n'est pas possible, dit-elle en frissonnant[15].

—Mais si. Tenez, remettez-vous de côté, je vais vous pousser. Vous effacerez bien la poitrine[16] et voilà.

Tout cela était affreux et pas du tout romanesque. Cependant, serrant *les*
30 dents, Fanny s'allongea à nouveau. Il la saisit fermement par le milieu *du* corps et l'introduisit dans la fente comme si elle avait été un simple outil.

Elle y était jusqu'à mi-corps maintenant, paralysée de terreur ; elle avait eu beau gonfler[17] *sa* poitrine, l'habileté de Richard avait eu raison de[18] cet obstacle. Elle était là, *les* bras collés au corps, dans la demi-obscurité. Elle en
35 était sûre à présent ; elle allait y rester[19], rester prisonnière dans ce trou, étouffer, *sa* poitrine prise entre deux parois de pierre humide.

Elle se mit soudain à hurler et il réussit, non sans écorchures[20], à l'extraire de l'ouverture.

—Mais qu'est-ce qu'il y a ? dit-il.

40 Elle avoua honteusement, cherchant par un réflexe instinctif *son* épaule pour s'y cacher :

—J'ai si peur...

—Peur de quoi ?

—Peur du trou.

45 —Mais pourquoi ? Pourquoi ?

C'était trop fort[21]. De toutes *ses* forces et avec un immense soulagement elle gifla cette joue ronde de bébé[22].

Il était si comique, dans *sa* stupéfaction naïve, *les* yeux arrondis[23], *la* bouche entrouverte[24], qu'elle éclata de rire. Et au bout de quelques instants, il rit aussi.

D'après Françoise Mallet-Joris. D'origine belge, membre de l'Académie Goncourt, elle est une des nombreuses et des plus remarquables femmes-écrivains d'aujourd'hui. (« Le Souterrain », dans *Cordelia*, Julliard, 1956)

Questions

1. De quelle utilité est Fanny pour Richard dans l'exploration de ce souterrain ?   2. Qu'est-ce que Fanny avait espéré trouver dans cette aventure ?

---

[12]**vous... épaules** *you get your shoulders in*   [13]*In this case,* **les** *could also have been used.*   [14]**Et si... ressortir ?** *Suppose she didn't manage to get out again !*   [15]*shuddering*   [16]**Vous... poitrine** *You must take in (i.e., shrink) your chest.*   [17]**elle... gonfler** *in spite of the fact that she had expanded*   [18]**avait eu raison de** *had overcome*   [19]**elle... rester** *she was going to have to stay there (and also she would die there)*   [20]*scratches*   [21]*It was just too much.*   [22]**cette... bébé** *his (that) baby face*   [23]**les yeux arrondis** *with his eyes wide-open*   [24]**la bouche entrouverte** *with his mouth half-open*

3. Pourquoi ses craintes et sa panique étaient-elles bien justifiées ?
4. Comment soulage-t-elle ses nerfs après ces émotions et cette déception ?
5. Pourquoi Richard a-t-il bien mérité ce qui lui est arrivé ? 6. Parlez d'une des nombreuses histoires, dans la réalité ou dans la littérature, où il s'agit de la recherche d'un trésor.

> NOTE: Voir aussi les sujets de composition dans le *Manuel d'exercices*.

A possessive is a word that shows possession. English has possessive adjectives : *my, your, his, her, its, our, their*, and possessive pronouns : *mine, yours, his, hers, its, ours*, and *theirs*.

I. POSSESSIVE ADJECTIVES

1. What are the French possessive adjectives ?

SINGULAR		PLURAL		SINGULAR		PLURAL	
Masculine	*Feminine*			*Masculine*	*Feminine*		
mon	ma	mes	*my*	notre	notre	nos	*our*
ton	ta	tes	*your*	votre	votre	vos	*your*
			{ *his*				
son	sa	ses	{ *her*	leur	leur	leurs	*their*
			{ *its*				

2. How and with what do the French possessive adjectives agree ?

J'ai perdu *mon* portefeuille et *ma* montre.	I've lost *my* billfold and *my* watch.
Jacques est allé voir *son* cousin Paul chez *sa* tante.	Jack went to see *his* cousin Paul at *his* aunt's.
Elle a mis *son* courrier et *sa* revue sur la table.	She put *her* mail and *her* magazine on the table.

The French possessive adjectives agree in gender and number with the thing possessed. They do not agree with the possessor.

In English, the possessive adjectives agree with the possessor, not with the thing possessed.

3. When are *mon, ton,* and *son* used for *ma, ta,* and *sa* ?

Son auto est belle.	*His* car is beautiful.
Mon ancienne maison était plus commode que celle-ci.	*My* former house was more convenient than this one.

The forms **mon, ton**, and **son** are used to modify feminine singular nouns when the word immediately following these forms, whether a noun or an adjective, begins with a vowel sound.

4. How is the French usage in respect to the possessive adjective different from the English in a sentence such as the following:

Son père et sa mère sont partis ce matin.	*Her father and mother* left this morning.

In English, the same possessive adjective may refer to two or more connected nouns, whereas in French, the proper possessive adjective must be used before each noun.

A. *Remplacez les mots anglais par l'adjectif français convenable.*

1. (*My*) parents et (*my*) oncle sont partis pour le Canada.   **2.** (*His*) livre est en bien mauvais état.   **3.** (*tu*) Je n'ai pas beaucoup aimé (*their*) remarque à (*your*) sujet.   **4.** As-tu passé (*your*) examen ?   **5.** Que pensez-vous de (*my*) tableaux ?   **6.** (*Our*) existence est ce que nous la faisons.   **7.** (*vous*) (*Your*) références sont bonnes, mais (*your*) expérience est insuffisante. **8.** Avez-vous vu (*their*) nouveaux chapeaux ?   **9.** Il veut me vendre (*his*) voiture, mais elle marche mal.   **10.** Elle m'a montré (*her*) maison et (*her*) jardin.   **11.** (*Her*) adresse est inconnue.

B. *Traduisez en français.*

1. (*vous*) My parents would like to invite you to our party[1].   **2.** (*tu*) Do we take my car or your motorcycle ?   **3.** (*vous*) Do you know whether her brother and sister speak German ?   **4.** (*tu*) Did you notice how[2] his voice has changed ?   **5.** (*vous*) Would you do everything for your country ? **6.** My grandchildren are my greatest joy.   **7.** I hope that her son and daughter will have her good looks and intelligence.

II. POSSESSIVE ADJECTIVES WITH NOUNS

Parts of the Body

5. How, in general, does French express possession with nouns denoting parts of the body ?

---

[1]**soirée** [2]**comme**

Marie a baissé *les* yeux.	Marie lowered *her* eyes.
Nous avons mal à *la* gorge.	*Our* throats are sore.
Il dort toujours *la* bouche ouverte.	He always sleeps with *his* mouth open.

In French, the definite article is often used with nouns denoting parts of the body, where English would use the possessive adjective. However, French does employ the possessive adjective with parts of the body in certain cases : (a) if ambiguity would result from the use of the article; (b) usually if the part of the body is modified; (c) if the part of the body is the subject of the sentence.

The exact usage of the article with parts of the body is so complicated that at this stage we shall present only a few of the most frequently used constructions. (See §§6–10 in this chapter.)

6. How is possession indicated in French when the subject of the sentence performs an action <u>with a part of his/her body</u> ?

Marie lève *la* main.	Marie raises *her* hand.
Jean tourne *la* tête.	John turns *his* head.

When the subject of the sentence performs an action *with* a part of his/her body, in French that part of the body is modified by the definite article. English would use the possessive adjective in such a sentence.

> SUBJECT + VERB + $\dfrac{\text{DEFINITE}}{\text{ARTICLE}}$ + NOUN (part of body)

C. Vous êtes dans une classe. Vous remarquez ce qui s'y passe. Traduisez ces phrases en français en employant **vous** *pour exprimer* **you.**

1. The teacher told the pupils : If you know the answers, raise your hands[1].   **2.** Several pupils raised their hands[1].   **3.** Michelle opened her mouth but didn't say anything.   **4.** Jack was sleepy and closed his eyes. **5.** On seeing that, the teacher shrugged his shoulders.   **6.** Paul had injured himself playing[2] football.   **7.** The teacher told him : "Be careful. Don't move[3] your arm."   **8.** At the end of the hour the teacher had a headache.

7. How is possession indicated in French when the subject of the sentence performs an action <u>on some part of his/her body</u> ?

Marie *se* lave *la* figure.	Marie washes *her* face.
Je *me* suis cassé *la* jambe.	I broke *my* leg.

---

[1]In French use the singular.   [2]Use **en** + PRESENT PARTICIPLE + **au.**   [3]Use a form of **bouger.**

Jean, tu t'es brossé *les* dents ce matin ?	John, did you brush *your* teeth this morning ?

When the subject of the sentence performs an action *on* a part of his/her body, in French that part of the body is modified by the definite article where English would use the possessive adjective, and a reflexive pronoun is placed before the verb.

SUBJECT + REFLEXIVE PRONOUN + VERB + DEFINITE ARTICLE + NOUN (part of body)

NOTE: This reflexive pronoun is an indirect object.

D. *Traduisez en français.*

1. I rub my back every morning.   **2.** John broke his arm.   **3.** They (f.) brushed their hair.   **4.** I cut my finger yesterday.   **5.** (*tu*) Wash your face.

8. How is possession expressed in French when the subject of the sentence performs an action <u>on a part of someone else's body</u> ?

Marie *lui* lave *la* figure.	Marie washes *his* face.
L'infirmière *me* frotte *le* dos tous les matins.	The nurse rubs *my* back every morning.

When the subject of the sentence performs an action on <u>someone else's</u> body, that part of the body is modified by the definite article, and an indirect object pronoun is placed before the verb. English would use only a possessive adjective in such a sentence.

SUBJECT + INDIRECT OBJECT PRONOUN + VERB + DEFINITE ARTICLE + NOUN (part of body)

NOTE: Compare the above with what happens when a noun showing possession modifies the part of the body in the English sentence :

Marie lave *la figure <u>de Jean</u>.*	Marie washes <u>*John's*</u> face.
L'infirmière frotte *le dos <u>du malade</u>.*	The nurse rubs <u>*the patient's*</u> back.

E. *Traduisez en français.*

1. I rub his back every morning.   **2.** Michael twisted her arm.
3. (*vous*) Wash her face.   **4.** He shook my hand.   **5.** We cut their hair.

9. When a part of the body is the subject of an English sentence, how does French express possession ?

***Il a les cheveux** bruns.*	*His hair is dark.*
*J'ai **mal à la gorge.***	*My throat is sore.*

Whenever possible, the French avoid having a part of the body as the subject of the sentence. Generally, they use the verb *avoir* with the part of the body as the object of the sentence. The part of the body is often modified by the definite article.

F. *Traduisez en français.*

1. (*vous*) Your eyes are blue.   **2.** Her skin is soft.   **3.** My feet are sore.
4. (*tu*) Do your eyes hurt ?   **5.** His finger hurts.   **6.** I have a headache.

10. How does French express the attitude or state of being of a part of the body ?

Il est entré *la tête baissée.*	He entered *with his head down.*
Bernard aime lire *les pieds sur le bureau.*	Bernard likes to read *with his feet on the desk.*

French expresses the position or state of a part of the body simply by modifying the part of the body with the definite article. English often uses the preposition *with* in such cases.

G. *Traduisez en français.*

1. He eats with his elbows on the table.   **2.** The little boy stood in front of the teacher with his hands in his[1] pockets.   **3.** Marie was sitting there with her head in her arms.   **4.** John, with his hand in[2] the air, tried to stop a taxi.   **5.** Micheline was watching[3] me with her eyes almost closed.

III. POSSESSIVE PRONOUNS

11. What are the French possessive pronouns ?

---

[1]Use the article. French sometimes but not always uses the article with a piece of clothing where English uses the possessive adjective.   [2]**en l'air**   [3]Use a form of **observer**.

SINGULAR		PLURAL		
Masculine	*Feminine*	*Masculine*	*Feminine*	
le mien	la mienne	les miens	les miennes	*mine*
le tien	la tienne	les tiens	les tiennes	*yours*
le sien	la sienne	les siens	les siennes	*his, hers its*
le nôtre	la nôtre	les nôtres	les nôtres	*ours*
le vôtre	la vôtre	les vôtres	les vôtres	*yours*
le leur	la leur	les leurs	les leurs	*theirs*

12. How do the possessive pronouns agree ? How are they used ?

Vos leçons sont faciles; *les miennes* sont plus difficiles.	Your lessons are easy; *mine* are more difficult.
Elle expliquera cela à son père; je l'expliquerai *au mien*.	She will explain it to her father; I will explain it to *mine*.

Possessive pronouns, like possessive adjectives, agree in gender and number with the object possessed rather than the possessor. Possessive pronouns regularly take the place of nouns modified by a possessive adjective. Notice that the possessive pronouns contract with *à* and *de*.

H. *Remplacez les pronoms possessifs anglais par l'équivalent français*[1].

1. Il aime sa maison; j'aime (*mine*).   **2.** Je me souviens de mon premier bal; elles se souviennent du (*theirs*, s.).   **3.** Quelles aventures ! Je ris encore quand je pense à (*his*, p.).   **4.** Je m'occupe de mes affaires, occupe-toi de (*yours*).   **5.** J'aime bien son studio, mais je préfère (*ours*, s.).   **6.** Est-ce votre chien ? Non, c'est (*his*).   **7.** Sa robe est beaucoup moins jolie que (*yours*, s.).   **8.** Si vous trouvez nos enfants mal élevés, vous devriez voir (*their*, p.).   **9.** Ma voiture ne marche pas; nous prendrons (*theirs*, s.).

13. What are three ways of showing possession in a sentence such as *This book is mine* ?

Ce livre *est à moi*. **Ce livre *m'appartient*.** **Ce livre *est le mien*.** }	This book *is mine*.

The most common way of expressing possession after *être* is by *à* + DIS-JUNCTIVE PRONOUN. When the possessive pronoun is used instead, the idea of the possessor is stressed. Possession is also often expressed by using an indirect object with a form of the verb *appartenir*.

---

[1]In this exercise, s. = singular, p. = plural.

Exercice Oral

Madame Lepic, qui a cinq enfants, rentre un soir et trouve sa maison en désordre. Les enfants ont laissé leurs affaires et celles de leurs petits voisins traîner un peu partout. Elle commence à remettre de l'ordre et demande à qui sont ces choses qu'elle veut ranger.
Répondez aux questions qu'elle pose.

Exemple: Pierre, est-ce que ce livre est à toi ? (Non.) **Non, il n'est pas à moi.**

1. Marie, est-ce que ce bracelet est à toi ? (Oui.)

2. Pierre et Jean, est-ce que ces cassettes sont à vous ? (Oui.)

3. Claudine, est-ce que ce pull-over est à Isabelle ? (Non.)

4. Jean, est-ce que ces magazines sont à Michel et à Albert ? (Oui.)

5. Nicole, est-ce que cette écharpe est à toi ? (Non.)

6. Pierre, est-ce que cette radio est à ton ami Alfred ? (Oui.)

7. Claudine, est-ce que ces cahiers sont à Isabelle et à Martine ? (Oui.)

8. Nicole, est-ce que ce sac est à ton amie Marguerite ? (Oui.)

9. Jean, est-ce que ce stylo est à Yves ? (Non.)

10. Pierre, est-ce que ce béret est à Michel ? (Oui.)

11. Oh ! Par exemple ! Et ces clés ? Est-ce que ces clés sont à moi ? (Oui.)

See pages 271–314 for the *Exercices d'ensemble.*

. . . . . .

Problems Words

23. intend

The word *intend* may be expressed in several ways. Often, but not always, these expressions may be used synonymously.

Jacques *pense* partir demain matin.	Jack *intends to* leave tomorrow morning.
J'ai *l'intention de* lire l'article du professeur Dugard.	I *intend to* read Professor Dugard's article.
La secrétaire *compte* prendre ses vacances en juillet.	The secretary *intends to* take her vacation in July.

The word *intend* may be expressed by **penser** + INFINITIVE, **compter** + INFINITIVE, and **avoir l'intention de** + INFINITIVE.

24. introduce

How to say *introduce someone to someone*

Voulez-vous me *présenter* à Madame Leduc ?	Will you *introduce* me to Mrs. Leduc ?
Françoise m'*a présenté à* Isabelle.	Frances *introduced* me to Isabelle.
Qui vous *a présenté à* Michel ?	Who *introduced* you to Michael ?

The English *introduce a person* is expressed in French by **présenter**.

> CAUTION: DO NOT use the French verb « introduire » with the meaning of *introduce a person*. The verb **introduire** sometimes expresses the English *introduce* in less common connotations; also, it often means *insert*.

Il *a introduit* la clé dans la serrure.	He *inserted* the key in the lock.

25. a knock

How to say *a knock at the door*

On a frappé à la porte.	*There was a knock* at the door.
Avez-vous entendu frapper à la porte ?	*Did you hear a knock* at the door ?

French has no expression that corresponds to the English *a knock at the door*. Instead, it uses the verbal expression **frapper à la porte**, and *to hear a knock at the door* is **entendre frapper à la porte**.

> CAUTION: DO NOT try to use a French noun to express the English noun *knock*.

26. know

(a) When *know = be acquainted with*

—*Connaissez-vous* Geneviève Leroy ?	"Do you *know* Genevieve Leroy ?"
—Oui, je la *connais* depuis longtemps.	"Yes, I *have known* her for a long time."

The verb **connaître** is always used to indicate *knowing a person*.

(b) When *know* = *be familiar with something*

—Les jeunes *connaissent* bien les œuvres de Camus.	Young people *know* (*are well acquainted with*) the works of Camus.
Je *connais* Paris, mais je ne *connais* pas Marseille.	I *know* Paris, but I don't *know* Marseilles.

The verb *connaître* is used to indicate familiarity with works, places, etc.

(c) When *know* = *meet, get acquainted with*

Où *avez*-vous *connu* votre mari ?	Where did you *meet* your husband ? Where did you *get acquainted with* your husband ? Where did you *get to know* your husband ?

In the compound past and simple past, *connaître* sometimes means *to meet* in the sense of *to get to know* or *to get acquainted with*.

(d) When *know* = *know from memory*

Savez-vous les mois de l'année en français ?	*Do* you *know* the months of the year in French ?

Use *savoir* when *know* = *know from memory*.

(e) When *know* = *know from study*.

Cet élève *sait* toujours sa leçon.	That pupil always *knows* his lesson.

Use *savoir* when *know* = *know from study*.

(f) When *know* = *be aware of*

Je *sais* où Pierre a mis son calculateur.	I *know* where Peter put his calculator.

Use *savoir* when *know* = *be aware of*.

(g) How to say *to know how to*

Est-ce que Suzanne *sait* faire la cuisine ?	Does Suzanne *know how to* cook ?

The verb *savoir* + INFINITIVE often means *to know how to*.

I. *Remplacez les mots entre parenthèses par leur équivalent français.*

1. Les Beaulieu (*intend to*) faire construire une nouvelle maison de campagne. **2.** Tout le monde (*knows*) l'histoire de la femme du docteur. **3.** Veux-tu me (*introduce*) à la jeune fille qui est assise là-bas ? **4.** Je (*don't know how to*) jouer d'un instrument, mais j'aime beaucoup la musique. **5.** Je (*know*) parfaitement bien tout ce que vous avez dit. **6.** J'habite ici depuis très longtemps; je (*know*) les plus petites rues de la ville. **7.** Il (*intended to*) partir hier, mais il a manqué l'avion. **8.** Vous (*know*) l'arabe; pouvez-vous m'aider à faire cette traduction ? **9.** (*tu*) (*Do you know how to*) conduire ?

J. *Traduisez en français. Attention aux mots en italique.*

1. There was a *knock* at the door about midnight. **2.** Raymond *knows* a great many very important people. **3.** (*vous*) What do you *intend* to do this weekend ? **4.** Someone already *introduced* me to Mrs. Martel, but she probably doesn't remember me. **5.** (*tu*) What[1] ! You don't *know how to* swim ? **6.** Does Paul *intend* to spend his vacation in Corsica ? **7.** (*vous*) Do you *know* what happened to Mark ? **8.** (*tu*) Where did you *get to know* that artist ?

Verb Review

Review the verbs **croire** and **devoir** according to the outline on pages 326–327.

---

[1]**Comment !**

Participles

*Le narrateur parle de son grand-père, Renato Zaga, comédien, jongleur
et quelque peu voyant. Tout jeune garçon, il interroge son père sur cet
ancêtre original et notamment sur « le secret de toutes choses » qu'il a
transmis à ses fils avant de mourir.*

Pages blanches

Nous étions d'une famille de saltimbanques[1] vénitiens[2] qui *avait émigré* en
Russie à l'époque où Pierre le Grand ouvrait ce pays aux lumières de
l'Occident. Mon grand-père Renato Zaga *était arrivé* de Venise avec pour tout
bien[3] un singe savant, quelques saintes reliques, un costume d'Arlequin[4] et
5 cinq de ces masses creuses[5] qu'utilisent encore aujourd'hui les jongleurs[6]. Il
avait dû quitter Venise précipitamment, *fuyant* les menaces de l'Inquisition.
En effet, vers quarante-cinq ans, *ayant connu* une carrière fort honorable de
comédien et de jongleur, il se mit à prédire l'avenir, ce qui eut pour lui de bien
fâcheuses[7] conséquences. Quand il *se fut mis* à annoncer des événements
10 désastreux qui se produisirent vraiment, il en fut *tenu* responsable par les diri-
geants de la République, soucieux d'offrir au bon peuple un bouc émissaire[8].
Mon grand-père, *sachant* ce qui l'*aurait attendu en restant* à Venise, échappa
à une triste fin en *se sauvant* par une belle nuit de lune.
     Je ne me lassais[9] pas d'interroger mon père sur la vie et les exploits de mon
15 illustre aïeul[10]. Avait-il *passé* tout son temps *à amuser* le monde ? *Avait*-il
continué à prédire[11] le futur ? Les événements continuaient-ils à se réaliser
tels qu'il les *avaient annoncés* ? Sur ce point mon père était formel[12]. Renato
Zaga fuyait[13] la vérité comme la peste. Il *avait compris* que le plus grand don
qu'un artiste *désirant* s'attirer les bonnes grâces du public pouvait faire à ce
20 dernier[14], c'était un peu d'illusion, un peu d'espoir et non la vérité.
     Mon père me raconta un jour que mon aïeul, Renato, sentant à l'âge de
quatre-vingt-six ans, qu'il allait falloir quitter ce monde, fit venir auprès de lui
ses fils et leur communiqua alors « les deux secrets profonds et bienheureux

---

[1]*entertainers in a traveling show*   [2]*from Venice*   [3]**avec pour tout bien** *with nothing
more than*   [4]*Harlequin (a comic actor)*   [5]*hollow clubs*   [6]*jugglers*   [7]*unfortunate*
[8]**bouc émissaire** *scapegoat*   [9]*tired*   [10]*ancestor*   [11]*predict*   [12]*explicit*   [13]*avoided*   [14]*i.e.,
the public*

de toutes choses », ainsi qu'il s'*etait exprimé* avec ce fort accent italien dont
25 nous ne *nous sommes* jamais *débarrassés*[15]. Mon père se tut[16], comme
regrettant d'avoir trop parlé... Je ne voulais pas le presser. Mais je ne pouvais
rester ainsi *à attendre* et je lui demandai :

—Quel était le premier secret ?

Mon père sortit de sa rêverie.

30 —C'est un livre, dit-il. Un très beau livre, et s'il ne contient à l'intérieur que
quelques feuillets blancs, chacune de ces pages vides et *enivrantes*[17] nous
enseigne une admirable leçon et nous donne la clé de la vérité la plus profonde.
Les pages blanches signifient que rien n'*a* encore *été dit*, que rien n'est *perdu*,
que tout *reste* encore *à créer* et *à accomplir*. Elles sont pleines d'espoir. Elles
35 enseignent la confiance dans l'avenir.

J'étais terriblement *déçu*[18].

—C'est tout ? Il n'y a pas quelques mots magiques qu'il suffirait de
prononcer pour que tous nos vœux se réalisent[19]... ?

Je n'étais pas content du tout. Ce n'est pas ainsi que j'imaginais le secret
40 « profond et bienheureux de toutes choses ». Ce fameux[20] Livre ne me semblait
même pas capable de me révéler la formule qui m'aurait permis de faire
marcher, danser et jouer avec moi le bonhomme de neige que j'*avais bâti* dans
la cour et qui me désolait par son immobilité lourde et son air bêta[21].

Mon père, *sentant* que j'étais bien trop jeune pour tirer profit de la sagesse
45 *souriante* et ironique du grand-père Renato, m'offrit le lendemain un magnifique traîneau[22] avec des clochettes plus gaies encore que celles de notre
troïka[23], me *faisant* bien vite oublier ce Livre, lequel n'*étant* point *écrit*, nous
fait à chaque page de si merveilleuses promesses...

D'après Romain Gary, d'origine russe, diplomate et l'un des grands
romanciers contemporains. (*Les Enchanteurs*, Gallimard, 1973)

Questions

1. Pour quelles raisons Renato Zaga avait-il quitté Venise pour la
Russie ?   **2.** Pourquoi avait-il renoncé à prédire l'avenir ?   **3.** Qu'est-
ce qu'un artiste doit apporter au public pour obtenir ses bonnes grâces ?
4. Quelle est la signification du premier secret révélé par Renato Zaga à ses
fils ?   **5.** Pourquoi le jeune garçon est-il déçu ?   **6.** Il y avait autrefois
beaucoup d'amuseurs publics dans les foires, les carnavals. Qu'est-ce qui les
a remplacés aujourd'hui ?

NOTE: Voir aussi les sujets de composition dans le *Manuel d'exercices*.

---

[15]*got rid of*   [16]**se tut** is the third-person singular **passé simple** of **se taire** *to be quiet*
[17]*intoxicating* [18]*disappointed* [19]*our wishes come true* [20]*much talked of* [21]*stupid
(in an indulgent way)* [22]*sled* [23]*Russian sleigh with three horses*

A participle has properties of both a verb and an adjective. English and French have a present and a past participle.

VERB	PRESENT PARTICIPLE	PAST PARTICIPLE
(speak) **parler**	(speaking) ***parlant***	(spoken) ***parlé***
(finish) **finir**	(finishing) ***finissant***	(finished) ***fini***
(lose) **perdre**	(losing) ***perdant***	(lost) ***perdu***
(drink) **boire**	(drinking) ***buvant***	(drunk) ***bu***

Syntactically, the past participle offers almost no problems in spoken French and only the problem of agreement in written French.

The present participle is somewhat more complex, since French often expresses an English present participle by some construction other than the French present participle.

I. THE PAST PARTICIPLE

1. With what auxiliaries are French verbs conjugated in the compound tenses ?

(a) most verbs

Nous <u>*avons*</u> *donné* un livre à l'élève.
Robert <u>*a*</u> *vu* un film intéressant.
Les étudiants <u>*avaient*</u> beaucoup *travaillé*.

(b) intransitive verbs of motion

Vous <u>*êtes*</u> *venu* trop tard.
Nous <u>*sommes*</u> *arrivés* vers trois heures.
J'<u>*étais*</u> *parti* quand mon ami est arrivé chez moi.

(c) reflexive verbs

La voiture s'<u>*est*</u> *arrêtée* devant notre porte.
Nous *nous* <u>*sommes*</u> *échappés* par la fenêtre.
Je ne m'<u>*étais*</u> pas *rasé* ce matin-là.

Most verbs are conjugated with the auxiliary ***avoir***. Ordinarily, intransitive verbs of motion are conjugated with ***être***. All reflexive verbs are conjugated with ***être***.

A. *Remplacez les tirets par l'auxiliaire convenable pour former le passé composé.*

1. Qui _____ ouvert la porte pour laisser rentrer le chat ?
2. Pourquoi vous _____ -vous caché quand je _____ arrivé ?

3. Le président _____ reçu le nouvel ambassadeur aujourd'hui.
4. Cette pièce était ennuyeuse; je _____ parti après le premier acte.
5. Le chauffeur s' _____ arrêté brusquement pour éviter un accident.
6. _____ -vous monté sur la Tour de Pise ? **7.** A Paris nous nous _____ promenés le long de la Seine. **8.** Il était trois heures du matin quand Jacques _____ rentré. **9.** Ils ont une belle pelouse et ils _____ interdit aux enfants de jouer dessus.

B. Traduisez en français en faisant bien attention à l'auxiliaire des verbes au passé composé.

1. (*vous*) I recommend this hotel to you; we stayed there a month. **2.** I was so tired that I did not wake up early enough to go to[1] class. **3.** I have finished my exercises and now I can go out. **4.** (*tu*) You'll be sick; you were warm, and you drank some ice water. **5.** Henry did not remember[2] his date with Pierrette. **6.** After his retirement, he went back to[3] his little village. **7.** (*vous*) What have you learned up to now[4] ? **8.** Many children were born[5] during the last war. **9.** The little boys sat down in the[6] first row at the movies.

2. When and how does the past participle of a verb conjugated with *avoir* agree ?

Le père a *mené* ses enfants au cirque.	(No agreement. Why ?)
Il *les* a *menés* au cirque.	(Agreement. Why ?)
***Les enfants* qu'il a *menés* au cirque sont les siens.**	(Agreement. Why ?)
***Quels enfants* a-t-il *menés* au cirque ?**	(Agreement. Why ?)

The past participle of a verb conjugated with *avoir* is invariable unless a direct object precedes the verb. The past participle of a verb conjugated with *avoir* agrees with the preceding direct object in gender and number.

3. Does the past participle of a verb conjugated with *avoir* agree with a preceding *en* ?

Nous avons *mené* des enfants au cirque.	(No agreement. Why ?)
Nous *en* avons *mené* au cirque.	(No agreement. Why ?)

The past participle of a verb conjugated with *avoir* does not ordinarily agree with a preceding *en*.

---

[1]en [2]Use a form of **se souvenir de**. [3]**dans** [4]**ici** [5]What tense will this verb be in ? What will be the tense of the auxiliary ? [6]*in the* **au**

C. Remplacez l'infinitif par la forme convenable du participe passé.

1. Où sont ces belles photos que vous avez (prendre) ? 2. Nous avons (entendre) une bonne chanteuse. 3. —Avez-vous (voir) ma femme ? —Oui, je l'ai (voir) il y a un instant. 4. Qui est la personne que vous avez (saluer) ? 5. Quelles fleurs avez-vous (choisir) ? 6. —Où sont les gâteaux ? En avez-vous (acheter) ? 7. —Je n'en ai pas (voir) sur le buffet.

D. Traduisez en français.

1. (*tu*) You have told me an interesting story. 2. (*vous*) Where is the person that you introduced to me just now ? 3. (*vous*) What beautiful gifts you bought ! 4. (*vous*) I didn't receive your letter. When did you send it ? 5. I like his book. Has he written others[1] ? 6. (*tu*) You want some stamps ? I bought some yesterday.

4. Which common intransitive verbs of motion are conjugated with *être* ? When, how, and with what does the past participle of an intransitive verb of motion conjugated with *être* agree ?

> *Jacqueline* était déjà *revenue* quand   (Agreement. Why ?)
>   *nous* sommes *partis*.
> *Mes camarades* sont *morts* pendant   (Agreement. Why ?)
>   la guerre.
> *Ils* sont *allés* à Paris pour les fêtes   (Agreement. Why ?)
>   de Noël.

The common intransitive verbs of motion conjugated with *être* are : *aller, arriver, descendre, devenir, entrer, monter, mourir, naître, partir, passer, rentrer, rester, retourner, revenir, sortir, tomber,* and *venir.*

The past participle of an intransitive verb of motion conjugated with *être* always agrees in gender and number with the subject of its clause.

> NOTE 1: The verbs *descendre, monter, passer, rentrer,* and *sortir* are usually intransitive, that is, they do not ordinarily take a direct object. But these verbs sometimes do take a direct object. In that case, they become transitive and are conjugated with *avoir,* and the meaning is different.

USED INTRANSITIVELY	USED TRANSITIVELY
Elle *est descendue* au sous-sol.	Elle *a descendu* la chaise au sous-sol.
Nous *sommes montés* tout de suite.	Nous lui *avons monté* le petit déjeuner.

---

[1]d'autres

Ils *sont passés* par la porte.   Ils *ont passé* l'examen hier.
Denise *est rentrée* tard.   Denise *a rentré* la voiture dans
                                             le garage.
Es-tu *sorti* ce matin ?   As-tu *sorti* le chien ce matin ?

NOTE 2: Verbs of motion such as *courir*, *marcher*, *nager*, and *voler* show the
type of motion and are conjugated with *avoir*. Ex. : Jean *a couru*
pendant une heure autour du parc. J'*ai marché* des heures dans le
musée. Georgette *a nagé* dans la grande piscine. L'avion *a volé* à
30.000 mètres.

**5. In matters of agreement, is the pronoun *vous* considered singular or
plural ?**

Vous *êtes sorti(e)(s)* hier,   (Agreement. Why ?)
n'est-ce pas ?

The pronoun ***vous*** may be singular or plural, masculine or feminine. The
past participle of a verb agrees according to whether ***vous*** refers to one or more
than one person, and whether these persons are masculine or feminine. When
vous refers to both masculine and feminine nouns the masculine plural
agreement is used.

E. **Remplacez l'infinitif par la forme convenable du participe passé.**

1. Les élèves étaient déjà (partir) quand leur professeur est (arriver).
2. Marie est (sortir) sans se retourner.   **3.** Nous sommes (tomber) dans
un piège.   **4.** Mes chers amis, vous êtes (arriver) trop tôt.   **5.** Pourquoi
ne sont-ils pas (venir) ?   **6.** Êtes-vous déjà (monter) sur la Tour Eiffel,
Jacqueline ?

F. **Traduisez en français.**

1. He had said that he would come back, and he came back.   **2.** (*vous*)
Did you come back home[1] to[2] rest ?   **3.** Our friends became important
men.   **4.** Those who stayed all[3] died.   **5.** (*vous*) When did your sisters
arrive ?

**6. When and how does the past participle of a reflexive or reciprocal verb,
which is always conjugated with *être*, agree ?**

A reflexive verb is one in which the reflexive object refers back to the subject
of the sentence. Ex. : I see *myself* in the mirror. *She* washes *herself*.

---

[1]*come back home* **rentrer**   [2]either **pour** or no preposition at all   [3]Put this word between the auxiliary and the past participle.

A reciprocal verb is one whose reciprocal object has the connotation of *each other*. Ex. : *They* see *each other* every week. *We* spoke to *each other* yesterday.

In French, reflexive and reciprocal verbs have identical forms and follow the same rules for agreement.

French reflexive objects may be :

(a) direct objects

Elle s'est coupé̲e̲.	She cut *herself*.
Ils se sont lavé̲s̲.	They washed *themselves*.

(b) indirect objects

Elles se sont parlé.	They spoke to *each other*.
Elle s'est coupé le doigt.	She cut her finger. (lit : She cut the finger *to herself*).

(c) inherent objects

Some reflexive pronouns are neither direct nor indirect in function but simply an integral part of the verb. We may call the verbs with which they are used INHERENTLY REFLEXIVE VERBS.

Elle s'est souvenu̲e̲ de son rendez-vous.	She remembered her appointment.
Nous *nous* sommes échappé̲s̲.	We escaped.
Elles se sont douté̲e̲s̲ de ce qui se passait.	They suspected what was happening.

Let us now examine the agreement of such verbs.

Votre femme et la mienne se sont vu̲e̲s̲ hier.	(Agreement. Why ?)
Nous *nous* sommes levé̲s̲ à dix heures.	(Agreement. Why ?)
Janine s'est souvenu̲e̲ de ton adresse.	(Agreement. Why ?)
Nos amis se sont parlé longtemps.	(No agreement. Why ?)
Les enfants se sont lavé les mains.	(No agreement. Why ?)

The past participle of a reflexive or reciprocal verb agrees with the reflexive object unless it is an indirect object. In that case, the past participle remains invariable. In other words, the past participle of a reflexive verb agrees with the reflexive object when it is direct or inherent but not when it is indirect.

G. *Un jeune homme parle de son ami Daniel qui vient de se marier.*
   Remplacez les infinitifs entre parenthèses par la forme convenable du participe passé, en faisant attention à l'accord.

1. Sophie et Daniel se sont (marier) récemment.   **2.** Ils sont (aller) faire du ski pour leur lune de miel.   **3.** Ils se sont bien (amuser) dans la station d'hiver.   **4.** Un jour il y a (avoir) un orage, mais ils se sont (réfugier) à temps dans une cabane.   **5.** Après des heures en plein air, ils se sont (régaler) de ce qu'on leur servait à l'hôtel.   **6.** Ils se sont (demander) si cela durerait toujours.   **7.** Malheureusement Daniel avait (acheter) des skis trop longs.   **8.** Il est (tomber) sur la piste et il s'est (faire) très mal.   **9.** Le docteur a vu qu'il s'était (casser) la jambe.   **10.** Ils sont (revenir) hier.   **11.** Ils se sont (arranger) pour continuer leurs affaires chez eux.   **12.** Je suis (aller) leur rendre visite et nous nous sommes (revoir) avec grand plaisir.

H. Traduisez en français.

1. We met each other on[1] the street and we spoke to each other.   **2.** They rushed into the store.   **3.** Why didn't they write to each other?   **4.** She cut her finger yesterday.   **5.** Finally we all[2] found[3] each other again.   **6.** We were mistaken.   **7.** They blamed each other for the accident.   **8.** They related their adventures to each other.   **9.** (*vous*) You made fun of me, both of you[4].

II. THE PRESENT PARTICIPLE

7. How is the present participle formed ?

First Person Plural Present	Present Participle	First Person Plural Present	Present Participle
*donn**ons***	*donn**ant***	*dorm**ons***	*dorm**ant***
finiss**ons**	finiss**ant**	lis**ons**	lis**ant**
perd**ons**	perd**ant**	pren**ons**	pren**ant**
*buv**ons***	*buv**ant***	*voy**ons***	*voy**ant***

The present participle is formed by adding **-ant** to the stem of the verb, which is derived by taking away the **-ons** from the first person plural of the present tense.

8. What three verbs have irregular present participles ?

être   *étant*   avoir   *ayant*   savoir   *sachant*

The verbs **être**, **avoir**, and **savoir** have irregular present participles.

---

[1]**dans**   [2]*Place directly after the auxiliary.*   [3]*find again* **retrouver**   [4]**vous deux**

9. What is the nature of the present participle ?

***Voyant* la porte ouverte, je suis entré.**	*Seeing* the open door, I entered.
Beaucoup de gens, *profitant* de leur week-end, étaient à la plage.	Many people were at the beach, *taking advantage* of their weekend.

The present participle is a verbal adjective, that is, it partakes both of the nature of an adjective and of a verb. As an adjective, it modifies some noun or pronoun in the sentence; as a verb, it indicates action or state of being and may be followed by whatever types of constructions other forms of the same verb are followed by.

10. When and with what does the present participle agree ?

Les Michaud ont de la chance d'avoir des enfants si *obéissants*.	The Michauds are lucky to have such *obedient* children.

When the *-ant* form of the verb is used entirely as an adjective, it agrees in gender and number with the noun it modifies.

In that case, it has none of the functions of a verb, that is, it does not indicate action or state of being, and it cannot govern an object or be followed by constructions that could follow it when used as a verb.

Les enfants, *obéissant* à leurs parents, sont allés se coucher.	The children, *obeying* their parents, went to bed.

When the *-ant* word is used as a present participle, it is invariable. As a present participle, the *-ant* word is an adjective in that it is identified with some noun or pronoun in the sentence, and it is a verb in that it tells what someone is or is doing and may be modified by an adverb or may govern a noun or pronoun object.

11. The present participle is sometimes used without *en*, at other times with *en* or *tout en*. To what does it refer when used without *en* ? when used with *en* ?

De bonne heure ce matin il a rencontré *Marie sortant*[1] de la bibliothèque.	Early this morning he met *Marie leaving* the library.
De bonne heure ce matin *il* a rencontré Marie *en sortant* de la bibliothèque.	Early this morning *he* met Marie *while leaving* the library.

---

[1]More common than **sortant** in this sentence would be **qui sortait**. The use of a **qui** clause to express the English present participle is very common in French. See page 112, §14.

When the present participle is used without *en*, it generally refers to the nearest noun or pronoun. When it is used with *en* or *tout en*, its action regularly refers to the subject of the sentence.

12. How does the use of *en* or *tout en* with the present participle influence its relation to the action of the main verb in respect to time ?

Disant ces mots, le pasteur s'est levé.	*Saying* these words, the pastor *arose*.
En sortant de la poste, notre facteur *a glissé* sur le verglas.	*On leaving* the post office, our mailman *slipped* on the ice.
Tout en parlant, le docteur *a remis* son manteau.	*While he was talking*, the doctor *put on* his overcoat.
Tout en étant sévère, le professeur *aimait* beaucoup ses élèves.	*Although he was* strict, the teacher *was* very *fond* of his pupils.

When the present participle is used without *en*, its action is usually followed by another action. When it is used with *en*, the two actions are somewhat more simultaneous, and when it is used with *tout en*, the simultaneous nature of the action is emphasized still more.

Notice that *en* + PRESENT PARTICIPLE is expressed in English by *in, on, by*, and *while* + PRESENT PARTICIPLE and sometimes by *while, when*, or *as* + CLAUSE. The expression *tout en* + PRESENT PARTICIPLE is expressed in a variety of ways in English : *while* or *still* + PRESENT PARTICIPLE, *all the while* + CLAUSE, *even though* + CLAUSE, etc.

I. *Dans l'exercice suivant, le mot entre parenthèses se termine en -ant. Il peut être un adjectif pur ou un participe présent. Faites l'accord du mot entre parenthèses où il y a lieu[1].*

1. Nous avons passé une journée (fatigant) à l'exposition.   **2.** (Fatiguant) tout le monde, Jeanne a recommencé son histoire.   **3.** Il y a dans la pièce des scènes (étonnant).   **4.** (Étonnant) ses amies, Madame Delom a déchiré toutes les lettres.   **5.** Nous avons trouvé les pauvres enfants (tremblant) de peur.   **6.** Le malade mangeait encore avec peine, la main (tremblant). **7.** Nicole, (courant) vers la porte, a renversé la lampe.   **8.** Les Bérard ont l'eau (courant) dans leur ferme.

J. *Traduisez en français les phrases suivantes. La traduction française de chaque phrase comporte un participe présent — seul, avec en ou avec tout en.*

1. Closing her[2] eyes, Genevieve listened attentively to the music.
2. The painter hurt himself by falling from the ladder.   **3.** Even though he

---

[1]*where it is necessary*   [2]Not the possessive adjective in French.

was sick, George used to read a great deal.   **4.** Opening the door with care[1], Bernard looked into the room.   **5.** On seeing that Mr. Lambert was busy, we left at once.   **6.** I saw Frederick while coming back from the office. **7.** All the while that I was listening to him, I was thinking of something else. **8.** (*vous*) On arriving in Paris, go to see the Jamois.

13. How does French express the English present participle when it stresses the idea of *in the act of* ?

Marc était *en train de lire* le journal.   Mark $\begin{cases} \textit{was reading} \\ \textit{was busy reading} \\ \textit{was in the act of} \\ \textit{reading} \end{cases}$ the newspaper.

When the English present participle stresses the idea of *in the act of*, French often uses ***en train de*** + INFINITIVE. This may also be expressed in English by *be busy doing something*.

14. How is the English present participle expressed after French verbs of perception, such as *voir, entendre, sentir*, etc. ?

Nous avons vu Claire $\begin{cases} \textit{ouvrir} \textbf{ la lettre.} \\ \textit{qui ouvrait} \textbf{ la lettre.} \\ \textit{en train d'ouvrir} \\ \textbf{la lettre.} \end{cases}$ We saw Clara *opening* the letter.

Je les entends $\begin{cases} \textit{se préparer.} \\ \textit{qui se préparent.} \\ \textit{en train de se préparer.} \end{cases}$ I hear them *getting ready.*

After verbs of perception, the English present participle is usually expressed in French by either an INFINITIVE, a ***qui*** clause, or by ***en train de*** + INFINITIVE. The ***qui*** clause and the ***en train de*** + INFINITIVE constructions are also used after forms of the verb ***trouver***.

15. When is the English present participle expressed by *à* + INFINITIVE in French ?

Nous avons passé trois heures *à jouer* aux cartes.	We spent three hours *playing* cards.
Paul est resté là au moins dix minutes *à lire* l'affiche.	Paul stood there at least ten minutes *reading* the announcement.
L'enfant s'est amusé *à découper* des images.	The child amused himself *cutting out* pictures.

---

[1]prudence

The English present participle is not always expressed by a French present participle. English present participles and gerunds are expressed in a variety of ways in French. We give only a few of the most common of these.

When the English present participle expresses manner of passing time, French often uses *à* + INFINITIVE.

Especially after forms of the verb **passer** (*to spend time*), this construction must be used rather than a present participle.

K. Traduisez en français.

1. We spent two hours watching television. **2.** We saw them getting on[1] the bus. **3.** (*vous*) Will you spend the evening playing cards ? **4.** John was busy fixing his car when I came back. **5.** (*tu*) Don't spend so much time reading detective stories. **6.** (*vous*) Don't bother me now—I'm busy working. **7.** I heard John playing the[2] violin. **8.** We amused ourselves doing crossword puzzles. **9.** I found Philip looking for his keys. **10.** They see the children going to[3] school every morning.

EXERCICE ORAL

Monsieur Lafitte, petit employé de banque, pense à ce qu'il fera le lendemain. Au lieu du demain de la première phrase, mettez hier et remplacez le futur de chaque phrase par la forme convenable du passé composé, en faisant attention à l'auxiliaire des verbes.

1. Demain matin j'arriverai à la banque à huit heures et demie.

2. Je rangerai soigneusement mes affaires et je commencerai à travailler à neuf heures.

3. Le directeur m'appellera pour savoir où en est l'affaire Dubuc[4].

4. Ensuite, je m'occuperai de l'affaire Galand.

5. A une heure j'irai déjeuner au Cochon d'or que j'aime beaucoup.

6. Après quatre heures, quand les bureaux sont fermés au public, j'aiderai le trésorier à faire ses comptes.

7. Je sortirai de la banque à six heures et demie.

8. Je demanderai à mon collègue Verdoux de m'accompagner.

9. Nous sortirons et nous irons prendre un verre au café du coin.

---

[1]*get on* **monter dans** [2]**du** [3]**à l'** [4]**pour... Dubuc** *to find out the status of the Dubuc affair*

10. Nous nous assoirons à une table à la terrasse.

11. Quand le garçon viendra, nous commanderons un apéritif.

12. Nous resterons au café une bonne demi-heure à bavarder.

13. Nous regarderons passer les gens.

14. Enfin, je me lèverai, je serrerai la main à Verdoux et je rentrerai vite chez moi pour voir le match de boxe à la télévision.

See pages 271–314 for the *Exercices d'ensemble.*

· · · · · ·

PROBLEM WORDS

27. lack

(a) How *to lack* may be expressed by ***manquer de***

Cet agent *manque de* tact.   That policeman *lacks* tact.

One of the most common ways of expressing *to lack* is : SUBJECT + ***manquer de*** + *what is lacking. What is lacking* is an indefinite noun, and it therefore follows ***de*** without a definite article.

(b) How *lack* may be expressed by the impersonal ***il manque...***

***Il lui manque* de la farine pour faire son gâteau.**   *She lacks* flour to make her cake.

When using the impersonal ***Il manque...*** to begin the sentence, *what is lacking* is a partitive and the person who *lacks* is the indirect object.

(c) How ***manquer*** is used when *what is lacking* is the SUBJECT

***La volonté lui manque* pour réussir.**   *He lacks the will* to succeed.

When *what is lacking* is the SUBJECT of the sentence, it is modified by the definite article and the person who lacks is the indirect object.

28. last night

(a) When *last night* = *last evening*

***Hier soir* nous sommes allés au théâtre.**   *Last night* we went to the theater.

When *last night* = *last evening*, the French say **hier soir**.

(b) When *last night* is *late in the night*

Il a fait très chaud *cette nuit*.	It was very hot *last night*.
***Cette nuit* je n'ai pas pu dormir.**	*Last night* I couldn't sleep.
On a volé la banque *la nuit dernière*.	The bank was robbed *last night*.

When *last night* refers to something that happened later than the preceding evening, the French use the expression **cette nuit**. Also possible, but less common, is **la nuit dernière**.

29. late

(a) When *late* = *not early*

Il est *tard*; il faut partir.	It is *late*; we must leave.

When *late* means *not early*, use **tard**.

(b) When *late* = *not on time*

Il vaut mieux être en avance qu'*en retard*.	It is better to be early than *late*.

When *late* means *not on time*, use **en retard**.

30. leave

(a) How to say *to leave someone or something somewhere* (always with a direct object)

Nous *avons laissé Jean* à la bibliothèque.	We *left John* at the library.
Où avez-vous *laissé votre serviette* ?	Where did you *leave your briefcase* ?

The verb **laisser** is used when it is a question of *leaving someone or something somewhere*.

(b) How to say *to leave someone or something* (always with a direct object)

J'ai *quitté mes amis* à deux heures.	I *left my friends* at two o'clock.
Nous *avons quitté la maison* de bonne heure.	We *left the house* early.

The verb **quitter** is used when it is a question of *leaving someone or something*.

(c) How to say *to leave* (not usually followed by a place)

Je *m'en vais*.	I'm *leaving*.
Marianne *s'en ira* demain.	Marianne *will leave* tomorrow.

The verb **s'en aller** means *leave* in the sense of *go away, go off*. It is not usually followed by a place.

(d) How to say *to leave* (for more than just a moment)

Nous *sommes partis* hier soir.	We *left* last night.

The verb **partir** is sometimes used to mean *leave* or *go away* without indicating a place.

Quand *partirez*-vous *de New York* ?	When *will* you *leave New York* ?

When **partir** indicates *leaving a place*, it must be followed by **de**.

Jacques *est parti en Espagne*.	Jack *left for Spain*.
Michel *est parti pour la Grèce*.	Michael *left for Greece*.

The idea of *leaving for* + PLACE (proper noun) is expressed by **partir pour** or **partir** + PREPOSITION OF PLACE required by the proper noun. Purists prefer **partir pour**.

In general, **partir** means *to leave* in the sense of leaving for a trip or leaving a place for a certain length of time.

(e) When *leave* = go out

***Sortez* par la porte de derrière.**	*Leave* (*go out*) by the back door.
Le patron vient de *sortir*. Revenez dans une heure.	The boss has just *left*. Come back in an hour.

The verb **sortir** means *leave* in the sense of *go out*. It often implies leaving for a short time as contrasted with **partir**, which implies leaving for a somewhat longer time and not merely temporarily.

Qui *est sorti du bureau* tout à l'heure ?	Who *left the office* just now ?

Les gens *sont sortis du restaurant* en riant.	The people *left the restaurant* laughing.
Rentrez tout de suite *en sortant du cinéma.*	Come back home right away *after (leaving) the movies.*

To indicate *leaving a place*, use **sortir de** + *place*.

(f) Other uses of **sortir** = *go out*

Êtes-vous *sorti* ce matin ?	*Did* you *go out* this morning ?

When **sortir** is used with no indication of from what place or with whom, it often means *going out of the place* where one habitually is at a given time.

Marc *sort avec* Françoise.	Mark *is going out with* Frances.

To indicate *going out with* in the sense of "dating," use **sortir avec.**

L. *Remplacez les mots anglais par leur équivalent français.*

1. Bernard a une décapotable[1] et toutes les jeunes filles veulent (*go out*) avec lui.   **2.** Avez-vous vu ce clair de lune sur le lac (*last night*) ?   **3.** Je regrette d'être (*late*); j'ai été pris dans un embouteillage.   **4.** Par ce temps, je refuse de (*leave*) la maison.   **5.** Excusez-moi de vous presser, mais je ne voudrais pas que vous soyez (*late*).   **6.** Si les Couve ne sont pas là, nous (*will leave*) notre carte de visite.   **7.** Il y a eu un formidable incendie (*last night*) vers deux heures du matin.   **8.** Il est (*late*); rentrons.   **9.** Les oiseaux (*are leaving*); c'est la fin de la belle saison.   **10.** Si vous (*leave*), plusieurs de nos collègues (*will leave*) aussi.   **11.** Comment faites-vous pour être toujours (*late*) ?   **12.** (*Let's leave*) nos manteaux au vestiaire; nous serons plus à l'aise.   **13.** Avant de (*leave*) le bureau, fermez bien la porte et les fenêtres.

M. *Traduisez en français. Attention aux mots en italique.*

1. (*vous*) Take the book that I *left* on my desk.   **2.** The men didn't *lack* courage, but they were not able to gain ground.   **3.** There was a good film on[2] television at nine *last* night.   **4.** (*vous*) If you arrive too *late*, we won't be able to have dinner together.   **5.** (*tu*) Why didn't you come *last* night, Colette ?   **6.** (*vous*) Your plants *lack* sunlight.   **7.** I *left* the children at the movies.   **8.** Gilbert *left last* night at eight o'clock.   **9.** Roger always goes to bed *late*.   **10.** Oliver doesn't *lack* ideas.   **11.** (*tu*) Don't *leave* without saying good-bye.   **12.** (*vous*) Don't fail to *leave* your address.

---

[1]*convertible* [2]*à la*

13. The travelers *left* at[1] dawn.   **14.** (*vous*) I hope you will not arrive *late*, because the bus *will leave* at one o'clock sharp.

Verb Review

Review the verbs **dire** and **écrire** according to the outline on pages 328–329.

---

[1] à l'

Chapter 9

Demonstratives

Jérôme Bastide a, dès sa jeunesse, une forte vocation de peintre, mais ses idées très personnelles sur l'art le mènent à tenter d'incendier le musée du Louvre et à détruire la Joconde[1]. Pourtant, il semble retrouver la raison et peint des tableaux criants de vérité[2]. A-t-il donc renoncé à ses idées sur l'art ?

Le tableau soluble[3]

Tout jeune, mon ami Jérôme Bastide aimait peindre les nuages et *ces* saules[4] qui se reflètent si joliment dans les rivières. « J'aimais déjà, disait-il, *ce* qui bouge[5], *ce* qui avance ». *Il* était fils du boulanger de notre village. *Celui-ci* ne prit pas *cette* vocation au sérieux. Il lui donna le choix de travailler avec lui
5 ou de s'en aller. *C'est* ainsi que Bastide arriva à Paris. De quoi vivait-il ? *Il* est impossible de le dire mais nous savons qu'il allait chaque jour au musée du Louvre pour y copier les chefs-d'œuvre[6]. Une nuit d'hiver il tenta d'incendier le musée et il brûla la Joconde. « Les peintres d'aujourd'hui, expliqua-t-il au juge, répètent sans fin *ce* que d'autres ont déjà dit. Faisons table rase du passé[7],
10 non pas en essayant d'oublier *ce* passé, mais en le supprimant[8]. Ainsi le passé deviendra l'avenir et nous pourrons à nouveau le découvrir. »
   Enfermé dans un asile, il se montra calme, docile, poli et jouit bientôt d'un régime de faveur[9]. Il occupait une mansarde[10] et obtint le droit d'aller en ville. Le jour anniversaire de l'incendie du Louvre, il sortit et revint « chez lui » avec
15 des toiles[11] blanches, une palette et des tubes de couleur. La nouvelle circula aussitôt : *ce* fou, qui ne l'était plus[12], s'était mis à peindre. Doué[13] de génie, il peignit une Joconde aussi parfaite que l'original. L'ayant détruite autrefois, il n'avait pu résister au plaisir de la revoir. *Ce* tableau fut placé dans un lieu sûr. Il se mit ensuite à peindre des toiles d'une vérité frappante[14]. *C'est* ainsi que
20 *cet* homme, qui avait su reproduire le plus beau sourire[15] du monde, peignit « Médor[16] », un simple chat de gouttière[17]. Or, *il* est difficile de le croire, mais

---

[1]*the Gioconda (also known as the* Mona Lisa)   [2]**criants de vérité** *extremely realistic*   [3]*dissolvable painting*   [4]*willows*   [5]*moves*   [6]*masterpieces*   [7]**Faisons... passé** *Let's do away with the past*   [8]*eliminating it*   [9]*privileged status*   [10]*attic*   [11]*canvases*   [12]**qui... plus** *who was no longer (mad)*   [13]*endowed*   [14]*striking*   [15]*that is, the famous smile of the* Mona Lisa   [16]**Médor** *is usually a dog's name*   [17]**chat de gouttière** *alley cat*

c'est un fait, *ce* chat ronronnait[18] quand on mettait le tableau près d'un radiateur. Sitôt[19] que les journaux eurent diffusé la nouvelle, un collection-neur américain offrit d'acheter « Médor » à dix mille dollars. *Ce* fut ensuite
25 « La jeune fille au piano » qui jouait du Chopin pendant la nuit. Il y en eut bien d'autres...

A sa mort, on trouva dans sa chambre un portrait de lui-même si admirable que le musée du Louvre, lui ayant pardonné, l'acheta. Beaucoup regrettèrent que Bastide ait abjuré[20] ses erreurs passées. *Ceci*, disaient les critiques, est un
30 renoncement à ses théories. C'était sans doute la faute de l'âge.

L'autoportrait fut donc[21] pendu au Louvre. Le lendemain, un surveillant remarqua que la toile se couvrait d'une légère vapeur. « Il faut la vernir[22] », dit le conservateur. On s'aperçut alors que la signature de Bastide n'était plus visible. Qu'est-*ce* que *cela* signifiait ? Le matin suivant, une des mains avait
35 disparu. Dans la soirée *ce* fut les bras. Quand les experts et tous *ceux* qui pouvaient se dire compétents sur le sujet arrivèrent, ils purent constater que, durant la nuit, Bastide avait perdu son nez. Et puis ses oreilles, ses cheveux, son veston... C'était clair : le tableau disparaissait, s'effaçait, dans le sens inverse[23] de sa création. *C'est* pourquoi la signature et la main furent les
40 premiers atteints[24]. *Ce* phénomène s'était produit à l'heure précise où Bastide était entré au musée du Louvre.

J'ai oublié de raconter qu'il m'avait dit un jour : « Les statues des hommes célèbres devraient être faites d'un aggloméré[25] de sucre et de sel. Un jour de pluie, le ciel nous en débarrasserait[26] ».
45 Je suis certain qu'il méditait depuis longtemps « le tableau soluble »[27]. *Celui* qui avait brûlé la Joconde pensait nous laisser son chef-d'oeuvre en peignant une toile qui redeviendrait blanche.

D'après Claude Spaak, auteur belge de pièces de théâtre et de contes fantastiques comme *celui-ci*. (« De l'infini au zéro », dans *Le pays des miroirs*, Julliard, 1962)

Questions

1. Quels goûts montre, dès sa jeunesse, la conception de l'art de Jérôme Bastide ? **2.** Quelle explication donne-t-il au juge de sa tentative d'incen-dier le musée du Louvre ? **3.** Pourquoi Bastide a-t-il particulièrement visé la célèbre Joconde ? **4.** Pourquoi, l'ayant détruite, en a-t-il fait, une fois « guéri », une reproduction parfaite ? **5.** Comment les toiles qu'il a peintes ensuite sont-elles d'une vérité jamais atteinte auparavant ? (le chat, la jeune fille au piano...) **6.** Comment s'explique ce qui est arrivé à l'autoportrait de Bastide au moment précis où il entrait au musée du Louvre ?

Note: Voir aussi les sujets de composition dans le *Manuel d'exercices*.

---

[18]*purred* [19]*as soon as* [20]*renounced* [21]*was then* [22]*varnish* [23]*opposite order*
[24]*affected* [25]*mixture* [26]*deliver* [27]**il... « le tableau soluble »** *he had been considering (the possibility of) the dissolvable painting for a long time*

A demonstrative is a word that points out. The English demonstratives are *this, that, these,* and *those.*

A demonstrative may modify a noun; in that case, it is a demonstrative adjective. Ex. : *this* book, *that* table, *those* people.

A demonstrative may take the place of a noun; in that case, it is a demonstrative pronoun. Ex. : This book is red, *that one* is green. Don't do *that.*

In French, it is important to know whether the DEMONSTRATIVE is an ADJECTIVE or a PRONOUN. If it is a pronoun, it is necessary to know which type of demonstrative pronoun it is, since there are three types of demonstrative pronouns.

I. THE DEMONSTRATIVE ADJECTIVE

1. What are the demonstrative adjectives and how do they agree ?

MASCULINE

Ce **livre est bleu.**   *Cet* **arbre est vieux.**
Ces **livres sont bleus.**   *Ces* **arbres sont vieux.**

FEMININE

Cette **ville est grande.**
Ces **villes sont grandes.**

The demonstrative adjectives are :

		SINGULAR	PLURAL
MASCULINE	**ce**	used before masculine noun or adjective beginning with a consonant[1]	**ces**
	cet	used before masculine noun or adjective beginning with a vowel sound	**ces**
FEMININE	**cette**	used before all feminine nouns and adjectives	**ces**

---

[1]That is, all consonants except mute **h.**

2. When and how do the French distinguish between *this* and *that* ?

Ce professeur est excellent.	*That* teacher is excellent.
Ce professeur-*ci* est plus âgé que ce professeur-*là*.	*This* teacher is older than *that* teacher.
A *ce* moment-*là* il n'y avait pas beaucoup de travail.	At *that* time there was not much work.

In French there is one demonstrative adjective with several forms (*ce*, *cette*, etc.); in English there are two demonstrative adjectives (*this*, *that*).

French does not usually distinguish between *this* and *that* unless a contrast is desired. In other words, *ce* points out more definitely than *le*, but it does not make a contrast between *this* and *that*.

When two objects are mentioned and a contrast is desired, each of the nouns contrasted is preceded by a form of the demonstrative adjective, and the first noun is followed by *-ci* (to indicate *this*), the second noun is followed by *-là* (to indicate *that*). A hyphen connects *-ci* and *-là* to their nouns.

In certain time expressions referring to the past, *-là* is regularly appended to the noun modified by the demonstrative without their being any corresponding expression with *-ci*.

A. *Alain déménage. Ses amis l'aident à s'installer dans son nouvel appartement. Remplacez les tirets par un adjectif démonstratif, en mettant -ci ou -là après le nom où il y a lieu*[1].

1. Comment trouvez-vous _____ appartement ? **2.** Mettons toutes _____ boîtes dans _____ coin. **3.** Gilbert, passe-moi _____ lampe à pied[2] et nous y verrons plus clair. **4.** Robert, donne-moi _____ portrait de ma belle-mère. **5.** Vous pouvez mettre _____ livres sur _____ rayon et _____ livres dans la chambre. **6.** Philippe et Gérard, mettez la télévision sur _____ table roulante[3], s'il vous plaît. **7.** C'est le propriétaire qui a fait repeindre _____ pièce. **8.** Celui qui voudra emporter _____ boîtes vides me rendra service. **9.** _____ fauteuil me suffit; je donnerai _____ fauteuil à l'Armée du Salut. **10.** Marius, fais bien attention à _____ vase de cristal. **11.** _____ admirable miroir m'a été légué[4] par ma tante d'Angleterre. **12.** Je vois qu'il me faudra de nouveaux rideaux pour _____ grandes fenêtres.

B. *Traduisez en français. Soulignez les démonstratifs.*

1. Who is that gentleman ? **2.** (*vous*) Do you like that music ? **3.** At that time[5] I was only four years old. **4.** (*tu*) When did you do these exercises ? **5.** This car is really better than that car. **6.** At that time[6] there was no one in the street. **7.** (*vous*) Have you read those short stories ?

---

[1]*where it is necessary* [2]*floor lamp* [3]*table with wheels* [4]*willed* [5]**époque** [6]**heure**

8. That child is a real prodigy.   **9.** At that time[1] I was doing the housework.
10. (*vous*) Do you know if that hotel is comfortable ?   **11.** (*tu*) Give me this stamp and I'll give you that stamp.

II. THE INDEFINITE DEMONSTRATIVE PRONOUNS

3. What are the indefinite demonstrative pronouns ? When are they used ? When is *ça* used for *cela* ?

Lisez *ceci*, ne lisez pas *cela*.	Read *this*, don't read *that*.
Avez-vous vu *cela* ?	Did you see *that* ?
Ne fais pas *ça*.	Don't do *that*.

The indefinite demonstrative pronouns are *ceci*, *cela*, and *ça*. They refer to something without gender or number, such as an idea, or they point out something indefinite. The pronoun *ça* is a shortened and familiar form of *cela*, common in spoken style but to be avoided in elegant written style.

The indefinite demonstrative pronouns are not normally used in good French before a form of *être*. Before a form of *être*, the demonstrative pronoun *ce* is used instead of *ça*. For example, not « Ça sera facile », but rather *Ce sera facile*.

III. THE DEFINITE DEMONSTRATIVE PRONOUNS

4. What are the definite demonstrative pronouns ?

The definite demonstrative pronouns are :

	SINGULAR	PLURAL
MASCULINE	celui	ceux
FEMININE	celle	celles

---

[1] **moment**

5. How are the definite demonstrative pronouns used ?

Ces livres-ci sont meilleurs **que** *ceux-là.*	These books are better than *those.*

The definite demonstrative pronouns often refer to a noun already mentioned which has number and gender. They then agree with this noun in gender and number.

Celui **qui travaille gagne de** **l'argent.**	*He (The one)* who works earns money.
Ceux **qui veulent peuvent partir.**	*Those (The ones)* who want to can leave.

The definite demonstrative pronouns + *qui* are also used to express the English *he who, she who, the one who,* etc. In this case, the gender and number of the definite demonstrative depends on its meaning.

6. By what must the definite demonstrative pronouns be followed ?

Ceux qui **sont en retard sont** **obligés de rester après la classe.**	*Those who* are late are obliged to stay after class.
J'aime mieux mes chiens que *ceux du* **voisin.**	I like my dogs better than *the neighbor's (those of* my neighbor).
Choisissez les fleurs que vous **préférez.** *Celles-ci* **sont plus** **fraîches que** *celles-là.*	Choose the flowers you prefer. *These* are fresher than *those.*

The definite demonstrative pronouns are always followed by *-ci, -là,* by a relative pronoun, or by a preposition. They cannot be followed by *-ci* or *-là* if they are followed by either a relative pronoun or a preposition.

7. How are *the former* and *the latter* expressed in French ?

Connaissez-vous ces deux dames ? *Celle-ci* **est anglaise;** *celle-là* **est polonaise.**	Do you know these two ladies ? *The former* is Polish, *the latter* English.
Les chiens et les chats sont des **animaux domestiques; quand ils** **sont contents,** *ceux-ci* **ronronnent,** **tandis que** *ceux-là* **remuent la** **queue.**	Dogs and cats are domestic animals; *the former* wag their tails when they are pleased, while *the latter* purr.

In English, in referring to two persons or things just mentioned, we use *the former* and *the latter*. In French, *the former* is expressed by **celui-là, celle-là, ceux-là,** and **celles-là,** whereas *the latter* is expressed by **celui-ci, celle-ci, ceux-ci, celles-ci.** The **celui-ci** forms (*the latter*) precede the **celui-là** forms (*the former*). Therefore, to render a sentence with *the former* and *the latter* in French, the word order must be changed so that *the latter* precedes *the former*.

Je cherche des renseignements sur Jean Dubois et Pierre Petit. *Ce dernier* habite à Chartres.	I am looking for information concerning John Dubois and Peter Petit. *The latter* lives in Chartres.

In sentences where only *the latter* is used, a form of **ce dernier** may also be used. However, a form of **celui-ci** is quite correct in such cases.

C. Remplacez les mots entre parenthèses par le pronom démonstratif convenable. Mettez -ci ou -là s'il y a lieu.

1. (*This*) doit rester strictement entre nous. **2.** —Laquelle de ces dames est Madame Delatour ? —(*The one*) qui porte une robe bleue. **3.** Si je découvre (*the one*) qui a fait cela, gare à lui[1] ! **4.** Je l'avais dit — (*that*) devait arriver. **5.** Le Rhône et la Garonne prennent leur source hors de France; (*the latter*) se jette dans l'Atlantique, (*the former*) dans la Méditerranée. **6.** Ils sont partis; (*that*) me fait beaucoup de peine. **7.** Savez-vous ce que veut dire (*this*) ? **8.** J'envie (*those*) qui peuvent aller passer l'été en France. **9.** Si votre voiture ne marche pas, pourquoi ne prenez-vous pas (*your brother's*) ? **10.** Il y a beaucoup de robes dans le magasin, mais il faut te décider. Veux-tu (*these*) ou (*those*) ?

D. Traduisez en français. Soulignez les démonstratifs.

1. (*vous*) That belongs to me; don't take it. **2.** (*tu*) If you don't like that, leave it. **3.** This gift is not the one that I wanted. **4.** This interests me a great deal. **5.** That author wrote plays and novels. The former[2] are entertaining, whereas the latter are boring. **6.** Those who are not satisfied can go and see[3] the manager. **7.** (*vous*) I know those girls. Go out with this one but not with that one. **8.** My ideas are sometimes different from my partner's[4]. **9.** I like these two lamps, especially this one.

---

[1]**gare à lui** *he'd better look out* [2]In French, *the latter* (referring to novels) precedes *the former* (referring to plays). [3]In the sense of *going to complain, go and see* = **s'adresser à.** [4]French says *from those of my partner.*

IV. THE DEMONSTRATIVE PRONOUN *CE*

When used as a demonstrative pronoun, *ce* is invariable and is usually the subject of some form of the verb *être*. It has several distinct uses. In one of its functions, we call it the *indefinite ce*, in another the *introductory ce*.

> **NOTE 1:** A third function, sometimes called the *pleonastic ce*, will not be taken up here. Ex. : **La guerre, c'est la ruine. Ce que Roger fait, c'est son affaire**.

> **NOTE 2:** The demonstrative pronoun *ce* is also used in the combinations *ce qui*, *ce que*, and *ce dont*. This use of *ce* will be taken up in the chapter on relative pronouns. See page 137.

The Indefinite ce

8. How is the English *it* expressed in French when it refers back to an idea without gender or number ?

Elle nage bien. *C'est* difficile.	She swims well. *It*'s difficult.
—Venez avec moi. —*C'est* impossible.	"Come with me." "*It*'s impossible."
Il lit vite. *C'est* facile à voir.	He reads rapidly. *It*'s easy to see.
Ils vont partir. *C'est* bon à savoir.	They are going to leave. *It*'s good to know.

The *indefinite ce* refers back to an aforementioned idea. Since an idea has neither gender nor number, the indefinite and neuter *ce* is used to refer to such an idea. English uses *it* to refer back to an idea.

When the indefinite *ce* + a form of *être* has its meaning completed by an infinitive, the preposition *à* normally connects the infinitive to what precedes.

	form			
idea + Ce +	of	+ ADJECTIVE	+ à +	INFINITIVE
	être			

9. When, on the other hand, is the English *it* expressed by the impersonal *il* ?

Il **est difficile de bien chanter.**	*It* is difficult to sing well.
Il **est impossible de partir avec vous.**	*It* is impossible to leave with you.
Il **est facile de lire vite.**	*It* is easy to read rapidly.

When one would begin an English sentence with an *it* which does not refer to any previous idea, in French such a sentence is often introduced by the impersonal *il* followed by a form of *être* and an adjective. This construction is usually followed by *de* + INFINITIVE.

$$\text{Il} + \begin{array}{c} \text{form} \\ \text{of} \\ \text{être} \end{array} + \text{ADJECTIVE} + \textbf{de} + \text{INFINITIVE}$$

In conversational style, the French often replace the impersonal *il* by *ce*, so that *Il est difficile de bien chanter* often becomes *C'est difficile de bien chanter*. The latter is, however, more colloquial and less elegant.

E. *Remplacez les tirets par* ce *ou* il.

1. Jean n'est pas encore arrivé. _____ est ennuyeux. 2. Où tout cela nous mène-t-il ? _____ est triste à penser. 3. _____ est impossible de retourner chez elle maintenant. 4. Voilà ce que je vous ai promis. _____ est joli, n'est-ce pas ? 5. _____ est plus facile de critiquer que de créer. 6. Savez-vous vous servir d'un ordinateur ? _____ est tellement utile.

F. *Traduisez en français.*

1. (*tu*) Your father is angry. It's evident. 2. It's easy to make mistakes. 3. (*vous*) What you have written surprises me, but it's interesting. 4. It is pleasant to travel. 5. It is useful to learn a foreign language. 6. Lawrence knows what he is doing. It's true. 7. John won't come back any more. It is difficult to believe.

The Introductory ce

10. When is the introductory *ce* used ?

Qui est ce garçon ? *C'est mon fils.*	Who is that boy ? *He's my son.*
Qui est là ? *C'est lui.*	Who is there ? *It's he / him.*
Qui sont ces personnes ? *Ce* sont *mes nièces.*	Who are those people ? *They are my nieces.*
C'est Pasteur qui a découvert un vaccin contre la rage.	It is *Pasteur* who discovered a vaccine for rabies.

The *introductory ce* is used before a form of the verb *être* when what follows *être* could be the subject of the sentence. After *être*, normally a pronoun, a proper name, or a modified noun could be the subject of the sentence.

In such cases, the introductory *ce* is expressed in English sometimes by *it*, sometimes by *he, she,* or *they.*

> NOTE: In sentences like *C'est le plus beau des mois*, the introductory *ce* is also used when a superlative form of the adjective follows a form of *être*.

11. When, on the other hand, are the subject pronouns *il, elle, ils,* and *elles* used as the subject of the verb *être* ?

Où est Marie ? *Elle* est en classe.	Where is Marie ? *She* is in class.
Voyez-vous souvent Gilbert ? *Il* est très intelligent.	Do you often see Gilbert ? *He* is very intelligent.
Nous parlons de vos enfants. Sont-*ils* là ?	We are speaking of your children. Are *they* there ?

Whenever what follows a form of the verb *être* could not be the subject of the sentence, a third person subject pronoun must be used instead of the introductory *ce*. That is, whenever an adverb, an adjective, or a phrase follows *être*, it is NOT possible to use the introductory *ce*.

12. When is the personal pronoun and when is the introductory *ce* used with names of professions, nationalities, religions, etc., when they follow a form of *être* ?

Il est médecin.	*C'est un médecin.*
Elle est protestante.	*C'est une protestante fervente.*
Ils sont français.	*Ce* sont *des Français naturalisés.*

When the <u>unmodified</u> name of a profession, nationality, religion, or any like noun is used after the verb *être*, it is considered an adjective rather than a noun. In such cases, *il, elle, ils,* or *elles* are used before the form of *être*. But if such a noun is modified, it is then considered as a noun, and since it can thus be the subject of the sentence, the form of the verb *être* is preceded by the introductory *ce*.

G. *Remplacez les tirets par l'équivalent français du mot indiqué en anglais.*

1. —Où est Christophe ? —(*He*) est en France.   **2.** Voilà Solange. (*She*) est professeur.   **3.** Connaissez-vous M. Dupont ? (*He*) est un célèbre écrivain.   **4.** Est-(*she*) catholique ou protestante ?   **5.** Ne demandez pas cela à Jacques. (*He*) n'est pas riche.   **6.** —Que fait son père ? —(*He*) est médecin.   **7.** —Où est votre frère maintenant ? —(*He*) est à l'armée.   **8.** (*It*) sont[1] eux qui m'ont ramené à la maison.   **9.** —De quelle nationalité sont ces gens ? —(*They*) sont allemands.   **10.** (*They*) sont des célibataires endurcis[2], mais (*they*) semblent contents de leur sort.

H. *Traduisez en français.*

1. Who is this man ? He is Mr. Lefranc.   **2.** I like this snapshot a great deal. It is very beautiful.   **3.** (*vous*) Look at these children; they are so cute.   **4.** Who took his dictionary ? It wasn't[3] I.   **5.** I remember him; he is a teacher, isn't he?   **6.** Is he French or American ?   **7.** Who is this girl ? She is my sister-in-law.   **8.** (*vous*) Do you know Madame Dumont ? She is our lawyer's second wife.

I. *Remplacez les mots anglais par l'équivalent français. Choisissez un des mots: ce, il, elle, ils, elles.*

1. Voyez-vous cette femme au chapeau rouge ? (*She*) est la sœur d'Henri.   **2.** Je connais Pierre et sa femme; (*they*) sont des catholiques pratiquants.   **3.** J'aime beaucoup cet écrivain. (*He*) est mon préféré.   **4.** —Qui est là ? —(*It*) est moi, Françoise.   **5.** Je n'ai pas fait ce que j'aurais dû, (*it*) est vrai.   **6.** Parlez plus fort, s'il vous plaît; voilà, (*it*) est mieux.   **7.** Je voudrais voir votre professeur. Est-(*he*) ici ?   **8.** Qui a dit ces mensonges sur moi ? Est-(*it*) Brigitte ?   **9.** Venez tout de suite, (*it*) est très important.   **10.** Voyez-vous ce monsieur ? Qui est-(*he*)[4] ?

---

[1]In present-day French, **est** is also used before **eux**.   [2]*confirmed*   [3]Use present in French.   [4]Since **qui** is a pronoun, how must *he* be expressed here ?

EXERCICE ORAL

Il y a quatre enfants dans la famille Colin, deux fils et deux filles.
(a) L'après-midi Mme Colin fait des courses avec ses deux filles. (b) Le soir
à table, M. Colin pose des questions à ses enfants.
Répondez aux questions en employant un pronom démonstratif.

EXEMPLE: —Robert, aimes-tu mieux ce pull-over-ci ou le pull-over que tu as
essayé avant hier ? —**J'aime mieux celui que j'ai essayé avant hier.**

a

1. —Monique, veux-tu acheter la robe qui est dans la vitrine ou la robe
   que la vendeuse nous a montrée ? —Je veux acheter...

2. —Regardez ces deux tableaux. Suzanne, aimes-tu mieux le portrait
   de Matisse ou le portrait de Picasso ? —J'aime mieux...

3. —Monique, il te faut un sac. Préfères-tu le sac qui est en cuir ou le
   sac qui est en velours ? —Je préfère...

4. —Suzanne, tu as besoin d'une blouse. Prendras-tu la blouse qui est
   sur le mannequin ou la blouse que la vendeuse vient de te proposer ?
   —Je prendrai...

5. —Monique, allons-nous prendre ces fleurs-ci ou ces fleurs-là ? —
   Nous allons prendre...

b

6. —Michel, as-tu lu la revue que nous avons reçue hier ou la revue
   que je t'ai apportée ? —J'ai lu...

7. —Suzanne, iras-tu voir le film qu'on joue en ce moment ou le film
   qu'on jouera la semaine prochaine ? —J'irai voir...

8. —Robert, as-tu réparé la bicyclette de Michel ou la bicyclette de
   Monique ? —J'ai réparé...

9. —Monique, on donne une pièce de Molière et une pièce de Racine
   demain soir. Laquelle veux-tu voir ? —Je veux voir...

10. —Michel, partiras-tu à la plage dans la voiture d'Olivier ou dans la
    voiture de ton oncle Laurent ? —Je partirai...

See pages 271–314 for the *Exercices d'ensemble.*

· · · · · ·

Problem Words

31. little

(a) When to use *peu*

Jeannot lit *peu*, il préfère s'amuser.	Johnnie reads *little*, he prefers to have a good time.
J'ai *peu* d'argent.	I do *not* have *very much* money.

When *peu* is used alone, that is, unaccompanied by *un*, it means *little, only a little, not very much*.

(b) When to use *un peu*

Si tu as *un peu* d'argent, mets-le de côté.	If you have *a little* money, save it.

Note that *un peu* means *a little* or *some*.

32. live

(a) When to use *habiter*

Nos amis *habitent*	à Genève. Genève.	Our friends *live* in Geneva.

To indicate where one lives, the French commonly use the verb *habiter*, which may be followed either directly by the place or by the French equivalent of *in + place*. It is somewhat synonymous with the English *inhabit*, but it is much more common.

The verb *demeurer*, formerly very frequently used for *live* in the above sense, has now been almost entirely replaced by *habiter*.

(b) When to use *vivre*

Monsieur Seydoux *vit* de ses revenus.	Mr. Seydoux *lives* from his income.
Il est mort comme il *a vécu*.	He died as he *lived*.
Monsieur Rochebois *vivait* entièrement pour sa famille.	Mr. Rochebois *lived* entirely for his family.

The verb *vivre* means *live* in a larger and more general sense and is sometimes synonymous with *exist*. It is occasionally used in the sense of *habiter*, but the learner should avoid using it in this sense.

33. long

(a) How to say *as long as*

Tant que je serai là, il n'y aura rien à craindre.	*As long as I am* there, there will be nothing to fear.

The time expression *as long as* is rendered in French by **tant que** and is followed by the FUTURE whenever futurity is implied.

(b) How to say *how long*

Combien de temps avez-vous travaillé pour lui ?	*How long* have you worked for him ?
Pendant combien de temps êtes-vous resté en France ?	*How long* did you stay in France ?

The English *how long*, meaning *how much time*, may be expressed in French by **combien de temps** or **pendant combien de temps**.

Depuis quand êtes-vous ici ?	*How long* have you been here ?
Depuis combien de temps attends-tu ?	*How long* have you been waiting ?

The expression **depuis quand** and **depuis combien de temps** are often used with the PRESENT where English uses *how long* + PRESENT PERFECT PROGRESSIVE to express the same idea.

(c) How to say *for a long time*

Nous avons parlé *longtemps* de ton avenir.	We spoke about your future *for a long time.*
Il y a *longtemps* que je connais les Jourdan.	I have known the Jourdans *for a long time.*

The English *a long time* is expressed in French by the adverb **longtemps**.

(d) How to say *at length*

Nous avons parlé *longuement* de ton avenir.	We spoke *at length* of your future.

The English *at length* is expressed in French by the adverb **longuement**, when *at length* = *in detail*.

34. make

How to say *make someone* + ADJECTIVE

Vous *me rendez très heureux* en disant cela.	You *make me very happy* by saying that.

The French equivalent of *to make someone* + ADJECTIVE is **rendre quelqu'un** + ADJECTIVE.

> CAUTION: Do NOT use the construction « faire quelqu'un » + adjective. French uses **rendre** in such situations.

J. Remplacez les mots anglais par leur équivalent français.

1. Je ne conduis pas depuis (*a long time*), mais je suis très prudente. **2.** Inutile de se faire trop de soucis; il faut (*live*) au jour le jour. **3.** Henriette écrit (*little*), mais elle nous téléphone souvent. **4.** Votre présence (*made*) la soirée très agréable. **5.** J'ai (*at length*) réfléchi à ce que vous m'avez dit. **6.** Monsieur et Madame Renaud ont une belle auto, mais ils (*live*) dans une très vieille maison. **7.** Il faut faire (*a little*) de gymnastique tous les matins. **8.** J'observe vos progrès depuis (*a long time*) sans rien dire.

K. Traduisez en français. Attention aux mots en italique.

1. (*tu*) I know your friend Daniel *a little*. **2.** I *lived* in a large city for twenty years. **3.** (*vous*) If you remain here too *long*, you will forget your native language. **4.** (*vous*) Don't smoke so much, it[1] will *make* you sick. **5.** (*vous*) You really give me *little* time to[2] do that. **6.** People *live* a great deal *longer* today than formerly. **7.** The mayor spoke *at length* concerning the traffic problems. **8.** Mr. Mollet no longer reads the newspaper; it *makes* him nervous. **9.** Those young people went out for *a long time* together before getting married. **10.** (*tu*) Wait *a little*.

Verb Review

Review the verbs **envoyer** and **faire** according to the outline on pages 328–329.

---

[1]ça [2]pour

Relatives

Un jeune professeur au lycée de Lausanne raconte le scandale provoqué par le discours subversif d'un lycéen[1] pendant une cérémonie, les sanctions qui s'ensuivent[2] et la grande manifestation où s'opposent la foule des lycéens et le directeur, M. Grapp.

Manifestation au lycée de Lausanne

En ce temps-là eut lieu une manifestation *qui* fit parler tout le pays et donna une célébrité définitive à M. Grapp, le directeur du lycée.

Tout avait commencé au cours de la cérémonie des « Promotions » *qui* marque le passage de centaines de garçons et de filles du collège secondaire au
5 lycée. Un élève, Pierre Müller, *qui* devait réciter un poème à cette occasion, en profita pour critiquer le système scolaire, accuser les programmes[3], se moquer des professeurs —parmi *lesquels* j'étais — et engager ses camarades à se révolter. Ce fut un scandale épouvantable *auquel* personne ne s'était attendu[4]. Mais le jour même *où* cela arriva, M. Grapp et l'administration
10 prirent une décision spectaculaire : l'orateur contestataire[5] fut suspendu pour six mois. Ce fut le prétexte à toutes sortes d'événements *que* les groupes de gauche provoquaient sans cesse : défilés avec pancartes[6], réunions sur les petites places autour du lycée, tracts quotidiens. « Réintégrez[7] Pierre Müller », criait sur la grande place une foule colorée[8] et joyeuse à *laquelle* se mêlaient
15 de nombreux curieux. Les jeunes gens débouchaient[9] de la rue de l'Université en cortèges désordonnés *où* l'on dansait, *où* l'on chantait. Les filles avaient dans les cheveux des fleurs *qu'*elles avaient cueillies dans les parcs publics. Rien ne manquait, c'était une vraie fête. Je regardais les spectacles avec un intense plaisir.
20 Cependant, trois jours après, comme j'arrivais au lycée à huit heures, je sortis de ma voiture et je sentis qu'il se passait quelque chose. Un élève *dont* la figure ne m'était pas inconnue se cacha derrière un mur en m'apercevant. Des pancartes étaient entassées[10] contre une porte. Je ne pouvais imaginer *ce*

---

[1]*high school student* [2]*result* [3]*courses of study* [4]*had expected* [5]*protesting*
[6]*marches with signs* [7]**Réintégrez Pierre Müller** *Let Pierre Müller back in* [8]*colorful* [9]*came out* [10]*piled up*

que la matinée allait me révéler et l'effet fatal *qu'*elle devait exercer sur ma vie.
25 C'était la manifestation.

Des centaines de jeunes gens arrivent soudain en courant, en riant, en criant
des slogans. Au moment *où* un mégaphone appelle les lycéens à réagir contre
la décision du Directeur, des groupes se préparent à envahir le bâtiment de
l'administration. Tout à coup le silence se fait, chacun demeure pétrifié :
30 devant la porte est apparu M. Grapp, massif, immense, le crâne luisant[11], ses
terribles lunettes noires sur le nez. Il représente la force concentrée et
contemple l'adversaire. Mais *ce qui* stupéfie chacun, c'est qu'il tient à la main
un long fouet, bouclé[12] comme un serpent prêt à mordre, monstruosité sortie
du fond des âges[13]. Quand le mégaphone *qui* s'était tu[14] recommence ses
35 exhortations, la foule des manifestants reprend sa marche vers la porte
principale où l'attend M. Grapp. Alors celui-ci avance, lève le fouet, le fait
siffler, attaque les protestataires. *Ce qui* les fait céder, ils le diront plus tard,
ce n'est pas le respect ni même la peur mais l'étonnement, la panique
*qu'*inspire le spectacle de ce colosse armé de son fouet. Car il avance toujours
40 en poussant des cris inarticulés, le fouet siffle toujours. Le groupe entier se
sauve, M. Grapp court de l'un à l'autre, frappe les fuyards[15], arrive enfin à la
grande porte *dont* il ferme la grille. La cour est vide. M. Grapp est maître du
terrain.

D'après Jacques Chessex, éminent essayiste, critique et romancier suisse.
(*L'Ogre*, Grasset, 1973)

Questions

1. Qu'est-ce qui s'est passé le jour de la cérémonie des « Promotions » ?
2. Quelles ont été les conséquences de la réaction du directeur du
lycée ?   **3.** Pourquoi le jeune professeur prend-il un intense plaisir à regarder les manifestations ?   **4.** Décrivez les préparatifs de la bataille, son
déroulement et la victoire de M. Grapp.   **5.** Vous avez sans doute vous-
mêmes des critiques de votre système scolaire, de vos programmes. Quelles
réformes proposeriez-vous ?   **6.** Quel pourrait être « l'effet fatal » que cette
manifestation aura sur la vie du narrateur ?

NOTE: Voir aussi les deux sujets de composition dans le *Manuel d'exercices*.

A relative pronoun is one that connects a dependent to an independent
clause. The relative pronoun is part of the dependent clause, performs a
function in that clause, and usually begins the dependent clause. The English
relative pronouns are *who*, *whom*, *whose*, *which*, *that*, and *what*. Ex. : The
student *who* wrote that essay is a genius.

---

[11]*skull shining*   [12]*whip, curled*   [13]**monstruosité... âges** *a monstrosity dating from
prehistoric times*   [14]**tu** *is the past participle of* **taire**   [15]*fleeing students*

The relative pronoun normally refers back to some noun in the independent clause. The noun is called the antecedent of the pronoun. In the above example, the antecedent of *who* is "student."

> *I corrected the <u>exercise</u> **that** John wrote.*

independent clause	= *I corrected the exercise* This is an independent clause because it makes sense by itself.
dependent clause	= *that John wrote* This is a dependent clause because it is incomplete; it depends on the preceding clause.
relative pronoun	= *that* *that* connects the dependent to the independent clause and is the direct object of the dependent clause.
antecedent	= *exercise* This is the word to which *that* refers.

Sometimes, however, the relative pronoun is indefinite. In that case, there is no antecedent in the English sentence. Ex. : My father does not know *what* I am doing.

1. What relative pronoun is used as the subject of its clause ?

C'est le professeur *qui* parle.	It is the teacher *who* is talking.
C'est une voiture *qui* coûte très cher.	It is a car *which* costs a great deal.

The relative pronoun *qui* is used as the subject of its clause, whether it refers to a person or a thing.

2. What relative pronoun is used as the object of its clause ?

Je voudrais voir les malades *que* vous avez amenés.	I should like to see the sick persons *whom* you brought.
Montrez-moi la bague *que* vous voulez.	Show me the ring *that* you want.

The relative pronoun *que* is used as the object of its clause, whether it refers to a person or a thing.

The relative pronoun as direct object may be omitted in English but not in French. Ex. : *Is the book you bought interesting* ? **Est-ce que le livre *que* vous avez acheté est intéressant ?**

3. Which two relative pronouns are used after prepositions ?

Où habitent les amis *avec* { *qui* / *lesquels* } vous parlez français ?	Where do the friends *with whom* you speak French live ?
Montrez-moi la clé *avec laquelle* vous avez ouvert ma porte.	Show me the key *with which* you opened my door.
Les candidats *pour* { *qui* / *lesquels* } vous avez voté sont jeunes.	The candidates *for whom* you voted are young.
C'est la région *dans laquelle* elle vit.	It is the region *in which* she lives.

> After a preposition, either *qui* or a form of *lequel* may be used to refer to persons; a form of **lequel** is used to refer to things.
> The forms of **lequel** are : *lequel, laquelle, lesquels, lesquelles.*

4. How is the relative pronoun *what* expressed in French ?

(a) Subject

Ce qui est sur la table est à moi.	*What* is on the table is mine.
Il ne faut pas faire *ce qui* est défendu.	You mustn't do *what* is forbidden.

The English *what* is expressed by *ce qui* when it is the subject of its clause.

(b) Object

Ce que vous écrivez est intéressant.	*What* you are writing is interesting.
Savez-vous *ce que* Jean a dit ?	Do you know *what* John said ?

The English *what* is expressed by *ce que* when it is the object of its clause.

(c) After a preposition

Je ne comprends pas *de quoi* vous parlez.	I don't understand *what* you are talking *about*.

The English *what* is expressed by *quoi* when it is used after a preposition.

NOTE: When this construction begins a sentence, one finds *Ce* + PREPOSITION + *quoi*. Ex. : *Ce à quoi je pense ne vous regarde pas.* (*What* I am thinking *about* is none of your business.) The *ce* + PREPOSITION + *quoi* combination may often also be used in the interior of a sentence, but just when is beyond the scope of this text.

The relative *quoi*, used after a preposition, is sometimes an indefinite that is expressed in English by *which*.

Maurice a fini ses devoirs, *après quoi* il est sorti.	Maurice finished his home-work, *after which* he went out.

5. How is *everything that* expressed in French ?

Avez-vous lu *tout ce qui* est dans votre bibliothèque ?	Have you read *everything that* is in your library ?
Dites-moi *tout ce que* vous faites.	Tell me *everything that* you are doing.

The English *everything that* is expressed in French by

(a) **tout ce qui** when it is the subject of its clause;
(b) **tout ce que** when it is the object of its clause.

6. How can the relative pronouns be presented in graphic tabular form ?

FUNCTION	PERSONS	THINGS	*WHAT*
SUBJECT	qui	qui	ce qui
OBJECT	que	que	ce que
AFTER PREPOSITION	qui lequel*	lequel*	quoi**

A. Un jeune homme parle du voyage qu'il vient de faire en Grèce. Remplacez les mots anglais entre parenthèses par leur équivalent français.

1. Je viens de faire le voyage en Grèce _____ (*that*) mon père m'avait promis.   **2.** L'hôtel dans _____ (*which*) nous sommes descendus à Athènes était très agréable.   **3.** On nous a donné un guide _____ (*who*) était très gentil.   **4.** Il savait bien de _____ (*what*) il parlait et il nous disait _____ (*what*) il fallait voir.   **5.** Les touristes avec _____ (*whom*) je voyageais étaient sympathiques et ils voulaient savoir à _____ (*what*) je

---

*i.e., **lequel, laquelle, lesquels**, or **lesquelles**, according to the gender of the antecedent
**Sometimes *ce* + PREPOSITION + *quoi* is required.

m'intéressais.   **6.** _____ (*What*) m'a le plus frappé était le temple de l'Acropole _____ (*which*) domine la ville.   **7.** L'autocar dans _____ (*which*) nous avons vu les environs aurait pu être plus moderne.   **8.** La route par _____ (*which*) nous avons dû monter pour aller à Delphes était très raide.   **9.** C'est à Delphes qu'il y avait la prophétesse _____ (*whom*) les Grecs venaient consulter.   **10.** Le temple _____ (*which*) s'élevait là est détruit, mais _____ (*what*) reste est un beau théâtre.

B. Traduisez en français.

1. (*vous*) The dress[1] you are wearing is very pretty.   **2.** The carpenter to whom I spoke is very nice.   **3.** (*vous*) My father, who is a businessman, will come to see you.   **4.** What we are studying is very useful.   **5.** (*tu*) The friend whom you invited is charming.   **6.** (*vous*) I do not understand what you are speaking of.   **7.** The road by which he came is very bad.   **8.** (*tu*) Show me everything that you have in your drawer.   **9.** (*vous*) Tell me what you are thinking of[2].   **10.** The parents gave the children some cookies, after which they left.   **11.** (*vous*) What is on the table is yours, but everything that is on the desk is mine.

7. How is *de* + RELATIVE normally expressed in French ?

Le livre *dont* vous parlez est connu.   The book *of which* you are speaking is well known.

The form ***dont*** normally replaces ***de*** + RELATIVE.

NOTE: When a preposition or a prepositional phrase comes between the antecedent and the relative, then *de* + RELATIVE are used instead of *dont*. The relative *dont* must follow its antecedent immediately and therefore must stand first in its clause. Ex. : **C'est <u>un livre</u> au milieu *duquel* il y a de jolies illustrations.** Also, *from which* (meaning *whence*) is usually expressed by *d'où* rather than *dont*. Ex. : **Je n'ai jamais visité la ville *d'où* il vient.**

8. Sentences with the relative pronoun *dont* present certain problems of word order. What is a practical way of determining the word order of such sentences ?

Voici le docteur Galand   Here is Dr. Galand

dont le fils est mon meilleur ami.   { *whose* son is my best friend. *of whom* the son is my best friend.

---

[1]The relative pronoun is missing in English but must be expressed in French. See page 136, §2.   [2]Not **de.**

Note that in French, when **dont** is identified with the subject of its clause, the subject is modified by the definite article.

Montrez-moi le livre	Show me the book
dont vous connaissez l'auteur.	{ *whose* author you know.
	{ *of which* you know the author.

Note that when **dont** is identified with the object of its clause, that object is in quite a different position than it is in the corresponding English clause. The word order of a French clause introduced by **dont** is :

dont + SUBJECT + VERB + rest of sentence

In order to arrive at the French word order in **dont**-clauses, instead of using *whose* in the English sentence, substitute *of whom* or *of which*. The rest of the English sentence will then fall into exactly the same word order that the French clause normally has.

C. *Traduisez en français.*

1. That is a decision of which he will be proud.   **2.** Jack is a young boy whose parents are very strict.   **3.** (*vous*) We know the lady whose husband you saw in Paris.   **4.** I finally found the book the title of which I had forgotten.   **5.** I recommend the doctor whose office[1] is on the first floor[2]. **6.** He has trouble[3] with the neighbors whose dogs bark so much.   **7.** (*vous*) The family whose address you sent me has moved.   **8.** That actress, whose talent I admire so much, lives in Sweden now.   **9.** The friend whose children George adopted died ten years ago.

9. How is the relative *when* expressed in French ?

Au moment *où* nous sommes	At the time *when* we arrived,
arrivés ils étaient tous à table.	they were all at the table.
Je vous dirai cela le jour *où* vous	I'll tell you that the day *when*
vous marierez.	you get married.

The ordinary French word for *when* is **quand**. But when the English word *when* modifies a preceding noun — usually a time expression — it is normally expressed by **où** in French.

---

[1]Not **bureau.**   [2]Not **premier étage.**   [3]The plural form of **ennui, histoire,** or **difficulté.**

The relative *où* also means *where* and indicates place, but this *où* constitutes no problem to the English-speaking student. Ex. : **J'ai visité la ville *où* ce poète a vécu.**

D. *Traduisez en français.*

1. (*vous*) Show me the house where Balzac was born.   **2.** (*tu*) Do you remember the day when we saw each other for the first time ?   **3.** I'll leave the moment[1] he arrives[2].   **4.** (*tu*) I did not feel well the evening when you came to see me.   **5.** (*vous*) Have you forgotten the winter when it was so cold ?   **6.** I prefer the months when there is sun.

EXERCICE ORAL

Monsieur Laforêt est au cirque avec son petit-fils Nicolas. De temps en temps, il fait remarquer ceci ou cela à Nicolas.
Chaque phrase a deux éléments. Combinez ces deux éléments avec le pronom relatif convenable.

EXEMPLE: J'aime voir les lions. Ils sont si majestueux. **J'aime voir les lions qui sont si majestueux.**

1. Vois-tu tous ces éléphants ? Ils vont entrer maintenant.

2. J'aime beaucoup ces chevaux blancs. Ils savent si bien danser.

3. J'admire ces quatre acrobates. Ils n'ont peur de rien.

4. Regarde les singes. Ils demandent des bananes à leur entraîneur.

5. Si tu pouvais, achèterais-tu cet âne savant ? Il sait bien compter.

6. Il y a beaucoup d'animaux dans la ménagerie. Nous irons les voir après le spectacle.

7. Voilà les clowns [klun]. Tu aimes toujours bien les regarder.

8. Je connais cet homme au premier rang. Le clown le taquine.

9. Regarde ce gros ours. Tu n'aimerais certainement pas l'avoir dans ta chambre.

10. Ça ne t'étonne pas de voir sauter ces petits chiens ? Ta grand-mère voudrait sûrement les adopter.

---

[1]French uses **au moment** followed by a relative pronoun.   [2]What tense ? See page 49, §6.

11. Je suis un ami du directeur. Son frère était étudiant avec moi.

12. Je trouve très adroits ces jongleurs. Nous parlions d'eux à midi.

See pages 271–314 for the *Exercices d'ensemble.*

· · · · · ·

PROBLEM WORDS

35. marry

(a) How to say *to get married*

Michelle *s'est mariée* au mois de juin.	Michelle *got married* in the month of June.

French expresses *to get married* by ***se marier.***

(b) How to say *to marry someone*

Robert *s'est marié avec la fille du patron.*	Robert *married the boss's daughter.*
Isabelle devrait *épouser un homme riche.*	Isabelle should *marry a rich man.*

French expresses *to marry someone* by either ***se marier avec quelqu'un*** or ***épouser quelqu'un.***

(c) How to say *to marry someone to someone*

Les Moreau *vont marier leur fille* à l'aîné des Duparc.	The Moreaus *are going to marry their daughter to* the oldest Duparc boy.

French expresses *to marry someone to someone* by ***marier quelqu'un à*** + PERSON.

36. miss

(a) When *miss* = *feel the absence of*

Nous *regrettons* notre ancienne maison.	We *miss* our former house.

The verb ***regretter*** may be used in the sense of *miss;* in that case, the subject of the English and French sentences is the same.

Ma voiture *me manque* beaucoup ici. I *miss* my car a great deal here.
Ses amis *lui manquent*. *He misses* his friends.

The verb ***manquer*** may also be used in the sense of *miss*, but in that case, the object missed becomes the subject of the French sentence.

(b) When *miss* = *fail to reach*

Gérard *a manqué* l'autobus; il va Gerard *missed* the bus; he is
   encore être en retard.   going to be late again.
Pourquoi *avez*-vous *manqué* la Why did you *miss* (*cut*) class ?
   classe ?
J'*ai raté* le train ! I *missed* the train !

French uses the verb ***manquer*** to express the idea of missing a means of transportation or of missing a gathering of some kind. With this sense, the subject of **manquer** is the person and the object of the sentence is the thing missed. Note that ***manquer la classe*** means *to cut class*. The verb ***rater*** is also used familiarly to express the idea of missing a means of transportation or a gathering.

37. more

(a) How to say *more and more*

Je m'intéresse *de plus en plus* à la I am becoming *more and more*
   politique.   interested in politics.
Je suis *de plus en plus* étonné. I am *more and more* surprised.

The English *more and more* + ADJECTIVE is expressed by ***de plus en plus*** modifying an adjective, an adverb, or a verb.

NOTE: The formula *more and more* is really an intensive comparative, so that
   it also includes the English comparatives in *-er* :

Georges devient *de plus en plus* George is getting *taller and*
 grand.   *taller.*

(b) How to say *the more... the more...*

Plus je connais Marianne, plus *The more* I know Marianne,
   j'apprécie ses qualités.   *the more* I appreciate her
    good qualities.

Plus Georges est riche, plus il *The richer* George is, *the more*
   veut d'argent.   money he wants.

French expresses *the more... the more* by ***plus*** + CLAUSE, followed by ***plus*** + CLAUSE.

CAUTION: DO NOT express *the more... the more* by « le plus... le plus ». The correct formula is ***plus..., plus....***

NOTE: The formula *the more... the more* is a type of comparative, so that it also includes the English comparatives in *-er*, as in the sentence :

Les gens croient que *plus* on est riche, *plus* on est *heureux*.	People think that *the richer* one is, *the happier* one is.

38. next

(a) When *next* is expressed by ***prochain***

Nous irons voir vos amis en France l'été *prochain*.	We'll go to see your friends in France *next* summer.
Est-ce que Toulon est le *prochain* arrêt ?	Is Toulon the *next* stop ?

The ordinary French word for *next* is ***prochain***. In general, it can be used, except when one could substitute *following* for *next* in the English sentence without changing the meaning of the sentence.

(b) When *next* is expressed by ***suivant***

J'ai expliqué à Robert pourquoi nous étions retournés en Suisse l'été *suivant*.	I explained to Robert why we had returned to Switzerland the *next* (= *following*) summer.
Regardez la page *suivante*.	Look at the *next* (= *following*) page.

Whenever *next = following* and when *following* can be substituted for *next* without changing the meaning of the sentence, French uses ***suivant***.

CAUTION: DO NOT use « prochain » for *next* when *next = following*. This is a very common error.

(c) How to say *the next day*

Le lendemain		
Le jour suivant	} **nos invités sont partis.**	*The next day* our guests left.
Le jour après		

The next day may be expressed by ***le lendemain, le jour suivant***, or ***le jour après***.

CAUTION: DO NOT say « le jour prochain » for *the next day*.

(**d**) How to say *the next morning* (*afternoon, evening*, etc.)

Le lendemain matin
Le matin suivant } **il a plu sans arrêt.**
Le matin après

The next morning it rained continually.

The adverb **lendemain** is used with times of day to express the English *next*.

E. Remplacez les mots anglais par leur équivalent français.

1. On ne demande plus beaucoup aujourd'hui l'avis de ses parents pour (*get married*). **2.** Allons bon ! Nous (*missed*) le train de sept heures quarante-cinq. **3.** (*The more*) ça change, (*the more*) c'est la même chose. **4.** Je serai à New York à minuit, et je m'envolerai pour Paris (*the next night*). **5.** On dit que cet acteur va (*marry*) une ancienne camarade d'enfance. **6.** Quand je voyage, je (*miss*) le confort de ma maison. **7.** Je suis (*more and more*) étonné par ton indifférence. **8.** Madame Drouet passera (*next week*) chez nous, et elle ira chez vous (*the next week*). **9.** Paul (*got married*) beaucoup trop jeune. **10.** J'ai passé mon baccalauréat et (*the next year*) j'ai fait mon service militaire. **11.** Suivez mon conseil : (*marry*) une jeune fille de votre condition.

F. Traduisez en français. Attention aux mots en italique.

1. (*vous*) Why don't you *marry* Albertine ? **2.** Robert will spend *next* year in Italy. **3.** *The more* I know Paris, *the more* I like it. **4.** Do the children *miss* the television set ? **5.** Mr. Martel would like to *marry* his daughter to a doctor. **6.** (*vous*) If you *miss* your bus[1], you will have to wait until tomorrow morning. **7.** That child is becoming *more and more* unbearable. **8.** Edmond went to bed late and the *next* morning he didn't hear his alarm clock. **9.** (*tu*) I *miss* you a great deal these days. **10.** If they arrive at midnight, they will certainly not leave again[2] the *next* day. **11.** Michael and Colette met at Nice and will *get married* in Paris. **12.** I arrived in London on[3] June 7 and the *next* week I went to Brussels. **13.** *The older* one is, *the harder* it is to get around.

Verb Review

Review the verbs **falloir** and **lire** according to the outline on pages 328–329.

---

[1]In French, a city bus is **un autobus**, whereas an interurban bus is **un autocar**. [2]*leave again* **repartir** [3]For ways of expressing French dates, see pages 170–171.

Chapter 11

The Subjunctive

*L'auteur, venu aux États-Unis avec un groupe d'intellectuels français,
donne ses impressions sur les vastes espaces qu'il survole[1] et qui lui
expliquent la formation et le caractère des villes d'Amérique.*

Villes d'Amérique

Pour apprendre à vivre dans les villes américaines, à les aimer comme les
Américains les aiment, il a fallu que je *survole* d'immenses déserts[2] de l'Ouest
et du Sud. En Europe, nos cités se touchent, elles sont situées dans des
campagnes humaines[3] dont chaque mètre carré est cultivé. Et puis, très loin
5 de nous, de l'autre côté des mers, nous savons vaguement qu'il y a le désert,
un mythe. Ce mythe, pour l'Américain, est une réalité quotidienne. Entre la
Nouvelle-Orléans et San Francisco, nous avons volé pendant des heures au-
dessus d'une terre rouge et sèche. Tout à coup une ville surgissait[4] et puis, de
nouveau, la terre rouge, la savane, le Grand Canyon, les neiges des Rocky
10 Mountains.
    Au bout de quelques jours, j'ai compris qu'une ville américaine était, à
l'origine, un campement dans le désert. Des gens qui venaient de loin, attirés
par une mine, du pétrole, un terrain fertile, arrivaient un beau jour et
s'installaient au plus vite, dans une clairière[5], au bord d'un fleuve. Pour que
15 la vie *puisse* s'organiser, on construisait les organes essentiels, banque,
mairie, église et puis, par centaines, des maisons de bois à un étage. La route,
s'il y en avait une, servait d'épine dorsale[6], et puis, perpendiculairement à la
route, on traçait des rues, comme des vertèbres. Il serait difficile de compter
les villes américaines qui ont ainsi la raie au milieu[7].
20   Rien n'a changé depuis le temps des caravanes vers l'Ouest; on fonde chaque
année des villes aux États-Unis et il semble que cela se *fasse* selon les mêmes
procédés[8].

    Dans ces villes qui vont vite[9], qui ne sont pas construites pour vieillir,
qui progressent en encerclant les îlots de résistance[10] qu'elles ne peu-
25 vent pas détruire, le passé ne se manifeste pas, comme chez nous, par des

---

[1]*fly over* [2]*wildernesses* [3]*inhabited* [4]*suddenly appeared* [5]*clearing* [6]**épine dorsale**
spinal column [7]**ont... milieu** *thus have their hair parted in the middle* [8]*methods*
[9]**qui vont vite** *which develop rapidly* [10]**îlots de résistance** *pockets of resistance*

« monuments », mais par des « résidus[11] », que l'on n'a pas pris le temps de démolir, et par des terrains vagues[12] qui servent du moins de parcs à autos.

Je voudrais que le touriste européen *soit* prévenu : il a tort de visiter les villes américaines comme il visite Paris ou Venise, car elles ne sont pas faites pour
30 cela. En Europe, une rue est intermédiaire entre la grande route et le centre de la ville. Elle est au niveau[13] des cafés, comme le prouve l'usage de la « terrasse »[14] aux beaux jours. Aussi change-t-elle d'aspect sans cesse car la foule qui la peuple se renouvelle toujours, quel que *soit* le moment de la journée. La rue américaine, elle, est un tronçon de grand'route[15]. Elle s'étend parfois sur
35 plusieurs kilomètres. Elle n'invite[16] pas à la promenade; elle n'a pas de secrets. C'est une ligne droite, sans mystère. D'ailleurs les distances sont si grandes qu'on ne se déplace presque jamais à pied.

Pourtant on se met rapidement à aimer les villes d'Amérique. Quoiqu'elles *aient* des ressemblances, on apprend vite qu'il est possible de les distinguer.
40 Et puis on finit par aimer ce qu'elles ont en commun : cet air de provisoire. C'est dommage qu'on *étouffe*[17] un peu dans nos villes fermées, que nos rues *viennent* buter[18] contre des murs, contre des maisons. En Amérique, ces longues rues droites sans obstacle conduisent le regard[19] jusqu'en dehors de la ville. Où que vous *soyez*[20], vous voyez au bout de chacune d'elles la montagne
45 ou les champs ou la mer... Parce que leurs boulevards sont des routes, elles n'oppressent pas, elles n'enferment jamais[21]. Vous sentez, du premier coup d'œil, que votre contact avec elles est provisoire; ou bien vous les quitterez ou bien elles changeront autour de vous.

N'exagérons pas; nous avons connu les dimanches étouffants[22] de la pro-
50 vince américaine... Mais ces villes légères, si semblables encore aux campements du Far West, montrent l'autre face des États-Unis : leur liberté. Chacun est libre ici, non de critiquer ou de réformer les mœurs, mais de les fuir[23], de s'en aller dans le désert ou dans une autre ville. Les villes sont ouvertes. Ouvertes sur le monde, ouvertes sur l'avenir... C'est ce qui leur
55 donne à toutes un air aventureux et, dans leur désordre, dans leur laideur[24] même, une sorte d'émouvante[25] beauté.

> D'après Jean-Paul Sartre, célèbre philosophe de l'existentialisme, dramaturge, romancier, essayiste, un des écrivains les plus importants de sa génération. (« Villes d'Amérique » dans *Situations III*, Gallimard, 1949)

Questions

1. Quelle est la première impression la plus frappante de Sartre en survolant l'Amérique ? **2.** Étant donné cette observation, comment se sont formées les villes américaines ? **3.** Dans quelle mesure ces facteurs géographiques

---

[11]*remains* [12]**terrains vagues** *vacant lots* [13]*level with* [14]*refers to the terrace of French cafés* [15]*tronçon de grand'route part of the main highway* [16]*entice* [17]*suffocates* [18]**viennent buter** *come to an end* [19]**conduisent le regard** *allow you, indeed invite you, to see* [20]**Où que vous soyez** *Wherever you may be* [21]**elles... jamais** *they don't stifle anyone, they never confine anyone* [22]*stifling* [23]*escape* [24]*ugliness* [25]*stirring*

et historiques ont-ils une influence sur la psychologie des habitants et sur la politique du pays ?   **4.** Quelles différences Sartre mentionne-t-il entre les villes américaines et les villes européennes ?   **5.** Commentez la conclusion de Sartre sur la liberté et l'ouverture sur l'avenir des villes d'Amérique. **6.** Parlez de votre ville, de sa topographie, de son peuplement, de son développement.

NOTE: Voir aussi les deux sujets de composition dans le *Manuel d'exercices.*

In connection with the subjunctive, we must consider four important questions :

(a) What is the basic function of the subjunctive as compared with that of the indicative ?

(b) Under what specific circumstances is the subjunctive used in French, and how do those uses fit into the basic concept of the function of the subjunctive ?

(c) When is the present subjunctive used and when is the past subjunctive used; in other words, what is the concept of time in the subjunctive tenses ?

(d) When must the infinitive be used instead of the subjunctive, even though the nature of the main clause seems to indicate a subjunctive in the subordinate clause ?

1. What is the essential difference between the indicative and the subjunctive mode when they deal with facts ?

INDICATIVE	SUBJUNCTIVE
Jean _est_ à la maison.	*Nous sommes contents* que **Jean _soit_ à la maison.**
John *is* at home.	*We are glad* that John *is* at home.
Pierre ne _sait_ pas la leçon.	*Je regrette* que **Pierre ne _sache_ pas la leçon.**
Peter *does* not *know* the lesson.	*I regret* that Peter *does* not *know* the lesson.
Les enfants _ont perdu_ leur ballon.	*C'est dommage* que **les enfants _aient perdu_ leur ballon.**
The children *lost* their ball.	*It is too bad* that the children *lost* their ball.

The INDICATIVE states an objective fact. It is concerned with the fact as a fact. The SUBJUNCTIVE sometimes deals with facts, but in such cases it deals with them not objectively, but from the point of view of the speaker in the main clause. It indicates the subjective attitude of the speaker in the main clause toward the action in the subordinate clause.

2. **What other types of state or action does the subjunctive deal with ? Compare it with the indicative in this respect.**

INDICATIVE	SUBJUNCTIVE
Vous *faites* votre travail.	***Je voudrais* que vous *fassiez* votre travail.**
You *do* your work.	*I wish* that you *would do* your work.
Monsieur Texier *viendra* demain.	***Il est possible* que Monsieur Texier *vienne* demain.**
Mr. Texier *will come* tomorrow.	*It is possible* that Mr. Texier *will come* tomorrow.
Nous *sommes arrivés* trop tard.	***Roger avait peur* que nous *soyons arrivés* trop tard.**
We *arrived* too late.	*Roger was afraid* that we *arrived* too late.

The INDICATIVE states an objective fact, whether in the present, past, or future.

The SUBJUNCTIVE often deals with hypothetical actions; that is, actions that have not occurred and may never occur. It often states the attitude of the subject in the main clause toward such hypothetical actions.

3. **Which types of verbs in the main clause are followed by the subjunctive in the subordinate clause, and why ?**

Nous *craignons* qu'il *pleuve* toute la journée.	We *fear* that it *will rain* all day long.
Roland *a suggéré* que nous *soyons* au stade une heure à l'avance.	Ronald *suggested* that we *be* at the stadium an hour ahead of time.
Je *suis content* que vous *sachiez* ce qui s'est vraiment passé.	I *am glad* that you *know* what really happened.
Le docteur Bertrand *préférerait* que sa fille *fasse* sa médecine à Paris.	Dr. Bertrand *would prefer* that his daughter *study* medicine in Paris.

Verbs of wishing, preferring, suggesting, etc., and verbs and expressions of emotion, such as fearing, being glad, being sorry, etc., all of which indicate the attitude of the subject of the main clause toward either a fact or a hypothetical action, are followed by the subjunctive in the subordinate clause, that is, in the clause introduced by *que*.

> NOTE 1: In affirmative statements, the verb *espérer* is always followed by the indicative. Ex. : *J'espère* **que nos invités *viendront*.** In interrogative sentences, it is usually followed by the indicative but may be followed by the subjunctive. In negative statements, it is followed by the subjunctive.

> NOTE 2: Verbs of advising, commanding, permitting, preventing, requesting, etc., may be followed by a subjunctive clause, but they are usually followed by *de* + INFINITIVE.

USUAL CONSTRUCTION	POSSIBLE CONSTRUCTION
L'avocat *a conseillé* <u>à son client d'être</u> moins exigeant.	L'avocat *a conseillé* <u>que son client *soit*</u> moins exigeant.
L'inspecteur <u>vous</u> *permettra* <u>de téléphoner</u> à votre femme.	L'inspecteur *permettra* <u>que vous téléphoniez</u> à votre femme.
Nous <u>les</u> avons empêchés <u>d'aller</u> plus loin.	Nous avons empêché <u>qu'ils aillent</u> plus loin.

A. Choisissez la forme convenable du verbe et expliquez oralement pourquoi vous avez choisi la forme indicative ou subjonctive.

1. Nous préférons que vous (restez, restiez) ici; ce serait plus prudent.
2. Comment pouvez-vous permettre que vos voisins (font, fassent) tant de bruit à cette heure ?   **3.** J'ai peur que tu ne me (comprends, comprennes) pas.   **4.** Vous savez que Brigitte ne (viendra, vienne) pas.   **5.** La radio dit qu'il (pleuvra, pleuve) demain.   **6.** Nous sommes contents que vous (avez, ayez) de bonnes nouvelles de votre famille.   **7.** Nous regrettons que Gilbert (n'est, ne soit) pas avec nous; nous aurions pu jouer au bridge.   **8.** Je vois que vous (êtes, soyez) pressé. Avez-vous encore une minute ?
9. Qu'est-ce qu'il y a ? J'espère que vous (n'êtes, ne soyez) pas malade.

B. Mettez les infinitifs entre parenthèses au subjonctif ou à l'indicatif, selon le cas.

1. Je suggère que vous (rentrer) immédiatement.   **2.** Ils savent que nous (être) à cet hôtel depuis deux jours.   **3.** Vous devez être bien content que votre belle-mère (être) si agréable.   **4.** Vos créanciers ont entendu dire que vous (aller) déménager le plus tôt possible.   **5.** Je m'étonne que vous (avoir) tant à faire maintenant que vous êtes à la retraite.   **6.** Nous espérons que vous (pouvoir) faire votre voyage au Canada cet été.

4. Certain constructions with the English verb *want* are handled differently in French. How does French express a sentence such as *George wants me to do everything* ?

Georges *veut que je fasse* tout moi-même.	George *wants me to do* everything myself.
Je *veux que tu partes* tout de suite.	I *want you to leave* at once.

An English sentence consisting of a form of *want* + OBJECT + INFINITIVE is expressed in French by a form of **vouloir** + **que** + SUBJUNCTIVE.

C. *Traduisez en français.*

1. We want the baby to sleep for an hour.   **2.** I wanted Colette to learn her lesson.   **3.** *(tu)* Who wants you to be the judge ?   **4.** I wanted Albert to return[1] my books.

5. When is the present subjunctive used in French ? When is the past subjunctive used ? What is the concept of time in the subjunctive ?

Je suis content que Maurice *puisse* le faire maintenant.	I am glad that Maurice *can* do it now.
Je suis content que Maurice *puisse* le faire demain.	I am glad that Maurice *will be able* to do it tomorrow.
Je suis content que Maurice *ait pu* le faire hier.	I am glad that Maurice *could* do it yesterday.

The only two tenses of the subjunctive used in conversational French are the present and the past. The PRESENT SUBJUNCTIVE is used if the action of the subordinate clause takes place <u>at the same time</u> as the action of the main clause or <u>after</u> the action of the main clause. The PAST SUBJUNCTIVE is used if the action of the subordinate clause took place <u>before</u> the action of the main clause. In other words, time in the subjunctive is relative to time in the main clause.

The past subjunctive (**passé du subjonctif**) is a compound tense corresponding to the compound past in the indicative. Ex. : (COMPOUND PAST OF INDICATIVE) : **j'ai vu, tu as parlé, il est parti;** (PAST SUBJUNCTIVE) : ... **que j'aie vu, ... que tu aies parlé, ... qu'il soit parti,** etc.

D. *Remplacez les infinitifs entre parenthèses par le présent ou le passé du subjonctif, selon le cas.*

1. Je suis content que tu (venir) à notre réunion demain.   **2.** Je suis content que tu (venir) à notre réunion hier.   **3.** Est-ce que ton père regrette

---

[1]Use a form of **rendre**.

que tu (partir) en Australie l'année prochaine ?   **4.** Est-ce que ton père regrette que tu (partir) en Australie l'année dernière ?   **5.** Nous avons peur que Georges (perdre) son argent quand il est sorti avec ce type.   **6.** Nous avons peur que Georges (perdre) son argent s'il sort avec ce type. **7.** Philippe s'étonne que nous (se lever) de si bonne heure avant-hier. **8.** Philippe s'étonne que nous (se lever) de si bonne heure demain.   **9.** Je suggère que vous (téléphoner) tout de suite.   **10.** Nous regrettons que vous ne (pouvoir) pas venir demain soir.

6. When must the infinitive be used instead of a *que*-clause with the subjunctive even after constructions which seem to require a subjunctive ?

SUBJUNCTIVE	INFINITIVE
Avez-*vous* peur *que Marcel fasse cela* ?	Avez-*vous* peur *de faire cela* ?
Are *you* afraid *that Marcel will do it* ?	Are *you* afraid *that you will do it* ?
Anne-Marie veut *que vous le sachiez.*	*Anne-Marie* veut *le savoir.*
Anne-Marie wants *you to know it.*	*Anne-Marie* wishes *that she might know it.*
Je suis content *que vous ayez gagné.*	*Je* suis content *d'avoir gagné.*
I am glad *that you won.*	*I* am glad *that I won.*
Nous regrettons *que vous soyez parti si tôt.*	*Nous* regrettons *d'être partis si tôt.*
We are sorry *that you left so soon.*	*We* are sorry *that we left so soon.*

When the subject of a subordinate clause requiring the subjunctive would be the same as the subject of the main clause, the INFINITIVE is normally required instead of *que* with the SUBJUNCTIVE.

NOTE 1: Both *ne* and *pas* precede a present infinitive. Ex. : **J'ai peur de *ne pas* arriver à l'heure.**

NOTE 2: Both *ne* and *pas* usually precede the auxiliary of a past infinitive. Ex. : **J'ai peur de *ne pas* avoir vu le vrai responsable. Nous regrettons de *ne pas* être partis de bonne heure ce matin.**

Verbs of wishing are followed directly by the infinitive without a preposition; verbs of emotion require *de* before an infinitive.

E. Écrivez les phrases suivantes en mettant à la forme convenable les mots entre parenthèses.

1. (tu) Raymond est content (*that you will finish*) ce travail demain. **2.** Raymond est content (*that he will finish*) ce travail demain.   **3.** N'êtes-

vous pas heureux (*that we will spend*) l'année prochaine en Europe ?
4. N'êtes-vous pas heureux (*that you will spend*) l'année prochaine en
Europe ?   **5.** (*vous*) Nous sommes contents (*that you went*) en ville.
6. Nous sommes contents (*that we went*) en ville.   **7.** Je suis étonné (*that
I found*) ma montre.   **8.** Je suis étonné (*that Philip found*) sa montre.
9. Je crains (*that John does not know*) ce que tu veux.   **10.** Je crains (*that
I do not know*) ce que tu veux.   **11.** Robert regrette (*that he does not
understand*) l'italien.   **12.** Robert regrette (*that we do not understand*)
l'italien.   **13.** Est-ce que votre père est content (*that he has retired*) ?
14. Nous sommes contents (*that we did not go*) à cette conférence.   **15.** Je
regrette (*that I arrived*) trop tard.

7. **When is the indicative and when is the subjunctive used after impersonal expressions ?**

INDICATIVE

Il est certain que Louis <u>est</u>
  intelligent.
  It is certain that Louis *is*
    intelligent.
Il est évident que vous <u>savez</u>
  votre leçon.
  It is obvious that you *know*
    your lesson.
Il est exact que Monsieur et
  **Madame Minard <u>vont</u> en
  France cet été.**
  It is true that Mr. and Mrs.
    Minard *are going* to France
    this summer.

SUBJUNCTIVE

Il est possible que Louis <u>soit</u>
  intelligent.
  It is possible that Louis *is*
    intelligent.
Il est important que vous
  <u>sachiez</u> **votre leçon.**
  It is important that you
    know your lesson.
Il est naturel que Monsieur et
  **Madame Minard <u>aillent</u> en
  France cet été.**
  It is natural that Mr. and
    Mrs. Minard *should go* to
    France this summer.

Impersonal expressions that insist on a fact or on the certainty of a fact are
followed by the INDICATIVE.

Impersonal expressions where not the fact but the attitude or opinion of the
speaker toward a hypothetical state or action is given are followed by the
SUBJUNCTIVE.

AMONG THE IMPERSONAL EXPRESSIONS FOLLOWED BY THE <u>INDICATIVE</u> ARE:	AMONG THE IMPERSONAL EXPRESSIONS FOLLOWED BY THE <u>SUBJUNCTIVE</u> ARE:	
Il est certain	*Il est bien*	*Il est préférable*
Il est clair	*Il est bon*	*Il est peu probable*
Il est évident	*Il est douteux*	*Il est rare*
Il est exact	*Il est étonnant*	*Il est temps*

INDICATIVE	SUBJUNCTIVE	
Il est probable	*Il est étrange*	*Il faut*
Il est sûr	*Il est important*	*Il importe*
Il est vrai	*Il est impossible*	*Il se peut*
Il me semble	*Il est juste*	*Il semble*
	Il est naturel	*Il suffit*
	Il est nécessaire	*Il vaut mieux*
	Il est possible	

F. Monsieur Favier lit son journal. Il fait des réflexions à haute voix sur des événements qui viennent d'arriver en Cerdagne (pays imaginaire). Mettez les infinitifs indiqués entre parenthèses soit au présent soit au passé du subjonctif ou au temps convenable de l'indicatif. Justifiez oralement votre choix du temps et du mode.

1. Il est évident que les choses ne _____ (être) pas toutes roses en Cerdagne. **2.** Il est possible que nous _____ (faire) erreur en soutenant ce pays l'année dernière. **3.** Il est étonnant qu'on _____ (envoyer) des troupes dans ce pays à cette époque-là. **4.** Il est certain que la situation _____ (paraître) explosive aujourd'hui. **5.** Je voudrais que le gouvernement nous _____ (dire) bientôt toute la vérité sur cette affaire. **6.** Il est impossible que les diplomates ne _____ (savoir) pas les dangers que nous courons. **7.** Il serait bon que les États-Unis _____ (faire) connaître leur position en Cerdagne. **8.** Il est aussi grand temps que les Nations unies _____ (être) informées de cette affaire. **9.** Il suffirait qu'elles _____ (vouloir) vraiment assurer la paix en Cerdagne. **10.** J'espère que cela ne _____ (compromettre) pas les Jeux Olympiques de l'année prochaine.

G. Traduisez en français. Justifiez oralement l'emploi du temps et du mode.

1. (*vous*) It is rare that your wife comes to see us. **2.** (*vous*) It is clear that you are mistaken. **3.** (*vous*) It[1] is important for you[1] not to speak of this story. **4.** It is probable that the treaty will be signed this week. **5.** (*tu*) It is good that you have already finished your work. **6.** It is surprising that he is so hateful[2]. **7.** (*tu*) It[1] is necessary for me[1] to think[3] before answering you. **8.** It is time that the president act energetically. **9.** It is doubtful that they have found the money. **10.** (*tu*) It is natural that you should wish to have a good time. **11.** It is fantastic that man can go to[4] the moon. **12.** It is correct[5] that he has never read a single book. **13.** I am surprised[6], but it is possible that I said that. **14.** (*vous*) It is evident that you do not work too much.

---

[1]Rearrange the wording before translating. [2]**méchant** [3]Use a form of **réfléchir**. [4]**dans** or **sur** [5]Not **correct** [6]**Ça m'étonne**

8. What mode follows verbs of "thinking" and "believing" in French ?

AFFIRMATIVE	NEGATIVE AND INTERROGATIVE
Je *crois* que vous *êtes* malade.	Je *ne crois pas* que vous $\begin{cases} \text{êtes} \\ \text{soyez} \end{cases}$ malade.
Il *pense* que sa femme *partira.*	Il *ne pense pas* que sa femme $\begin{cases} \text{partira.} \\ \text{parte.} \end{cases}$
Nous *croyons* que Paul *a lu* cela.	*Croyez-vous* que Paul $\begin{cases} a \ lu \ \text{cela ?} \\ ait \ lu \ \text{cela ?} \end{cases}$
Moi, je *trouve* qu'il *a* bien *fait.*	*Trouvez-vous* qu'il $\begin{cases} a \ \text{bien } fait \ ? \\ ait \ \text{bien } fait \ ? \end{cases}$

Affirmative forms of verbs of thinking and believing are ALWAYS followed by the indicative — NEVER by the subjunctive.

Negative and interrogative forms of verbs of thinking and believing may be followed by the subjunctive when there is considerable doubt on the part of the speaker, and when the speaker is grammatically precise in the use of the subjunctive. When the element of doubt is minor and especially when the idea in the subordinate clause is of a future nature, the indicative is normally used. This also applies to negative and interrogative forms of impersonal expressions, which are always followed by the indicative in the affirmative form.

Forms of the verb *douter* are normally followed by the subjunctive.

> NOTE: It is true that the subjunctive after forms of the verb *douter* and after expressions such as *Je ne crois pas* indicates <u>doubt</u>. However, in the great majority of cases, the subjunctive is used to show attitudes other than those of doubt. For instance, the subjunctive after *Il faut que...* or *Je suis content que...* does not give the slightest indication of doubt. Students should not try to justify the use of a given subjunctive by saying that it expresses doubt, except in cases where doubt actually exists.

H. Mettez les infinitifs à la forme convenable et expliquez oralement le temps et le mode que vous aurez choisis.

1. Je trouve que cette robe vous (aller) très bien.   **2.** Nous doutons que votre idée (valoir) grand-chose.   **3.** Je ne pense pas que nous (pouvoir) nous révoir.   **4.** Ils croient que leur fils (être) toujours un enfant.   **5.** Ne croyez-vous pas que vos amis (savoir) cela ?   **6.** Je ne crois pas que Jean (venir) demain.   **7.** Je trouve qu'elle (conduire) très bien.   **8.** Je crois que cet homme (connaître) bien métier.   **9.** Nous ne pouvons pas croire que Jacques (venir) hier soir.

I. *Traduisez en français.*

1. He thinks we are stupid. **2.** *(vous)* Do you think that he will do that ? **3.** I do not believe that he can get to the airport in time. **4.** He believes that they are going to Paris. **5.** *(tu)* Do you believe that they will invite us ? **6.** *(vous)* I don't think that you understand the problem.

9. What are the subordinate conjunctions that are always followed by the subjunctive in French, and what in the nature of their meaning causes them to be followed by a subjunctive rather than an indicative ?

afin que *pour que* } *in order that, so that*	*à moins que*	*unless*
bien que *quoique* } *although*	*sans que*	*without*
	avant que	*before*
pourvu que *à condition que* } *provided that*	*jusqu'à ce que*	*until*

Each of these expressions embodies a concept that is concerned either with a hypothetical action or with an attitude toward a real action :

(a) *afin que* and *pour que* indicate purpose, and the intended purpose is hypothetical, not yet real.

(b) *bien que* and *quoique* indicate concession on the part of the speaker toward what is either a reality or something that could be so and is therefore hypothetical.

(c) *pourvu que* and *à condition que* introduce a restrictive condition that is not a reality.

(d) *à moins que* and *sans que* also introduce a restrictive condition that is not a reality.

(e) *avant que* and *jusqu'à ce que* are conjunctions concerned with actions to take place at some time after the action of the main clause and which, in the mind of the speaker, depend on some other action taking place. Thus, they are restrictive to a certain extent.

10. Under what conditions are these conjunctions replaced by a corresponding preposition followed by an infinitive ?

Je lui écrirai *pour qu'il sache* cela.
I will write him *so that he may be aware of* that.

Je lui écrirai *pour* savoir cela.
I will write him *so that I may find out about* that.

Je conduirai vite *afin que* **vous arriviez** à l'heure.
I'll drive fast *so that you arrive* on time.

Je conduirai vite *afin d'arriver* à l'heure.

I'll drive fast { *in order to arrive* on time. / *so that I may arrive* on time. }

Je viendrai *à moins que* **Marc soit malade.**
I'll come *unless Mark is sick.*

Je partirai *avant que* **Georges apprenne** les résultats de l'examen.
I'll leave *before George learns* the results of the examination.

Je viendrai *à moins d'être* **malade.**
I'll come *unless I am sick.*

Je partirai *avant d'apprendre* **les résultats de l'examen.**
I'll leave *before learning* the results of the examination.

Je ferai cette affaire *sans que* **vous perdiez** un sou.
I'll carry this thing out *without your losing* a penny.

Je ferai cette affaire *sans* **perdre** un sou.
I'll carry this thing out *without losing* a penny.

When the subject of the subordinate clause introduced by conjunctions requiring the subjunctive in French would be the same as the subject of the main clause, French normally uses a preposition with an infinitive if such a construction exists.

The most common conjunctions with a prepositional counterpart are :

CONJUNCTION	PREPOSITION	
à moins que + SUBJUNCTIVE	*à moins de* + INFINITIVE	*unless*
afin que + SUBJUNCTIVE	*afin de* + INFINITIVE	*in order that (to)*
pour que + SUBJUNCTIVE	*pour* + INFINITIVE	*so that*
avant que + SUBJUNCTIVE	*avant de* + INFINITIVE	*before*
sans que + SUBJUNCTIVE	*sans* + INFINITIVE	*without*

NOTE: In a few cases, such as in sentences with *bien que, quoique, pourvu que,* and *jusqu'à ce que,* it is impossible to replace a clause in the subjunctive by an infinitive construction even when the subject of the main clause and that of the dependent *que*-clause would be the same, since there is no prepositional construction that corresponds to the subordinate conjunctions. In these cases the subjunctive must be used even when the subject of the main clause and that of the dependent clause are the same. Ex. : **Nous viendrons *bien que nous soyons* fatigués. Jean-Paul le fera *pourvu qu'il soit* libre.**

However, in the case of *à moins que,* one finds both *à moins que* + SUBJECT OF MAIN CLAUSE and *à moins de* + INFINITIVE.

J. *Écrivez les phrases suivantes en mettant à la forme convenable les mots entre parenthèses.*

1. Je te conseille de finir (*before your father comes back*).   **2.** Il est dur d'oreille. Parlez-lui plus fort (*so that he can hear you*).   **3.** J'ai pu quitter la salle (*without the lecturer noticing*[1] *it*).   **4.** Je passerai par le bureau (*before I come*) vous voir.   **5.** Daniel sera toujours pauvre (*unless his uncle should die*).   **6.** Elle refuse de parler (*although she knows*) toute l'histoire. **7.** Il est parti (*without having done*) la moitié du travail.   **8.** J'ai envoyé cette lettre hier (*so that I might have*) une réponse demain.   **9.** Amuse-toi bien (*before it is too late*).

K. *Traduisez en français les phrases suivantes. Attention au temps et au mode.*

1. (*tu*) I'll go with you although I am very busy.   **2.** (*vous*) Do something so that they will go away sooner.   **3.** (*vous*) Do what you please[2] provided that you do not make any[3] noise.   **4.** She truly loves me, although she doesn't tell me so[4].   **5.** How can we leave[5] without their being angry ? **6.** They did everything[6] so that their children might be happy.   **7.** I'll work until I understand these rules.

11. Why do the sentences on the left use the indicative in the subordinate clause, while those on the right use the subjunctive ?

INDICATIVE	SUBJUNCTIVE
	(a) the antecedent is as yet unattained
J'ai un domestique *qui sait* **tout faire.**	**Je cherche un domestique** *qui sache* **tout faire.**
	(b) doubt is expressed as to the attainability of the antecedent
Vous avez un collègue *qui est* **très au courant de ces choses.**	**Avez-vous un collègue** *qui soit* **trés au courant de ces choses ?**
	(c) the antecedent is negative
Je connais quelqu'un *qui peut* **vous accompagner.**	**Je ne connais personne** *qui puisse* **vous accompagner.**
Il y a des professeurs *qui vont* **en Europe tous les ans.**	**Il n'y a pas de professeur** *qui aille* **en Europe tous les ans.**

---

[1]Use a form of **s'apercevoir de**.   [2]Either **vous voulez** or **vous voudrez**   [3]**de**   [4]**le**   [5]*How can we leave* **Comment partir**   [6]Place between auxiliary and past participle.

The INDICATIVE is normally used in dependent relative clauses, since relative clauses normally state a fact.

The SUBJUNCTIVE is often used in relative clauses where there is some doubt or denial of the existence or attainability of the antecedent, but certain tenses of the indicative are also found in such clauses.

L. Remplacez l'infinitif entre parenthèses par le temps convenable de l'indicatif ou du subjonctif, selon le cas.

1. Avez-vous une amie qui (pouvoir) venir avec nous dimanche ?   **2.** Il y a à la porte un homme qui (vouloir) vous voir.   **3.** Pouvez-vous m'indiquer un film qui (plaire) à tout le monde ?   **4.** Il cherche quelqu'un qui (vouloir) bien acheter sa vieille maison.   **5.** Y a-t-il ici un étudiant qui (savoir) parler chinois ?   **6.** Connaissez-vous une seule personne qui (être) capable de se sacrifier pour cela ?   **7.** Nous cherchons un cadeau qui lui (faire) plaisir.   **8.** Je vous apporte un livre qui vous (intéresser).   **9.** Y a-t-il quelque chose que je (pouvoir) faire pour vous ?

M. Traduisez en français.

1. (*vous*) We do not know anyone who is able to solve your problem. **2.** He is looking for someone who can help him.   **3.** I know a very young boy who drives very well.   **4.** (*vous*) Can you tell me the name of a student who knows how to type ?   **5.** Is there a restaurant near here that is not too expensive ?   **6.** (*tu*) Bring me a book that is not too long.   **7.** We are looking for an apartment that is near a shopping center.   **8.** I see no one I know.   **9.** There are many people who know how to speak several languages.   **10.** There is nothing that can save that man.

12. When and why is the subjunctive used in the following examples ?

C'est *le plus beau* musée que je *connaisse*.	It is *the most beautiful museum* that I *know*.
Quel est *le plus grand* édifice qu'on *ait* (*a*) *construit* à Paris ?	What is *the largest building* that they *have built* in Paris ?
C'est *le seul* homme qui *puisse* (*peut*) faire cela.	He is *the only man* who *can* do that.
C'est *le plus long* voyage que nous *avons* (*ayons*) jamais *fait*.	It is *the longest trip* that we *have* ever *taken*.

In clauses whose antecedent is modified by a superlative or by adjectives such as **premier, dernier**, and **seul**, the verb may be in either the indicative or subjunctive. The INDICATIVE is used when the speaker wishes to state an objective fact. When there is an element of doubt or personal opinion or of subjective feeling, the SUBJUNCTIVE may be used.

N. *Traduisez en français.*

1. (*vous*) Who[1] is the most interesting author that you have read ?   **2.** It is the first thing that he must do.   **3.** Here are the only oranges that we were able to find.   **4.** Is France the only country where one is really free ? **5.** It's the last book that I am obliged to read for this course.   **6.** (*tu*) What is the most beautiful opera you ever heard ?   **7.** Here is the only person who saw the accident.   **8.** (*vous*) Who is the best teacher you have had ?

13. How does French express the English indefinites *whoever, whatever, wherever, however*, etc. ? Why is the verb of French clauses introduced by such indefinites in the subjunctive ?

Qui que ce soit, il n'a pas le droit de fumer ici.	*Whoever* he $\begin{cases} is, \\ may\ be, \end{cases}$ he does not have the right to smoke here.
Quel que soit son métier, il faut qu'il fasse son service militaire.	*Whatever* his trade $\begin{cases} is, \\ may\ be, \end{cases}$ he must do his military service.
Quoi qu'il en soit, vous devez revenir.	*However* that *may be*, you must come back.
Où que nous soyons, nous n'oublierons pas nos parents.	*Wherever* we $\begin{cases} are, \\ may\ be, \end{cases}$ we will not forget our parents.
Si riches qu'ils soient, ils ne sont pas heureux.	*However rich* they $\begin{cases} are, \\ may\ be, \end{cases}$ they are not happy.
Quelles que soient vos objections, il s'en ira.	*Whatever* your objections $\begin{cases} are, \\ may\ be, \end{cases}$ he will go away.

The common French indefinites that correspond to the English indefinites in -*ever* are :

qui que	*whoever*	**quoi que**	*whatever*
quel que	*whoever, whatever*	**si** + ADJECTIVE + **que**	*however* + ADJECTIVE

When a clause introduced by one of the above indefinites indicates concession, that is, admits that something is or may be the case, its verb is in the subjunctive. Clauses of this kind have a certain vagueness, which places them in the realm of the hypothetical subjunctive rather than in that of the factual indicative.

---

[1]Quel

NOTE 1: The idea of concession is illustrated in the above examples. For instance, ***Quel que soit son métier*** concedes that he does or may have a trade. ***Si riches qu'ils soient*** admits that they are or may be rich.

NOTE 2: The ***quel*** of the expression ***quel que*** agrees with the noun it modifies in gender and number. Ex. : ***Quelle que*** soit <u>votre préférence</u>... (*Whatever your preference* is / may be...); ***Quelles que*** soient <u>ses</u> <u>raisons</u>... (*Whatever* <u>his reasons</u> are / may be...).

NOTE 3: The English *However* + ADJECTIVE is expressed in current spoken French by ***Si*** + ADJECTIVE. Ex. : ***Si*** <u>intéressant</u> que soit ce roman... (*However* <u>interesting</u> this novel is / may be...); ***Si*** <u>grands</u> que soient ces jeunes gens... (*However* <u>tall</u> these young men are / may be...).

O. Traduisez en français.

1. (*tu*) Whoever he is[1], tell him to come to see me at once.   **2.** (*vous*) Whatever[2] your religion may be, you must help your neighbor[3].   **3.** (*vous*) Whatever[2] your ideas are, keep them to yourself[4].   **4.** Whatever he does, he will not be able to change the situation.   **5.** However[5] lazy they may be, they are obliged to work in order to live.   **6.** (*vous*) However that may be, you must come to class every day.   **7.** Wherever he goes, he makes[6] friends easily.   **8.** Whatever he does, fate is against him.   **9.** However[5] good[7] they may be, their mother is never satisfied[8].

EXERCICE ORAL

Un homme quelque peu hypocondriaque va voir son docteur avant de partir en voyage. Voici ce qu'il lui dit.
Répétez chaque phrase en la faisant précéder par l'expression indiquée entre parenthèses. Faites les changements nécessaires dans les verbes s'il y a lieu.

1. Docteur, j'ai besoin d'un examen avant de partir en voyage. (Je crois...)

2. Je bois trop de café. (Il est probable...)

3. Je prends aussi trop de cocktails. (Il est possible...)

4. Je dors bien. (Il est rare...)

5. Nous ne vivons pas vieux dans ma famille. (Il est vrai...)

---

[1]Use either **Qui que ce soit** or **Quel qu'il soit**.   [2]In such constructions, the **Quel** must agree with the noun that follows.   [3]**prochain**   [4]*to yourself* **pour vous**   [5]Use *si* + ADJECTIVE.   [6]Use a form of **se faire**.   [7]**sages**   [8]**contente**

6. Dites-moi la vérité. (Je voudrais...)

7. Je me mettrai au lit. (Serait-il préférable...)

8. Je suis un petit régime. (Faut-il...)

9. Je prends plusieurs pilules tous les jours. (Est-il nécessaire...)

10. Permettez-moi de partir comme je l'avais prévu. (Je serais content...)

11. J'ai une entière confiance en vous. (Vous savez...)

12. Vous ne pouvez pas venir en voyage avec moi. (Je regrette...)

13. Je vivrai encore dix ou vingt ans. (Pourvu...)

See pages 271–314 for the *Exercices d'ensemble.*

· · · · · ·

PROBLEM WORDS

39. notice

(a) When *to notice* is expressed by **remarquer**

Avez-vous remarqué ces deux personnes au premier rang ?	*Did* you *notice* those two people in the first row ?
J'ai remarqué tout de suite que tu n'avais pas reconnu Monsieur Lévêque.	I *noticed* right away that you had not recognized Mr. Lévêque.

The verb **remarquer** may be used for *notice* in almost any circumstance.

(b) When *to notice* is expressed by **apercevoir**

J'ai aperçu Elizabeth dans un taxi.	I *noticed* Elizabeth in a taxi.

The verb **apercevoir** means *notice* in the sense of *catch sight of.*

(c) When *notice* is expressed by **s'apercevoir**

Le conférencier ne s'aperçoit pas qu'on ne l'écoute plus.	The lecturer doesn't *notice* (= *realize*) that people are no longer listening to him.
Je me suis aperçu de son inquiétude.	I *noticed* (= *realized*) his uneasiness.

The verb *s'apercevoir* is synonymous with *realize* or *be aware of*. When *s'apercevoir* is followed by *de*, the object of *de* is something intangible.

40. opportunity

(a) When *opportunity* = *l'occasion*

J'espère que nous aurons souvent *l'occasion* de nous revoir.	I hope that we will often have *the opportunity* to see each other.

When *opportunity* means a favorable conjunction of circumstances, it is expressed by *l'occasion*.

(b) When *opportunity* = *la possibilité*

Ces étudiants n'ont pas encore eu *la possibilité* d'aller en France.	Those students haven't yet had *the opportunity* to go to France.

The English *opportunity* is expressed by *la possibilité* when *opportunity* means *possibility*.

> CAUTION: DO NOT use the « opportunité » for *opportunity*. The word *opportunité* means *opportuneness* and is relatively uncommon.

41. paper

(a) When *paper* = *a piece of paper*

Jacques dit qu'il ne peut pas finir son devoir parce qu'il n'a plus de *papier*.	Jack says that he can't finish his homework because he doesn't have any more *paper*.
Votre livre est imprimé sur un beau *papier*.	Your book is printed on very good *paper*.

When *paper* means *material to write on* it is expressed by *le papier*.

(b) When *paper* = *newspaper*

Avez-vous lu *le journal* ce matin ?	Did you read *the paper* this morning ?

When *paper* is used in the sense of *newspaper*, it is *le journal*.

> CAUTION: DO NOT use « papier » for *newspaper*.

(c) When *paper* is *a classroom exercise*

Remettez vos *copies* à la fin de l'heure.	Hand in your *papers* at the end of the hour.

For *papers* to be handed in to the teacher one can say **les copies, les devoirs**, or **les exercices**. The classroom expression : *Hand in your papers* is : **Remettez vos copies** or **Donnez-moi vos copies**.

> Caution: Do not use « papier » for *classroom exercise*, and do not say « Passez les papiers » for *Hand in your papers*. The classroom exercise is **la copie**; say **Remettez les**[1] **copies** for *Hand in your papers*.

(d) When *paper* is *a classroom report*

J'ai *un travail* à préparer.	I have *a paper* to prepare.

In French, there are various names for *classroom report*, such as **un travail**, **un compte rendu**, **une composition**, **une dissertation**, or **une étude** — but NOT « un papier ».

42. people

(a) When *people* is expressed by **personnes**

Ses idées ont offensé plusieurs *personnes*.	His ideas offended several *people*.

When *people* means *a few persons*, French uses **personnes**.

(b) When *people* is expressed by **gens**

Il y a trop de *gens* sur la Côte d'Azur en été.	There are too many *people* on the French Riviera in summer.
Il y a des *gens* qui n'ont aucun scrupule.	There are *people* who have no scruples.

When *people* means *a considerable number of persons*, French often uses **les gens**.

(c) When *people* is expressed by **monde**

Il y avait beaucoup de *monde* au concert.	There were many *people* at the concert.

---

[1]Either the definite article or the possessive adjective may be used in this sentence.

To state that there were *many people* at some function, French often uses **monde**. When used in this sense, **monde** cannot be modified by a relative clause.

(d) When *people* is expressed by **peuple**

> **Les Italiens sont un peuple très musicien.**
>
> The Italians are a very musical *people*.

The English *a people*, in the sense of *a nation*, is expressed by **le peuple**. Note that **le peuple** also sometimes means *the masses*.

> CAUTION: DO NOT use « peuple » to express *people* except when it means *nation* or *the masses*.

(e) When *people* is expressed by **on**

> **Qu'est-ce qu'on dirait si on savait ça ?**
>
> What would *people* say if they knew that ?

When *people* has the very indefinite sense of *people in general*, French uses the indefinite pronoun **on**.

P. Remplacez les mots anglais par leur équivalent français.

1. (*vous*) (*Notice*) que nous sommes presque du même avis.   **2.** (*People*) n'aime pas conduire quand il neige.   **3.** Venez me voir à la première (*opportunity*).   **4.** Étienne corrige des (*papers*) pour le professeur Grémillot. **5.** Les Hongrois sont un (*people*) très artiste.   **6.** Nous (*noticed*) un renard au bord de la route cette nuit.   **7.** Deux (*people*) sont venues pendant que vous étiez absent.   **8.** Ce (*paper*)-là a des tendances libérales. **9.** J'aimerais vivre dans ce pays, mais je n'aurais pas la (*opportunity*) d'y travailler.   **10.** D'où vient tout ce (*people*) ?   **11.** Ce (*paper*) n'est pas assez bon pour taper une thèse.   **12.** Tous ces (*people*) attendent la sortie des artistes[1].   **13.** Il lui a fallu longtemps pour (*notice*) qu'on le volait. **14.** (*People*) aime bien prendre des vacances l'été.

Q. Traduisez en français. Attention aux mots en italique.

1. Anne always writes on purple *paper*.   **2.** Several *people* came to see me this morning.   **3.** Irene *noticed* the new painting as soon as she entered the house.   **4.** A *people* should know its history.   **5.** I have never had the *opportunity* to visit Sweden.   **6.** I *noticed* too late that I had left my briefcase in the taxi.   **7.** One mustn't believe everything one reads in the

---

[1]*are waiting for the artists to come out*

paper.   **8.** I saw many *people* that I didn't know.   **9.** I *noticed* Guy at the theater last evening.   **10.** Would there be an *opportunity* to see the director ?   **11.** Were there many *people* at the reception ?   **12.** (*vous*) Don't forget to hand in your *papers*.   **13.** The teacher didn't *notice* that I was finishing my exercises in class.   **14.** (*vous*) Don't believe everything that *people* tell you.

Verb Review

Review the verbs **mettre** and **mourir** according to the outline on pages 330–331.

The Article

Brassens[1], *un des chansonniers*[2] *les plus aimés des Français, poète, lauréat du Grand prix de poésie de l'Académie française, est interviewé par une journaliste à la suite d'un sondage*[3] *où il est choisi comme l'homme le plus heureux dans une longue liste de personnalités proposées aux lecteurs.*

Moi, le *plus heureux des Français* ?

L'EXPRESS—*Un* sondage nous indique que pour 65%[4] des Français vous représentez *l'*homme heureux.

GEORGES BRASSENS—Ah ! *les* idiots...

EXP—Sans doute parce que vous symbolisez à travers vos chansons *une*
5 forme de liberté à *la* limite de *l'*anarchie dans laquelle beaucoup de Français aiment à se reconnaître. Il y a *la* fidélité aux copains d'abord, à *la* bonne langue populaire et poétique ensuite. Vous êtes *un* peu libertin[5], *un* peu libertaire[6].

G. B. —Mon bonheur à moi, c'est de faire des chansons. *Le* bonheur, c'est deux vers agréables à entendre. Si je n'étais pas célibataire, mes enfants
10 auraient eu plus d'importance que mes chansons mais comme je n'en ai pas... J'écris des chansons depuis *l'*âge de 14 ans. J'essaie d'en faire *une* par semaine, en tout cas *une* par mois. En dehors de ça, je n'existe pas. J'aurais d'ailleurs été plus pleinement heureux si j'avais été <u>musicien</u>*. *Les* vrais bonheurs physiques et psychiques que j'ai éprouvés, c'est en écoutant *une* nouvelle mélodie
15 qui me touche. *La* musique me donne des frissons[7] que je n'éprouve pas autrement... C'est quelque chose qui me donne envie de pleurer comme *un* veau[8], *une* vibration...

EXP —Y a-t-il *une* période de votre vie dont vous ayez *la* nostalgie ?

G. B. —*Le* passé est *un* thème pour moi, je ne *l'*évoque que dans mes
20 chansons, pas dans *la* vie. J'ai eu *une* enfance heureuse mais gâchée[9] par *l'*école. Ma mère était sévère, elle exigeait de moi de bonnes notes. Ça

---

[1]Pronounce [brasɛ̃s] [2]*writers and performers of popular songs and songs dealing with social and political satire* [3]*poll* [4]% *pour cent* [5]*sensualist* [6]*partisan of absolute and total freedom* *Underscored words are examples of THE NOUN ALONE not preceded by an article. [7]*shivers* [8]**pleurer... veau** *i.e., cry like a baby* [9]*spoiled*

m'embêtait[10] de ne pas lui faire plaisir mais, <u>en égoïste</u>, je préférais lui déplaire[11] et ne rien faire !

EXP —Vos débuts ont été difficiles. *Le* confort, c'est nécessaire ?

25 G. B. —Non. Quand j'étais dans *le* besoin, il se trouvait toujours quelqu'un pour me donner *un* paquet de tabac ou de quoi manger *le* lendemain. J'étais plus heureux alors que *le* type que je suis aujourd'hui qui s'achète *une* paire de chaussures.

EXP —*L'*amour est-il indispensable au bonheur ?

30 G. B. —*L'*amour ? Je ne sais pas bien ce que c'est. Je ne fais pas *la* différence entre *l'*amour que j'ai pour *une* femme et celui que j'ai pour mes amis ou pour mes chats. J'ai *une* somme de sentiments à donner. A qui que ce soit que je les dispense, ils sortent du même coin, non ?

EXP —Vous donnez *l'*impression d'être *un* homme libre.

35 G. B. —Quelle liberté ? Pendant *les* 20 ans que j'ai eu des coliques né- phrétiques[12], je n'étais plus libre. A ce moment-là, j'aurais donné toutes mes chansons pour cesser de souffrir. Je l'aurais regretté après... Mais j'étais limité par *la* maladie, donc, prisonnier. Si vous parlez de *la* liberté en pensant à *la* censure[13], il faut admettre que, sous *un* régime totalitaire, je serais <u>en prison</u>. 40 Et que, dans cette démocratie fatiguée qui est *la* nôtre, je peux dire à peu près tout ce que je veux. Comme tout *le* monde, d'ailleurs.

EXP —On vous a reproché de ne pas vous engager[14]...

G. B. —Mais c'est *un* engagement total que j'ai pris. Depuis *le* début, j'ai dans mes chansons *la* même attitude en face de *la* vie, en face de *l'*argent, en face 45 de *la* réussite, en face des grands[15], en face des humbles. Mais si on entend par là appartenir à *un* parti, je ne reconnais à aucun parti *le* droit de m'avoir[16].

EXP —Peut-on mesurer *le* bonheur des gens ?

G. B. —*La* notion que nous avons du bonheur est celle d'*une* midinette[17]. Il y a des gens qui sont heureux lorsque *la* sirène de *l'*usine sonne, parce qu'ils 50 vont sortir, cesser de bosser[18]. Pour *l'*ouvrier, qu'il soit payé au maximum ou au minimum de *l'*heure, c'est *une* plus grande joie, peut-être, *la* sirène qui sonne, que pour moi de trouver *un* quatrain[19]. <u>A vélo, en auto</u> ou <u>en métro</u> il va rentrer chez lui, trouver sa femme, ses enfants, sa télévision, sa pipe. Il est heureux, *le* type, si c'est son bonheur. Pour lui, pour *les* autres, pour moi, ce 55 n'est que *l'*accumulation des petites joies qui rend *la* vie possible. Et puis on ne devrait jamais demander à quelqu'un s'il est heureux.

EXP —Et pourquoi ?

G. B. —Parce que c'est indiscret.

D'après Georges Brassens. (« Moi, le plus heureux des Français ? » *l'Express,* 19 septembre 1977)

---

[10]*bothered me* [11]*displease* [12]*kidney pains* [13]*censorship* [14]**de ne pas vous engager** *for not getting involved* [15]*rich and powerful* [16]**de m'avoir** *to claim (as a member) and to dictate to me* [17]*working girl* [18]*work* [19]**que... quatrain** *than I do hitting on a good verse (lit., a verse of four lines)*

Questions

1. Quelles qualités symbolise Georges Brassens dans lesquelles les Français aiment à se reconnaître ?   **2.** Qu'est-ce qui constitue le bonheur pour Brassens ?   **3.** Quelles sont ses idées politiques et sociales ?   **4.** Commentez la conception de l'amour selon Brassens.   **5.** On dit que l'argent ne fait pas le bonheur. Quelle est votre opinion ?   **6.** Comment s'exprime, aux États-Unis, la satire politique et sociale ?

NOTE: Voir aussi les deux sujets de composition dans le *Manuel d'exercices.*

1. What are the forms of the definite and indefinite articles ?

	DEFINITE		**INDEFINITE**	
	Singular	*Plural*	*Singular*	*Plural*
MASCULINE	le	les	un	des
FEMININE	la	les	une	des

Before any singular noun or adjective beginning with a vowel or a mute *h*, *le* and *la* elide, that is, they become *l'*.

This elision must be made before a noun or adjective beginning with a vowel or mute *h*.

2. What is the most common use of the definite article in both French and English ?

Les œufs sont dans le réfrigérateur.   The eggs are in *the* refrigerator.
Le papier et les crayons sont sur   The paper and pencils are on
    la table.   *the* table.

The definite article is used to indicate a particular noun.

When there is more than one noun used with the definite article, the article must be repeated before each noun. English often uses the article before the first noun only.

3. How do English and French differ in their treatment of nouns used in a general sense ?

Les pommes sont bonnes pour   *Apples* are good for one's
    la santé.   health.
J'aime beaucoup les chiens.   I like *dogs* a great deal.

La justice **est une chose bien relative.**	*Justice* is a very relative thing.
Le travail **éloigne de nous trois grands maux :** *l'ennui, le vice* **et** *le besoin.* (*Voltaire*)	*Work* protects us from three great evils : *boredom, vice,* and *need.*

In French the definite article is placed before nouns used in a general sense. This is not the case in English.

A great many nouns used in a general sense are abstract.

4. In French, how is the definite article used with the days of the week ?

Lundi **nous aurons un examen.**	*Monday* we'll have a test.
Nous avons toujours un examen *le lundi.*	We always have a test on *Mondays.*

Days of the week are used without the article when they refer to an occurrence that takes place once on a given day. The definite article is used with the singular form of the day of the week when the occurrence takes place regularly every week on a given day.

5. How does French use the definite article with a division of the day, such as *in the morning, in the evening, in the night/at night* ?

Richard travaille *le matin* **mais il dort** *l'après-midi.*	Richard works *in the morning,* but he sleeps *in the afternoon.*
Les voleurs viennent rarement *le jour;* **ils viennent plutôt** *la nuit.*	Thieves come rarely *during the day;* rather, they come *in the/at night.*

NOTE 1: The expression *night and day* may be expressed either by *le jour et la nuit* or by *jour et nuit.* Ex. : **Bernard travaille** *le jour et la nuit,* or **Bernard travaille** *jour et nuit.* (Bernard words *day and night.*)

NOTE 2: But in expressions such as *two o'clock in the morning,* the English *in the* is expressed by *de* + DEFINITE ARTICLE + DIVISION OF THE DAY. Ex. : **deux heures** *du matin,* **trois heures** *de l'après-midi,* **huit heures** *du soir.*

6. How is the article used with dates ?

le lundi **30 avril**	*Monday,* April 30

When both the day of the week and the date are given, the definite article is normally placed before the day of the week, but not before the day of the month. No comma separates the day of the week from the day of the month. Also found is *lundi*, **30 avril**. In this case, a comma separates the day of the week from the day of the month.

> *le 30* **avril 1989**   April *30*, 1989

When the date alone is given, the article normally precedes the day of the month. No commas are used.

7. When is the article used with the seasons ?

Le printemps **est très beau.**	*Spring* is very beautiful.
Nous en parlerons *l'été* **prochain.**	We'll talk about it next *summer.*
Au printemps **nous avons beaucoup à faire.**	*In the spring* we have a great deal to do.
Où irez-vous *en hiver* **?**	Where will you go *in winter* ?

The article is used with names of seasons, except when they are preceded by *en*. Note the expressions *au printemps*, *en été*, *en automne*, *en hiver*.

8. When is the article used with names of languages ?

Le français **est une langue facile.**	*French* is an easy language.
Comprenez-vous *l'allemand* **?**	Do you understand *German* ?
Je ne parle pas *anglais.*	I do not speak *English.*
Marie parle bien (*le*) *russe.*	Marie speaks *Russian* well.
En italien **on prononce toutes les lettres.**	*In Italian* all the letters are pronounced.

The article is used with names of languages except when the language is preceded by *en* or when it follows a form of the verb *parler*.

When the language does not follow a form of the verb *parler* immediately, sometimes the article is used with the language, sometimes not.

All names of languages are masculine.

In each sentence of the English-to-French exercises of this lesson, there is some word with which the definite article must be either used or omitted. Identify this word and connect it with one of the rules in the preceding sections. Explain orally why you use or omit the definite article.

A. *Traduisez en français.*

1. Summer is a very beautiful season.   **2.** It is necessary to be patient with children.   **3.** For the United States the Second World War began on

December 7, 1941.   **4.** The flowers that I prefer are roses.   **5.** We celebrate our wedding anniversary Tuesday, February 28.   **6.** I like to hear my friend Sergio Tonelli speak Italian.   **7.** He loves animals.   **8.** In spring all nature awakens.   **9.** It is difficult to know Arabic well[1].   **10.** In English they use the word "sorry" a great deal.

B. *Traduisez en français.*

1. Men are truly curious.   **2.** (*vous*) Do you like French coffee ?
3. (*tu*) Are you free Saturday afternoon ?   **4.** Many Frenchmen speak Spanish.   **5.** Sundays I always go to church.   **6.** There are interesting concerts in winter.   **7.** French is a beautiful language.   **8.** We never have any class on Saturday.   **9.** Undeveloped countries need help.

9. When is the article used with nouns in apposition ?

Pasteur, *le grand savant français,* mourut en 1895.	Pasteur, *the great French scientist,* died in 1895.
Philippe, *le fils de notre voisin,* est parti à l'armée.	Philip, *our neighbor's son,* has left for the army.
Pierre Dupont, *étudiant en médecine,* habite à Paris.	Pierre Dupont, *a medical student,* lives in Paris.
Yvetot, *petite ville de Normandie,* se trouve entre Le Havre et Rouen.	Yvetot, *a little Norman town,* lies between Le Havre and Rouen.

In French, the definite article is normally used with nouns in apposition to state what the speaker considers a well-known fact. This is also English usage.

But in French the indefinite article is not often used with nouns in apposition. Whenever the noun in apposition furnishes additional and presumably unknown information, the noun in apposition tends to be used without any article.

10. What about the use of the article with a noun following the preposition *en* ?

Jacques est un étudiant *en droit.*	Jack is a *law* student.
L'Europe est divisée *en pays.*	Europe is divided *into countries.*

Normally, no article follows the preposition *en*. Note, however, the following :

L'Arc de Triomphe fut construit *en l'honneur* des armées de Napoléon.	The Arc de Triomphe was constructed *in honor* of Napoleon's armies.

---

[1]Place this adverb before *know*.

L'agent a tiré *en l'air*.	The policeman fired a shot *into the air*.
***En l'absence* du professeur les élèves ont fait beaucoup de bruit.**	*In the absence* of the teacher the pupils made a lot of noise.

In certain set expressions, the most common of which are ***en l'honneur*, *en l'air***, and ***en l'absence***, the article is used after ***en***.

11. Is the article used with given (first) names ?

Marie est partie hier avec son frère *Henri* et *le petit Claude*.	Mary left yesterday with her brother *Henry* and *little Claude*.

The article is not normally used with first names. But it is used with first names modified by an adjective.

12. When speaking of someone, how is the article used with titles ?

Hier, j'ai vu *le docteur Lemaître*.	Yesterday, I saw *Dr. Lemaître*.
***Le capitaine Lebeau* arrivera demain.**	*Captain Lebeau* will arrive tomorrow.
Connaissez-vous *le professeur Dupré* ?	Do you know *Professor Dupré* ?
***Le président Kennedy* est allé en Europe en 1961.**	*President Kennedy* went to Europe in 1961.

When speaking of a person, the definite article is used before titles indicating a profession.

***Monsieur Lebrun* habite 30, rue de Vaugirard.**	*Mr. Lebrun* lives at 30 Vaugirard Street.
Où est *Madame Rivière* ?	Where is *Mrs. Rivière* ?
Jacques sort souvent avec *Mademoiselle Moreau*.	Jack often goes out with *Miss Moreau*.

But no article is used before ***monsieur*, *madame***, or ***mademoiselle*** when they are followed by the person's name.

> CAUTION: When ***madame*** and ***mademoiselle*** are used as common nouns, they must not be accompanied by an article. Do not say : « La mademoiselle qui passe là-bas est une avocate. » Say : **La *demoiselle* qui passe là-bas est une avocate.**

monsieur = *M.*   madame = *Mme* or *M*ᵐᵉ   mademoiselle = *Mlle* or *M*ˡˡᵉ

A period is used after the abreviation for *monsieur*, but no period is used after the abbreviations for *madame* and *mademoiselle*.

13. How is the article used with titles when addressing a person ?

—*Docteur*, je ne me sens pas bien du tout.	"*Doctor*, I don't feel well at all."
—J'ai suivi vos conseils, *Dr. Perret*.	"I followed your advice, Dr. Perret."

In addressing a doctor, no article is used either with or without the name of the doctor.

—Bonjour, *mon capitaine*.	"Good morning, *captain*."
—Je suis à vos ordres, *mon commandant*.	"I am at your disposal, *major*."

In the military, when a soldier of lower rank or an officer speaks to an officer of higher rank, the possessive adjective is used before the title.

—Bonsoir, *Monsieur*.	"Good evening, *Mr. Jones*."
—Bonjour, *Madame*.	"Good morning, *Mrs. Leroque*."
—*Mademoiselle*, j'espère que nous nous reverrons.	"*Miss Smith*, I hope that we'll see each other again."

In French, a person is usually addressed as *Monsieur*, *Madame*, or *Mademoiselle*, and no last name is normally used when addressing a person, although the last name is sometimes heard in familiar speech.

—Je n'ai pas encore lu ce livre, *monsieur*.	"I haven't yet read that book, *Professor Lemercier*."

In addressing teachers in France, including professors, neither the title nor the name is used, but simply *monsieur*, *madame*, or *mademoiselle*.

—*Monsieur le Président*, vous avez toujours raison.	"*Mr. President*, you are always right."
—*Monsieur le professeur*, voulez-vous nous donner votre opinion ?	"*Professor Bruce*, will you give us your opinion ?"

With certain titles, the formula *Monsieur le*... is sometimes used in address.

C. *Traduisez en français*.

1. He was speaking of Mr. Leduc, a publisher from Strasbourg. **2.** There will be a big dinner in honor of Senator Amieux. **3.** (*tu*) Have you invited

beautiful Sylvia to the dance ?   **4.** She knows Prince Louis very well[1].
5. General Lacaze will inspect the troops tomorrow morning.   **6.** Pasteur,
the great French scientist[2], was a very generous man.   **7.** They spent the
night in prison.   **8.** In the absence of the manager, his assistant will make[3]
the decisions.   **9.** Doctor, I don't know what[4] is the matter with me.
10. (*vous*) I'll do what you wish, colonel.   **11.** Miss Duneau, a mathematics professor at the university, has just written a new book.   **12.** We'll go
to France by[5] plane.   **13.** She loves Roger and would like to marry him.
14. The best specialist in that field[6] is Dr. Petit.   **15.** (*vous*) I'll follow you,
lieutenant.

14. When is the article used before names of countries and continents ?

La France est un grand pays.	*France* is a large country.
Je suis allé *en Angleterre.*	I went *to England.*
Il vient *de Grèce.*	He comes *from Greece.*
L'Europe et *l'Afrique* sont sépa-rées par la Méditerranée.	*Europe* and *Africa* are sepa-rated by the Mediterranean.
Nous sommes arrivés *au Portugal.*	We arrived *in Portugal.*
Il vient *du Danemark.*	He comes *from Denmark.*

The article is normally used before names of countries and continents.
But the article is not used after *en* (which expresses *in* or *to* with feminine
countries) nor after *de* (meaning *from*) when it precedes a feminine country.

Note: For the gender of countries, see page 229, §2. For how to express *in* and
to with countries, see pages 229–230, §3 and §4. For how to express
from with countries, see pages 231–232, §7 and §8.

15. Is the article used with names of cities ?

Il va à *Paris.*	He is going to *Paris.*
Avez-vous vu *Londres* ?	Have you seen *London* ?
La Nouvelle-Orléans est en Louisiane, *Le Havre* en France.	*New Orleans* is in Louisiana, *Le Havre* in France.

The article is not usually found with names of cities. However, a few cities,
such as *La Haye* (*The Hague*), *La Nouvelle-Orléans*, *Le Havre*, *La Rochelle*,
etc., have the article as part of the name. The prepositions **à** or **de** contract in
the usual manner with the article : *au Havre, du Havre.*

---

[1]Where will these words come in relation to the verb ?   [2]Not « scientiste »   [3]Not a
form of « faire »   [4]This is an idiom.   [5]**en** or **par**   [6]**domaine**

16. When is the article used before names of streets and avenues ?

Dites-moi où est *la rue Racine.*	Tell me where *Racine Street* is.
Le Boulevard Saint-Germain est très tranquille.	*Saint-Germain Boulevard* is very quiet.
Connaissez-vous *l'avenue des Champs-Élysées* ?	Do you know *Champs-Élysées Avenue* ?

The article is normally used before names of streets and avenues.

Nous sommes arrivés *Boulevard Saint-Michel.*	We arrived at *Saint-Michel Boulevard.*
On me trouvera au café *rue Royale.*	They'll find me in the café on *Royal Street.*

When the prepositions *in* or *on* precede the street name in English, the French tend to omit the preposition and article. However, the preposition and the article may be used.

The French say :

dans la rue	*on the street*
dans ⎫ ***l'avenue*** ***sur*** ⎭	*on the avenue*
sur la place	*in the square*
sur le boulevard	*on the boulevard*

17. How is the English word *per* expressed in French with various types of units of measure ?

(a) speed per hour

Le train roulait à cent soixante kilomètres *à l'heure.*	The train was going at a hundred miles *per hour.*

With expressions of *time indicating speed, à* + ARTICLE is used, and this is especially common with *à l'heure.*

(b) money per hour

Marie gagne cinq dollars *de l'heure.*	Mary earns five dollars *per hour.*

Money per hour is expressed by ***de l'heure.***

(c) something accomplished per unit of time

Dans ce pays on travaille huit heures *par jour* et quarante heures *par semaine*.	In this country they work eight hours *a day* and forty hours per week.
Jacques gagne deux mille dollars *par mois*.	Jack earns two thousand dollars *per month*.

In general, French expresses *per* + UNIT OF TIME by *par* + UNIT OF TIME : *par jour*, *par semaine*, *par mois*, *par an*. No article is used after *par*.

(d) expressions of dry measure, weight, etc.

Les pommes de terre coûtent dix francs *la livre*.	Potatoes cost ten francs *per pound*.
Le sucre coûte quatre francs *le kilo*.	Sugar costs four francs *per kilogram*.

French expresses *per* with expressions of *dry measure, weight*, and so on, by placing the definite article before the expression.

18. What prepositions are used with expressions of means of locomotion, and when is the article used ?

Nous sommes venus <u>*en*</u> *train* (or <u>*par***</u> *le train*), <u>*en*</u> *voiture*, <u>*en*</u> *avion* (or <u>***par***</u> *avion*), <u>*à*</u> *pied*, <u>*à*</u> *bicyclette*.**	We came <u>on</u> the train, <u>in</u> a car, <u>by</u> plane, <u>on</u> foot, <u>on</u> a bicycle.

The prepositions used with means of locomotion must often be learned. In general, *dans* or *en* is used if one can enter the vehicle, *à* if one is on the vehicle. However, for *on a motorcycle* the French say *en moto*.

19. What about the use of the article in stating the profession, nationality, or religion of the subject of the sentence ?

M. Badin est *avocat*.	Mr. Badin is *a lawyer*.
Sa femme est *américaine*.	His wife is *(an) American*.
Mlle Bajard est *un excellent professeur*.	Miss Bajard is *an excellent teacher*.

After forms of the verb *être*, French designates profession, religion, nationality, etc., by an unmodified noun. English uses the noun modified by an indefinite article.

In French, if the name of the profession, nationality, or religion is modified, the indefinite article is used as in English.

D. Deux amies bavardent sur un docteur de leurs connaissances. Remplacez les mots anglais entre parenthèses par leur équivalent français.

1. Tu sais que _____ (*Dr. Texier*) est considéré comme le spécialiste par excellence des maladies de foie.   **2.** Il est curieux. Au lieu de se déplacer _____ (*by car*), il circule _____ (*on a motorcycle*).   **3.** Il fait faire ses costumes _____ (*in Portugal*).   **4.** Il paraît qu'il y a un célèbre tailleur _____ (*in Lisbon*).   **5.** Tous les ans il va faire un stage _____ (*in the United States*).   **6.** Sais-tu s'il est _____ (*a Catholic**) ou _____ (*a Protestant**) ?   **7.** Il a son cabinet _____ (*on Avenue de l'Opéra*). **8.** Il doit bien voir une dizaine de malades _____ (*per day*).   **9.** Sur sa moto il aime faire plus de cent kilomètres _____ (*per hour*).   **10.** Moi, je préfère voyager _____ (*by car*) ou _____ (*by plane*). Et toi ?   **11.** Il paraît que son père vient _____ (*from Belgium*) et que sa mère est _____ (*an American*).

E. Traduisez en français.

1. These toys come from Germany.   **2.** Formerly, there was a prison in the Place de la Bastille.   **3.** There are many lakes in Canada.   **4.** I caught a fish which I'll sell for a dollar a pound.   **5.** Our neighbors came back from Poland yesterday.   **6.** She charges[1] ten dollars an hour, which[2] seems expensive.   **7.** My mother-in-law comes to see us twice a year. **8.** I should like to go to Italy.   **9.** They left[3] for Brazil yesterday.   **10.** In Paris life has a special charm.   **11.** He earns $550 a week, but that will not last.

EXERCICE ORAL

Deux dames amies se rencontrent en se promenant rue Victor Hugo. Après des salutations, elles bavardent un moment.
Répétez chaque phrase en ajoutant l'équivalent français des mots anglais entre parenthèses.

1. —Je vois que vous aimez aussi vous promener... (*on Victor Hugo Street*)

2. —Oui, c'est tellement agréable... (*in the spring*)

3. —J'ai entendu dire que vous avez été à Nice voir votre fille, celle qui est... (*a teacher*)

---

*In French names of religions are usually not capitalized.   [1]Use a form of **prendre**.   [2]**ce qui**   [3]Use a form of **partir**.

4. —Oui, j'ai été heureuse de la revoir avec ses deux enfants, Jacques et... (*little Peter*)

5. Le petit est mignon, mais il se promène toujours le nez... (*in the air*)

6. Quant à Jacques, il a une grosse moto et il file dans la campagne à plus de cent kilomètres... (*per hour*)

7. Du moins, il travaille dans l'usine de son père et il gagne 120 francs... (*per hour*)

8. —Êtes-vous allée à Nice en auto ou... (*by plane*)

9. —Pas en auto, c'est trop long. Mais vous-même, je crois que vous êtes allée avec votre mari... (*to Spain*)

10. —En effet et maintenant il veut, je ne sais pas pourquoi, visiter... (*Russia*)

11. J'irai sans doute avec lui, car j'aime beaucoup... (*trips*)

12. —Oh ! excusez-moi, je dois me dépêcher car je vais voir ce matin... (*Dr. Lefèvre*)

13. —Il est très renommé mais je pense que vous avez pris rendez-vous avec sa secrétaire... (*Miss Arnaud*)

14. —Allez ! Bonne journée !

15. —Vous aussi.

See pages 271–314 for the *Exercices d'ensemble*.

. . . . . .

PROBLEM WORDS

43. piece

(a) How to say *piece* in general

Aimez-vous ce *morceau* de musique ?	Do you like this *piece* of music ?

The general word for *piece* is **le morceau**.

(b) Ways of saying *a piece of paper*

Donnez-moi *un bout de papier*. **Donnez-moi *un morceau de papier*.** **Donnez-moi *une feuille de papier*.**	Give me *a piece of paper*.

The word *piece* in *piece of paper* may be expressed by **morceau** or **feuille** (*sheet*) or **bout** (somewhat familiar).

The noun **bout** is also used with **fil** (*thread, wire*) and **ficelle** (*string*) to mean *piece*.

> CAUTION: DO NOT use « la pièce » for piece; **la pièce** means play (to be acted) or room.

44. place

(a) When *place* is expressed by **endroit**

Le guide nous fera voir les *endroits* les plus curieux.	The guide will show us the most curious *places*.
Il y a bien des *endroits* où la vie est plus facile qu'ici.	There are many *places* where life is easier than here.

The common word for *place* is **l'endroit** (*m*.).

(b) When *place* is expressed by **lieu**

Il paraît qu'on revient toujours au *lieu* de son crime.	It seems that one always returns to the *place* (=*scene*) of one's crime.

The word **le lieu** means *place* in the sense of *spot*. It is literary and not very common, but it is used specifically in certain instances and also in some compound expressions such as **le chef-lieu** (*county seat*). It is also used in the idiomatic expression **avoir lieu**. It is best to avoid using **lieu** in other cases.

(c) When *place* means *space*

Avez-vous *de la place* pour ma voiture dans votre garage ?	Do you have *a place* for my car in your garage ?

When *place* means *space*, French uses **la place**.

(d) When *place* means *a seat*

Montez vite dans le train si vous voulez *une place* près de la fenêtre.	Get on the train right away if you want *a place* near the window.

When *place* means *a seat*, often a paid accommodation, *place* is expressed by **la place**.

(e) When *place* means *a job*

Jean-Paul a une bonne
$\left\{\begin{array}{l}\textbf{\textit{situation.}}\\\textbf{\textit{position.}}\\\textbf{\textit{place.}}\end{array}\right.$

Jean-Paul has a good *place*
(= *job*).

When the English word *place* means *job*, it may be expressed by **la situation**, **la position**, or **la place**.

> CAUTION: DO NOT use « place » to express *place* in general. The ordinary word for *place* is **endroit**.

45. rather

(a) How to say *rather than*

Je voudrais une revue **plutôt qu'**un journal.

Allez vous promener **plutôt que de rester** ici par ce beau temps.

I would like a magazine *rather than* a newspaper.

Go and take a walk *rather than stay* here in this nice weather.

The expression *rather than* is often rendered in French by **plutôt que**, and when it precedes an infinitive, it may be rendered by **plutôt que de**.

(b) How to say *rather* + ADJECTIVE or ADVERB

Je suis **assez fatigué** ce soir après cette longue journée.

Après un an d'étude vous parlerez **assez couramment**.

I am *rather tired* this evening after this long day.

After a year of study you will speak *rather fluently*.

When the adverb *rather* modifies an adjective or another adverb, French uses **assez**.

(c) How to say I would rather...

Nous **aimerions mieux** rester à la maison ce soir.
Nous **préférerions** rester à la maison ce soir.

We *would rather* stay home this evening.

J'**aimerais mieux** jouer au bridge qu'au poker.
Je **préférerais** jouer au bridge **plutôt** qu'au poker.

I *would rather* play bridge *than* poker.

The English *would rather* + VERB may be expressed in French by the conditional of **aimer mieux** + INFINITIVE or of **préférer** + INFINITIVE. In comparisons, **plutôt** is required to complete the meaning of **préférer**.

46. reason

(a) How to say *the reason for*

Quelle est *la raison de* votre refus ?	What is *the reason for* your refusal ?

French expresses *the reason for* by **la raison de**.

(b) How to say *the reason that*

Philippe m'a expliqué *la raison pour laquelle* il n'a pas pu venir. **Philippe m'a expliqué *pour quelle raison* il n'a pas pu venir.** **Philippe m'a expliqué *pourquoi* il n'a pas pu venir.**	Philip explained to me *the reason that* he could not come.

French expresses *the reason that* (colloquially *the reason why*) by **la raison pour laquelle** or **pour quelle raison** or simply by **pourquoi**.

CAUTION: DO NOT say « la raison pourquoi », which is incorrect.

F. Remplacez les mots anglais par leur équivalent français.

1. Je ne peux pas être dans deux (*places*) à la fois.   **2.** Béatrice est (*rather*) découragée par tout ce qui s'est passé.   **3.** Je voudrais savoir (*the reason*) Monsieur Béraud a changé d'avis.   **4.** Allez en avant et gardez-nous une (*place*).   **5.** Il me faut un petit (*piece*) de cette étoffe.   **6.** Les enfants (*would rather*) passer leurs vacances à la mer qu'à la montagne.   **7.** Il n'y a pas assez de (*place*) pour deux dans ce bureau.   **8.** Le beau vase chinois s'est cassé en mille (*pieces*).   **9.** Juliette a laissé une lettre pour expliquer (*the reason for*) son départ.   **10.** On ira voir (*the place*) de l'accident. **11.** Faisons quelque chose chez nous (*rather than*) d'aller au restaurant ce soir.

G. Traduisez en français. Attention aux mots en italique.

1. I know a *place* where we can work in peace.   **2.** Lucien works *rather* well, but he could do better.   **3.** (*vous*) Now you know the *reason* I came back.   **4.** The children don't have enough *space* to play.   **5.** What are those *pieces* of paper on the floor ?   **6.** (*tu*) Johnnie, give your *place* to that lady.   **7.** I would *rather* leave this evening than tomorrow morning.

8. What is the *reason* for his absence ?   **9.** (*vous*) Do you take one *piece* of sugar or two ?   **10.** I decided that Jack should do that work *rather* than George.

Verb Review

Review the verbs **ouvrir** and **pouvoir** according to the outline on pages 330–333.

Indefinite Nouns

*Une jeune femme fait toutes les nuits le même rêve[1] d'une certaine
maison très belle dans un jardin bien soigné. Plus tard, elle voyage et
cherche à « retrouver » cette maison de ses rêves.*

La maison

Il y a deux ans, dit-elle, quand je fus malade, je faisais toutes les nuits le même
rêve. Je me promenais dans la campagne; j'apercevais de loin une maison
blanche, basse et longue, qu'entourait un groupe *de** tilleuls[2]. A gauche de la
maison, un pré bordé *de* peupliers[3] rompait agréablement la symétrie du décor,
5 et la cime[4] de ces arbres, que l'on voyait de loin, se balançait[5] au-dessus des
tilleuls.

Dans mon rêve, j'étais attirée par cette maison et j'allais vers elle. Une
barrière peinte en blanc fermait l'entrée. Ensuite on suivait une jolie allée
bordée *d'*arbres sous lesquels je trouvais les fleurs du printemps : *des* prime-
10 vères[6], *des* pervenches[7], beaucoup *d'*anémones[8] qui se fanaient[9] dès que je les
cueillais. Devant la maison s'étendait une grande pelouse bien tondue[10], en-
tourée *d'*une bande *de* fleurs violettes.

La maison, bâtie *de* pierres blanches, portait un toit *d'*ardoises[11]. Une porte
de chêne[12] clair était au sommet d'un petit perron[13]. J'avais <u>envie</u>** de visiter
15 cette maison, mais personne ne répondait à mes appels. J'étais profondément
désappointée, je sonnais, je criais, et enfin je me réveillais.

Tel était mon rêve et il se répéta, pendant *de* longs mois, avec une précision
et une fidélité telles que je finissais par penser que j'avais certainement, dans
mon enfance, vu ce parc et ce château. Pourtant je ne pouvais en retrouver le
20 souvenir, et cette recherche devint pour moi une obsession si forte qu'un été,
ayant appris à conduire une petite voiture, je décidai de passer mes vacances
sur les routes de France, à la recherche de la maison de mon rêve.

---

[1]**fait... rêve** *has the same dream every night*   *The italicized **de** and **des** indicate that
an indefinite noun follows.   [2]*linden trees*   [3]**pré bordé de peupliers** *meadow lined
with poplar trees*   [4]*top*   [5]*swayed*   [6]*primroses*   [7]*periwinkles*   [8]*windflowers*   [9]*wilted*
[10]*a well-kept lawn*   [11]*slate*   [12]*oak*   [13]*flight of stairs at the top of which is a landing*
Underscored words are examples of THE NOUN ALONE not preceded by **de.

Je ne vous raconterai pas mes voyages. J'explorai la Normandie, la Touraine, d'autres provinces et ne trouvai rien. En octobre je rentrai à Paris et, pendant
25 tout l'hiver, je continuai à rêver de la maison blanche. Au printemps, je recommençai mes promenades aux environs de Paris. Je n'avais pas eu *de* chance mais je ne me décourageai pas. Un jour, comme je traversais une vallée voisine de l'Isle-Adam, je sentis tout d'un coup un choc agréable, cette émotion curieuse que l'on reconnaît, après une longue absence, *des* personnes
30 ou *des* lieux que l'on a aimés.

Bien que je ne fusse jamais venue dans cette région, je connaissais parfaitement le paysage qui s'étendait à ma droite, les cimes *de* peupliers qui dominaient la masse *de* tilleuls, le tapis *de* fleurs, la pelouse verte, le petit perron, la porte *de* chêne clair... Je sus sans aucun doute que j'avais trouvé le
35 château de mes rêves. Je sortis de ma voiture, montai rapidement les marches et sonnai.

J'avais très <u>peur</u> que personne ne répondît, mais, presque tout de suite, un domestique parut. C'était un homme au visage triste, fort vieux et vêtu d'un veston noir. En me voyant, il parut très surpris et me regarda avec <u>attention</u>,
40 sans parler.

—Je vais, lui dis-je, vous demander une faveur un peu étrange. Je ne connais pas les propriétaires de cette maison, mais je serais heureuse s'ils pouvaient m'autoriser à la visiter.

—Le château est à louer, Madame, dit-il, comme à regret[14], et je suis ici pour
45 le faire visiter.

—A louer ? dis-je. Quelle chance ! Comment les propriétaires eux-mêmes n'habitent-ils pas une maison si belle ?

—Les propriétaires l'habitaient, Madame. Ils l'ont quittée depuis que la maison est hantée[15].
50 —Hantée ? dis-je. Voilà qui ne m'arrêtera guère. Je ne savais pas que, dans les provinces françaises, on croyait encore aux revenants[16].

—Je n'y croirais pas, Madame, dit-il sérieusement, si je n'avais moi-même si souvent rencontré dans le parc, la nuit, le fantôme qui a mis mes maîtres en fuite[17].
55 —Quelle histoire ! dis-je en essayant de sourire.

—Une histoire, dit le vieillard d'un air *de* reproche, dont vous au moins, Madame, ne devriez pas rire, puisque ce fantôme, c'était vous.

D'après André Maurois, membre de l'Académie française, auteur très connu pour ses écrits sur la civilisation anglo-saxonne et ses biographies de grandes figures littéraires et politiques. (« La Maison » , dans *Toujours l'inattendu arrive*, Éditions de la Maison française, 1943)

---

[14]**comme à regret** *as if he regretted saying it*   [15]*haunted*   [16]*ghosts*   [17]**le fantôme... fuite** *the ghost that caused my masters to flee*

Questions

1. Décrivez la maison — ou le jardin — dont rêve la narratrice pendant sa maladie.   **2.** Comment se terminait chaque fois ce rêve ?   **3.** Pourquoi veut-elle absolument « retrouver » cette maison ?   **4.** Décrivez la personne qui vient lui ouvrir la porte.   **5.** Pourquoi ce château n'est-il plus habité par ses maîtres ?   **6.** Racontez un rêve significatif (réel ou imaginaire) que vous avez pu faire.

NOTE: Voir aussi les sujets de composition dans le *Manuel d'exercices*.

1. A noun may be definite, general, or indefinite. How is an indefinite noun expressed in English and in French ?

Il y a *du papier* sur mon bureau.	There is (*some*) *paper* on my desk.
Vous trouverez *des cartes postales* dans le tiroir.	You will find (*some*) *postcards* in the drawer.
Avez-vous *des enfants* ?	Have you any children ?

In English, a noun is made indefinite either by the use of <u>the noun alone</u> or by the use of *some* or *any* with the noun.

In French, a noun is usually made indefinite by the partitive construction.

NOTE: In both French and English, a noun modified by the indefinite article is also indefinite. Ex. : *un livre* (*a book*), **une pomme** (*an apple*).

2. What are the partitive articles ?

	SINGULAR	PLURAL
MASCULINE	du	des
FEMININE	de la	des
MASCULINE OR FEMININE	de l'	des

If the word following the partitive singular begins with a vowel or a mute *h*, the form *de l'* must be used.

The partitive construction is, in effect, *de* + DEFINITE ARTICLE, but as a partitive it has lost its original meaning of *of the*.

3. What is the partitive construction ?

Vous trouverez *du beurre* et *de* **la *crème* au supermarché.**	You will find *butter* and *cream* at the supermarket.
Y a-t-il *des chevaux* dans la ferme ?	Are there *any horses* on the farm ?

The partitive construction indicates that an indefinite quantity of a given noun (part of all there is) exists in the sentence at hand.

In French, a noun is made indefinite by the partitive construction except in certain cases, when the noun alone indicates indefiniteness. The fact that there are times when the noun alone rather than the partitive is used complicates the problem.

4. When an indefinite noun is modified by a preceding adjective, how is the partitive construction modified ?

(a) when the noun is singular

Nous avons entendu *de la* **belle musique.**	We heard *some beautiful music.*
Avez-vous *du bon vin* ?	Do you have *any good wine* ?

When an adjective precedes an indefinite singular noun, the partitive construction is normally used.

(b) when the noun is plural

Nous avons vu *de jolies fleurs* **dans le bois.**	We saw *some pretty flowers* in the woods.
Il y a *de magnifiques châteaux* **dans ce pays.**	There are *some magnificent castles* in that country.

When a preceding adjective modifies a plural indefinite noun, *de* takes the place of the partitive construction. One normally finds *de* + ADJECTIVE + PLURAL NOUN.

5. When does one find *des* + ADJECTIVE + PLURAL NOUN ?

Ils ont vu *des jeunes gens* sur **la plage.**	They saw *some young men* on the beach.
Y a-t-il *des jeunes filles* dans **cette pension ?**	Are there *any girls* in that boardinghouse ?
Voulez-vous *des petits pois* ?	Do you want *any peas* ?

When ADJECTIVE + NOUN constitute a unit, so that the adjective has lost its identity as an adjective, the construction is treated like a single word, and as a single word it is modified by the partitive article *des* with the plural noun.

A. *Bertrand est allé chez le bijoutier avec Odette pour lui acheter un petit quelque chose. Remplacez les tirets par l'article partitif ou par de. Expliquez oralement votre choix.*

1. On nous a montré _____ bagues et _____ bracelets.   **2.** Il y avait dans le magasin _____ jeunes filles qui ne pouvaient pas se décider. **3.** Elles avaient passé _____ longues heures à regarder les bijoux.   **4.** On trouve quelquefois _____ bonnes occasions dans ce magasin.   **5.** Il faisait chaud et le bijoutier est allé chercher deux verres d'eau et _____ glace pour Odette et moi.   **6.** Nous l'avons apprécié, car nous avions aussi bu _____ bon vin avec notre repas de midi.   **7.** _____ jeunes gens sont entrés pour retrouver les jeunes filles toujours indécises.   **8.** Nous étions un peu inquiets parce qu'il y avait beaucoup _____ bijoux à voler. **9.** Enfin Odette a choisi _____ belles perles pour faire un collier.

B. *Traduisez en français. Expliquez oralement chaque article partitif et chaque de.*

1. (*vous*) I saw some cats and dogs in your garden.   **2.** There were some girls in the group who did not know how to speak French.   **3.** One finds good milk in Denmark.   **4.** Is there any ice in the refrigerator ?   **5.** We drank some good cider in Normandy.   **6.** (*tu*) Were there any young men[1] on your boat ?   **7.** There were numerous tourists on the beach. **8.** They spent long hours in the[2] library.

6. Is an indefinite noun always modified by a partitive article ?

J'ai *faim.*	I'm *hungry.* (lit., I *have hunger.*)
Jacques a travaillé avec *soin.*	Jack worked with *care* (carefully).
Nous sommes arrivés sans argent.	We arrived without *money.*
La maison est pleine de poussière.	The house is full of *dust.*

There are several cases in which an indefinite noun is not modified by a partitive but rather in which the noun stands alone.

We shall now examine each of these cases — and their exceptions.

---

[1]The plural of **jeune homme** is NOT « jeunes hommes ».   [2]**à la**

7. When is <u>the noun alone</u> used in idiomatic sentences with *avoir*?

Marie *a soif*.	Mary *is thirsty*. (lit., Mary *has thirst*.)
J'*ai mal* à la gorge.	I *have a sore throat*. (lit., I *have a pain* in my throat.)

Certain set expressions made up of a form of ***avoir*** + <u>the noun alone</u> came into the language before there was any partitive article. Many of these expressions still exist.

8. When is the preposition *avec* used with <u>the noun alone</u>?

Pierre a accepté cette offre <u>avec</u> hésitation.	Peter accepted that offer <u>with</u> hesitation (i.e., *hesitatingly*, in a hesitating manner).
Sa femme l'a reçu <u>avec</u> *joie*.	His wife received him <u>with</u> *joy* (*joyfully*).

The preposition ***avec*** is used with abstract <u>nouns alone</u> when the resulting prepositional phrase indicates manner. Often this phrase can be expressed by an adverb in English.

9. When is <u>the noun alone</u> used with *sans* and *ni... ni...*?

Paul est parti <u>sans</u> *livres*.	Paul left <u>without</u> books.
Nous n'avons <u>ni</u> *crayons* <u>ni</u> *papier*.	We have <u>neither</u> pencils <u>nor</u> paper.

<u>The noun alone</u> follows ***sans*** and ***ni... ni...*** when it is an indefinite noun.

C. *Traduisez en français. Expliquez oralement chaque omission de l'article partitif devant un nom indéfini.*

1. The poor child is hungry.   **2.** Without friends life is not pleasant.
3. They fought with courage, but they lost.   **4.** Was he able to fix the faucet without tools?   **5.** What are we going to do? There are neither chairs nor tables here.   **6.** He claims that he has a headache.   **7.** We left their house without regret.   **8.** (*vous*) What are you afraid of?   **9.** (*vous*) If you are right, I must be wrong.   **10.** (*tu*) We need your dictionary.
11. (*tu*) Did you go out without a hat?   **12.** (*vous*) Are you sleepy? You are yawning[1] all the time[2].   **13.** (*tu*) "Will you help me move?" "Sure."
14. They are ashamed of their mistakes.   **15.** He is a lawyer; he speaks with ease.   **16.** I am cold and I have a sore throat.

---

[1]*yawn* **baillez**   [2]Use **sans** with the noun **arrêt** (*m*).

10. How is an indefinite noun expressed when it is immediately preceded by the preposition *de* ?

J'ai beaucoup *de travail*.	I have a lot *of work*.
Jacques n'a pas *de chance*.	Jack doesn't have *any luck*.
Ne me privez pas *de cigarettes*.	Don't deprive me *of cigarettes*.
Elle porte une robe *de soie*.	She is wearing a *silk dress*.

Whenever the preposition *de* precedes an indefinite noun for any reason whatever, the noun follows *de* immediately, without any partitive article.

We will now examine the cases in which *de* most often precedes an indefinite noun.

11. What construction follows adverbs of quantity ?

Nous avons *beaucoup de livres*.	We have *many books*.
Avez-vous *assez d'argent* ?	Have you *enough money* ?
Il y a *trop de voitures* dans la rue.	There are *too many cars* in the street.

Adverbs of quantity are followed by *de* because of the nature of their meaning (*much of, enough of, too much of, more of,* etc.). The noun alone follows *de*.

NOTE 1: However, the adverb of quantity *bien* (meaning *many*) is followed by the partitive *des* before a plural indefinite noun. Ex. : **Il a *bien des* ennuis**. (He has *many* troubles.) ***Bien des* fois nous restons à la maison**. (*Many* times we stay home.)

The adverb *bien* is simply an intensifier; it does not affect the partitive article of the construction that follows it.

NOTE 2: *La plupart des* (*the majority of*) is followed by a definite noun and the plural form of the verb. Ex. : *La plupart des* **romans sont intéressants**. Here, *des* = *de* + *les* means *of the* and is not a partitive.

The only singular construction with *la plupart* is *la plupart du temps*. Otherwise, say : *la plus grande partie*. Ex. : *la plus grande partie de l'été*, etc.

12. What construction follows the negative *pas* when it indicates negative quantity ?

Je n'ai *pas de temps* à perdre.	I don't have *any time* to lose.
Nous ne voyons *pas de bateaux*.	We see *no boats*.

When *pas* indicates negative quantity, it is followed by *de*, as are other adverbs of quantity. Then *pas* is translated into English as *not... any* or *no*.

NOTE: Therefore, in most cases *pas* is followed by *de* rather than the partitive article. By analogy, *de* also follows other negatives used quantitatively. Ex. : **Il *n'a jamais d'argent*.** (He *never* has *any* money.)

13. When is *pas* followed by the partitive article ?

Ce n'est *pas du beurre*.	That isn't *butter*.
Ce ne sont *pas des soldats*.	Those aren't *soldiers*.
Il est rare qu'il ne se produise pas *des aventures extraordinaires* sur un bateau.	It is rare that *extraordinary adventures* do not occur on a ship.

When *pas* is used as an absolute negative and indicates type or quality, *pas* is followed by the partitive article before the noun, and in that case is translated into English as *not*. This construction is most often found in sentences such as : *Ce n'est pas...* and *Ce ne sont pas...*

14. How is the indefinite noun expressed after verbs and adjectives regularly followed by *de* ?

Les enfants seront *privés de dessert*.	The children will be *deprived of dessert*.
Leur maison est *entourée d'agents*.	Their house is *surrounded by policemen*.
Il y a encore trop de gens qui *manquent de pain*.	There are still too many people who *lack bread*.
Le pays *manque de ressources*.	The country *lacks resources*.
Il *a rempli* le sac *de billets* de mille francs.	He *filled* the bag *with* thousand-franc *bank notes*.
J'ai besoin de timbres.	I *need stamps*.

Whenever a verb, adjective, or special construction is followed by *de*, the indefinite noun alone follows *de*.

15. How are English adjectives or phrases indicating material expressed in French ?

une maison *de bois*	a *wooden* house
un chapeau *de paille*	a *straw* hat

Where English uses an adjective or a phrase of "material," French uses an adjectival phrase consisting of *de* + NOUN.

NOTE: Sometimes *en* is used to indicate material. One can say : **une maison de pierre** or **une maison en pierre.** But distinguish between **un sac d'argent** (*a bag of money*, or, *a bag of silver*) and **un sac en argent** (*a silver bag*, i.e., a bag made of silver).

D. *Remplacez les tirets par l'article partitif ou par* de. *Expliquez oralement votre choix.*

1. J'aimerais avoir un bon pull-over _____ laine.   **2.** Ces arbres ne sont pas _____ orangers, ce sont des pommiers.   **3.** Bien _____ étrangers viennent visiter l'Amérique.   **4.** Ses parents lui laissent trop _____ liberté pour son âge.   **5.** Donnez-moi une tasse_____ thé avec _____ citron, s'il vous plaît.   **6.** Ils ont plus _____ ressources que vous.   **7.** Nous ne mangeons pas _____ viande le soir.   **8.** Nous avons tous besoin _____ affection pour vivre.   **9.** Il y a bien _____ gens qui seraient heureux d'aller en France avec vous.   **10.** Cet arbre est plein _____ oiseaux tous les soirs.   **11.** Ce ne sont pas _____ maisons, ce sont des taudis.   **12.** Je me passerai _____ café parce qu'il m'empêche de dormir.

E. *Traduisez en français. Expliquez oralement chaque emploi de l'article partitif ou du* de.

1. We'll give them a silver tray for their wedding.   **2.** These men aren't spies.   **3.** Many[1] times I regretted my indifference.   **4.** They are students, and they have few distractions.   **5.** The room was full of people. **6.** He bought a new silk shirt to go to Florida.   **7.** Those aren't mountains; they are hills.   **8.** That house is very quiet; one doesn't hear any noise there.   **9.** Today they use[2] machines for all sorts of things.   **10.** They always watch television and do not read any books.   **11.** He has good qualities[3], but he lacks initiative.   **12.** We know few people in our building[4].   **13.** They sent him a package[5] filled with toys.   **14.** The majority of people like to travel.

EXERCICE ORAL

Un couple, venu passer des vacances dans une villa à Nice, va faire des provisions.

Répétez chaque phrase en y introduisant le mot entre parenthèses et en faisant les changements nécessaires.

1. On dit qu'il y a des centres commerciaux à Nice. (grands)

2. Tu vois ? Il y a là-bas des magasins. (nombreux)

3. Entrons là. Oh, zut ! Il y a du monde dans ce supermarché ! (tant)

---

[1]Use **bien**.   [2]Use a form of **se servir de**.   [3]*good qualities* **qualités**   [4]Use **immeuble**.
[5]Use **colis**.

4. Tu es venu avec de l'argent ? (sans)

5. Nous achèterons des produits frais. (beaucoup)

6. Nous prendrons de la viande. (pas)

7. Je voudrais des œufs et du jambon. (ni... ni...)

8. Regarde ces gros fruits ! Ce sont des pamplemousses ? (pas)

9. Achetons des bananes pour demain matin. (très mûres)

10. Il y a des légumes en cette saison. (peu)

11. Il y a des restaurants à Nice, tu sais. (bons, petits)

12. Allons-y, au lieu de faire des histoires. (tant)

See pages 271–314 for the *Exercices d'ensemble.*

. . . . . .

Problem Words

47. return

(a) When *return = give back*

Guy ne m'*a* pas encore *rendu* mon magnétophone.	Guy *has* not yet *returned* my tape recorder to me.

The verb **rendre** means *to return* in the sense of *give back.*

(b) When *return = come back*

***Revenez* le plus tôt possible.**	*Return* } as soon as *Come back* } possible.

The verb **revenir** means *return* in the sense of *come back.*

(c) When *return = go back*

Je ne *retournerai* pas tout de suite à Paris.	I will not { *return* { *go back* } to Paris at once.

The verb **retourner** means *return* in the sense of *go back.*

> Caution: Do not use « retourner » when you mean *return* in the sense of *come back* or *give back*. The verb **retourner** does not have the all-inclusive meaning of the English *return*. It also means *turn over.*

(d) When *return* = *return home*

> **Tu devrais parler à Georges;** | You should speak to George; he
> **il *est rentré* à trois heures** | *returned*   } at three in the
> **du matin.** | *came back home* } morning.

The verb **rentrer** means *return* in the sense of *to return home*.

48. room

(a) How to express *room* without indicating the type of room

> **Combien de *pièces* y a-t-il dans** | How many *rooms* are there in
> **ce château ?** | that castle ?

The general word for *room* is **la pièce**.

(b) When *room* = *bedroom*

> **Est-ce que Madame Renaud loue** | Does Mrs. Renaud rent
> **des *chambres* ?** | *rooms* ?

The word **chambre** indicates a *bedroom*.

(c) When a *room* is used for meetings

> **Nous avons besoin d'une grande** | We need a large *room* for our
> ***salle* pour notre prochaine** | next meeting.
> **réunion.** |

The word **salle** indicates a room used for meetings.

(d) When *room* = *space*

> **Il n'y a pas beaucoup de *place*** | There isn't much *room* in
> **dans ta voiture.** | your car.

When *room* = *space*, the French use **place**.

Note that **le salon** is the formal living room, but the room where the family lives is **la salle de séjour**, also called **le séjour**.

49. save

(a) When *save* means *to save from destruction*

> **Marius m'*a sauvé* la vie.** | Marius *saved* my life.
> **L'inondation a tout emporté;** | The flood took everything;
> **on n'a rien pu *sauver*.** | we couldn't *save* anything.

The verb **sauver** indicates *saving a person or a thing from destruction*. It is most often used to refer to saving persons.

(b) When *save* means *to keep*

Nous *avons gardé* quelques fruits pour vos amis.	We *saved* some fruit for your friends.

The verb **garder** means *save* in the sense of *to keep*.

(c) How to say *save money*

Jean *a fait des économies* pour s'acheter une moto.	John *has been saving up* in order to buy himself a motorcycle.
J'ai donné une tirelire aux enfants pour les encourager à *économiser*.	I gave a piggy bank to the children to encourage them *to save*.
Économisez votre argent au lieu de le dépenser inutilement.	*Save* your money instead of spending it uselessly.

The expression **faire des économies** is often used to mean *to save money* in the sense of *to save up*; the verb **économiser** is used with or without an object to mean *to save money*.

(d) When *save* is expressed by **mettre de côté**

Je *mettrai* mes notes *de côté*; elles pourront vous être utiles plus tard.	I will *save* my notes; they can be useful to you later.
Les Berger *ont mis* assez *de côté* pour se faire construire une belle maison.	The Bergers *saved* enough to have a nice house constructed for themselves.

The expression **mettre de côté** means *save* in the sense of *put aside* something for later use, whether it be money or something else.

50. sit

(a) How to say that *something is sitting = seated*

La dame *assise* devant moi avait une coiffure si haute que je ne pouvais rien voir.	The lady { *sitting* / *seated* } in front of me had such a high hairdo that I couldn't see anything.

When *assis* is used as a pure adjective, it means *sitting* or *seated*.

Tout le monde *est assis*; Everyone is { *sitting down*; *seated*; } we can begin.
on peut commencer.

When *assis* follows the verb *être*, it is also an adjective. When *is sitting* (or its equivalent in other tenses) expresses a state rather than an action, it must be expressed by a form of *être assis*.

> CAUTION: Do NOT express *is sitting* by the verb « s'asseoir »; rather, use a form of *être assis*.

(b) How to say that *someone is sitting down*

Après avoir chanté l'hymne After singing the national
national, tout le monde *s'est assis*. anthem, everyone *sat down*.

When *sit down* indicates an action rather than a state, a form of the verb *s'asseoir* must be used.
Note the difference between :

Elle *est assise*. She *is sitting* (= *is seated*).
Elle *s'est assise*. She *sat down*.

Dans les exercices **F** *et* **G** *remplacez les mots anglais par leur équivalent français.*

F.

1. Est-ce que le voisin nous (*returned*) notre échelle ? **2.** Les enfants sont trop grands; il leur faut une (*room*) à chacun. **3.** Il y a bien des façons de (*save*). **4.** Ouf ! Quelle journée ! Je suis content de (*sit down*). **5.** Cela vaut toujours la peine de (*save*). **6.** Le maire devrait faire construire une plus grande (*room*) pour les fêtes. **7.** Attendez-moi; je (*will return*) dans un instant. **8.** On a pu (*save*) tous les papiers importants de l'incendie.

G.

1. On est content de se remettre au travail en (*returning*) de vacances. **2.** Inutile d'acheter ce buffet; il n'y aurait pas de (*room*) dans la salle à manger. **3.** Même dans les moments les plus durs, je (*saved*) de l'argent. **4.** Les Ponsard ont acheté une maison de dix (*rooms*) dans la banlieue. **5.** Les Arnoux (*will not return*) à l'Hôtel Terminus, parce qu'il est devenu trop cher. **6.** Lucie a fait un grand nettoyage; elle ne (*saved*) que quelques objets. **7.** L'étudiant qui (*is sitting*) au cinquième rang s'endort toujours pendant le cours.

Traduisez les phrases des exercices H *et* I *en français. Attention aux mots en italique.*

H.

1. (*tu*) If you didn't smoke, you would *save* a great deal of money.   **2.** How can that family live in those two *rooms*?   **3.** Guy will *return* to Japan next year.   **4.** Marie-Claire bought some pretty green curtains for her *room*.   **5.** I *save* all the stamps I receive from abroad for Regis.   **6.** Juliette *sat down* on the sofa and listened to the music. **7.** (*vous*) *Save up* for your old age.

I.

1. In what *room* will the tournament be held?   **2.** (*tu*) *Return* home early this evening, since we are going out.   **3.** I like houses with a lot of *room*.   **4.** My old grandmother *was sitting* in her armchair near the window.   **5.** Their dog *saved* a child's life.   **6.** (*vous*) I am willing to lend you that book if you promise to *return* it to me.   **7.** When Roland receives his check, he always *saves* ten percent of it.   **8.** (*vous*) I didn't know that you had already *returned*.

Verb Review

Review the verbs **prendre** and **rire** according to the outline on pages 332–333.

The Passive Voice and The Causative Construction

Une jeune fille de dix-sept ans, Cécile, très proche de son père, passe avec lui et des amis des vacances heureuses sur la Méditerranée. Le père, un veuf¹, a invité Anne Larsen, une ancienne amie de la famille, femme séduisante et autoritaire. Elle jette le trouble dans les relations entre le père qui lui fait la cour² et Cécile qui veut alors se débarrasser³ d'elle et qui ne peut plus maintenant compter que sur elle-même dans la vie.

Émancipation

Mon père avait loué sur la Méditerranée une grande villa blanche, isolée, ravissante⁴. Les premiers jours furent éblouissants⁵. Nous passions des heures sur la plage, prenant peu à peu une couleur saine et dorée⁶. Dès l'aube, j'*étais plongée* dans l'eau, une eau fraîche et transparente où je faisais des mouve-
5   ments furieux pour me laver de toutes les poussières de Paris. Je m'allongeais dans le sable, en prenais une poignée⁷ dans ma main, le laissais couler de mes doigts en un jet jaunâtre et doux; je me disais qu'il coulait comme le temps, que c'était une idée facile et qu'il était agréable d'avoir des idées faciles. C'était l'été... Et puis Anne Larsen arriva...
10   J'avais raté mon baccalauréat en juin. Anne disait qu'il fallait absolument que je le passe en octobre. Elle voulait me *faire travailler*, ces vacances, ces vacances qui pourraient me faire tant de bien, et par ces chaleurs !... J'eus beau faire⁸, c'était une femme de tête⁹. J'aurais voulu *être appuyée*¹⁰ par mon père, mais il ne répondait à mes regards désespérés que par de petits sourires gê-
15   nés¹¹. Je *fus* donc *obligée* d'ouvrir quelquefois, distraitement, mes livres de philosophie...

---

¹widower   ²courts her   ³get rid of   ⁴delightful   ⁵fascinating, dazzling   ⁶bronzed
⁷handful   ⁸**J'eus beau faire** *In spite of anything I could do*   ⁹**une femme de tête** *a strong-willed woman*   ¹⁰be supported   ¹¹embarrassed

Un jour, cependant, où je me reposais sur la plage, après le bain du matin, mon père s'assit auprès de moi et me regarda. Je sentais son regard posé sur moi. J'allais me lever et lui proposer d'aller dans l'eau, avec un air faus-
20 sement enjoué[12], quand il posa sa main sur ma tête et éleva la voix d'un ton lamentable :

—Anne, venez voir cette sauterelle[13], elle est toute maigre. Si le travail lui fait cet effet-là, il faut qu'elle s'arrête.

Anne s'approchait. Elle s'assit près de nous et murmura :
25 —C'est vrai que ça ne lui réussit pas[14]. D'ailleurs, il lui suffirait de travailler vraiment au lieu de tourner en rond[15] dans sa chambre.

Je m'étais retournée, je les regardais. Comment savait-elle que je ne travaillais pas ? Peut-être même avait-elle deviné mes pensées hostiles à son égard. Je *fus prise* d'une peur subite à cette idée.
30 —Je ne tourne pas en rond dans ma chambre, protestai-je.

—Est-ce ton ami Cyril qui te manque[16] ? demanda mon père.

—Non !

C'était un peu faux. Mais il est vrai que je n'avais pas eu le temps de penser à Cyril. Et il n'était pas question de le *faire revenir*.
35 —Tu ne te portes pas bien, dit mon père sévèrement. Anne, vous la voyez ? On dirait un pauvre poulet tout maigre qu'on *ferait rôtir* au soleil.

—Ma petite Cécile, dit Anne, faites un effort. Travaillez un peu et mangez beaucoup. Cet examen est important...

—Je me fous de[17] mon examen, criai-je, vous comprenez, je m'en fous !
40 Je la regardai désespérément, bien en face[18], pour qu'elle comprît que c'était plus grave qu'un examen. Il fallait qu'elle me dise : « Alors, qu'est-ce que c'est ? », qu'elle me harcèle[19] de questions, qu'elle me force à tout lui raconter. Et là, elle me convaincrait, elle déciderait ce qu'elle voudrait, mais ainsi je ne *serais* plus *infestée* de ces sentiments acides et déprimants. Ma détresse devait
45 pourtant *se voir* sur mon visage, *s'entendre* dans mes paroles. Elle me regardait attentivement, je voyais le bleu de ses yeux assombris[20] par l'attention, le reproche. Et je compris que jamais elle ne penserait à me questionner, à me délivrer parce qu'elle estimait que cela ne *se faisait* pas...

Je me rejetai sur le sable avec violence, j'appuyai ma joue sur la douceur
50 chaude de la plage, je tremblai un peu. La main d'Anne, tranquille et sûre, *se posa* sur ma nuque[21] un moment.

—Ne vous compliquez pas la vie, dit-elle. Vous qui étiez si contente, vous qui n'avez pas de tête[22], vous devenez cérébrale[23] et triste. Ce n'est pas un personnage pour vous[24]... Venez déjeuner...

---

[12]**faussement enjoué** *seemingly jovial* [13]*grasshopper* [14]**ça... pas** *that doesn't agree with her* [15]**tourner en rond** *walk around* [16]"*Do you miss your friend Cyril ?*" [17]**Je me fous de** *I don't give a damn about* [18]**bien en face** *straight in the eye* [19]*pester, harass* [20]*darkened* [21]*nape of the neck* [22]**vous... tête** *you who are not an intellectual* [23]*intellectual* [24]**Ce... vous** *That's out of character for you...*

55   Mon père s'était éloigné; il n'*était* pas *fait* pour ce genre de discussions;
dans le chemin, il me prit la main et la garda. C'était une main dure et récon-
fortante : elle m'avait mouchée[25] à mon premier chagrin d'amour, elle avait
tenu la mienne dans les moments de tranquillité et de bonheur parfait, elle
l'avait serrée furtivement dans les moments de complicité et de fou-rire[26].
60 Cette main sur le volant[27], ou sur les clés, le soir, cherchant vainement la
serrure[28], cette main sur l'épaule d'une femme ou sur des cigarettes, cette main
ne pouvait plus rien pour moi. Je la serrai très fort. Se tournant vers moi, il me
sourit.

> D'après Françoise Sagan. Depuis *Bonjour tristesse* écrit à vingt ans, elle
> connaît un grand succès avec des œuvres sensibles et élégantes, écrites
> dans la meilleure manière traditionelle. (*Bonjour tristesse*, Julliard, 1954)

Questions

1. Quels sont les plaisirs de Cécile sur cette belle plage de la Méditerranée ?
2. Pourquoi tout est-il gâté par l'arrivée d'Anne Larsen ?   **3.** Pourquoi l'in-
troduction d'un examen d'état à la fin des études secondaires (comme le
baccalauréat en France) serait-elle une innovation utile aux États-Unis ?
4. Racontez la scène entre Cécile et Anne Larsen.   **5.** Qu'est-ce que Cécile
espérait qu'une explication provoquerait ?   **6.** Quelles sont les caractéristiques du père de la jeune fille ou de la jeune fille elle-même ?

Note: Voir aussi les deux sujets de composition dans le *Manuel d'exercices*.

I. THE PASSIVE VOICE

When the subject of the sentence acts, we say that the sentence is in the ACTIVE
VOICE. When the subject of the sentence is acted upon, we say that the sentence
is in the PASSIVE VOICE.

ACTIVE VOICE	PASSIVE VOICE
John *found* <u>the money</u>.	<u>The money</u> *was found* by John.
The teacher *will correct* <u>that examination</u>.	<u>That examination</u> *will be corrected* by the teacher.

In the two examples above, note :

---

[25]**elle m'avait mouchée** it (*the hand*) *had consoled me* (lit. : *had blown my nose*)
[26]*uncontrolled laughter*   [27]*steering wheel*   [28]*keyhole*

(a) The subject of the sentence in the active voice (*John, teacher*) becomes the object of the preposition *by* and is called the "agent" of the sentence in the passive voice.

(b) The object of the sentence in the active voice (*money, examination*) becomes the subject of the sentence in the passive voice.

(c) The verb of the sentence in the passive voice is in the same tense as the verb of the sentence in the active voice.

(d) The verb of the sentence in the passive voice is made up of a form of the auxiliary *to be* + THE PAST PARTICIPLE of the verb in the active voice.

1. How is the passive voice formed in French ?

Cet escroc *sera mis* en prison.	That swindler *will be put* in prison.
Les enfants *étaient* toujours *récompensés pour leurs bonnes notes.*	The children *were* always *rewarded* for their good marks.
La maison *a été vendue* hier.	The house *was sold yesterday.*

In French, the passive voice is made up of :

> a form of auxiliary verb ***être*** + PAST PARTICPLE

2. How and with what does the past participle of a verb in the passive voice agree ?

(See examples in §1.)

The past participle of a verb in the passive voice agrees in gender and number with the subject of the sentence.

3. By what preposition is the agent usually introduced in French ?

Cet article sera certainement lu *par* tout *le monde.*	That article will certainly be read *by* everyone.
Ce roman a été écrit *par* un Russe.	That novel was written *by* a Russian.
Cette maison a été détruite *par* l'incendie.	This house was destroyed *by* the fire.

In French, *par* usually introduces the phrases indicating the agent.

The agent is the person or the thing by which the action of a sentence in the passive voice is caused or performed.

4. When is *de* used to introduce the phrase indicating the agent ?

Elle était aimée *de tous*.	She was loved *by all*.
Le Président était suivi *de* plusieurs ministres.	The president was followed *by* several ministers.
Il sera accompagné *de deux* secrétaires.	He will be accompanied *by* two secretaries.
La maison était entourée *d'un* jardin.	The house was surrounded *by* a garden.

The preposition *de* is less strong than *par*. It usually follows verbs that indicate a state, a mental action, or an habitual action, where the role of the agent is less dynamic.

Also, certain verbs are normally followed by *de*, as, for example, *entourer de*, *couvrir de*, *remplir de*, etc.

5. If a verb can be followed by both *par* and *de*, what determines whether *par* or *de* should introduce the phrase indicating the agent ?

Les verres ont été de nouveau remplis *par* le garçon.	Les verres étaient remplis *de* vin.
L'enfant qui allait tomber a été saisi *par* son frère.	L'enfant était saisi *de* peur.
Irène était très aimée *par* son fiancé.	Irène était aimée *de* ses amis.

One can almost always use *par* to introduce a phrase indicating the agent unless the past participle is habitually followed by *de*.

The preposition *par* is dynamic, the preposition *de* is weaker. When the role of the agent is forceful, *par* is likely to be used; when the role of the agent is less active, *de* is often found. The preposition *par* is likely to indicate an action that took place at one time; both *par* and *de* may indicate habitual actions.

A. *Mettez les verbes des phrases suivantes à la voix passive en employant le temps indiqué.*

1. (PASSÉ COMPOSÉ) Cette chambre (réserver) par Monsieur et Madame Amieux, mais ils ne peuvent pas venir. **2.** (PRÉSENT DE L'INDICATIF) Les fleurs (récolter) pour en faire des parfums. **3.** (PRÉSENT DU SUBJONCTIF) J'aimerais que Charlotte (inviter) à votre soirée. **4.** (FUTUR) Les manifestations (interdire) à l'Université. **5.** (IMPARFAIT) Ce restaurant (tenir) par les parents de

Pierre.   **6.** (FUTUR) Si le coup réussit, ce peuple (gouverner) par des gens capables de tout.   **7.** (PASSÉ DU SUBJONCTIF) Je ne crois pas que ce poème (écrire) par Georges.   **8.** (IMPARFAIT) Les hommes les plus influents (inviter) chez le maire.   **9.** (PASSÉ COMPOSÉ) Le petit garçon du voisin (mordre) par son chien.   **10.** (FUTUR) Dépêchez-vous, sinon toutes les cerises (cueillir).

B. Traduisez en français.

1. I wonder why Mr. Lenoir is being watched by the police.   **2.** Considerable sums are being spent each year by the state.   **3.** The criminal was being defended by Maître Olivier.   **4.** Everything they had was lost in this fire.   **5.** The new ambassador was received by the president.

6. How does French often avoid an English passive when there is no agent expressed in the English sentence ?

On a donné **le prix au meilleur élève.**	The prize *was given* to the best pupil.
On verra **l'éclipse demain soir.**	The eclipse *will be seen* tomorrow evening.

Although the passive is by no means uncommon in French, it is not used as frequently as in English. There are certain verbs with which it is never used, there are other verbs with which it is not used in certain tenses, and there are still others where it could be used but sounds somewhat unnatural. Long experience in speaking French is necessary to develop a precise feeling for when a French sentence sounds natural in the passive and when it does not. But French has various other ways of expressing certain sentences that English puts into the passive.

To express an English passive in a sentence where there is no agent, French often uses the indefinite pronoun *on* + VERB IN ACTIVE VOICE.

C. Traduisez en français en évitant la voix passive.

1. Why was I awakened at six o'clock ?   **2.** How is this sentence translated ?   **3.** That was said at the beginning of the hour.   **4.** The prizes will be distributed to the winners Saturday morning.   **5.** The door was opened to allow[1] a little more air to come in.   **6.** Bridge will be played after the reception.   **7.** Christmas carols are sung everywhere in the month of December.   **8.** That evening[2] the doors were locked at 8:30.   **9.** French is spoken in that store.   **10.** His name was taken out[3] of the telephone book.

---

[1]*allow... to come in* **laisser entrer**   [2]In time expressions referring to the past, how is *that* expressed ?   [3]*take out* **enlever**

7. How does French often avoid an English passive when an agent is expressed in the English sentence ?

Un célèbre humoriste *a dit* cela.	That *was said* by a famous humorist.
Ceux qui l'ont vu n'*oublieront* pas cet incident.	That incident *will not be forgotten* by those who saw it.

French often uses the active voice to express an idea that English might express with a sentence in the passive voice. Some French verbs are not normally used in the passive voice.

D. *Traduisez en français en évitant la voix passive.*

1. That explosion was heard by several persons.   **2.** The boss would be liked by everyone if he were more patient.   **3.** All the money for the family was earned by the oldest brother.   **4.** This doctor had been criticized by several of his colleagues.   **5.** The problem was explained to the students by the teacher.   **6.** That talk will be given[1] by a well-known specialist. **7.** The car was driven by a sixteen-year-old boy[2].   **8.** By whom was that man seen ?

8. How does French express an English passive sentence whose subject would be the indirect object in the active sentence ?

Le notaire montrera le testament *aux héritiers* jeudi.	*The heirs* will be *shown* the will *by the notary* Thursday.
On a permis à Suzanne de passer le week-end chez les Grillet.	*Suzanne* was *allowed* to spend the weekend at the Grillets'.

Consider the passive and active forms of the following English sentence :
PASSIVE: *I was given* the book by a friend.
ACTIVE: A friend *gave* the book *to me*.

The subject of the passive sentence is *I*. This *I* would become *to me* in the active sentence. Thus, the subject of the passive sentence is the indirect object of the active sentence. As you can see from the preceding examples, this is not the case in French.

The indirect object of the active form of a French sentence CANNOT become the subject of the passive form of that sentence. Instead, French expresses the sentence in the active voice only.

---

[1]Use a form of **faire**.   [2]The French say : *a boy of sixteen years.*

E. Traduisez en français.

1. We were forbidden to enter that room.   **2.** The workmen were promised a raise in[1] pay.   **3.** *(vous)* You will be given the necessary information by my secretary.   **4.** We were served coffee and sandwiches on the plane. **5.** The delegates were told to come back the next day.   **6.** The defendant was asked by the lawyer where he had been that evening.   **7.** *(vous)* You will be sent some samples by the salesman[2] of that company[3].   **8.** We were shown some snapshots at the Arnauds'[4].   **9.** The children were allowed to go to the movies yesterday evening.

9. When is the English passive expressed by a French reflexive ?

Ce produit *se vend* partout.	That product *is sold* all over.
Ça ne *se fait* pas ici.	That *isn't done* here.

The reflexive form of a French verb is often used to express an English passive when the sentence describes a general rather than a specific action.

Compare the following three sentences, each of which has a different meaning, although English uses approximately the same construction in each.

(a) **Ce livre *se vend* partout.**   That book *is sold* everywhere.

Here, French uses the reflexive form of the verb to describe a general action.

(b) **Ce livre *est vendu*.**   That book *is sold*.

Here, a form of *être* + PAST PARTICIPLE describes a state, so that **vendu** is an adjective, and the sentence is not in the passive voice at all.

(c) **Ce livre *a été vendu* hier.**   That book *was sold* yesterday.

Here, **a été vendu** is a real passive, which describes one specific action.

10. In what other way is the reflexive form of a French verb used to express an English passive ?

Mon ami *s'appelle* Jean Colin.	My friend *is called* Jean Colin.
Orléans *se trouve* au sud de Paris.	Orléans *is located* to the south of Paris.

---

[1]**de** [2]**représentant** [3]**maison** [4]In French, proper names do not take an **-s** in the plural. The plural is indicated by the plural form of the definite article.

The reflexive forms of certain French verbs are used idiomatically where English uses the passive voice. Each verb of this type must be learned individually with its meaning.

F. Traduisez en français.

1. Everything is done automatically in that factory.   **2.** The Pyrenees are situated[1] between France and Spain.   **3.** That telephone is used[2] only in case of an[3] emergency.   **4.** Green[4] was worn a great deal last year. **5.** That is said, but it[5] isn't written.   **6.** Hundreds[6] of novels are published each year.

II. THE CAUSATIVE CONSTRUCTION

11. **What is the causative construction ? With what verb does French express it ?**

Le professeur *fera lire* les élèves.	The teacher *will have* the pupils *read*.
Notre voisin *a fait peindre* la maison.	Our neighbor *had* the house *painted*.

The causative construction expresses the idea of *having something done* or of *having someone do something*—of causing something to be done or of causing someone to do something—or, at times, of making someone do something.

> NOTE: When the English infinitive follows a form of *have*, it is used without *to*. For example, in the sentence *The teacher will have the pupils read*, *read* is an infinitive without *to*.

In English, this idea is expressed by *have* + INFINITIVE or *have* + PAST PARTICIPLE. In French, the causative is expressed by *faire* + INFINITIVE.
The causative always has at least one object and often it has two objects.

> NOTE: Consider the sentence : *Le professeur fera lire les élèves*. In this sentence, *les élèves* is the object of the verb *fera*, and the subject of the infinitive *lire*.

---

[1]Use a form of **trouver**.   [2]Use a form of **employer**.   [3]Omit in French.   [4]Supply the definite article.   [5]ça   [6]Here, *hundreds* is a noun.

Now consider the sentence : ***Notre voisin a fait peindre la maison***. Here, ***la maison*** is the object of the verb ***peindre***.

In a sentence with a causative construction, the object is sometimes governed by a form of ***faire***, sometimes by the INFINITIVE following ***faire***.

12. When the causative has only one object, what kind of object is it ?

Nous *ferons écrire <u>les enfants</u>*.	We'll *have <u>the children</u> write*.
Ils *faisaient écrire <u>des lettres</u>*.	They *used to have <u>letters</u> written*.

When a causative has only one object, it is always a direct object—whether a person or a thing.

G. *Traduisez en français.*

1. The teacher isn't making Roger[1] work because he was sick.   **2.** Our neighbors are having a garage[1] built.   **3.** (*vous*) Why did you have your father-in-law[1] intervene ?   **4.** (*tu*) When will you have the television[1] repaired ?   **5.** We'll have those records[1] played later.

13. When a causative construction has two objects—usually a person and a thing—what kind of objects are they ?

Nous avons fait étudier *sa leçon <u>à Lucie</u>*.	We had <u>Lucy</u> study *her lesson*.
Je ferai ranger *ses affaires <u>à Jean</u>*.	I'll have <u>John</u> put *his things* in order.

When a causative construction has two objects, the thing is the direct object and the person the indirect object.

NOTE: Occasionally, a causative construction has two personal objects. In such cases, the person receiving the action is the direct object of the infinitive, and the person performing the action is the agent and is introduced by ***par***.

Le président fera présenter *le conférencier <u>par son collègue</u>*.	The president will have <u>his colleague</u> introduce *the speaker*.

---

[1]In the causative construction in French, the noun object directly follows the infinitive.

14. Sometimes the use of the indirect object for the person causes ambiguity. How may this ambiguity be avoided ?

J'ai fait écrire une lettre *par* mon frère.	I had *my brother* write a letter.
Il fait lire ce roman *par tous ses amis*.	He has *all his friends* read that novel.

In cases where the use *à* + PERSONAL OBJECT could result in ambiguity, it is not incorrect to use that construction for the causative, but such a sentence is often made clearer by using instead *par* + PERSONAL OBJECT.

> NOTE: Equally correct is : ***J'ai fait écrire une lettre à mon frère***. But this could mean either : *I had a letter written to my brother* or *I had my brother write a letter*. Likewise, equally correct is : ***Il fait lire ce roman à tous ses amis***. But this could mean either : *He has all his friends read that novel* or *He has that novel read to all his friends*.

H. *Traduisez en français.*

1. We had his parents correct his mistakes.   **2.** Mr. Géré had his wife pack his suitcase[1].   **3.** Businessmen have their secretaries[2] write their letters.   **4.** I will have the chauffeur wash the car.   **5.** That teacher has all his students copy the same poem.

15. When the causative construction governs a pronoun object, what is the position of the pronoun object ?

Jacques *fera lire* <u>*le testament de son oncle*</u>.	**Jacques *<u>le</u> fera lire*.**
Nous *ferons réparer* <u>*notre voiture*</u> demain.	**Nous *<u>la</u> ferons réparer* demain.**
La ville *a fait abattre* <u>*cette vieille maison au propriétaire*</u>.	**La ville *<u>la lui</u> a fait abattre*.**
Mon père *<u>m</u>'a fait recommencer <u>mes devoirs</u>*.	**Mon père *<u>me les</u> a fait recommencer*.**

The pronoun objects of a causative construction normally precede the form of the verb *faire*. Pronouns come in their usual order.

> NOTE: When the causative construction is in the affirmative imperative, pronoun objects follow the form of *faire*. Ex. : ***Faites-le lire***.

---

[1]*pack a suitcase* **faire une valise**   [2]Use the singular in French.

16. When the verb *faire* is used in a compound tense, what about the agreement of its past participle with a preceding direct object ?

Je *les ai fait* vendre.   I *had them* sold.

Où sont *les lettres que* nous *avons*   Where are *the letters* that we

  fait copier ?   had copied ?

When the past participle of the verb *faire* is followed by an infinitive, the past participle of *faire* is always invariable. In other words, when it is used as part of the causative construction, the past participle of *faire* does not agree with its preceding direct object.

I. Copiez les phrases françaises et traduisez en français les phrases anglaises. Attention à la position et à l'ordre des pronoms compléments.

> EXEMPLE: Votre frère a-t-il fait réparer sa vieille voiture la semaine passée ?
> (Oui,...) Oui, il l'a fait réparer la semaine passée.

1. Avez-vous fait construire le garage cette année ? (*Yes, I had it constructed this year.*)   **2.** Ferez-vous envoyer ce paquet par avion ? (*Yes, I'll have it sent by plane.*)   **3.** Faisiez-vous travailler vos élèves pendant les week-ends ? (*Yes, I used to have them work during the weekends.*)   **4.** M. Duchamp a-t-il fait couper ces beaux arbres ? (*No, he didn't have them cut down.*)   **5.** Le médecin vous a-t-il fait prendre un nouveau remède ? (*No, he didn't have me take any.*)   **6.** Claude vous a-t-il fait conduire sa voiture ? (*Yes, he had me drive it.*)   **7.** Leur mère a-t-elle fait ranger leurs jouets aux enfants ? (*Yes, she had them put them away.*)

EXERCICE ORAL

Monsieur Benoît fait un voyage de quelques jours. Pendant ce temps il pense à ce qui se fera pendant son absence. En rentrant, il voit ce qui s'est passé.
Mettez les phrases suivantes à la voix passive.

A. Pendant que je serai loin...

1. ma femme commandera de nouveaux tapis.

2. des ouvriers répareront le toit de notre garage.

3. mon fils Arthur tondra soigneusement la pelouse.

4. la bonne lavera les grandes fenêtres du salon.

5. ma fille Annette invitera ses amis anglais à une soirée dansante.

B. Quand je serai de retour...

6. l'électricien aura réparé ma télévision japonaise.

7. ma fille aura acheté un manteau de fourrure.

8. ma femme aura organisé une fête pour ses charités.

9. Arthur aura planté des fleurs dans le jardin.

10. la bonne aura préparé un bon dîner de bienvenue.

C. Quand je suis rentré, j'ai vu que...

11. le chien avait creusé un énorme trou devant la maison.

12. des enfants avaient cassé une vitre du salon en jouant avec leur ballon.

13. ma fille avait démoli ma nouvelle voiture.

14. la police avait arrêté mon fils pour excès de vitesse.

15. ma femme avait réservé deux billets d'avion pour Tahiti.

See pages 271–314 for the *Exercices d'ensemble.*

. . . . . .

PROBLEM WORDS

51. soon

(a) When *soon* is expressed by **bientôt**

Ma fille aura *bientôt* vingt ans.	My daughter will *soon* be twenty years old.

The common word for *soon* is **bientôt**. But **bientôt** is not usually modified.

(b) When *soon* is expressed by *tôt*

Ne venez pas <u>si</u> tôt.	Don't come <u>so</u> soon.
Vous avez parlé <u>trop</u> tôt.	You spoke <u>too</u> soon.
Il aurait fallu faire cela <u>plus</u> tôt.	You should have done that *soon<u>er</u>.*

To express *soon* modified by an adverb, use **tôt**. Also, **tôt** is used in the expression **tôt ou tard**, which means *sooner or later*.

(c) Expressions embodying *soon*

dès que (common) **aussitôt que** (mainly literary) }	*as soon as*
dès que possible **aussitôt que possible** **le plus tôt possible** **au plus tôt** }	*as soon as possible*

52. spend

(a) When it is a question of *spending money*

Vous *dépensez* beaucoup trop d'*argent* pour des choses superflues.	You *spend* much too much *money* for superfluous things.

The verb ***dépenser*** is used when it is a question of *spending money*.

(b) When it is a question of *spending time*

Nous *avons passé deux semaines* au Portugal.	We *spent two weeks* in Portugal.
J'*ai passé une heure* à écrire cette lettre.	I *spent an hour* writing that letter.

The verb ***passer*** is used when it is a question of *spending time*.

> CAUTION: The verb ***passer*** must NOT be followed by the present participle to express the idea of spending a given amount of time doing something. French expresses this construction by *à* + INFINITIVE.

53. stop

(a) When *stop* may be expressed by ***cesser***

Le bruit *a cessé*.	The noise *stopped*.
Tiens ! Il *a cessé de neiger*.	Look ! It *has stopped snowing*.
Quand est-ce que les gens du dessus *cesseront de faire* tout ce bruit ?	When will the people upstairs *stop making* all that noise ?

The verb ***cesser*** never takes a direct object. It is most often used with ***de*** + INFINITIVE, although it may be used as in the first example when a thing is the subject of the verb.

(b) When *stop* may be expressed by ***arrêter***

Arrêtez donc *la voiture* un peu plus doucement.	*Stop the car* a little more gently.
Arrête donc *de prendre* tous ces médicaments !	*Stop taking* all that medicine !

The verb ***arrêter*** is usually followed by a direct object. It is sometimes followed by ***de*** + INFINITIVE.

(c) When *stop* may be expressed by ***s'arrêter***

Nous *nous sommes arrêtés* pour admirer la vue.	We *stopped* to admire the view.
Je ne peux pas *m'arrêter* si près du carrefour.	I can't *stop* so near the crossing.
Il *s'est arrêté de parler*.	He *stopped talking*.

The reflexive form ***s'arrêter*** is used when no object follows. It is sometimes followed by ***de*** + INFINITIVE.

54. such

(a) How to say *such a* + NOUN

Avez-vous jamais entendu *une histoire pareille* ?	
Avez-vous jamais entendu *une histoire comme ça* ?	Have you ever heard *such a story* ?
Avez-vous jamais entendu *une telle histoire* ?	

The English *such a* + NOUN may be expressed by ***un*** + NOUN + ***pareil***, by ***un*** + NOUN + ***comme ça***, and by ***un tel*** + NOUN.

(b) How to say *such a* + ADJECTIVE

Je n'ai jamais entendu une histoire *aussi* (*tellement*) *drôle*.	I never heard *such a funny story*.
Je n'ai jamais entendu une histoire *aussi drôle que ça*.	

The English *such a* + ADJECTIVE may be expressed by ***aussi*** (or ***tellement***) + ADJECTIVE or ***aussi*** + ADJECTIVE + ***que ça***.

J. Remplacez les mots anglais par leur équivalent français.

1. Pourquoi Nicolas est-il rentré (*sooner*) que toi ?   **2.** (*tu*) Où (*will you spend*) les trois mois d'été ?   **3.** Voulez-vous (*stop*) votre taxi au coin de la rue ?   **4.** Si Marcel ne revient pas (*soon*), je m'en vais.   **5.** J'ai dû (*stop*) plusieurs fois en route pour me reposer.   **6.** Personne ne peut (*spend*) tant d'argent sans se ruiner.   **7.** (*As soon as*) vous recevrez sa lettre, préve-nez-moi.   **8.** Je ne peux rien entendre; (*stop*) l'aspirateur, s'il te plaît.   **9.** Quand Thomas (*stops*) de travailler, c'est pour dormir.

K. Traduisez en français. Attention aux mots en italique.

1. (*vous*) You'll come to see me *soon*, won't you ?   **2.** Ah, that Micheline ! She never *stops* talking !   **3.** I never saw *such* a hard exercise !   **4.** (*tu*) *Stop* making that noise !   **5.** (*vous*) If you *spend* your money like that, you won't go far[1].   **6.** (*vous*) Come *soon* enough to have dinner[2] with us.   **7.** (*tu*) If you need information, *stop* someone on[3] the street.   **8.** *Such a* person should be the mayor of the city.   **9.** I *stopped* to have lunch[4] at the Hôtel de la Poste.   **10.** We are invited to *spend* the evening at Dr.[5] Beaugendre's.   **11.** (*vous*) Come[6] and see me *as soon as possible*.   **12.** Won't it ever *stop* raining ?   **13.** I have rarely heard *such a* boring lecture.   **14.** (*tu*) Have you ever seen *such a* monster ?

Verb Review

Review the verbs **savoir** and **suivre** according to the outline on pages 332–333.

---

[1]Use a form of **aller loin**.   [2]*have dinner* **dîner**   [3]**dans**   [4]*have lunch* **déjeuner**   [5]Use the article before such titles.   [6]French uses **venir** + INFINITIVE.

The Verb *Devoir*

Les grands-parents de la narratrice sont originaires du Québec. Un jour, le grand-père se représente les grandes plaines de l'Ouest et veut partir. La grand-mère résiste longtemps et accepte enfin. « C'est presque toujours, dans une famille, le rêveur qui l'emporte », écrit Gabrielle Roy. De nombreux Québécois ont ainsi quitté leur province, autrefois, pour des plaines plus fertiles.

L'écrivain parle ici de la visite qu'elle fait avec sa mère dans la belle ferme de son oncle et raconte la conversation entre sa mère et son oncle rappelant le voyage du Québec au Manitoba et l'image de la grand-mère.

Souvenirs du Canada

De nouveau, l'année suivante, à l'automne, à l'époque des moissons[1] qu'elle aimait tant, je partis avec ma mère pour notre visite annuelle à son frère.

Nous arrivâmes chez l'oncle Cléophas en plein temps des battages[2].

Quelle activité régnait alors dans nos fermes du Manitoba ! Douze à quinze
5 hommes, loués[3] pour la saison, logeaient à la ferme; quelques-uns *devaient* coucher dans de petites granges[4] qui servaient de dortoirs[5], avec la porte toujours ouverte pour admettre l'air.

Ces gens, à la fois serviteurs, hôtes et amis, venaient de tous les coins du Canada, je *devrais* dire du monde peut-être, car chose bien étonnante, des
10 hommes de nationalité et de caractère les plus divers s'étaient assemblés dans nos terres lointaines pour récolter[6] le blé : jeunes étudiants, vieux bougres revenus de tout[7], voyageurs de passage[8], conteurs nés[9], émigrés de toutes sortes.

En cette maison perdue au milieu de la plaine, pendant les soirées, vibrait
15 quelque chose de l'univers. Car jamais la fatigue de ces hommes ne *devait* les empêcher, le soir venu, de raconter un peu leur vie, essayer de se communiquer quelque chose d'unique en chacun d'eux et qui les rapprochait[10].

---

[1]*harvests* [2]**en... battages** *in the middle of the threshing season* [3]*hired* [4]*barns*
[5]*dormitories* [6]**récolter le blé** *harvest the wheat* [7]**bougres... tout** *disillusioned fellows*
[8]**voyageurs de passage** *travelers passing through* [9]**conteurs nés** *born storytellers*
[10]*brought them nearer to each other*

C'est de ces soirées de chants et d'histoires que date sans doute mon désir d'apprendre à bien raconter car j'avais saisi alors le poignant[11] et miraculeux
20 pouvoir de ce don[12].

Maman, il est vrai, m'en avait toujours donné l'exemple, mais jamais comme en ces temps de forte stimulation où le passé revivait en elle avec une force particulière...

Plus d'une fois, déjà quand j'étais enfant, elle m'avait raconté l'arrivée des
25 grands-parents dans l'Ouest; elle m'avait redit comment, *ayant dû* quitter notre village, tous entassés[13] dans le chariot couvert[14], serrés les uns contre les autres, grand-mère ayant emporté quelques-uns de ses meubles, son rouet[15] et d'innombrables paquets, ils s'en allaient à travers l'immense pays.

—La plaine alors, me disait-elle, paraissait encore plus immense qu'aujour-
30 d'hui, et le ciel aussi, plus immense; car il n'y avait pour ainsi dire pas de village le long de la piste[16] et même très peu de maisons. En apercevoir une, tout au loin, à une grande distance, était déjà toute une aventure...

Ce soir-là, dans la grande salle de la ferme, j'écoutais ma mère et l'oncle Cléophas un peu à l'écart[17] et occupés à évoquer le souvenir de grand-mère.
35 Un tout jeune homme réfugié dans un coin de la salle jouait doucement de l'harmonica. L'air un peu traînant[18] formait un accompagnement discret aux paroles et peut-être les poussait-il quelque peu à la nostalgie.

—Te souviens-tu, Eveline, rappela mon oncle, de sa colère subite le premier soir où en chariot vers notre destination, n'ayant pas trouvé en route de
40 maison pour nous loger, nous *avons dû* camper à la belle étoile[19] ? Était-ce à cause du feu qui prenait mal[20] ? Était-ce la peur de la plaine nue tout autour ? Elle se dressa, nous traitant de bohémiens[21] et nous menaça : « Tiens, j'en ai assez de vous suivre, bande d'inconnus[22] ! Allez donc votre chemin[23]; moi, j'irai le mien ».
45 Maman souriait avec un peu de tristesse.

—Avant de quitter son village, elle n'avait sans doute pas entrevu toute l'ampleur du changement[24]. C'est le soir dont tu parles qu'elle *a dû* en saisir la portée[25].

—Mais nous traiter d'inconnus ! Et d'ailleurs, *il fallait* partir, insista mon
50 oncle. Là-bas, dans les collines, rappelle-toi, Eveline, ce n'était que cailloux, maigre terre...

—Sans doute, dit maman, mais elle y était attachée, et toi-même tu *dois* savoir à présent que l'on ne s'attache pas uniquement à ce qui nous est doux et facile.

---

[11]*intense, gripping* [12]*gift* [13]*huddled* [14]**chariot couvert** *covered wagon* [15]*spinning wheel* [16]*trail* [17]**à l'écart** *aside* [18]*slow* [19]**à la belle étoile** *in the open* [20]**qui prenait mal** *which wouldn't start* [21]*gypsies* [22]*strangers* [23]**Allez... chemin** *You go your way* [24]**n'avait... changement** *doubtless had not realized the extent of the change* [25]**qu'elle... portée** *that she must have understood the significance of it*

55 —Qu'aurions-nous pu faire d'autre que ce que nous avons fait ? reprit mon
oncle. L'Ouest nous appelait. C'était l'univers alors. Du reste, il nous a donné
raison.

D'après Gabrielle Roy, une des romancières les plus en vue d'un groupe
brillant d'écrivains canadiens aussi estimés en France que dans leur pays
d'origine. (*La Route d'Altamont*, Éditions H. M. H. Montréal and Éditions
Flammarion, 1966)

Questions

1. Décrivez la ferme de l'oncle Cléophas.   **2.** D'où la narratrice a-t-elle
tiré son don d'écrivain ?   **3.** Qu'est-ce qui avait fait de ce voyage du Québec
au Manitoba une grande aventure ?   **4.** Qu'est-ce qui est arrivé dans cette
soirée mémorable passée à la belle étoile au cours de ce voyage ?   **5.** Pourquoi l'oncle Cléophas ne manifeste-t-il aucun regret d'être parti ?   **6.** Beaucoup de gens quittent leur pays, volontairement ou non. D'où sont venus les
immigrants qui ont peuplé les États-Unis ?

NOTE: Voir aussi les deux sujets de composition dans le *Manuel d'exercices*

The verb ***devoir*** constitutes a difficulty for an English-speaking person
because no one English verb corresponds exactly to the French verb ***devoir***.
Each tense of ***devoir*** has its own translation, and in some tenses ***devoir*** may
have several meanings, according to the context.

1. What meanings may *devoir* have in the present tense ?

M. Guillot *doit* arriver demain.	Mr. Guillot *is to* arrive tomorrow.
Vous *devez* partir tout de suite.	You *must* (*have to*) leave at once.
Anne *doit* beaucoup aimer la musique.	Anne *must* like (*probably likes*) music a great deal.
Votre fils *doit* lire beaucoup.	Your son *must* read (*has to read /probably* reads) a great deal.

In the present tense, ***devoir*** means either *is to* (*am to, are to*) or *must*. But
must itself has two possible meanings : *has to* and *probably does*. In the
second example above, *must* clearly means *have to*. The *must* of the third
example clearly means *probably does*. But in the fourth example, there are
two possibilities. *Your son must read a great deal* may mean : *Your son <u>has
to</u> read a great deal*, or : *Your son <u>probably</u> reads a great deal*. When the two
possible interpretations exist, the context decides.

A. Traduisez en anglais les phrases suivantes. Attention au verbe devoir. Si vous traduisez ce verbe par *must,* **indiquez le sens de** *must.*

1. Mon collègue *doit* me rendre mon livre demain, et je vous le passerai. **2.** Si vous *devez* leur écrire, faites-le tout de suite.   **3.** Il *doit* y avoir des ours dans cette forêt.   **4.** On *doit* toujours faire de son mieux.   **5.** Le professeur *doit* nous expliquer ces règles cette semaine.   **6.** Vous *devez* avoir beaucoup d'argent.

2. What meanings may *devoir* have in the imperfect ?

M. Guillot *devait* arriver ce matin.	Mr. Guillot *was* to arrive this morning.
Gilbert *devait* travailler plus dur pour se rattraper.	Gilbert *had to* work harder to catch up.
Ces gens-là *devaient* être très riches.	Those people *must have* been (*probably* were) very rich.
Votre fils *devait* lire beaucoup.	Your son *used to have to* (*probably used to*) read a great deal.

In the imperfect, **devoir** sometimes means *was to* (*were to*), sometimes *had to,* and sometimes *must have.* (Occasionally, the imperfect of **devoir** has other less common meanings.)

3. When does the imperfect of *devoir* mean *had to* and when *must have* ?

Claude *devait* finir son travail avant de s'occuper de nous.	Claude *had to* finish his work before turning his attention to us.
Cet homme *devait* savoir plusieurs langues.	That man *must have* known (*probably* knew) several languages.

When the imperfect of **devoir** represents the past of the English *must,* meaning *have to,* it is often translated by *had to.*

When the imperfect of **devoir** is the past of the English *must,* meaning *probably does,* it is usually translated by *must have,* meaning *probably did.*

When the imperfect of **devoir** is expressed by the English *must have,* it normally represents a habitual state or action. Even though *must have* looks like an English present perfect, it corresponds to the French imperfect of **devoir.** The best way to determine the proper translation is to rephrase the sentence, using the word *probably* + THE MAIN VERB.

B. *Traduisez en anglais les phrases suivantes. Attention au verbe* devoir.

1. Nous *devions* partir demain, mais c'est impossible.   **2.** Avant de sortir le soir, nous *devions* montrer à nos parents ce que nous avions fait. **3.** Votre neveu *devait* être bien embarrassé chaque fois que vous racontiez cette histoire.   **4.** Quand Florence habitait chez nous, elle *devait* passer l'après-midi à garder les enfants.   **5.** Les Lemaire *devaient* faire le tour du monde cet été, mais ils n'ont pas pu.

4. What two meanings may *devoir* have in the compound past ?

J'*ai dû* travailler toute la nuit pour faire mes devoirs.	I *had to* work the whole night to do my homework.
Guy *a dû* se faire mal en tombant.	Guy *must have* hurt himself (*probably* hurt himself) when he fell.
Leurs portes étaient fermées à clé; les voisins *ont dû* entrer par la fenêtre.	Their doors were locked; the neighbors *must have* (*probably*) entered through the window.

In the compound past, the verb ***devoir*** sometimes means *had to*, which is the past of *must* meaning *has to*. This is clearly the case in the first example. It sometimes means *must have* meaning *probably did*, which is the past of *must* meaning *probably does*. This is clearly the case in the second example. But in the third example, either possibility is present, and the context must decide.

When the imperfect of ***devoir*** means *must have*, it describes a customary state or action, whereas when the compound past of ***devoir*** means *must have*, it indicates a past action at one definite past time.

C. *Traduisez en anglais les phrases suivantes. Attention au verbe* devoir.

1. Si vous étiez chez les Lagarde, vous *avez dû* voir Pierre.   **2.** Personne ne parlait anglais ici; Agnès *a dû* aller en Angleterre pour l'apprendre. **3.** Comme il n'y avait pas assez de place dans la voiture, nous *avons dû* laisser les enfants à la maison.   **4.** Julien n'est pas encore là; il *a dû* se tromper de route.

5. What does *devoir* mean in the conditional ?

On annonce le froid; vous *devriez* mettre un manteau.	They say it will be cold; you *should* put on an overcoat.
Les Lepic *devraient* être plus patients avec leurs enfants.	The Lepics *ought to* be more patient with their children.

In the conditional, ***devoir*** means *should, ought to*.

6. What does *devoir* mean in the past conditional ?

Les Aubry n'*auraient* pas *dû* acheter cette voiture.	The Aubrys *should* not *have* bought that car.
Vous *auriez dû* nous dire que vos parents seraient là.	You *ought to have* told us that your parents would be there.

In the past conditional, **devoir** means *should have, ought to have.*

D. *Traduisez en anglais. Attention au verbe* devoir.

1. Les Bréger *auraient dû* prendre l'avion pour venir ici.   **2.** Nous *devrions* leur dire de quoi il s'agit.   **3.** Georges, tu *devrais* aider ton frère à finir sa leçon.   **4.** Robert *aurait dû* faire cela quand je le lui ai demandé.
5. Ce film est très drôle; vos amis *devraient* aller le voir.

7. In what other ways does French express the idea of *must* meaning
has to ?

Il faut que vous **vous couchiez plus tôt.**	You *must* go to bed earlier.
Nous étions obligés de **surveiller cet enfant tout le temps.**	We *used to have to* watch that child all the time.

Note the following equivalents :

Je dois + INFINITIVE	*Il faut que je* + SUBJUNCTIVE	*Je suis obligé de* + INFINITIVE
Je devais + INFINITIVE	*Il fallait que je* + SUBJUNCTIVE	*J'étais obligé de* + INFINITIVE
J'ai dû + INFINITIVE	*Il a fallu que je* + SUBJUNCTIVE	*J'ai été obligé de* + INFINITIVE
Je devrai + INFINITIVE	*Il faudra que je* + SUBJUNCTIVE	*Je serai obligé de* + INFINITIVE

In the present, imperfect, compound past, and future, the appropriate tenses of *must* meaning *have to* may also be expressed by forms of *il faut que* + SUBJUNCTIVE and by forms of *être obligé de* + INFINITIVE.

The *il faut que* construction is somewhat stronger than **devoir**. When *must* is expressed by forms of *être obligé de*, it is about the equivalent of *to be obliged to.* Sometimes, but not always, any of the three forms may be used to express the same idea.

> NOTE: In affirmative statements the verb *falloir* has two meanings : *must* and *be necessary.* For instance, **Il faut être là** and **Il faut que vous soyez là** means both You *must* be there and *It is necessary* for you to be there.

But in negative statements, *falloir* means only *must not*. For instance, *Il ne faut pas* *être là* and *Il ne faut pas* *que vous soyez là* mean only *You must not be there*. They do not mean *It is not necessary that you be there*.

E. *Traduisez en français chaque phrase de trois façons différentes.*

1. We used to have to work every day except Sunday.   **2.** Yesterday I had to leave at five o'clock.   **3.** Our friends have to stay in Bordeaux this evening.   **4.** The Leclercs[1] will have to move next week.

EXERCICE ORAL

Une mère de famille vient de rentrer chez elle pour être là quand les enfants sortiront du lycée. Elle pense à diverses choses à leur sujet.
Répétez chaque phrase en remplaçant l'idée du premier verbe de la phrase par la forme convenable du verbe devoir, *tout en gardant le sens de la phrase.*

EXEMPLE: Mon mari travaille probablement tard au bureau ce soir. **Mon mari doit travailler tard au bureau ce soir.**

1. Étant mère de famille, c'est mon devoir d'être chez moi tous les jours avant quatre heures.

2. J'ai été obligée de me dépêcher pour être ici avant les enfants.

3. Il aurait fallu que je fasse mes courses plus tôt.

4. Georgette n'est pas encore ici; elle est probablement chez son amie Cécile.

5. Il aurait fallu qu'elle rentre tout de suite après être sortie du lycée.

6. Mais je ne peux pas trop me plaindre; mes enfants savent ce qu'ils sont obligés de faire à la maison.

7. Ils savent qu'ils ont l'obligation de bien travailler.

8. Je dirai pourtant à Roland qu'il faut qu'il apprenne ses leçons avant d'aller chez son ami Jacques.

9. Mais ils pensent probablement que c'est plus intéressant de s'amuser avec leurs camarades.

10. Il faut peut-être que je sois plus stricte avec eux.

---

[1]In French, the plural form of proper names does not take an **-s**.

11. Il serait bon que je limite les heures où ils peuvent regarder la télévision.

12. Demain il faudra que j'aille au lycée parler à leurs professeurs.

13. Je suis quand même obligée de dire que ce sont de bons enfants.

14. Mais il faudrait que leur père soit plus souvent ici avec nous.

See pages 271–314 for the *Exercices d'ensemble*.

. . . . . .

PROBLEM WORDS

55. take

(a) When *take* is expressed by **prendre**

Qui *a pris* la voiture ?	Who *took* the car ?

The verb **prendre** is the most common way to express *take*. But it cannot be used indiscriminately to express *take*.

(b) When *take* is expressed by **porter** or **apporter**

Le chauffeur *a porté* nos valises au taxi.	The driver *took* our suitcases to the taxi.

When *take* is the equivalent of *carry to*, it is usually expressed by **porter** or **apporter**.

(c) When *take* is expressed by **emporter**

N'*emporte* pas <u>la télévision</u> dans ta chambre.	Don't *take* <u>the television</u> into your room.

When *take* means *to carry something away*, it may be expressed by **emporter**.

(d) When *take* is expressed by **mener**

Nous *avons mené* <u>nos invités</u> au restaurant.	We *took* our <u>guests</u> to the restaurant.

French has several ways of expressing *to take a person (somewhere)*. When the verb **mener** is used, the destination must be indicated.

(e) When *take* is expressed by **emmener**

J'emmène <u>Françoise</u> ce soir.	I *am taking* <u>Frances</u> (with me) this evening.
J'emmène <u>Françoise</u> *au cinéma* ce soir.	I *am taking* <u>Frances</u> *to the movies* this evening.

The verb **emmener** means *to take someone away*. It may be used either with or without the destination.

> NOTE: In certain cases, forms of the verb **amener** may also be used to express the idea of *taking a person or thing away*, but **amener** also has the meaning of *bringing a person or a thing*.

(f) How to say *to take time to...*

Le menuisier *a mis* cinq jours $\left.\begin{array}{l} \textbf{à} \\ \textbf{\textit{pour}} \end{array}\right\}$ *faire* ce travail.	The carpenter *took* five days *to do* that work.

The idiomatic **mettre** + period of time + *à* (or **pour**) + INFINITIVE expresses *to take (so much) time to do something.*

(g) How to say *to take an examination*

Nous *passons notre examen* à deux heures.	We *take our test* at two o'clock.

The expression **passer un examen** means *to take an examination.*

> NOTE: In present-day French, **passer un examen** is also often used to mean *to pass an examination.*

(h) How to say *to take a course*

Suivez-vous *des cours* intéressants ?	Are you *taking* interesting courses ?

The expression **suivre un cours** means *to take a course.* It is becoming more and more common to say **prendre un cours**, but it is best for the learner to avoid this expression.

(i) How to say *to take a magazine*

Je vais *m'abonner à* plusieurs revues.	I am going *to take* several magazines.
Je *suis abonné* au journal du matin.	I *take* the morning paper.

When *take = subscribe to*, French uses **s'abonner à** to indicate the action of subscribing or the state of being a subscriber, and **être abonné à** to indicate the state of being a subscriber.

(j) How to say *to take (away) from*

Ce jouet est dangereux. Enlevez-le à cet enfant.	That toy is dangerous. *Take* it *away from* that child.
A qui *as-tu *pris* cet argent ?	Who(m) *did* you *take* that money *from* ?

When *to take from* has the clear implication of *to take away from,* **enlever** is usually found <u>with an indirect object</u>. Otherwise, **prendre** may be often used <u>with an indirect object</u>.

(k) How *take* is expressed by **faire** in some expressions

There are many idiomatic expressions with **faire** which English expresses with *to take,* such as :

faire une promenade	take a walk
faire un tour	take a stroll
faire un voyage	take a trip

56. teach

(a) When *teach* is expressed by **enseigner**

Qui *a enseigné votre classe* pendant votre absence ?	Who *taught your class* during your absence ?
Mademoiselle Bouillet *enseigne les mathématiques* au lycée.	Miss Bouillet *teaches mathematics* in high school.

The verb **enseigner** is used with a direct object to mean *teach.* The direct object may be the subject taught, but not normally the person taught. For instance, to express in French : *Mr. Duparc teaches John,* one would have to say something like : **Monsieur Duparc est le professeur de Jean.**

Qui *enseignera* le latin *à Philippe* ?	Who *will teach* Latin *to Philip* ?

The verb **enseigner** may also be used with a direct object indicating <u>what</u> is taught and an indirect object indicating <u>who</u> is taught.

(b) When *teach* may be expressed by ***apprendre***

Ç'est un ami brésilien qui *nous* *a appris* le portugais.	It is a Brazilian friend who *taught us Portuguese.*
C'est un ami brésilien qui *a appris* le portugais à Brigitte.	It is a Brazilian friend who *taught Brigitte Portuguese.*

The basic meaning of ***apprendre*** is *learn*. But it means *teach* when it is followed by a direct object denoting the thing taught and an indirect object indicating the person taught.

Ma mère *a appris à ma sœur à jouer* du piano.	My mother *taught my sister to play* the piano.

The verb ***apprendre*** means *teach* when followed by a PERSONAL INDIRECT OBJECT + *à* + INFINITIVE.

57. time

(a) When *time* is expressed by ***le temps***

Je n'ai pas *le temps* de réparer la radio.	I don't have *the time* to repair the radio.
Combien de *temps* faut-il pour faire cela ?	How much *time* is needed to do that ?

The general word for *time* is ***le temps***.

The following expressions are used with ***temps***:

à temps	*in time (for)*
en même temps	*at the same time*
de temps en temps	*from time to time*

In certain contexts ***le temps*** means *weather*.

(b) When *time* is expressed by ***la fois***

Robert a dû répéter son explication trois *fois*.	Robert had to repeat his explanation three *times.*
Chaque *fois* que tu viens il pleut.	It rains each *time* you come.

The word ***fois*** is somewhat synonymous with *occasion*. It is used with numerals as well as with other words that indicate quantity.

(c) When *time* is expressed by **heure**

Quelle _heure_ est-il ?	What *time* is it ?
C'est _l'heure_ du thé.	It is tea *time*.

The word **heure** is used to ask *what time it is* and sometimes to indicate the *time* of a given function. When it tells time in sentences such as **Il est cinq heures**, it is expressed by *o'clock* in English.

(d) When *time* is expressed by **le moment**

En ce moment nous apprenons le latin.	At this time we are learning Latin.
A _ce moment-là_ j'étais en France.	At that time I was in France.

The word **moment** indicates *a point in time*; **en ce moment** means *now* or *at this time*; **à ce moment-là** means *then* or *at that time*.

(e) When *time* is expressed by **l'époque**

A _cette époque-là_ nous n'avions pas le téléphone.	At that time we didn't have a telephone.

The word **époque** indicates a longer period of time than does **moment** and usually refers to a time that is farther in the past.

(f) How to express *have a good time*

Passez une bonne soirée.	Have a good time this evening.
Nous _avons fait un excellent séjour_ en France cet été.	We *had a very good time* in France this summer.
Les enfants _se sont bien amusés_ au cirque.	The children *had a very good time* at the circus.

The French have no word-for-word translation of the English expression *to have a good time*. The verb **s'amuser** is often used to express this idea, especially when referring to younger people, but, depending on the occasion, other expressions such as those found in the preceding examples are also used.

Dans les exercices F et G remplacez les mots anglais par leur équivalent français.

F.

1. Il faut (*take*) Pierrot à sa leçon de danse tous les jeudis. **2.** Nous parlions justement de vous (*at the time*) où vous êtes entré. **3.** Lucienne voudrait (*take*) une revue de mode de Paris.   **4.** Il ne faut jamais regretter le (*time*) passé.   **5.** Cette lettre est importante; je la (*will take*) moi-même à la poste.   **6.** Il faut réussir à ce concours pour (*teach*) dans un lycée. **7.** Ce film est excellent; je l'ai vu trois (*times*).   **8.** En juin la plus grande partie des élèves (*take*) des examens.   **9.** Je crois que nous (*will have a good time*) chez les Barois.

G.

1. Si tu veux me faire plaisir, (*take*) les enfants au jardin zoologique. **2.** C'est Florence qui me (*taught*) à nager quand j'avais quatre ans. **3.** Nous n'avons plus besoin de ces affaires; vous pouvez les (*take*) chez vous.   **4.** (*At the time*) où j'habitais Londres, les choses n'étaient pas faciles.   **5.** Il faut (*take*) les choses un peu plus au sérieux, mon ami. **6.** C'est toi qui a permis à Pierre de (*take*) l'auto ?   **7.** A quelle (*time*) est le dernier métro ?   **8.** Jeannot (*takes*) un journal de sport.   **9.** Depuis son mariage, Lucie n'a plus le temps de (*take*) des cours.

Dans les exercices **H** *et* **I**, *traduisez en français. Attention aux mots en italique.*

H.

1. Someone *has taken* the silverware.   **2.** (*vous*) If you don't have *time* to write, telephone me Sunday.   **3.** (*vous*) Will you *take* Mr. Galant to the laboratory ?   **4.** (*vous*) At what *time* do you want to see me ?   **5.** I wonder who *taught* Rose to cook.   **6.** I think I am going to *take* another magazine.   **7.** (*tu*) Did you have a good *time* last night ?   **8.** (*tu*) Don't forget to *take* your suit to the cleaner's.   **9.** Louise *teaches* art, and her sister *teaches* history.

I.

1. Susan *is taking* some Spanish courses[1].   **2.** Claude can't *take* us; his car broke down.   **3.** Felix arrived just at the *time* when I was leaving. **4.** Did Peter pass the examination he *took* last week ?   **5.** Every *time* he comes, Paul brings us something.   **6.** (*tu*) When are you going to *take* your vacation ?   **7.** At the *time* of my grandparents there wasn't any television[2]. **8.** I *took* an hour to read that book.

Verb Review

Review the verbs **tenir** and **valoir** according to the outline on pages 332–335.

---

[1] **cours d'espagnol**   [2] Use the definite article.

Constructions With Prepositions

Simone de Beauvoir parle de la force de sa vocation d'écrivain. Déjà adolescente elle savait qu'elle serait un jour un auteur célèbre.

Pourquoi j'ai choisi d'écrire

Pourquoi ai-je choisi *d'*écrire ? Lorsque j'étais enfant, je n'avais pas attaché beaucoup d'importance à mes gribouillages[1]; mon véritable souci avait été *de* m'instruire; j'aimais écrire mes compositions françaises, mais « ces demoiselles », mes professeurs, me reprochaient *d'*avoir un style guindé[2]; je ne me
5 sentais pas « douée[3] ». Cependant, quand à quinze ans, une amie me demanda d'écrire sur son album les prédilections, les projets qui devaient définir ma personnalité, je n'hésitai pas. À la question : « Que voulez-vous faire plus tard ? » je répondis : « Être un auteur célèbre ». Pour mon musicien favori, ma fleur préférée, je m'étais inventé des goûts plus ou moins artificiels. Mais sur
10 ce point je n'hésitai pas : je convoitais[4] cet avenir à l'exclusion de tout autre. Il m'est facile *de* l'expliquer.
    La première raison, c'est l'admiration que m'inspiraient les écrivains; mon père les mettait bien au-dessus des savants, des érudits[5], des professeurs. J'étais convaincue moi aussi de leur suprématie; l'œuvre d'un spécialiste,
15 même si son nom était largement connu, ne s'ouvrait qu'*à* un petit nombre; mais tout le monde lisait les livres : ils touchaient l'imagination, le cœur; ils valaient à leur auteur la gloire la plus universelle. En tant que[6] femme, ces sommets me semblaient en outre plus faciles *à* atteindre que les pénéplaines[7]; les plus célèbres de mes sœurs s'étaient illustrées dans la littérature.
20   Et puis j'avais toujours eu le goût de[8] la communication. Sur l'album de mon amie, je citai comme divertissements favoris : la lecture et la conversation. J'aimais beaucoup parler. Tout ce qui me frappait au cours d'une journée, j'essayais *de* le raconter. Je craignais la nuit, l'oubli; c'était une agonie *d'*abandonner au silence ce que j'avais vu, senti, aimé. Émue par un clair de

---

[1]*scribblings* [2]*stilted* [3]*gifted* [4]*set my heart on* [5]*scholars* [6]**en tant que** *as a*
[7]*slopes* [8]**le goût de** *a propensity, an inclination for*

25 lune, je souhaitais avoir une plume, du papier et savoir m'en servir. J'aimais, à quinze ans, les correspondances, les journaux intimes[9] qui s'efforcent *de* retenir le temps[10]. J'avais compris aussi que les romans, les nouvelles, les contes ne sont pas des objets étrangers à la vie mais qu'ils l'expriment à leur manière.

30 Si j'avais souhaité autrefois me faire institutrice, c'est que je rêvais *d'*être ma propre cause et ma propre fin[11]; je pensais à présent que la littérature me permettrait *de* réaliser ce désir. Elle m'assurerait une immortalité qui compenserait l'éternité perdue; il n'y avait plus de Dieu *pour* m'aimer, mais je brûlerais dans des million de cœurs[12]. En écrivant une œuvre nourrie de mon 35 histoire, je me créerais moi-même à neuf[13] et je justifierais mon existence. En même temps, je servirais l'humanité : quel plus beau cadeau lui faire que des livres ? Je m'intéressais à la fois *à* moi et *aux* autres; ce projet conciliait tout; il flattait toutes les aspirations qui s'étaient développées en moi au cours de ces quinze années.

> D'après Simone de Beauvoir. Professeur comme Sartre et comme lui philosophe existentialiste, elle est dramaturge, essayiste, romancière et elle a écrit une importante autobiographie. (*Mémoires d'une jeune fille rangée*, Gallimard, 1958)

Questions

1. Quelle influence a pu avoir sur Simone de Beauvoir enfant l'attitude de ses maîtresses ? **2.** Pourquoi Simone de Beauvoir avait-elle cette admiration sans bornes pour les écrivains ? **3.** Mentionnez des savants dont la gloire a aussi été universelle. **4.** De quelles façons se manifestaient dès son adolescence les signes de la vocation de Simone de Beauvoir ? **5.** Parlez d'une grande figure que vous connaissez de la littérature féminine. **6.** Comment ce projet de devenir écrivain conciliait-il chez l'auteur son intérêt pour elle-même et son intérêt pour les autres ?

NOTE: Voir aussi les deux sujets de composition dans le *Manuel d'exercices*.

I. PREPOSITIONS OF PLACE

To, In, At

In French, *in*, *at*, and *to* are all expressed by the same preposition before proper nouns used as place names. The preposition used depends on whether the place name is a city, a masculine country, or a feminine country or continent.

---

[9]**journaux intimes** *diaries* [10]**s'efforcent... temps** *try to make time stand still* [11]**d'être... fin** *that I was a law unto myself* [12]**je... cœurs** *I would shine like a beacon* [13] *anew*

1. What preposition of place is used to express *in*, *at*, and *to* with cities ?

Nous sommes *à* Paris.	We are *in* (*at*) Paris.
Gérard va *à* Tours.	Gerard is going *to* Tours.

The preposition *à* is used before cities to express the English prepositions *in*, *at*, or *to*.

2. How can one determine the gender of countries in French ?

la France	*la* Grèce	*la* Belgique
la Chine	*la* Suisse	*la* Bolivie

All countries ending in *-e* are feminine except **le Mexique**, **le Cambodge**, and **le Zaïre**.

le Canada	*le* Japon	*le* Portugal	*le* Danemark	*le* Pérou

All countries not ending in *-e* are masculine.

> NOTE: These rules hold usually with the well-known and well-established countries, but they do not always seem to apply to the so-called "emerging countries," where uniform usage has not yet been well determined. Likewise, *en* is used to express *in* or *to* with certain masculine countries beginning with a vowel, as, for instance *en* Israël.

3. What preposition of place is used to express *in* or *to* before feminine countries and continents ?

Michel est *en* France.	Michael is *in* France.
Louise va *en* France.	Louise is going *to* France.
Maurice a passé deux ans *en* Afrique.	Maurice spent two years *in* Africa.

French uses *en* to express both *in* and *to* before feminine countries and continents.

4. What preposition of place is used to express *in* or *to* before masculine countries ?

Monique est *au* Danemark.	Monica is *in* Denmark.
Gilbert va *au* Danemark.	Gilbert is going *to* Denmark.
Restez-vous longtemps *aux* États-Unis ?	Are you staying *in* the United States for a long time ?
Nous allons *aux* États-Unis l'année prochaine.	We are going *to* the United States next year.

French uses *à* + DEFINITE ARTICLE to express *in* or *to* before masculine countries.

NOTE 1: Although the same prepositions *à* and *en* are used to express both *in* and *to* with French place names, this does not ordinarily lead to ambiguity. *Je suis allé en France* clearly means *I went to France*; *Je suis allé au Canada* clearly means *I went to Canada*. *J'ai passé un an en France* clearly means *I spent a year in France*; *J'ai passé un an au Canada* clearly means *I spent a year in Canada*.

NOTE 2: In sentences with the verb *voyager*, however, a problem does exist. *J'ai voyagé en France cet été* means *I traveled in France this summer*, and not *I traveled to France this summer*. To avoid ambiguity in expressing the idea of traveling *to a place*, it is best to use the verb *aller*. Ex. : *Je suis allé en France cet été*.

NOTE 3: However, *in*, or *to Cuba* is expressed by *à* alone. Ex. : **Nous sommes allés *à* Cuba avant la révolution. Le sucre est une industrie très importante *à* Cuba.**

Note 4: French makes certain states of the United States feminine by ending them in *-e*. Ex. : *la Californie*, *la Géorgie*, *la Floride*. With such states, *in* and *to* are therefore expressed by *en*. With other states, which are considered masculine, *dans le* is most often used, although one sometimes finds *au*. Ex. : <u>*dans l'Ohio*</u>, <u>*dans le* Texas</u>, <u>*dans le* Michigan</u>.

5. **What preposition of place is used before modified countries, cities, and continents ?**

(a) if the modifying phrase or adjective is an integral part of the place name

Il habite *à* la Nouvelle-Orléans.	He lives *in* New Orleans.
Nous allons *en* Amérique du Sud.	We are going *to* South America.
Le Maroc, l'Algérie et la Tunisie sont *en* Afrique du Nord.	Morocco, Algeria, and Tunisia are *in* North Africa.

If the modifying phrase or adjective is an integral part of the place name, the same preposition would be used as if the place were not modified.

(b) if the modifying phrase or adjective is not an integral part of the place name

Quelle université est située *dans* la Belgique flamande ?	What university is located *in the* Flemish part of Belgium ?
Nous avons passé des journées *dans le* vieux Paris.	We spent days *in* old Paris.

When a place name is modified by an adjective or phrase that is not an integral part of the name, **dans** + DEFINITE ARTICLE is used to express *in* or *to*. But this construction is rather rare.

A. *Remplacez les tirets par la préposition convenable.*

1. Beaucoup de catholiques vont _____ Rome pour voir le Vatican.
2. Quand vous serez _____ Naples, allez donc voir les ruines de Pompéi.
3. Quand j'étais _____ Angleterre, j'aimais prendre le thé à quatre heures.
4. Puisque vous aimez les sports d'hiver, allez passer l'hiver _____ Colorado.   **5.** Nous avons renoncé à aller _____ Chine, c'est un trop long voyage.   **6.** Ces jeunes Français passeront un mois _____ États-Unis pour étudier la chimie.   **7.** Quand vous serez _____ Danemark, vous verrez que presque tout le monde parle anglais.

B. *Traduisez en français.*

1. They want to spend their vacation in Madrid, but they do not know Spanish.   **2.** (*vous*) If you want to go to Canada, I advise you to take the train at eight in[1] the evening.   **3.** Many Americans go to Florida to spend the winter.   **4.** Our friends were[2] to come back, but they want to stay in Portugal in April.   **5.** A large number of American engineers work[3] in Mexico.   **6.** I took some very beautiful photographs on arriving in Japan and some others[4] while I was in China.   **7.** We did not stay in Russia long enough to[5] learn Russian.   **8.** This old man would now like to go back to Italy to see his relatives.

From

6. How is *from* expressed with cities ?

Je suis parti *de* Paris hier pour voir les environs.

I left Paris yesterday to see the surrounding country.

With cities, *from* is expressed by **de.**

7. How is *from* expressed with feminine countries and continents ?

**Nous sommes revenus *de* France la semaine dernière.
Philippe partira-t-il *d'*Angleterre la semaine prochaine ?**

We returned *from* France last week.
Will Philip leave England next week ?

Before feminine countries and continents, *from* is expressed by **de.**

---

[1]**du** [2]Use a form of **devoir.** [3]This verb is in the plural. [4]**d'autres** [5]**assez longtemps pour**

8. How is *from* expressed with masculine countries ?

Nos cousins sont partis *du* Canada hier.	Our cousins left Canada yesterday.
Quand reviendrez-vous *du* Portugal ?	When will you come back *from* Portugal ?

Before masculine countries, *from* is expressed by *de* + DEFINITE ARTICLE (*du, de l', des*).

C. Remplacez les tirets par l'équivalent français de **from**.

1. Il part _____ Japon la semaine prochaine à cause de la situation politique.   **2.** A leur accent, je devine qu'ils viennent _____ Belgique. **3.** Des avions partent tous les jours _____ Canada pour l'Europe. **4.** Ces messieurs viennent _____ Lyon pour montrer leurs étoffes de soie. **5.** Beaucoup de gens qui reviennent _____ Mexique sont contents de retrouver la cuisine américaine.   **6.** Les Russes peuvent aujourd'hui sortir librement _____ Russie.   **7.** Si vous allez _____ France en Angleterre, prenez donc l'avion.

D. Traduisez en français.

1. How much time does it take[1] to go from Japan to the United States ? **2.** It is sometimes difficult to say whether someone comes from the United States or from England.   **3.** We are coming back from Greece delighted by[2] the beauty of that country.   **4.** He is coming back from Spain, where he spent the whole month of July.   **5.** (*tu*) When you come[3] back from Portugal, we'll go to Wisconsin to spend the summer.

II. VERB + PREPOSITION + INFINITIVE

9. What words does French use to join a verb to a following infinitive ?

Je *voudrais aller* en France.	I *should like to go* to France.
Nous *avons commencé à lire*.	We *began to read*.
Les ouvriers *ont refusé de travailler*.	The workmen *refused to work*.

Some verbs are followed directly by an infinitive, some verbs require *à* before an infinitive, some require *de* before an infinitive, a few require still other prepositions.

---

[1]Use a form of **falloir**.   [2]**enchantés par**   [3]Not the present tense.

10. How can one determine which construction to use before an infinitive ?

Ils *viendront voir* leur nouveau petit-fils la semaine prochaine.	They *will come to see* their new grandson next week.
Nous *voulons régler* cette affaire le plus tôt possible.	We *want to take care of* this matter as soon as possible.

Verbs of motion (*aller*, *venir*) and the common verbs of wishing (*vouloir*, *désirer*) are followed directly by the infinitive.

Le mari de Janine lui *a demandé de faire des économies.*	Janine's husband *asked* her *to be saving.*
Nous *avons regretté d'apprendre* son départ si précipité.	We *were sorry to learn* of his very hasty departure.

Verbs of telling, asking, ordering, advising, etc. (someone to do something) and most verbs of emotion (*craindre, avoir peur, regretter, s'étonner*, etc.) are followed by *de* before an infinitive.

But except for these, the preposition to be used after each verb before an infinitive must be learned.

11. Which verbs require no preposition before an infinitive ?

The following are the most common verbs that are followed directly by the infinitive

aimer	like	*falloir*	be necessary
aimer mieux	prefer	*laisser*	leave, allow, let
aller	go, be going	*oser*	dare
compter	intend	*pouvoir*	can, be able
croire	believe	*préférer*	prefer
désirer	desire, wish	*savoir*	know, know how
devoir	am to, must, should	*sembler*	seem
entendre	hear	*venir*	come
espérer	hope	*voir*	see
faire	do, make, have	*vouloir*	want, wish

12. Which verbs require *de* before an infinitive ?

The following are the most common verbs that require *de* before an infinitive :

avoir peur de	be afraid	*craindre de*	fear
cesser de	cease	*décider de*	decide

défendre de	*forbid*	*oublier de*	*forget*
*demander de**	*ask*	*permettre de*	*permit*
se dépêcher de	*hurry*	*prier de*	*beg, ask, pray*
dire de	*tell*	*promettre de*	*promise*
écrire de	*write*	*refuser de*	*refuse*
empêcher de	*prevent*	*regretter de*	*regret*
essayer de	*try*	*remercier de*	*thank*
finir de	*finish*	*tâcher de*	*try*
ordonner de	*order*		

13. Which verbs require *à* before an infinitive ?

The following are the most common verbs that require *à* before an infinitive :

aider à	*help*	*enseigner à*	*teach*
s'amuser à	*amuse oneself*	*s'habituer à*	*accustom oneself*
apprendre à	*learn, teach*	*hésiter à*	*hesitate*
arriver à	*succeed*	*inciter à*	*encourage someone,*
s'attendre à	*expect*		*prompt, incite*
avoir à	*have*	*inviter à*	*invite*
commencer à	*begin*	*recommencer à*	*begin again*
consentir à	*consent*	*renoncer à*	*give up, renounce*
continuer à	*continue*	*réussir à*	*succeed*
se décider à	*decide*	*songer à*	*think, dream*
*demander à**	*ask*	*tarder à*	*delay in*
échouer à	*fail, flunk*		

E. Remplacez les tirets par une préposition s'il y a lieu**.

1. —Allô chérie, j'ai invité le patron _____ dîner chez nous ce soir.
2. J'avais un oiseau en cage, mais je l'ai laissé _____ s'envoler.
3. Essaie _____ finir ton travail pour qu'on puisse sortir.   **4.** Je n'aime pas qu'il s'amuse _____ faire des expériences de chimie dans la maison.
5. Dépêche-toi, ils peuvent _____ arriver d'un moment à l'autre.
6. Cessez_____bavarder avec votre voisin ou prenez la porte.   **7.** Il faut _____ vivre mieux que ça; je vais _____ essayer _____ gagner un peu plus d'argent.   **8.** Il vient d'avoir cinquante ans et il a décidé _____ se remarier.   **9.** Commencez _____ économiser de l'argent dès que possible.   **10.** J'aime mieux _____ sortir quand il pleut, l'air est plus pur.   **11.** Oseriez-vous _____ répéter ce que vous venez de dire ?
12. Beaucoup de réfugiés refusent absolument _____ retourner dans leurs pays.

---

*The verb **demander** + AN INDIRECT OBJECT meaning *to ask* to requires **de** before an infinitive. Compare: **Il demande à venir. Il demande à son ami de venir.**   **If one is necessary.*

F. Remplacez les tirets par une préposition s'il y a lieu.

1. Le professeur est malade, mais il continue _____ faire ses cours.
2. J'ai été un peu brusque, je crains _____ l'avoir vexé.   **3.** Faites un
petit effort pour apprendre _____ parler correctement.   **4.** A partir de
demain, je veux _____ travailler dix heures tous les jours.   **5.** Je regrette
_____ ne pas être plus riche.   **6.** Il est bon de savoir _____ faire
plusieurs métiers.   **7.** Bien des Américains espèrent _____ aller un jour
en Europe.   **8.** J'ai cru qu'ils ne se décideraient jamais _____ partir.
9. Il faut s'habituer _____ vivre dans l'incertitude.   **10.** Si vous voulez
un chat, nous cherchons _____ placer les nôtres.   **11.** S'il tarde _____
rentrer, sa femme imagine qu'il a eu un accident.   **12.** On doit _____
réfléchir avant de parler.

G. Traduisez en français. Attention aux prépositions.

1. His work prevents him from playing poker with his friends this
evening.   **2.** I completely forgot to telephone him[1] today, and it's[2] too late
now.   **3.** Several friends will help me paint my house.   **4.** (vous) Don't
hesitate to interrupt me if you have a question.   **5.** As soon as one speaks
of France, Anne begins[3] to dream.   **6.** He is stubborn; I didn't succeed in
convincing him.   **7.** Few people like to write long letters.   **8.** (tu) If you
want to see him, come quickly, because he is going to leave.   **9.** (vous)
Look at that man; he seems to want to speak to us.

III. THE *À* + *DE* VERBS

14. **How does French express the idea *to tell someone to do something* ?**

*J'ai dit **à** mon frère **de** partir tout de suite.*	I *told my brother to* leave immediately.
Michel *a promis **à** ses enfants **de** leur apporter des jouets.*	Michael *promised his children to* bring them some toys.

Certain verbs require *à* before a noun object and *de* before a following
infinitive in French but not necessarily in English. These may be called the
à + *de* verbs. Among these are :

conseiller à quelqu'un **de**	*advise someone to*	Je **conseille à Paul de** partir.
défendre à quelqu'un **de**	*forbid someone to*	Il **défend à Marie de** sortir.

---

[1]Which type of object is this?   [2]Either *il est* or *c'est*.   [3]Use a form of *se mettre*.

demander *à* quelqu'un *de*	*ask someone to*	Elle **demande** *à* **sa mère** *de* venir.
dire *à* quelqu'un *de*	*tell someone to*	Je **dis** *à* **mon frère** *de* se taire.
écrire *à* quelqu'un *de*	*write someone to*	Nous **écrivons** *à* **Guy** *de* rester.
ordonner *à* quelqu'un *de*	*order someone to*	Il **ordonne** *au* **soldat** *de* se lever.
permettre *à* quelqu'un *de*	*permit someone to*	Je **permets** *à* **Jean** *d'*entrer.
promettre *à* quelqu'un *de*	*promise someone to*	Elle **promet** *à* **Henri** *de* lui écrire.
téléphoner *à* quelqu'un *de*	*telephone someone to*	Il **téléphone** *à* **Claude** *de* revenir.

H. *Traduisez en français.*

1. (*vous*) Telephone your father to send you some money. **2.** After that trouble[1], I advised Gerard to leave town[2]. **3.** (*vous*) If you want to marry my daughter, promise me to come to work here every day. **4.** There are always people who want to forbid others[2] to do what they wish. **5.** (*tu*) Ask your uncle to buy you a car, since he is rich. **6.** (*vous*) If he comes, tell Mr. Fondeville to leave his address and I'll write him. **7.** (*vous*) You are wrong to[3] permit your children to do everything[4] they wish. **8.** (*vous*) I'll write my friends to come to get[5] you at the airport.

IV. VERB + PREPOSITION + NOUN

15. How do the VERB + NOUN constructions in French compare with those in English ?

Nous *attendons* le train.	We *are waiting for* the train.
Je *suis entré dans* la maison.	I *entered* the house.
Il *pense à* ses examens.	He *is thinking of* his examinations.

While many VERB + NOUN constructions are the same in French and English, some verbs require a preposition before a noun in French but not in English, and others require a preposition before a noun in English but not in French. Still other verbs require one preposition in English, another in French.

---

[1]**histoire** [2]Use the definite article. [3]*de* [4]**tout ce que** [5]**chercher**

16. What are some common verbs that require a direct object in French but a preposition before the object in English?

attendre	*wait for*	Paul **attend** son ami.
chercher	*look for*	Marie **cherche** son livre.
demander	*ask for*	Pierre **demande** cinq cents francs.
écouter	*listen to*	Nous **écoutons** la musique.
payer	*pay for*	Il **a payé** cet objet mille francs.
regarder	*look at*	Je **regarde** le plan de Paris.

The verbs listed above require a direct object in French.

17. What are some common verbs that require a preposition before the object in French, but a direct object in English?

approcher *de*	*approach*	Nous **approchons** *de* la rivière.
assister *à*	*attend*	Il **assiste** *à* la réunion.
changer *de*	*change*	Elle a **changé** *de* robe.
entrer *dans*	*enter*	Qui **entre** *dans* la salle?
échapper *à*	*escape*	Le soldat a **échappé** *à* la mort.
s'échapper *de*	*escape*	Le voleur **s'est échappé** *de* prison.
jouer *à*	*play*	Je **joue** *au* football, lui *aux* échecs.
jouer *de*	*play*	Elle **joue** *du* piano et *du* violon.
manquer *de*	*lack*	Je **manque** *de* renseignements.
se marier *avec*	*marry*	Denise **se marie** *avec* Jean-Pierre.
obéir *à*	*obey*	Paul **obéit** toujours *à* son père.
plaire *à*	*please*	Yvonne **plaît** *à* tout le monde.
répondre *à*	*answer*	Je **réponds** *à* la lettre.
résister *à*	*resist*	Il **résiste** *à* la tentation.
ressembler *à*	*resemble*	Maurice **ressemble** *à* son frère.
se servir *de*	*use*	Ils **se servent** *de* la machine à écrire.
se souvenir *de*	*remember*	Je **me souviens** *de* cette affaire.

The verbs listed require a preposition before the object in French.

NOTE: The verb *échapper à* means *to escape getting into something*; *s'échapper de* means *to escape from something one has gotten into*. The construction *jouer à* means *to play a game*; the construction *jouer de* means *to play a musical instrument*.

18. What are some common verbs that require one preposition in French and another in English?

s'intéresser *à*	be interested *in*	Il **s'intéresse** *à* la musique.
s'occuper *de*	busy oneself *with*	Je **m'occupe** *de* la maison.
penser *à*	think *of*	Il **pense** *à* son travail.

penser *de*	think *of*	Que **pensez-vous** *de* cet homme ?
remercier *de*	thank *for*	Il a **remercié** sa mère *de* son cadeau.
rire *de*	laugh *at*	Nous **rions** *de* sa réponse.
songer *à*	think *of*	Il **songe** *à* son voyage en France.

The verbs listed above require one preposition in French and another in English.

> NOTE: The construction **penser** *à* means *to think of someone or something*; the construction **penser** *de* is most often used in questions *to ask one's opinion of someone or something.*

The verb **remercier** may also be followed by **pour** before a noun. Ex. : **Il a remercié sa mère pour son cadeau.**

I. Remplacez les expressions anglaises entre parenthèses par les équivalents français.

(Each sentence has a verb that entails the use or omission of a preposition. In certain sentences, it may be necessary to combine a preposition with the definite article.)

1. Je (*am looking for*) une bonne réponse à sa lettre, mais c'est difficile. **2.** Certains élèves peuvent travailler en (*listening to*) la radio. **3.** (*Look at*) bien le ciel et vous verrez peut-être des satellites. **4.** Avec cette foule il sera impossible de (*approach*) la scène. **5.** Victor (*escaped from*) la maison qui brûlait juste à temps. **6.** Il faut de longues années d'étude pour (*play*) le violon en virtuose. **7.** Trop de familles (*lack*) argent. **8.** Chacun rêve de (*marry*[1]) la personne idéale. **6.** Il y a des gens qui croient pouvoir (*escape*) la maladie. **10.** Tout évolue et il est impossible de (*resist*) longtemps les changements. **11.** (*Concern yourself with*[2]) vos affaires. **12.** Il faut le (*thank for*) les fleurs qu'il m'a envoyées. **13.** Ce n'est pas gentil de (*laugh at*) une personne qui tombe. **14.** Il (*is waiting for*) son amie, mais je sais qu'elle ne viendra pas.

J. Traduisez en français. Attention aux prépositions.

1. (*vous*) Live in the present; do not think too much of the past. **2.** I attended a fine concert last evening. **3.** They change cars every other year. **4.** I have lost my key, and I can't get into the house. **5.** It is amusing to[3] play chess. **6.** Teenagers often refuse to obey their parents. **7.** He is spending a fortune to please that woman. **8.** (*vous*) Do not wait to[4] answer those letters. **9.** He does not resemble his father at all[5]. **10.** Today one uses[6] knives and forks[7] to[4] eat. **11.** She doesn't like poetry;

---

[1]Use a form of **se marier**. [2]Use a form of **s'occuper**. [3]de [4]pour [5]Place directly after **pas**. [6]Use a form of **se servir**. [7]Repeat the preposition before the second noun.

she is interested in sports.   **12.** (*tu*) What do you think of the work of that painter ?

V. THE *IT IS* + ADJECTIVE + INFINITIVE CONSTRUCTIONS

19. What construction follows the impersonal *Il est* + ADJECTIVE ?

Il est impossible *de* partir aujourd'hui.	*It is* impossible *to* leave today.
Il serait difficile *de* lui donner cet argent.	*It would be* hard *to* give him that money.

The construction used with the impersonal *il est* + ADJECTIVE is :

> (impersonal) *il est* + ADJECTIVE + *de* + INFINITIVE (+ idea)

NOTE: In conversational French, this impersonal *il* may always be replaced by *ce*, and the following construction is exactly the same as though the impersonal *il* were used.

20. What construction follows IDEA + *c'est* + ADJECTIVE ?

Est-ce que cet écrivain écrit vraiment bien ? *C'est* **difficile** *à* **dire.**	Does that author really write well ? *It's* hard *to* say.
Votre frère est-il bon élève ? Non, et *c'est* **impossible** *à* **comprendre.**	Is your brother a good student ? No, and *that's* impossible *to* understand.

When *c'est* + ADJECTIVE refers to a preceding idea without gender or number, the following construction is used :

> IDEA in preceding sentence + *c'est* + ADJECTIVE + *à* + INFINITIVE

K. *Remplacez les tirets par à ou de, selon le cas.*

1. —Les planètes sont-elles habitées ?—Peut-être, mais c'est impossible _____ prouver.   **2.** Il est maintenant possible _____ aller dans la lune.   **3.** Il est agréable _____ prendre un petit cognac après un bon repas.   **4.** —Comment avez-vous fait pour apprendre à jouer si bien ? —C'est difficile _____ expliquer.   **5.** Les candidats ont discuté pendant une heure. C'était intéressant _____ écouter.   **6.** Il n'est pas toujours facile _____ dire ce qui est bien et ce qui est mal.   **7.** Vous l'avez vraiment vu voler cette montre ? C'est difficile _____ croire.

L. Traduisez en français.

1. It is interesting to see a football game[1] between two good teams. **2.** Man is master of his destiny. It's easy to say.   **3.** It is necessary to write a great many letters, even if it is sometimes boring to do.   **4.** It is difficult to understand certain scientific theories.   **5.** It is amusing to observe people in the street.   **6.** Maurice wants to buy an airplane. That's impossible to believe.   **7.** I'm going to paint my house. It's easy to do.   **8.** It is restful to interrupt one's[2] work from time to time.   **9.** Mark is so stubborn that it is useless to try to convince him.   **10.** Jack says that he is capable of writing a novel. It is hard to imagine.   **11.** Mr. Laroque does not believe that his son was at my house last night, but it's easy to prove.   **12.** It is impossible to get[3] to the top of that mountain.

VI. VERBAL CONSTRUCTIONS AFTER PREPOSITIONS; CONSTRUCTIONS WITH *POUR*

Most English prepositions are followed by the present participle. One says *on arriving, in coming, by working, without leaving,* etc., but this is not usually the case in French.

21. What verbal construction usually follows a French preposition ?

Ne partez pas *sans laisser* votre adresse.	Don't go away *without leaving* your address.

All French prepositions except *en* are followed by the infinitive.

When we use the term infinitive, we mean SIMPLE INFINITIVE, for it is by far the most common infinitive to be used. But there is also a COMPOUND INFINITIVE, which is made up of the infinitive of *avoir* or *être* and the past participle of the main verb. The compound infinitive is also known as the PAST INFINITIVE.

---

[1]*football game* **match de football**   [2]Use a form of **son**.   [3]Use a form of ***arriver à***.

SIMPLE INFINITIVE	COMPOUND INFINITIVE
parler	*avoir parlé*
finir	*avoir fini*
venir	*être venu(e)(s)*
se laver	*s'être lavé(e)(s)*

22. By what verbal construction is the preposition *en* followed ?

En entrant dans le café, nous avons vu Robert et Marie.	*On entering* the café, we saw Robert and Marie.

The preposition *en* is followed by the present participle. (For a complete treatment of *en* + PRESENT PARTICIPLE, see pages 111–112.)

23. When is a French preposition followed by the compound infinitive ?

Les voisins ont puni leur fils *pour avoir cassé* nos vitres.	The neighbors punished their son *for having broken* our windowpanes.

When the verbal action after a preposition clearly takes place before the action of the main verb of the sentence, the compound infinitive is used in order to preserve the time distinction.

24. What French construction is used to express the English *before* + VERB + *-ing* ?

Regardez à droite et à gauche *avant de traverser* la rue.	Look left and right *before crossing* the street.

French uses *avant de* + INFINITIVE for the English *before* + VERB + *-ing*.

25. What French construction is used to express the English *after* + VERB + *-ing* ?

Après avoir lu le journal, je me suis mis au travail.	*After reading* the newspaper, I got down to work.

French uses *après* + COMPOUND INFINITIVE to express the English *after* + VERB + *-ing*.

26. How does French express purpose ?

Mon voisin a acheté ce terrain *pour planter* des arbres fruitiers.	My neighbor bought this land *to plant* some fruit trees.

To express purpose, English uses $\begin{cases} to \\ in\ order\ to \end{cases}$ + VERB.

French uses the preposition *pour* + THE INFINITIVE to indicate purpose.

27. When may the preposition *pour* be omitted before the infinitive in purpose phrases ?

Jean *est venu* **(*pour*)** *travailler* **avec Daniel aujourd'hui.**	John *came* (*in order*) *to work* with Daniel today.
Nous *sommes allés* **à la ferme (*pour*)** *chercher* **du lait.**	We *went* to the farm (*in order*) *to get* some milk.

In purpose phrases, the preposition *pour* is usually omitted after forms of *aller* and *venir* and sometimes after other verbs of motion. When *pour* is used after forms of *aller* and *venir*, it emphasizes the idea of purpose much as *in order to* does in English. The preposition *pour* is also often used when several words separate the main verb and the infinitive.

28. How does French express the idea of *enough... to* and *too much... to* or *too... to* ?

Louise chante *assez* **bien** *pour* **faire partie du chœur.**	Louise sings well *enough to* be in the choir.
Nous avons *trop* **à faire** *pour* **partir maintenant.**	We have *too much to* do to leave now.
Jacques est *trop* **jeune** *pour* **rester dehors après neuf heures du soir.**	Jack is *too* young *to* stay out after nine o'clock at night.

French expresses the idea of *enough... to* by *assez... pour* and of *too much... to* and *too... to* by *trop... pour*.

M. *Remplacez l'infinitif entre parenthèses par la forme convenable du verbe, s'il y a lieu.*

1. Pourquoi êtes-vous venu ici sans (téléphoner) d'avance ? **2.** Il faut aller au Maroc pour (acheter) un beau tapis. **3.** Après (monter) dans ma chambre, j'ai réfléchi à ce qui venait de se passer. **4.** En (parler) à l'agent, j'ai appris ce qui s'était passé. **5.** Faites peser mes lettres avant de les (mettre) à la poste. **6.** Nous avons commencé par (ouvrir) toutes les fenêtres. **7.** Michel a répondu après (réfléchir) un moment. **8.** Au lieu de (se[1] plaindre), vendez donc votre voiture. **9.** Je me suis intéressé à la science en (lire) la biographie des Curie. **10.** Jean est encore parti sans (fermer) la porte. **11.** On apprend mieux quelque chose en l'(expliquer) à d'autres.

[1] Even in the infinitive form, the reflexive object must agree in person with the subject of the sentence. In what person is the subject of an imperative sentence?

N. *Traduisez en français.*

1. Paul is too proud to admit his error. **2.** Someone came to ask for some information[1] concerning[2] Jack. **3.** We left after hearing the results of the election. **4.** Robert is old[3] enough to have a motorcycle. **5.** (*vous*) Did you come to our house only to talk business ? **6.** The children went to play at the neighbor's. **7.** (*vous*) Before leaving for Paris, reserve a room in a good hotel. **8.** (*tu*) You are intelligent enough to understand those things. **9.** Paul went to get[4] some books at the library. **10.** I am too tired to go out this evening. **11.** (*vous*) Correct your mistakes before erasing the sentences. **12.** (*tu*) At what time will you come to get[4] me ?

EXERCICE ORAL

Pierre Leroux envisage d'acheter une voiture. Il pense à divers aspects de l'affaire.

Remplacez le premier verbe de la phrase par la forme convenable de l'infinitif donné entre parenthèses, en mettant la préposition qui suit cet infinitif s'il en faut une.

EXEMPLE: Je consentirais à prendre une auto japonaise. (accepter) **J'accepterais de prendre une auto japonaise.**

1. J'ai décidé d'acheter une nouvelle voiture. (se décider)

2. Je crains de demander toujours à mon père de me prêter la sienne. (refuser)

3. Je crois avoir maintenant assez d'argent pour m'offrir une auto. (espérer)

4. Je désire dépenser une bonne somme pour cet achat. (préférer)

5. Car je voudrais avoir une voiture assez chic. (aimer)

6. On m'a dit d'acheter une marque américaine. (conseiller)

7. J'ai commencé à examiner tous les modèles. (essayer)

8. Un vendeur a cru me faire signer un contrat. (chercher)

9. J'ai promis de lui téléphoner. (oublier)

10. Mais je refuserai d'acheter sa voiture sans en avoir vu plusieurs autres. (hésiter)

11. Je pourrai sans doute obtenir une réduction de prix. (devoir)

12. Tout cela semble prendre beaucoup de temps. (commencer)

---

[1]Use the plural. [2]**sur** [3]**âgé** [4]**chercher**

13. Mon ami Roland acceptera de venir avec moi. (consentir)

14. Je me dépêcherai de prendre une décision. (réussir)

15. Je voudrais avoir cette nouvelle voiture dimanche prochain. (tenir)

See pages 271–314 for the *Exercices d'ensemble.*

. . . . . .

PROBLEM WORDS

58. very much

Ways of expressing *very much* and *very many*

J'ai *énormément* à faire.

J'ai $\begin{cases} \textbf{\textit{un tas}} \\ \textbf{\textit{des tas}} \end{cases}$ *de choses* à faire. } I have *very much* to do.

J'ai *une quantité de choses* à faire. }

Ces étudiants ont *énormément de* livres à lire. }

Ces étudiants ont *des tas de* livres à lire. } Those students have *very many* books to read.

Ces étudiants ont *une quantité de* livres à lire. }

Depending on the exact sentence, *very much* and *very many* may be expressed by *énormément de*, *une quantité de*, *un tas de*, *des tas de*[1], and other similar expressions. In familiar speech, the French sometimes say **beaucoup** twice, so that one might hear : **J'ai beaucoup beaucoup à faire**, and **Ces étudiants ont beaucoup beaucoup de livres à lire**. This latter construction should be avoided in writing.

French often expresses *not very much* by **pas grand-chose**. This is somewhat colloquial. Ex. : **Je n'ai pas fait grand-chose ce matin.**

> CAUTION: In French, **très** cannot modify **beaucoup**. Therefore, *very much* and *very many* can<u>not</u> be expressed by « très beaucoup ».

59. visit

(a) How to say *to visit a person*

Hier je suis allé voir Monsieur Moreau.   Yesterday I *visited* Mr. Moreau.

---
[1]The expressions **un tas de** and **des tas de** are colloquial.

The most common way of saying *to visit a person* is **aller voir quelqu'un**.

Il faudra *faire une visite aux voisins*.   We must *visit the neighbors*.

A more formal way of saying *to visit a person* is ***faire une visite à quelqu'un***.

Nous **avons rendu visite à** **Madame de Rosemont**.	We *visited (paid a visit to)* Mrs. de Rosement.

Also more formal and therefore less common is **rendre visite à quelqu'un**.

> CAUTION: DO NOT use the verb « visiter » to express the idea of *visiting a person*. The most common way of saying *to visit a person* is **aller voir une personne**.

(b) How to say *to visit a place*

Avez-vous *visité le Louvre* ?	Did you *visit the Louvre* ?
Quand nous étions en Italie, **nous *avons visité Naples*.**	When we were in Italy, *we visited Naples*.
Ne manquez pas de *visiter les* *vieux quartiers* de Paris.	Don't fail *to visit the old sections* of Paris.

The verb **visiter** is used to express the idea of *visiting a place*.

60. while

(a) When to express *while* by **pendant que**

Attendez-moi dans la voiture ***pendant que* je vais chercher** **les enfants.**	Wait for me in the car *while* I go and get the children.

When *while* means *during the time that*, it is expressed by **pendant que**.

(b) When to express *while* by **tandis que**

Marc travaille bien, *tandis que* **Joseph ne fait pas grand-chose.**	Mark works well, *while* Joseph doesn't do much of anything.

When *while* means *whereas*, it is expressed by **tandis que** (pronounced either [tãdikə] or [tãdiskə]).
Sometimes **tandis que** is also used in the sense of *during the time that*, but it is best for the learner to reserve **tandis que** for *while* meaning *whereas*.

61. wish

(a) How to *wish someone something*

Je vous *souhaite* un bon voyage.   I *wish* you a good trip.

The verb **souhaiter** is used to *wish someone something*.

(b) How *désirer* expresses *wish*

> **Pauline *désire* toujours avoir   Pauline always *wishes to have*
> ce qu'ont les autres.**   *what others have.*

The verb **désirer** *means wish or desire. It may be used in the spoken language but is much less common than the verb* ***vouloir***.

(c) How to express *wish* by the conditional of ***vouloir*** and ***aimer***

> **François** $\begin{cases} \textbf{\textit{voudrait}} \\ \textbf{\textit{aimerait}} \end{cases}$ **être riche.**   Francis *wishes* that he were
> very rich.

The conditional of ***aimer*** *and* ***vouloir*** *is used with the* INFINITIVE *to express* wish *when the subject of the main and subordinate clauses are the same in the English sentence.*

> **Nous** $\begin{cases} \textbf{\textit{voudrions}} \\ \textbf{\textit{aimerions}} \end{cases}$ **que Roger vienne**   We *wish* (that) Roger would
> ***avec nous.***   come with us.

The conditional of ***aimer*** *and* ***vouloir*** *+* ***que*** *+* SUBJUNCTIVE *is used to express* wish *when the subject of the main and subordinate clauses is different in both the English and French sentences.*

O. Remplacez les mots anglais par leur équivalent français.

1. Vincent est marié, mais il *(visits)* sa mère tous les jours.   **2.** Vous avez accepté sa proposition tout de suite *(while)* vous auriez dû la discuter. **3.** Le directeur *(wishes)* vous parler.   **4.** Il peut bien être fatigué, il a *(very much)* travaillé.   **5.** Nous *(visited)* plusieurs musées à Rome.   **6.** Je travaillerai au bureau *(while)* tu seras chez Martine.   **7.** Les Marcellin sont revenus de la mer; nous devrions *(visit them)*.   **8.** Je *(wish)* que tu m'apprennes à jouer de la guitare.   **9.** Il fait bon chez vous *(while)* il fait toujours froid chez nous.   **10.** Si vous n'avez pas le temps de *(visit)* la ville, montez au moins sur la colline.   **11.** *(tu)* Jean a un examen aujourd'hui; *(wish)*-lui bonne chance.

P. Traduisez en français. Attention aux mots en italique.

1. *(vous)* If I have time, I will *visit* you Friday afternoon.   **2.** *(tu)* I *wish* you a Happy New Year[1].   **3.** Louis learned Arabic *while* he was in Africa. **4.** This morning I *visited* my former teacher.   **5.** I have always *wished* to travel.   **6.** I speak only one language, *while* Alexander speaks several.

---

[1]**une bonne année**

7. (*vous*) Have you ever *visited* Athens ?   **8.** I *wish* I could go to Portugal this year.   **9.** I would be glad to see Madeleine again; I like her *very much.*

Verb Review

Review the verbs **venir** and **vivre** according to the outline on pages 334–335.

Problem Prepositions

Ce texte a été écrit en 1936 par Jules Romains, un des écrivains les plus importants des années 1930. Il prend une signification particulière car les douze nations qui constituent la Communauté européenne ont ouvert en 1992 toutes les frontières entre elles, créant ainsi un « espace d'Europe » analogue à « l'espace d'Amérique ».

L'Espace d'Amérique

Que les États-Unis soient un pays de grande dimension, nous le savons *depuis* l'école. On nous a enseigné que leur surface égalait *à peu près* celle de l'Europe. Bien des écrivains nous ont dit aussi le sentiment d'immensité, d'augmentation générale des proportions, qui saisit le voyageur *dès qu'*il met le pied sur
5 le sol américain. Mais il est impossible de s'attendre[1] au dépaysement[2] extraordinaire que l'on éprouve et que la répétition n'affaiblit pas...
Un exemple : les Rocheuses. Dieu sait si j'avais entendu parler des Rocheuses par des amis fort bons narrateurs qui les avaient passées. Mais certaines choses ne se conçoivent pas *avant qu'*on en ait soi-même l'ex-
10 périence. Un jour j'ai quitté Kansas City, *avec* le train. Nous étions partis *à* midi. Je savais que Kansas City, *au bord de* son fleuve, peut être considéré comme le point de départ *de* la traversée des Rocheuses *en direction de* Los Angeles. J'avais la crainte que le trajet *de* nuit qui allait *à peu près* de la huitième à la vingtième heure du parcours, ne me fasse manquer une partie
15 spectaculaire de la « traversée des Rocheuses ». Or, le lendemain matin, quand j'ai regardé *hors du* wagon, je n'ai aperçu encore que les signes les plus vagues d'un changement d'altitude. Nous montions *depuis* vingt heures, et toute cette nature avait monté avec nous si lentement que rien n'évoquait les violences *de* la montagne. Il faudrait encore des milliers de kilomètres pour
20 avoir enfin traversé les Rocheuses...

---

[1]*expect* [2]*strangeness*

Il peut y avoir l'accablement[3] de l'espace mais il y a surtout l'ivresse[4] qu'il vous donne. J'ai senti un jour cette ivresse *en* touriste, dans « l'observation car » d'un train qui roulait *du côté de* Saint-Louis. Cela m'est arrivé comme une bouffée[5] de vent. Il m'a semblé soudain que j'étais Américain, un
25 Américain *en* voyage dans ce même wagon. Et un bien-être extraordinaire, d'une profondeur organique, s'emparait[6] de moi *à* l'idée de cet immense pays, *de* tous côtés, qui était le mien. Ces centaines *de* kilomètres offertes *dans* toutes les directions. Le train alerte, silencieux (aussi bien qu'une voiture *sur* les grandes routes) peut filer[7] *à* toute vitesse *sur* les lignes droites *sans* risquer
30 de se cogner[8] bêtement *à* une frontière, *à* une douane.

Avancez tant que vous voulez. Vous serez toujours comme un jeune homme allègre[9] qui marche, la poitrine dégagée[10] et les cheveux flottants. Libre parcours[11] *à* tous, libre aventure.

Il se peut que toutes les richesses ne soient plus à prendre, *comme* autrefois.
35 Mais l'espace est une richesse. Des millions *d'*hommes sont une richesse quand ils ne s'écrasent[12] pas les uns *contre* les autres, quand ils ne se gênent[13] pas mutuellement *pour* respirer, et qu'ils laissent *entre* eux tant *d'*espace où votre destin *à* vous peut faire sa trajectoire[14]. Surabondance d'espace, c'est aussi abondance de hasards, mauvais ou bons. Aucune partie n'est jouée
40 définitivement. Celui *à* qui reste tant *d'*espace *devant* lui n'a jamais tout perdu. L'avenir est grand... *De* tout ce qu'on appelle "les charmes *d'*une civilisation", est-ce que le plus profond, le plus vital, n'est pas la quantité *d'*espérance qu'elle vous donne ?

D'après Jules Romains, auteur notamment de *Knock, ou le Triomphe de la médecine* et des *Hommes de bonne volonté* (*Visite aux Américains*, Flammarion, 1936).

Questions

1. Qu'est-ce qui frappe le voyageur dès qu'il met le pied sur le sol américain ? **2.** Qu'est-ce que l'auteur craignait en partant à midi pour la traversée des Rocheuses ? **3.** Pourquoi est-il surpris malgré les descriptions que lui avaient faites ses amis ? **4.** Quelles sont certaines des richesses dont parle l'auteur qui ne sont plus à prendre ? **5.** Comment se manifeste l'accablement possible de l'espace auquel il fait allusion ? **6.** En quoi est-ce que l'espace est un des « charmes » les plus importants d'une civilisation ?

NOTE: Voir aussi les deux sujets de composition dans le *Manuel d'exercices*.

---

[3]*overwhelming weight* [4]*intoxication* [5]*puff* [6]*seized* [7]*speed* [8]*bump into* [9]*light-hearted* [10]*freed* [11]*course* [12]*bump* [13]*be in each other's way* [14]*course*

I. ENGLISH WORDS THAT ARE BOTH PREPOSITIONS AND CONJUNCTIONS

Certain English words, such as *after, as, before,* and *since* are sometimes used as prepositions to introduce a prepositional phrase, and sometimes as conjunctions to introduce a dependent clause, which has its own subject and verb. It is important to know when such English words are used as a preposition and when as a conjunction, for French often uses one word to express the English preposition and another to express the English conjunction.

Among the most common English words used as both a preposition and a conjunction are :

Preposition	**Conjunction**

1. after

après[1]	après que
Nous sommes partis *après* l'annonce des résultats.	**Nous sommes partis *après que* le directeur a annoncé les résultats.**
We left *after* the announcement of the results.	We left *after* the director announced the results.

Après is used to express English *after* when a preposition, and *après que* when a conjunction.

2. as

comme	**comme**
Comme **mécanicien, il est excellent.**	*Comme* **j'ai du travail à finir, je ne peux pas aller chez vous.**
As a mechanic, he is excellent.	*As* I have work to finish, I cannot go to your house.

Sometimes **comme** is used to express the English *as* both when a preposition and a conjunction.

---

[1]For *après* + VERBAL CONSTRUCTION, see page 241, §25.

The preposition **comme**, meaning *as*, is normally followed by the noun alone, without **un**, **une**, or **des** and is used in a phrase which has a general sense.

On the other hand, when **comme** is followed by **un**, **une**, or **des** plus a noun, it means *like* and is used in a phrase implying a comparison. Ex. : **Il parle comme un professeur.** (He talks *like* a teacher.) **Il conduit comme un fou.** (He drives *like* a madman.)

As a conjunction, **comme** means *as* in the sense of *because*.

en	à mesure que
Il s'est conduit en véritable ami.	**A *mesure qu*'il vieillissait, il devenait moins sévère.**
He behaved *as* a true friend.	*As* he got older, he became less strict.

The preposition **en** followed by the noun unmodified by **un**, **une**, or **des** means *as* in the sense of *in the character of*.

The conjunction **à mesure que** means *as* = *in proportion as*.

3. because

à cause de	parce que
Je suis resté à la maison *à cause de* la pluie.	**Je suis resté à la maison *parce qu*'il pleuvait.**
I stayed home *because of* the rain.	I stayed home *because* it was raining.

The English preposition *because of* is expressed in French by **à cause de** and is followed by a noun or pronoun, whereas the English conjunction *because* is expressed in French by **parce que** and is followed by a clause.

4. before

avant	avant que
Nous sommes partis *avant* l'annonce des résultats.	**Nous sommes partis *avant que* le directeur annonce les résultats.**
We left *before* the announcement of the results.	We left *before* the director announced the results.

The conjunction **avant que** is always followed by the subjunctive, and both the present and past subjunctive are found with it. Thus, **Nous sommes partis *avant que* le directeur *ait annoncé* les résultats** is also correct.

5. but

sauf	mais
Tout le monde est parti *sauf* Suzanne.	**Georges est parti, *mais* où est-il allé ?**
Everyone left *but* Suzanne.	Georges left, but where did he go ?

The word *but* is usually a conjunction. However, it is occasionally used as a preposition, and then it is equivalent to the English *except*. The preposition *but* may be expressed in several ways[1], the most common of which is probably *sauf*.

6. for

pour	car
Nous avons fait cela *pour* vous.	**Nous avons fait cela *car* vous n'étiez pas ici.**
We did that *for* you.	We did that, *for* you were not here.

The most common way of expressing *for* as a preposition is *pour*[2].

The conjunction *for* is always expressed by *car*, and its meaning is somewhat similar to that of *because*.

7. since

depuis	depuis que
Philippe est chez nous *depuis* jeudi.	**Philippe est chez nous *depuis que* ses parents sont partis pour la Suisse.**
Philip has been with us *since* Thursday.	Philip has been with us *since* his parents left for Switzerland.

When *since* indicates time, it is expressed by *depuis* as a preposition and by *depuis que* as a conjunction.

Note that the preposition *depuis* and its equivalents are usually followed by the present tense in French where English uses the present perfect tense.

---

[1]For other ways, see page 258, §18.   [2]For other ways, see page 259, §19.

puisque

Puisque **vous partez pour la Suisse, Philippe peut venir chez nous.**
Since you are leaving for Switzerland, Philip can come to our house.

When *since* = *because*, it is a conjunction and is expressed in French by *puisque*.

8. until

jusqu'à	**jusqu'à ce que**
Nous resterons ici *jusqu'à* dimanche.	**Nous resterons ici *jusqu'à ce que* vous reveniez.**
We'll stay here *until* Sunday.	We'll stay here *until* you come back.

In affirmative sentences, the English *until* is expressed by *jusqu'à* when used as a preposition; as a conjunction, French expresses *until* by *jusqu'à ce que*, and the verb of the dependent clause is always in the subjunctive.

pas avant	**pas avant que**
Nous n'irons <u>pas</u> à Paris *avant* dimanche.	**Nous n'irons <u>pas</u> à Paris *avant que* vous soyez rétabli.**
We will <u>not</u> go to Paris *until* Sunday.	We will <u>not</u> go to Paris *until* you are better.

In negative sentences, the English *not until* (meaning *not before*) is expressed by *pas avant*; as a conjunction, French expresses *not until* (meaning *not before*) by *pas avant que*, and the verb of the dependent clause is always in the subjunctive.

> CAUTION: DO NOT use *jusqu'à* or *jusqu'à ce que* to express *until* in a negative sentence.

A. *Remplacez les mots anglais indiqués entre parenthèses par l'équivalent français.*

1. Nous vous traiterons tout à fait (*as a*) camarade.   **2.** Marie a retrouvé toutes ses clés (*but*) celle de sa voiture.   **3.** Roland regrette de ne pas avoir connu Françoise (*before*) elle se marie.   **4.** Vous viendrez me voir (*after*) la classe.   **5.** Je m'ennuyais (*before*) votre arrivée.   **6.** Il ne faut pas renoncer à un projet (*because*) on a des difficultés.   **7.** (*Since*) nous sommes ici, il pleut tous les jours.   **8.** Cherchez (*until*) vous trouviez la solution de ce problème.   **9.** Ma colère montait (*as*) son avocat parlait.

B. Remplacez les mots anglais indiqués entre parenthèses par l'équivalent français.

1. Il ne faut pas négliger votre famille (*because of*) vos affaires.   **2.** Je vous dirai mon opinion (*after*) vous aurez vu ce dossier.   **3.** (*Since*) votre séjour en Orient, vous n'êtes plus le même.   **4.** Je voulais vous voir, (*but*) je n'ai pas pu.   **5.** (*Before*) son accident, il faisait toutes sortes de sports.
6. (*Since*) vous êtes debout, voulez-vous m'apporter le dictionnaire ?
7. Cet argent leur permettra de vivre (*until*) la fin du mois.   **8.** Tu ne peux pas trouver mieux (*as a*) ami.   **10.** Ne partez pas (*until*) je revienne.

C. Traduisez en français.

1. The children will come home[1] immediately after the movies.   **2.** I visited every country in Europe but Spain.   **3.** Juliette was becoming more and more worried[2] as time went by.   **4.** (*vous*) Mr. Forestier will give you a good job after you have done[3] your military service.   **5.** We'll not go out this evening because of the snow.   **6.** Since my operation, I am much better[4].   **7.** Almost everyone left before Mr. Ponsard's lecture.
8. Mark and Irene danced until six o'clock in[5] the morning.

D. Traduisez en français.

1. As a minister, Mr. Carré was remarkable.   **2.** Anne cannot come until five o'clock.   **3.** Peter has many shortcomings, but he is very nice.
4. (*tu*) All that happened because you were careless.   **5.** As we have little time, we'll take an[6] airplane.   **6.** (*vous*) Since you like the theater, why don't you go there more often ?   **7.** (*vous*) The director would like to speak to you before you hand in[7] your resignation.   **8.** The astronaut was received in his native city as a hero.

II. OTHER ENGLISH PREPOSITIONS THAT POSE PROBLEMS IN FRENCH

Certain English prepositions pose problems in French (1) because they may also be used as another part of speech, in which case they are expressed by two different words according to their function; (2) because some English prepositions have several connotations, each of which is expressed in a special way in French.

---

[1]*come home* **rentrer**   [2]*become worried* **s'inquiéter**   [3]What tense does French use here ?
[4]*be much better* **aller beaucoup mieux**   [5]**du**   [6]Use the definite article.   [7]*hand in* **donner**

The words presented in this section are all used as prepositions some of the time. Sometimes it seems sufficient to give just the French equivalent, at times examples best show the differences, other times an explanation of usage appears clearest.

9. about

(a) *concerning* = *de, sur, au sujet de, à propos de*

Nous parlions *de* votre nouvelle maison de campagne.	We were speaking *about* your new country house.
Paul nous a écrit plusieurs lettres *sur* son voyage.	Paul wrote us several letters *about* his trip.
Qu'est-ce que vous avez à dire *au sujet de* votre conduite ?	What do you have to say *about* your behavior ?
Personne n'a rien dit *à propos de* mon absence.	No one said anything *about* my absence.

When *about* means *concerning*, it is a preposition and is sometimes expressed by *de* (especially after forms of *parler*), sometimes by *sur*, and sometimes by *au sujet de* or *à propos de*. At times, but not always, several of these words could express *about* in the same sentence.

(b) *approximately* = *environ, vers, à peu près, -aine* (appended to a cardinal numeral)

J'ai vu *environ* dix appartements.	I saw *about* ten apartments.
Michel est arrivé *vers* six heures.	Michael came at *about* six o'clock.
Il est *environ* dix heures.	It is *about* ten o'clock.
C'est *à peu près* ce que j'ai dit.	That's *about* what I said.
Il s'est passé une *vingtaine* d'années.	*About twenty* years went by.

The word *environ* modifies a numeral. The preposition *vers* is usually found in sentences with the time of day except when the verb of such sentences is a form of *être*. In that case, *about* is expressed by *environ*. When the suffix *-aine* is appended to a cardinal numeral, it indicates an approximation. The expression *à peu près* may be used for *environ*, but it may also modify words other than numerals.

(c) *be about to* = *être sur le point de*

Nous étions *sur le point de* partir.	We were *about* to leave.

10. above

En général les avions volent *au-dessus des* nuages.	Airplanes generally fly *above* the clouds.

The preposition *above*, meaning *over*, *in*, or *to a higher place*, is expressed in French by **au-dessus de**.

11. according to

Selon
Suivant } **Voltaire, il faut cultiver**   *According to* Voltaire, one
D'après   **son jardin.**   must cultivate one's garden.

The English preposition *according to* is expressed by **selon**, **suivant**, and **d'après**,[1] which are normally interchangeable.

12. across

Marc a couru après son chien *à travers* **les champs.**	Mark ran after his dog *across* the fields.
Je l'ai vu *traverser* **la place** *en courant.*	I saw him *run across* the square.
Je l'aurais salué, mais il était *de l'autre côté* **de la rue.**	I would have greeted him, but he was *across* the street.
Nous *avons traversé* **le pont.**	We *went across* the bridge.

The preposition *across* is often expressed by **à travers**. But when *across* means *on the other side of*, the French say **de l'autre côté de**, and *to run across* is **traverser en courant**. The idea of *to go across* is often expressed by using the verb **traverser**.

13. after

On l'a appelé Victor *d'après* **son parrain.**	They *named* him Victor *after* his godfather.

The preposition *after* is usually **après**, but *to name after* is **appeler d'après**.

14. along

Il est agréable de se promener *le long de* **la Seine.**	It is pleasant to walk *along* the Seine.
Il y a des voitures stationnées tout *le long de* **la rue.**	There are cars parked all *along* the street.
Il *a suivi le chemin* **jusqu'au pont.**	He *went along the road* up to the bridge.

---

[1]See §13 on this page for another use of **d'après**.

The preposition *along* is usually expressed by **le long de**. But *to go along the road* is **suivre le chemin (la route)** and *to go along the street* is **suivre la rue**.

E. Remplacez le mot anglais indiqué entre parenthèses par l'équivalent français.

1. Georges fume (*about*) deux paquets de cigarettes par jour.   **2.** Claude et Sophie se promènent (*along*) la rivière.   **3.** Avez-vous vu ce qui se passe (*across*) la frontière ?   **4.** Hier, j'ai entendu parler (*about*) votre voyage. **5.** C'est (*about*) la même chose.   **6.** (*According to*) le traité, il n'y aura plus de douane entre ces pays.   **7.** Il y avait des fleurs tout (*along*) le sentier. **8.** J'ai entendu une conférence (*about*) l'énergie atomique.   **9.** Ils se sont revus (*at about*) six heures et demie.   **10.** (*After*) qui avez-vous appelé votre fils Christian ?   **11.** (*According to*) les experts, on ne peut pas construire un pont à cet endroit.   **12.** Donnez-moi (*about twenty*) francs. **13.** Qu'est-ce que c'est que ce fil (*above*) le pont ?   **14.** Il ne faut pas vous inquiéter (*about*) vos enfants.   **15.** (*According to*) les journaux, on trouvera bientôt le coupable.   **16.** Je n'aime pas avoir des gens bruyants dans l'appartement (*above*) moi.   **17.** Je voudrais vous demander des renseignements (*about*) les hôtels à Paris.   **18.** Il est (*about*) trois heures du matin.

F. Traduisez en français.

1. According to his father, Francis doesn't work enough.   **2.** It is about five o'clock now, but Mr. Dupont locked the door at about four thirty. **3.** We went along the road up to the white house.   **4.** After the lecture, we went home.   **5.** Have you heard about George's accident ?   **6.** Our friends traveled across the whole country on a motorcycle.   **7.** There were about two hundred people in the library.   **8.** We had some good discussions about modern music.   **9.** We named my daughter Rose after her grandmother.

G. Traduisez en français.

1. The little boy ran across the street.   **2.** Louise spoke to the class about her trip to Mexico.   **3.** According to Mr. Parrain, they are going to build a new city hall.   **4.** Our friends were about to telephone us when we arrived. **5.** My friend lives across the street.   **6.** The sun was directly above us. **7.** There are about thirty girls in the dormitory.   **8.** It's about all I have to do.   **9.** Professor Martin wrote me about my examination.

15. at

With nouns, *at* is usually expressed by **à** or **dans**.
The preposition *at* with place names is taken up on pages 228–229.

With the connotation of *at the home of, at the place of business of,* or *in the country of, at* is often expressed by **chez**. Note the uses of **chez** in the following sentences.

Nous irons passer la soirée *chez* les Moreau.	We'll go to spend the evening *at the Moreaus'.*
***Chez nous*[1] on dîne à six heures du soir.**	*In our country* we eat at six in the evening.
N'oublie pas de passer *chez le boulanger* à ton retour.	Don't forget to go *to the bakery* on your return.
On retrouve cette même idée *chez tous les grands écrivains.*	One finds this same idea *in the works of all the great writers.*

16. before

Il y a un écran *devant* la classe.	There is a screen *before* (*in front of*) the class.
Venez *avant* huit heures.	Come *before* eight o'clock.
Nous avons *déjà* fait ça. } **Nous avons fait ça *avant*.** }	We did that *before.*

The preposition *before* is expressed by ***devant*** when it indicates place and means *in front of,* and by ***avant*** when it indicates *time.* As an adverb, *before* may be expressed by ***déjà***, ***avant***, and ***auparavant***.

17. down

Ils *sont*[2] *descendus* tout de suite.	They *came down* at once.
Nous *avons*[2] *descendu* la rue.	We *went down* the street.

The English *down* is often part of the French verb ***descendre***, which may mean *to come down* or *to go down.* The English *to go down the street* is expressed in French by ***descendre la rue***.

18. except

Tout le monde m'a félicité **sauf** **à part** } **M. Picard.** **excepté** }	Everyone congratulated me except Mr. Picard

The English *except* may be expressed by ***sauf***, ***à part***, and ***excepté***.

---

[1]In this sentence, **chez nous** may also mean *at our house.*   [2]Intransitive verbs of motion are usually conjugated with **être**, but when a verb of motion governs a direct object, it becomes transitive and is then conjugated with **avoir**.

19. for (time)

Nos amis sont chez nous *depuis* **quinze jours.**	Our friends have been with us *for* two weeks.

When an action begins in the past and is still going on in the present, French uses *depuis* with the present to express *for*.[1]

Nos amis sont restés chez nous (*pendant*) **quinze jours.**	Our friends stayed at our house (*for*) two weeks.

A completed action describing a certain duration of time uses *pendant* with the compound past, where English uses *for*. This *pendant* may be omitted, just as *for* may be omitted in the English sentence.

Ces jeunes gens voyageront en Afrique *pendant* **quinze jours.**	These young men will travel in Africa *for* two weeks.

In the future *for* is usually expressed by *pendant*.

J'irai à Paris *pour* **quinze jours.**	I'll go to Paris *for* two weeks.
***Pour* combien de temps partirez-vous ?**	*For* how long will you be gone ?

However, with verbs of motion and the verb *être* the future is often used with *pour* to express duration of time.

20. in

(a) The preposition *in* with place names is taken up on pages 228–231.

(b) *in* + COMMON NOUN

Nos amis sont *au* restaurant.	Our friends are *in* the restaurant.
Jacques est *dans* sa chambre.	Jack is *in* his room.

The usual word for *in* is *dans*, but *à* + DEFINITE ARTICLE is often used to express *in the*.

(c) *in* + *matin, après-midi, soir*

Ne faites pas de bruit *le soir* après dix heures.	Don't make any noise *in the evening* after ten o'clock.

---

[1]For other ways of expressing this idea, see pages 47–48.

For *in the morning, in the afternoon,* and *in the evening,* French say
le matin, l'après-midi, and *le soir* without the preposition *dans.*

(d) *in* to express time required to do something

> **Monsieur Goulet travaille très vite;** Mr. Goulet works very fast; he
> **il pourrait réparer votre télévision** could fix your television set
> **en une heure.** *in an hour.*

To indicate the length of time required to do something. French uses *en* to
express the English *in.*

(e) *in* to express time at which an action can begin

> **Je n'ai pas le temps maintenant,** I don't have time now, but I
> **mais je pourrais réparer votre** could fix your television set
> **télévision *dans trois jours.*** *in* (meaning *"after"*) *three
> days.*

To indicate the moment at which an action can begin, French uses *dans* to
express the English *in.*

(f) *in* used to introduce a phrase of manner

> **Madame Renard parle *d'une*** Mrs. Renard speaks *in a very*
> **voix très douce.** *soft voice.*

Phrases of manner are often introduced by the preposition *de.*

(g) —*o'clock in the*—

> **Je me suis réveillé *à deux heures*** I woke up *at two o'clock in*
> **du matin.** *the morning.*

In expressions such as ***deux heures du matin, trois heures de l'après-midi,***
and ***huit heures du soir,*** the English *in the* is expressed in French by *de* +
DEFINITE ARTICLE.

H. Remplacez les mots anglais indiqués entre parenthèses par leur équivalent français.

1. Paul fait tout bien (*except*) ses leçons de musique.   **2.** Vous êtes fou
de dépenser votre argent (*in*) une façon aussi extravagante.   **3.** Couchez-
vous de bonne heure (*in the evening*).   **4.** Jean a passé le week-end (*at*) les
Biéville.   **5.** (*For*) dix jours on ne savait pas où ils étaient.   **6.** Je viens de
parler à Nicole; elle était (*in*) mauvaise humeur.   **7.** Le petit a dormi

jusqu'à quatre heures (*in the afternoon*).   **8.** Nous partirons (*for*) huit jours.
9. (*In*) Molière il y a toujours des choses amusantes.   **10.** Marc a fait
ses devoirs (*in*) vingt minutes.   **11.** Nous regardons la télévision (*for*)
deux heures.   **12.** Dépêchez-vous, le train part (*in*) une demi-heure.
13. Cela ne se passe pas comme ça (*at*) les Italiens.   **14.** Son mari lui a
répondu (*in*) un ton ferme.   **15.** (*For*) combien de temps partirez-vous à
Londres ?

I. *Traduisez en français.*

1. Those boys have been playing here for an hour.   **2.** My alarm clock
rang at six o'clock in the morning.   **3.** I will go to England for three days.
4. (*vous*) Your little boy went down the street a little while ago.   **5.** (*vous*)
Do you want to see me at your home or in your office ?   **6.** I saw Mr. Lebrun
at the barber's.   **7.** I'll begin that work in a half hour.   **8.** We get up early
in the morning.   **9.** I slept a great deal during my illness.   **10.** Everyone
came except Michael.   **11.** In Balzac one finds extraordinary characters[1].
12. I can finish that book in an hour.   **13.** One is always well received at
their home.   **14.** We read that before.

21. in spite of

**Malgré le mauvais temps, je vais
    sortir ce soir.**

In spite of the bad weather,
I'm going out this evening.

The English *in spite of* is expressed in French by **malgré**.

22. instead of

**Au lieu d'un cadeau, j'ai donné
    de l'argent à Jacques.**

Instead of a gift, I gave Jack
some money.

The English *instead of* is expressed in French by **au lieu de**, which may be
followed by a noun, a pronoun, or an infinitive.

23. out of

(a) *out of* = **hors de**

**Votre ami est *hors de* danger
    maintenant.**

Your friend is *out of* danger
now.

The most common equivalent of *out of* is **hors de**.

---

[1]Not « caractères ». See page 42.

(b) *out of* meaning *without*

> **Vous êtes toujours *sans* argent.**   You are always *out of* money.

When *out of* means *without*, it is expressed by ***sans***.

(c) *out of* between numerals (one *out of* three)

> **Un étudiant *sur* cinq a déjà été   One student *out of* five has
> en France.**   already been in France.

When *out of* is used idiomatically between numerals in phrases such as *two out of three*, French expresses *out of* by ***sur***.

(d) *go out of, come out of, fall out of*

> **Louis *est sorti de* la maison avec   Louis *came out of* the house
> son chien.**   with his dog.
> **Votre carte d'identité *est tombée*   Your identification card *has
> de* votre portefeuille.**   fallen out of* your billfold.

The verbs *come out of* and *go out of* are expressed by ***sortir de***, and *fall out of* is expressed by ***tomber de***.

24. toward

> **Tout le monde s'est précipité   Everyone rushed *toward* the
> *vers* la porte.**   door.
> **Vers la fin de la journée, je suis   *Toward* the end of the day I
> contente de m'asseoir.**   am glad to sit down.

The word *toward* is usually expressed by ***vers***, whether it indicates motion or means *about* with an expression of time.

> **Il faut être loyal *envers* ses amis.**   One must be loyal *toward*
>   one's friends.
> **Quelle est son attitude *envers*   What is his attitude *toward*
> ses parents ?**   his parents ?

Used figuratively in referring to a person, *toward* is expressed by ***envers***.

25. under

> **Le métro passe *sous* la Seine.**   The subway goes *under* the
>   Seine.

The most common way of expressing *under* is ***sous***.

La famille Delorme habite *au-dessous de* nous.	The Delorme family lives *under* us.
Raymond a quinze employés *au-dessous de* lui.	Raymond has fifteen employees *under* him.

However, *under* and *underneath* are expressed by *au-dessous de* when used figuratively and when *under* does not mean *immediately under*.

J'ai travaillé *sous* la direction du professeur Moreau.	I worked *under* Professor Moreau.

But when *under* is used in the sense of *under the supervision of*, it is expressed by *sous la direction de*.

26. up

Je *monte* cet escalier cinq fois par jour.	I *go up* that stairway five times a day.
En sortant de son bureau, Monsieur Clément *a remonté la rue.*	On leaving his office, Mr. Clement *went up the street*.

The English *up* is often part of the French verb. Two of the common expressions that express *up* are *monter*, meaning *to go up*, and *remonter la rue*, which means *to go up the street*.

27. with

(a) *with* = *avec*

Je vous ai vu *avec* une dame hier soir.	I saw you *with* a lady yesterday evening.

The common way of expressing *with* is *avec*.

(b) *with* = *de* after verb or adjective

Son bureau est toujours *couvert de* poussière.	His desk is always *covered with* dust.
Es-tu *content de* ta voiture ?	Are you *satisfied with* your car ?

Certain verbs and adjectives are regularly followed by *de* in French, and their English equivalents are followed by *with*.

(c) *with* = *chez*

Louise habite *chez* sa tante.	Louise lives *with* her aunt.
Chez Verlaine, la qualité musicale des mots est très importante.	*With* Verlaine, the musical quality of the words is very important.

When *with* means *at the house of* or *in the case of* + A PERSON, French generally uses *chez*.

(d) *with* in phrases of manner = *de*

Françoise regardait sa montre *d'un air anxieux.*	Frances was looking at her watch *with an anxious air.*

French phrases of manner are introduced by *de*. Sometimes this *de* is expressed in English by *with*, sometimes by *in*.

(e) *with* in phrases of characteristic = *à* + ARTICLE

Cette brune *aux yeux bleus* a beaucoup de charme.	That brunette *with blue eyes* has a great deal of charm.

French uses *à* + DEFINITE ARTICLE to indicate a characteristic of a person. English uses the preposition *with* in the same way.

(f) *with* to express attitude or manner of a part of the body = DEFINITE ARTICLE

Louis dort toujours *les bras sous les couvertures.*	Louis always sleeps *with his arms under the blankets.*

English uses *with* to express attitude or manner of a part of the body, whereas French uses the DEFINITE ARTICLE without a preposition.

J. Remplacez par l'équivalent français les mots anglais entre parenthèses.

1. Restez à la maison (*instead of*) vous fatiguer.   **2.** Je suis allé en classe (*in spite of*) la neige.   **3.** Connaissez-vous ce jeune homme (*with*) cheveux roux ?   **4.** Les enfants (*under*) sept ans paient demi-place.   **5.** Cet homme est toujours (*out of*) travail.   **6.** Nous nous sommes dirigés (*toward*) le centre de la place.   **7.** Nous sommes très satisfaits (*with*) vos progrès.   **8.** Êtes-vous toujours indulgents (*toward*) vos amis ?   **9.** Comment trouvez-vous la famille qui habite (*under*) vous ?   **10.** Nous habitons (*at*) mes beaux-parents.   **11.** Dans ce pays, deux personnes (*out of*) cinq savent une langue étrangère.   **12.** La terre était couverte (*with*) neige.   **13.** Aidez-moi à porter ce bureau (*toward*) la fenêtre.   **14.** Achetez une voiture (*instead of*) une moto.

K. *Traduisez en français.*

1. He was so surprised that he looked at me with his mouth open.
2. Read instead of watching television.   **3.** Who is that girl with bare feet ?
4. (*vous*) What is your attitude toward foreigners ?   **5.** (*vous*) Are you
satisfied[1] with your new job ?   **6.** (*tu*) What fell out of your pocket ?
7. My son lives at his grandmother's.   **8.** Toward the end of the play,
everybody was laughing.   **9.** (*vous*) What do you have under your coat ?
10. The room was filled with smoke.   **11.** (*tu*) Don't forget to go to the
dentist's before going to the movies.   **12.** Our friends came to see us in
spite of the bad weather.   **13.** One girl out of three gets married before the
age of twenty[2].   **14.** Who just came out of the office ?   **15.** (*vous*) I hope
that your father is out of danger.   **16.** My brother-in-law has been out of
work for a month.   **17.** When Mr. Saunier came out of the hotel, he went
up the street.

EXERCICE ORAL

*La femme de Michel Bertrand est partie pour quelques jours et Michel
pense à diverses choses.*
  *Chaque phrase se termine par une proposition subordonnée. Répétez la
phrase en remplaçant la proposition subordonnée par la préposition
indiquée entre parenthèses en faisant les changements nécessaires.*

EXEMPLE: Nous nous sommes beaucoup amusés pendant que Jacques nous
rendait visite. (pendant) **Nous nous sommes beaucoup amusés pendant
la visite de Jacques.**

1. Voyons, que vais-je faire pendant que ma femme est absente ?
(pendant)

2. J'ai bien des affaires à régler avant qu'elle revienne. (avant)

3. Il y a beaucoup de choses que je fais seulement parce que ma femme
me les conseille.[3] (à cause de)

4. Je ne suis pas à mon aise depuis qu'elle est partie. (depuis)

5. Je travaillerai au bureau jusqu'à ce que la nuit tombe. (jusqu'à)

6. Je jouerai au golf samedi parce que mon patron m'a invité. (à cause de)

7. Les enfants sont au lycée. Je rentrerai à la maison seulement après
qu'ils seront revenues. (après)

---

[1]**content** [2]Supply **ans**. [3]The noun **conseil** is used in the plural to denote advice in
general.

8. Marc aura besoin d'argent car il va entrer à l'université. (pour)

9. Mes fils veulent aller à l'université, mais Pascal, lui, a d'autres idées. (sauf)

10. Ma femme et moi resterons dans notre maison jusqu'à ce que nos enfants se marient. (jusqu'à)

See pages 271–314 for the *Exercices d'ensemble.*

. . . . . .

PROBLEM WORDS

62. would

(a) When *would* is used to express a condition

Je *partirais* tout de suite si j'avais le temps.	I *would leave* immediately if I had time.

The word *would* is often a part of the conclusion of an English conditional sentence. In this case, French puts the verb in the CONDITIONAL.

Que *ferais*-tu à ma place ?	What *would* you *do* in my place ?

Sometimes *would* is the auxiliary of the verb of an implied condition, that is, one in which the *if*-clause is missing but implied. The above sentence, for instance, means : *What would you do if you were I ?* In an implied condition, French uses the CONDITIONAL of the verb of the sentence to express the English *would.*

(b) When *would* means *used to*

Je *partais* de bonne heure tous les matins.	I *would* (*used to*) leave early every morning.

When *would* = *used to*, it indicates a customary past action, and in such cases the IMPERFECT of the verb must be used.

> CAUTION: Whenever you find *would* in an English sentence that you wish to express in French, determine whether *would* is part of a condition or whether it is used to describe a customary action and is the equivalent of *used to.* If *would* is the equivalent of *used to*, use the imperfect rather than the conditional.

63. year

(a) When *year* is expressed by *année*

En quelle *année* êtes-vous né ?	In what *year* were you born ?
Cette *année*-là il a beaucoup neigé.	That *year* it snowed a great deal.
J'ai passé beaucoup d'*années* en France.	I spent many *years* in France.
Ma troisième *année* à l'université a été très amusante.	My third *year* at the university was very entertaining.

The most common word for *year* is ***année***. It should be used except in the cases stated in (b).

(b) When *year* is expressed by *an*

Nous avons passé *trois ans* en France.	We spent *three years* in France.
Nous y retournons *tous les ans*.	We go back there *every year*.
Sans indiscrétion, combien gagnez-vous *par an* ?	If it isn't indiscreet to ask, how much do you earn *a year* ?

The word ***an*** is used for *year* when it is modified by a cardinal numeral, in the expressions ***tous les ans*** (*every year*) and ***par an*** (*per year*) and occasionally in other circumstances.

64. yes

(a) When *yes* is expressed by *oui*

— Êtes-vous arrivé hier ?	"Did you arrive yesterday ?"
—*Oui*, je suis arrivé hier.	"*Yes*, I arrived yesterday."

The usual word for *yes* is ***oui***; it indicates the speaker's agreement with the previous statement or question.

(b) When *yes* is expressed by *si*.

—*N'êtes*-vous *pas* arrivé hier ?	"*Didn't* you arrive yesterday ?"
—*Si*, je suis arrivé hier.	"*Yes*, I arrived yesterday."
—Guy *ne* comprend *pas* bien l'anglais.	"Guy *doesn't* understand English well."
—*Si*, il le comprend bien.	"*Yes*, he does understand it well."

After a negative statement or question, *si* is used for *yes*. It contradicts the preceding statement or question.

65. young men

How to express the plural of *jeune homme*

Il y avait *des jeunes gens* et des jeunes filles à cette réception.	There were *some young men* and some young ladies at that reception.
Lucile voudrait connaître *des jeunes gens* avec qui elle puisse sortir.	Lucille would like to get acquainted with *some young men* with whom she could go out.

The plural of *jeune homme* is *jeunes gens*. A frequent meaning of *jeunes gens* is therefore *young men*. The expression ***les jeunes hommes*** seldom occurs, and you should avoid using it.

Les *jeunes gens* s'amusent beaucoup pendant les vacances de printemps.	*Young people* have a very good time during spring vacation.

The term *jeunes gens* also means *young people*. The context must decide where *jeunes gens* means *young men* and where *young people*.

L. Remplacez les mots anglais par leur équivalent français.

1. Dans quelques (*years*) j'espère savoir plusieurs langues.   **2.** Ces (*young men*) avec leurs cheveux longs ressemblent à des filles.   **3.** Nos amis mexicains ne sont pas retournés dans leur pays depuis dix (*years*).
4. —Pourquoi ne prenez-vous pas le train de cinq heures ? —Parce que je (*would arrive*) au milieu de la nuit.   **5.** —Je ne parle pas bien le français. —(*Yes*), vous le parlez fort bien.   **6.** Agnès ne veut sortir qu'avec des (*young men*) de son âge.   **7.** Le patron change de voiture (*every year*).
8. Quand je préparais mes examens, je (*would get up*) à six heures du matin.
9. —Voulez-vous m'accompagner chez les Bridoux ? —(*Yes*), volontiers.

M. Traduisez en français. Attention aux mots en italique.

1. I think I could go to France in[1] two *years*.   **2.** (*vous*) *Would* you lend me your car this weekend ?   **3.** Our cousins from Pontigny come to see us twice a *year*.   **4.** (*tu*) "Do you like that music ?" "*Yes*, very much."
5. Robert and Roger are very serious *young men*.   **6.** (*vous*) In[2] what *year*

---

[1]dans   [2]en

did you come to the United States ?   **7.** When we were young, we *would* play tennis[1] every Saturday.   **8.** I found the first *year* of medicine the most difficult.   **9.** (*tu*) "Haven't you seen Alain ?" "*Yes*, he's coming[2]."

Verb Review

Review the verbs **voir** and **vouloir** according to the outline on pages 334–335.

---

[1]**faire du tennis**   [2]*he's coming* **il arrive**

Exercices d'Ensemble 1

A. Ces questions se rapportent au texte au début du Chapitre 1. Vous rentrez chez vous. Vous êtes étonné de ne pas entendre les bruits habituels au moment d'ouvrir la porte de votre appartement, et vous apprenez qu'il y a une grève de la télévision.

1. (*What*) _____ est donc la raison de ce silence ?

2. (*What*) _____ a pu se passer ?

3. (*What*) _____ sont les demandes des grévistes ?

4. (*Who*) _____ aurait de l'appétit dans ces conditions ?

5. De (*what*) _____ pourrait-on parler ?

6. (*Who*) _____ a une idée pour passer la soirée ?

7. (*Which*) _____ d'entre vous veut aller au cinéma ?

8. (*What*) _____ nous empêcherait de jouer aux cartes ?

9. (*Whom*) _____ pourrions-nous aller voir ?

10. (*What*) _____ mauvais temps pour sortir !

11. (*What*) _____ ennui de ne pas avoir la télévision !

12. (*What*) _____ il me reste à faire ?

B. Mettez les phrases suivantes à la forme interrogative, remplaçant les mots en italique par un pronom ou un adjectif interrogatif selon le cas.

EXEMPLE: *Irène* a fermé la fenêtre. **Qui a fermé la fenêtre ?**
Roger a fermé *cette* fenêtre. **Quelle fenêtre Roger a-t-il fermée ?**

1. *La cathédrale* se trouve au centre de la ville.

_____

2. Il faut absolument voir *ce* film.

_____

3. Paul a laissé *son courrier* sur mon bureau.

_____

4. *Monsieur Galand* arrivera demain.

_____

5. *Votre* client a téléphoné il y une heure.

_____

6. Ils ont ouvert la porte avec *un passe-partout.*[1]

_____

7. Pierre a rencontré *leur fils* dans la rue ce matin.

_____

8. Jean-Paul a retrouvé *son* portefeuille dans la voiture.

_____

9. Les autres comptent toujours sur *Charles* pour les tirer d'affaire.[2]

_____

10. Claude a enfin rendu *ce* livre à la bibliothèque.

_____

C. *Remplacez les interrogatifs anglais par leur équivalent français.*

1. (*What !*) _____ Paul n'est pas encore là ?

2. —(*What is*) _____ un ordinateur ? —(*What ?*)

   _____

3. (*Who*) _____ vient de sortir ?

4. A (*whom*) _____ veux-tu donner notre vieux canapé ?

5. (*Which*) _____ sont les langues les plus utiles ?

6. (*What*) _____ sorte de pièce aimeriez-vous aller voir ?

7. (*Whom*) _____ le directeur veut-il voir ?

8. De (*what*) _____ parlez-vous ?

9. (*What*) _____ vous avez fait hier soir ?

10. (*What*) _____ fait ce bruit ?

_____

[1]**passe-partout** *master key*   [2]**tirer d'affaire** *get out of trouble*

11. (*What*) _____ as-tu appris dans ton voyage ?

12. (*Of which one*) _____ parles-tu ?

EXERCICES D'ENSEMBLE 2

A. *Ces phrases se rapportent au texte au début du Chapitre 2. Remplacez les tirets par la forme convenable de l'adjectif indiqué.*

1. Il y a cinquante ans les vols en avion étaient assez

_____ (dangereux).

2. Les pannes étaient _____ (nombreux) quand il fallait

traverser des déserts _____ (brûlant) ou des montagnes

_____ (glacé).

3. Saint-Exupéry, tombé dans le désert de Libye, a commencé une

marche _____ (épuisant).

4. Il a cru voir un homme qui dormait : c'était un rocher

_____ (noir).

5. Une croix sur une colline devait indiquer un établissement

_____ (religieux).

6. Un puits toujours _____ (plein) d'eau se trouvait à côté.

7. Mais très vite les _____ (beau) mirages disparaissaient.

8. Il partage une _____ (dernier) orange avec son
mécanicien.

9. Ce fruit _____ (lumineux) est une des plus

_____ (grand) joies de sa vie.

10. Il a perdu l'espoir d'être _____ (sauvé), mais il ne

regrette rien sauf la souffrance des personnes _____
(aimé).

B. *Remplacez les tirets par le mot convenable.*

1. Louise est la meilleure pianiste _____ groupe.

2. Paul dispose-t-il de plus de temps _____ vous ?

3. Nous avons moins _____ trois heures à passer à Dijon.

4. Je ne suis pas _____ riche que mon partenaire.

5. La Russie est-elle plus grande _____ le Canada ?

6. Le chinois est une des langues les plus difficiles _____ monde.

7. Monsieur Blanc a perdu plus _____ la moitié de sa fortune à la bourse.

C. *Remplacez l'adjectif indiqué entre parenthèses par la forme convenable du comparatif ou du superlatif, selon le cas. Faites l'accord de l'adjectif.*

1. Je trouve Claire beaucoup _____ (joli) que sa sœur.

2. Les produits _____ (cher) ne sont pas toujours

   _____ (bon.)

3. Les Italiens sont un des peuples _____ (musicien) du monde.

4. Les Morel sont _____ (riche) que nous, mais sont-ils

   _____ (heureux) ?

5. Mes examens sont bien _____ (dur) que les tiens.

D. *Introduisez dans la phrase les adjectifs indiqués pour modifier le nom en italique. Faites l'accord de l'adjectif avec le nom.*

EXEMPLE: (maigre) On nous a servi un *repas*.
On nous a servi un maigre repas.

1. (merveilleux[1]) J'aimerais revoir ces *payages* de Grèce.

   _____

2. (méchant) Cet *animal* devrait être attaché.

   _____

3. (propre) Avez-vous votre *rasoir* ?

   _____

4. (public) L'*opinion* favorise ce changement.

   _____

5. (humble) Je suis votre *serviteur*, comme on disait autrefois.

   _____

---

[1]Consider this as an adjective used to adorn its noun for stylistic effect, as described in Chapter 2, §21.

6. (amer) Vous devriez goûter ce *sirop* que je prends le soir.

_____

7. (sacré) Ce *chien* ! Il aboie tout le temps.

_____

8. (vrai) Ce vieux bonhomme est un *avare*.

_____

9. (grave[1]) Demain nous discuterons cette *affaire*.

_____

10. (intéressant[1]) Cette *hypothèse* a été condamnée par l'expérience.

_____

11. (profond) Avez-vous remarqué le *malaise* qui règne dans ce pays ?

_____

_____

[1]Consider this as an adjective used to adorn its noun for stylistic effect, as described in Chapter 2, §21.

EXERCICES D'ENSEMBLE 3

A. *Complétez la seconde phrase avec l'adverbe qui correspond à l'adjectif de la première phrase.*

1. Il est patient. Il attend _____.

2. Ils sont sérieux. Ils travaillent _____.

3. Il est amoureux. Il la regarde _____.

4. Il est triste. Il se promène _____.

5. Elle est élégante. Elle s'habille _____.

6. Il est violent. Il a réagi _____.

7. Il est affreux. Il s'est conduit _____.

8. Elle est polie. Elle répond _____.

9. Il est furieux. Il s'est débattu _____.

10. Ils sont sévères. Ils jugent tout _____.

11. Il est énorme. Il mange _____.

12. Ils sont attentifs. Ils écoutent _____.

B. *Introduisez dans les phrases suivantes les adverbes entre parenthèses.*

1. (beaucoup) Nous nous sommes amusés à cette soirée.

   _____

2. (mal) Vos camarades ont compris vos intentions.

   _____

3. (encore) Guy n'a pas acheté ma vieille motocyclette.

   _____

4. (lentement) Il faut traverser ce vieux pont.

   _____

5. (évidemment) Ces travailleurs sont entrés chez nous sans passeports.

   _____

6. (hier) Il a plu toute la journée.

   _____

7. (là-bas) J'arriverai vers dix heures au plus tard.

   _____

8. (ailleurs) Allez jouer du tambour.

_____

9. (partout) Nous avons vu de belles fleurs.

_____

C. Introduisez dans les phrases suivantes les adverbes entre parenthèses.

1. (tard) Georges est-il rentré cette nuit ?

_____

2. (peut-être) Solange est allée au cinéma.

_____

3. (à peine) Pierrette a seize ans et elle veut sortir seule.

_____

4. (déjà) Avez-vous payé la note ?

_____

5. (souvent) Nous avons visité l'Italie.

_____

6. (toujours) Les alpinistes retenaient le même guide.

_____

7. (suffisamment) Avez-vous étudié la question ?

_____

8. (rarement) Mon oncle nous a donné de bons conseils.

_____

9. (récemment) Il a neigé; nous aurons un rude hiver.

_____

D. Traduisez les phrases suivantes en français. Attention aux mots en italique.

1. *Obviously* they will no longer travel in Europe.

_____

2. The doctor *always* told me to[1] take two aspirins at bedtime.

_____

_____

[1]**de**

3. *(vous)* —When will I be able to see[1] you again ? —*Never.*

_____

4. *Yesterday* we sold our car.

_____

5. Helen saw *no one* in the corridor.

_____

6. Our friends don't often watch television[2] and we don't *either.*

_____

7. I looked for[3] a long time but I found *nothing.*

_____

8. There are *only* twelve pupils in the class.

_____

----

[1]Use a form of **revoir**. [2]Use the definite article. [3]Either omit or express by **pendant**.

EXERCICES D'ENSEMBLE 4

A. *Cet exercice se rapporte à l'exercice* B *du Chapitre 4.*
L'ami de Marc est arrivé en Europe. Voici une partie d'une lettre qu'il a écrite à son ami d'Amérique. Remplacez les mots entre parenthèses par leur équivalent français. Employez la forme **tu** *pour exprimer* **you.**

1. J' _____ (*had hoped*) t'écrire plus tôt, mais je

   _____ *have been*) très occupé depuis un mois.

2. Nous _____ (*would have telephoned you*), mais

   ça _____ (*costs*) très cher.

3. La jolie fille d'un de nos amis parisiens _____ (*is getting married*[1]) au mois de juin.

4. Nous _____ (*had been planning*) d'aller à son

   mariage, mais malheureusement nous _____ (*will not be*) à Paris ce jour-là.

5. J' _____ (*would like*) te décrire les conditions économiques dans cette région assez pauvre du pays où nous

   _____ (*are*) maintenant.

6. _____ (*There is*) beaucoup de chômage, et cela

   _____ (*creates*) des problèmes.

7. Nous _____ (*know*) plusieurs hommes qui

   _____ (*have not been able*) trouver du travail depuis le commencement de l'année.

8. Ils _____ (*would have gone*) ailleurs, mais leurs

   familles _____ (*want*) rester ici.

9. Ils _____ (*have often told us*) combien ils

   _____ (*are*) mécontents.

10. L'un d'eux _____ (*asked me*) si je

    _____ (*would be able*) lui prêter de l'argent.

11. Je _____ (*told him*) que ça me

    _____ (*would be*) impossible parce que

---

[1]Use a form of **se marier.**

j'_____ (*am buying*) une voiture qui

m'_____(*is*) indispensable pour mon travail.

12. Entre nous, à la fin de ce mois j'_____ (*will have paid*) la moitié de ce que je _____ (*owe*).

B. Remplacez les infinitifs entre parenthèses par la forme convenable du verbe.

1. Quand mes parents ne _____ (être) plus là, je ne sais pas ce que je ferai.

2. Voilà un mois que vous _____ (avoir) mon livre. Pouvez-vous me le rendre ?

3. Quel sale temps ! Il _____ (pleuvoir) depuis ce matin.

4. Nous _____ (préparer) un excellent dîner quand les invités ont téléphoné qu'ils ne pouvaient pas venir.

5. Georges _____ (aller) obtenir son diplôme quand il est tombé malade.

6. Je garderai cette grammaire quand j' _____ (finir) mon cours.

7. Si tu _____ (épouser) cette jeune fille, tes parents seraient très heureux.

8. J'ai toujours pensé que cela _____ (finir) mal.

9. Dès que je _____ (apprendre) cela, je suis parti.

10. Donnez-moi la main si vous _____ (avoir) peur.

11. Encore un mot et je _____ (s'en aller).

12. Quand vous _____ (écrire) à Suzanne, faites-lui mes amitiés.

13. Si j'avais su, évidemment, j'_____ (agir) tout autrement.

14. Quand ces jeunes gens _____ (partir), je vous montrerai quelque chose d'intéressant.

C. Dans les deux devoirs qui suivent, traduisez chaque phrase en faisant très attention aux temps des verbes.

1. I must hurry; I am leaving this evening.

2. I wrote our friends[1] that we would go to see them Sunday.

_____

3. Our neighbors had already washed the car when it began to rain.

_____

4. (*tu*) Tell me what Anne says[2] to you as soon as you have seen her.

_____

5. (*vous*) If you were willing to see Gilbert, he would be very happy.

_____

6. Thomas has been studying Russian for two years, but he doesn't know it very well.

_____

7. Alfred will be horrified when he learns what has happened.

_____

8. If Janine had understood me, things[3] would have been very different.

_____

9. (*vous*) I'll talk to her only if you come with me.

_____

D.

1. As soon as Mary had won the contest, she left for Paris.

_____

2. (*vous*) Did you tell Louise that we would not be home tomorrow ?

_____

3. I'll speak to the boss about that matter as soon as I see him.

_____

4. We had finished our meal when we heard the newscast.

_____

5. I will travel when I have saved enough[4].

_____

---

[1]This is an indirect object. [2]Does this verb express something happening now or something that will happen ? [3]Use the definite article. [4]*save enough* **faire assez d'économies**

6. If the weather[1] is good, I always take a walk.

   _____

7. (*tu*) What are you doing tonight ?

   _____

8. When George realized that he was wrong, he changed his mind

   _____

9. (*tu*) When you speak to him, be very polite.

   _____

---

[1]Use an idiomatic expression with **faire**.

EXERCICES D'ENSEMBLE 5

A. *Les pronoms compléments entre parenthèses sont en ordre alpha-*
   bétique. L'ordre est parfois juste, parfois faux. Mettez les pronoms
   dans l'ordre convenable, en changeant l'ordre quand c'est nécessaire.

1. Voilà les renseignements que j'ai obtenus. Donnez-_____ (les, lui).

2. Vous avez acheté un nouveau jeu vidéo. Montrez- _____ (le, moi).

3. Je ne sais pas où est cette rue. L'agent _____ (le, me) dira.

4. Ce crime est révoltant. Ne _____ (le, nous) racontez pas.

5. J'aimerais savoir où ils sont allés. Je _____ (le, leur) demanderai
   demain.

6. Nous aurons besoin de ces deux documents. Paul _____ (les, nous)
   rapportera la semaine prochaine.

7. Ils connaissent le règlement. Je ne _____ (le, leur) répéterai pas.

8. Ce paquet est trop lourd. Il est impossible de _____ (le, lui) envoyer
   par la poste.

9. Vous avez appris son secret. Dites- _____ (le, nous).

10. Vous avez vu mes timbres. Si vous en faites une collection, vous
    n'avez pas besoin de _____ (les, me) rendre.

11. Voilà les disques que j'ai promis à Michel. Il _____ (en, lui) faut six
    pour sa soirée.

B. *Remplacez les tirets par le pronom qui convient au sens.*

1. Nicole a acheté un cadeau pour _____ hier et elle me l'a offert ce
   matin.

2. Marie est fâchée contre son mari et elle refuse de _____ parler.

3. Cet acte aura de graves conséquences; il faut _____ penser.

4. —Avez-vous un cendrier ? —Bien sûr, j' _____ ai plusieurs.

5. —Vous intéressez-vous à l'art moderne ? —Oui, nous nous _____
   intéressons beaucoup.

6. Ce sont des ingrats. Tâchez de ne plus penser à _____ .

7. L'agent vous fait signe de vous arrêter. Vous feriez bien de _____
   obéir.

8. Ma femme voudrait aller à l'opéra. Mais _____ , je ne tiens pas à _____ aller.

9. Tu as reçu une lettre importante l'autre jour. Il faut _____ répondre tout de suite.

10. Avez-vous besoin de papier à lettre ? Je viens d' _____ acheter.

11. Vous connaissez Marc et Christophe ? C'est _____ qui sont dans la pièce à côté.

C. Traduisez les phrases suivantes, en faisant bien attention à la position et à l'ordre des pronoms compléments.

1. (*vous*) These books are too heavy. Don't take[1] them to them.

   _____

2. (*vous*) Tell them what happened to you.

   _____

3. Who will get[2] the first prize ? —I.

   _____

4. (*tu*) Do you like tea ? Yes, I prefer it to coffee.

   _____

5. (*vous*) You have only one car; we must have two.

   _____

6. (*tu*) Can you do this problem yourself ?

   _____

7. Helen is my best friend. I speak of her with pleasure.

   _____

8. They[3] are the ones who gave us this picture.

   _____

9. —Are there many pupils in this class ? —Yes, there are many.

   _____

10. (*tu*) Do you remember them ?

   _____

---

[1]Use a form of **apporter**.   [2]Use a form of **avoir**.   [3]lit. : *It is they...*

D. *Traduisez les phrases suivantes, en faisant bien attention à la place et à l'ordre des pronoms compléments.*

1. They too[1] can leave now.

---

2. His brother is not as ambitious as he.

---

3. (*tu*) Do you want to go to[2] Europe with me ?

---

4. Since they are late, let's leave without them.

---

5. (*vous*) Are you going to[2] France, or are you coming back from there ?

---

6. (*vous*) You and I agree on this point.

---

7. (*vous*) You like exotic countries, but do you go there from time to time ?

---

8. (*vous*) They want to know the truth; tell it to them.

---

9. They should[3] be here, but I do not see them.

---

10. *He* can do that, not I.

---

[1]Put *too* in this place in the sentence.   [2]**en**   [3]Use a form of **devoir.**

EXERCICES D'ENSEMBLE 6

Dans le passage suivant, Georges Simenon, auteur belge d'excellents romans, créateur du célèbre Inspecteur Maigret, évoque le souvenir de son père dans son livre : De la Cave au grenier. *Dans cet exercice nous donnons l'imparfait et le passé composé de la plupart des verbes. Barrez la forme qui vous paraît incorrecte. Dans quelques cas les deux formes peuvent être employées.*

Mon père *était / a été* comptable dans un petit bureau d'assurances où il n'y *avait / a eu* que cinq employés. C'est lui qui *restait / est resté* de garde de midi à une heure et demie car les bureaux et magasins *ne fermaient pas / n'ont pas fermeé* à midi.

5   Il m' *arrivait / est arrivé* souvent d'aller voir mon père, surtout, je l'avoue[1], pour lui réclamer un peu d'argent. Je *le trouvais / l'ai trouvé* là, installé devant son travail. Nulle part ailleurs je ne *le voyais / l'ai vu* si serein. On *le sentait / l'a senti* heureux d'avoir le poids du bureau[2] sur ses épaules, comme d'avoir ce bureau pour lui seul.

10   —Assieds-toi, fils, je suis à toi dans deux minutes.

Et un peu plus tard il *me demandait / m'a demandé* sans amertume[3], comme sans ironie : « Combien ? »

Il *aimait / a aimé* le matin partir pour son bureau et y rester. *C'était / Ça a été* lui qui en *possédait / a possédé* la clé et il en *était / a été* fier. Je
15   *retrouvais / J'ai retrouvé* cette fierté, ce plaisir de travailler, même à une tâche assez ingrate, chez mon grand-père, qui *travaillait / a travaillé* encore à soixante-quinze ans.

Si j'y pense aujourd'hui, c'est qu'on lit ou qu'on entend partout que le travail est une malédiction[4]. Moi, aussi, pendant toute ma vie, j' *avais / ai*
20   *eu* quotidiennement mes heures de solitude dans mon bureau aux rideaux fermés, devant ma machine à écrire que j' *astiquais[5] / ai astiqué* avec soin et que *je huilais[6] / j'ai huilé* avant chaque roman. Certes, *c'était / ça a été* dur de garder à la fois la ligne[7] des personnages et le rythme du récit. Je *m'usais / me suis usé* à ce travail que je *ne quittais / n'ai quitté* que le jour
25   de mes soixante-dix ans. Il n'empêche que cela constitue un des meilleurs souvenirs de ma vie.

---

[1]*I confess*   [2]*responsibility of the office*   [3]*bitterness*   [4]*curse*   [5]*polished*
[6]*oiled*   [7]*continuity*

EXERCICES D'ENSEMBLE 7

A. *Cet exercice se rapporte au texte au début du Chapitre 7. Richard et Fanny sont réconciliés après la gifle reçue par Richard. Remplacez le mot entre parenthèses par son équivalent français.*

1. Richard, tenant Fanny par _____ (*her*) bras, monte avec elle au sommet du château pour se reposer après _____ (*their*) exploration.

2. Richard prend dans son sac deux sandwiches, mais _____ (*his*) est tout écrasé.

3. —Prenez _____ (*mine*), dit Fanny, cela m'est égal.

4. De là-haut, ils aperçoivent _____ (*their*) amis sur la route.

5. Richard dit que la voiture de Luc est plus belle que _____ (*his*).

6. —Peut-être, répond Fanny, mais _____ (*yours*) est plus pratique pour _____ (*your*) expéditions.

7. Fanny déclare qu'elle aurait aimé avoir _____ (*her*) photo dans le journal s'ils avaient trouvé un trésor.

8. Richard dit que s'il y a un trésor, il le partagera avec _____ (*his*) amie Fanny.

9. Il donnera une moitié de _____ (*his*) part aux paysans qui l'avaient aidé.

10. Richard et Fanny se racontent _____ (*their*) rêves d'enfance et Fanny a _____ (*her*) visage plein de larmes.

11. Quand Richard l'embrasse sur _____ (*her*) joue, elle baisse _____ (*her*) jolis yeux bleus et _____ (*their*) aventure continue.

B. *Remplacez les mots entre parenthèses par leurs équivalents français.*

1. Pourquoi est-ce que vous _____ (*are shrugging your shoulders*) ?

2. Tous les élèves _____ (*raised their hands*[1]) pour répondre à la question.

3. Donnez-lui _____ (*your arm*); ça lui fera plaisir.

4. Si _____ (*your feet hurt*), repose-toi.

---

[1]French uses the singular here.

5. L'enfant nous regardait _____ (*with his thumb*[1] *in his mouth*).

6. (*tu*) J'ai quelque chose pour toi; _____ (*close your eyes*).

7. Adèle _____ (*broke her leg*) pour la troisième fois.

C. *Traduisez en français les phrases suivantes.*

1. (*vous*) Do you have a sore throat ?

_____

2. Her hairdresser will wash her hair tomorrow.

_____

3. It's his wife who cuts his hair.

_____

4. (*tu*) You can put down your hand.

_____

5. (*vous*) You are going to hurt him if you twist[2] his arm.

_____

6. (*vous*) It is not proper to sit[3] with your legs crossed.

_____

---

[1]**pouce** *m*   [2]**tordre**   [3]**d'être assis**

EXERCICES D'ENSEMBLE 8

A. *Une famille se lève le matin. Mettez en français les mots entre parenthèses, en faisant attention à l'accord du participe passé.*

1. Nous _____ (*had all slept well*) et nous _____ (*woke up*) à sept heures.

2. Dès que nous _____ (*got up*), nous _____ (*opened*) la porte au chat, qui _____ (*had spent*) la nuit dehors.

3. Nous _____ (*washed and dressed*[1]) et je _____ (*saw*) que Thérèse _____ (*had not brushed her hair*).

4. Félix et Claude _____ (*had not washed their ears*) comme il faut.

5. Ils _____ (*told each other*) leurs projets pour la journée.

6. Félix _____ (*cut his lip*[2] *while shaving*).

7. Nous _____ (*all got dressed*) avec soin.

8. Nous _____ (*went down*) dans la salle à manger.

9. Nous _____ (*took*) le petit déjeuner ensemble.

10. Nous _____ (*made for ourselves*) des œufs au plat et du pain grillé.

11. Thérèse _____ (*entertained*[3] *us by telling us*) ses rêves.

12. A un certain moment, nous _____ (*noticed*[4]) que la pendule était arrêtée.

13. Nous _____ (*realized*[5]) que nous allions être en retard.

---

[1]*to wash and dress* **faire sa toilette**   [2]**lèvre** *f*   [3]Use a form of **amuser.**   [4]Use a form of **s'apercevoir.**   [5]*realize* **se rendre compte,** lit. : *render account to oneself.* What is the function of the reflexive pronoun in **se rendre compte** ?

14. Nous _____ (*quickly finished*) notre petit déjeuner.

15. Nous _____ (*put on*) nos manteaux et nous

_____ (*looked at ourselves*) dans la glace.

16. Nous _____ (*said goodbye to each other*) et nous

_____ (*left*), chacun allant à ses affaires.

B. *Remplacez les infinitifs par la forme convenable du participe passé.*

1. Combien de tableaux avez-vous _____ (vendre) ?

2. J'en ai _____ (vendre) trois.

3. Quels tableaux avez-vous _____ (vendre) ?

4. Les touristes japonais nous ont _____ (demander) où était le Musée de l'Industrie et nous leur avons _____ (indiquer) le chemin le plus court.

5. Simone et Monique _____ (se chercher) en vain aux Galeries Lafayette.

6. Nous _____ (s'apercevoir) que quelque chose n'allait pas.

7. Ces deux écrivains _____ (s'écrire) souvent; ils nous

_____ (laisser) une belle correspondance, mais ils

_____ (ne jamais se rencontrer).

8. Nous _____ (se rendre compte[1]) qu'il serait impossible de passer plus d'un jour à Venise.

9. Mes amis _____ (se demander[2]) ce qui allait se passer après ce scandale.

10. Est-ce que vous et Roland _____ (se servir) de la scie électrique[3] que nous vous _____ (prêter) ?

---

[1]*realized*, lit. : *rendered account to ourselves* [2]*wondered*, lit. : *asked themselves.*
What kind of object is *themselves* ? [3]*electric saw*

C. *Barrez toutes les formes incorrectes.*

1. Ça m'a amusé de les entendre *parlant / parler* de leurs aventures.

2. Les autres sont restés *discutant / à discuter / en discutant* les élections.

3. Nous étions *en train de fermer / fermant / fermants* le magasin quand nous avons entendu une explosion.

4. Toto s'est amusé *lançant / à lancer / en train de lancer* des boules de neige aux passants.

5. Paul s'est endormi *en train d'écouter / en écoutant / à écouter* une conférence peu intéressante.

6. J'ai découvert l'élève *lançant / qui lançait / à lancer* des boulettes[1] de papier.

7. Robert a la mauvaise habitude de toujours lire *en mangeant / en train de manger*.

8. J'ai passé une heure *à parcourir / en parcourant / parcourant* ce livre.

9. Voilà Bernard *sortant / qui sort / en sortant* de la pharmacie.

10. Madeleine *voyant / voyante* que tout était fini est partie *pleurant / en pleurant / qui pleurait*.

11. Nous sommes restés un bon moment *nous demandant / en nous demandant / à nous demander* ce que nous allions faire après leur départ.

---

[1]*small balls*

EXERCICES D'ENSEMBLE 9

A. Remplacez les tirets par *c'est, il est, elle est, ils sont* ou *elles sont,* selon le cas.

1. _____ important de faire cette réparation immédiatement.

2. Je me souviens assez bien de lui. _____ un ancien camarade de classe.

3. _____ difficile de comprendre ce qu'il a essayé de nous expliquer hier.

4. _____ un très gros industriel.

5. —Avez-vous confiance en votre docteur ? —Oui, _____ un excellent médecin.

6. Où est ma serviette ? — _____ là, sur la table. Vous ne la voyez pas ?

7. _____ clair que cette fois vous avez raison.

8. —Apportera-t-il son stéréo ?— _____ probable.

9. _____ toujours bon de vous revoir. Revenez bientôt.

10. _____ malade, mais il est venu quand même.

11. Allez voir mes cousins si vous avez le temps. _____ très drôles.

B. Remplacez les mots anglais entre parenthèses par l'équivalent français.

1. Pardonnez-nous nos offenses comme nous pardonnons à _____ (*those*) qui nous ont offensés.

2. _____ (*It*) est un petit arbre qui a donné tous _____ (*those*) beaux fruits.

3. Je vous présenterai mon ami. _____ (*He*) est ingénieur.

4. Ne recommencez pas à m'ennuyer avec _____ (*that*).

5. _____ (*He*) est un ancien prince russe.

6. _____ (*This*) homme de science dit qu'il pourrait créer un être humain. _____ (*It*) est extraordinaire.

7. —Je me suis trompé de route.— _____ (*It*) est évident.

8. Connaissez-vous _____ (*those*) jeunes gens ? _____ (*They*) sont très amusants.

9. Quant à Florence, _____ (*she*) est fâchée de n'avoir pas été invitée.

10. Je connais plusieurs Belges. _____ (*They*) sont tous catholiques.

11. _____ (*It*) est une triste histoire.

12. Je retrouverai _____ (*the one*) qui m'a joué _____ (*that*) tour.

13. _____ (*She*) est japonaise.

14. _____ (*The one*) que je cherche n'est pas encore arrivé.

C. *Traduisez en français.*

1. I like that song a great deal.

_____

2. (*tu*) The ones who told you that lied.

_____

3. (*vous*) You do not need two ballpoint pens; lend me that one.

_____

4. I want to speak to those who couldn't come yesterday.

_____

5. I have already seen this man somewhere, but where ?

_____

6. (*vous*) Take[1] her those flowers.

_____

7. The ones I prefer are the pink carnations[2].

_____

8. (*tu*) Don't say that; it's not polite.

_____

---

[1]Use a form of **apporter.**   [2]**œillet** *m*

EXERCICES D'ENSEMBLE 10

A. Quelques élèves parlent de leurs problèmes avec un jeune professeur de lycée après une manifestation comme celle décrite en tête de ce chapitre. Remplacez les tirets par le pronom relatif qui convient.

1. Quelquefois des élèves du lycée viennent voir le jeune professeur

   _____ leur est sympathique.

2. Ils veulent discuter _____ ils pourront faire plus tard.

3. Le professeur leur demande _____ ils pensent.

4. Mais ils ne savent pas _____ sera le mieux pour eux.

5. Il y a plusieurs possibilités _____ ils ont entendu parler.

6. Le professeur leur dit qu'il y a un conseiller spécialisé avec

   _____ ils peuvent parler d'orientation.

7. Mais les élèves croient qu'il est complice du directeur

   _____ ils n'aiment pas, ni lui ni _____ il représente.

8. La plupart d'entre eux n'acceptent pas la société dans

   _____ ils vivent.

9. Ils veulent des changements _____ ne sont pas possibles.

10. Le professeur leur dit qu'il ne connaît pas un seul pays

    _____ les choses soient parfaites.

11. Les manifestations _____ les lycéens organisent ne servent pas à grand-chose pour le moment.

12. Mais ils sont jeunes, enthousiastes, idéalistes et ils sauront bientôt

    _____ ils peuvent devenir.

B. Dans les exercices B et C, remplacez les mots anglais entre parenthèses par leur équivalent français.

1. Pouvez-vous me prêter les livres _____ (which I need) ?

2. Connaissez-vous la femme _____ (who) vient de passer ?

3. Il est parti; c'est le mois _____ (*when*) il prend ses vacances.

4. Où est la montre _____ (*which*) je vous ai achetée ?

5. Racontez-nous seulement _____ (*what*) est important.

6. Je me demande avec _____ (*what*) ils ont pu faire cela.

7. Les élèves _____ (*of whom*) vous vous plaignez ne travaillent pas assez.

8. La sonnerie _____ (*that*) vous entendez marque la fin de la classe.

C.

1. Il fait _____ (*everything that*) il veut.

2. Je vous prêterai ma voiture le jour _____ (*when*) vous aurez du travail.

3. L'homme _____ (*who*) doit venir me voir ce matin est russe.

4. C'est un ami pour _____ (*whom*) je ferais n'importe quoi.

5. Puisque vous le pouvez, prenez donc _____ (*what*) est devant vous.

6. Je ne sais pas exactement à _____ (*what*) il pense.

7. Le train dans _____ (*which*) je me trouvais a eu un accident.

8. Il vous donnera _____ (*everything*) vous demanderez.

D. Traduisez en français en faisant attention aux pronoms relatifs.

1. (*vous*) The person you are making fun of is one of my friends.

_____

2. I remember the summer when we went to Europe for the first time.

_____

3. (*vous*) What you say concerning[1] them does not surprise me.

_____

---

[1]**à leur sujet**

4. (*tu*) He is very pale. Ask him what he is suffering from.

_____

5. She left the moment[1] I entered.

_____

6. The dress with which she had[2] so much success came from Paris.

_____

7. I can't stand the noise the neighbors[3] are making.

_____

8. I like people who are optimistic.

_____

9. Those who criticize his style should try to understand him.

_____

10. What we are thinking of[4] is not important.

_____

---

[1]The French say the equivalent of the English *at the moment when.* [2]Use the **passé composé.** [3]Place this subject after its verb. [4]Not **de.**

EXERCICES D'ENSEMBLE 11

A. *Monsieur et Madame Roussel envisagent de faire un voyage pendant leurs vacances. Ils discutent plusieurs possibilités. Remplacez les infinitifs entre parenthèses par la forme convenable de l'indicatif ou du subjonctif, selon le cas.*

1. Il est temps que nous _____ (faire) un petit voyage d'agrément.

2. Nous partirons bientôt quoique ce ne _____ (être) pas la saison des vacances.

3. Je suis sûr que nous _____ (obtenir) ainsi des prix plus avantageux.

4. Il faudra que nous _____ (chercher) des brochures à l'agence de voyage tout de suite.

5. Tout ira bien pourvu que nous _____ (prendre) nos billets à l'avance.

6. Mais il est important que nous _____ (décider) bientôt où aller.

7. C'est dommage que nos amis Benoît ne _____ (pouvoir) pas venir avec nous.

8. Il me semble que nous _____ (avoir) plusieurs possibilités.

9. Nous aimerions une belle plage pourvu qu'il n'y _____ (avoir) pas trop de monde.

10. Si nous allons à l'étranger, nous trouverons bien des gens qui _____ (savoir) parler français.

11. Il vaudrait mieux que nous _____ (éviter) les grands hôtels internationaux.

12. Il se peut même que nous _____ (aller) en Amérique.

13. Je ne connais pas d'écrivains qui _____ (écrire) sur l'Amérique aussi bien que Sartre il y a quelques années.

14. Mais je crois qu'il y _____ (avoir) aussi là-bas des villes historiques telles que Boston, la Nouvelle-Orléans ou Washington qui ressemblent à nos villes européennes.

15. Il est possible que nous _____ (faire) une croisière.

16. Mais qui sait ? Il se peut que nous _____ (changer)

    d'avis et que nous (rester) _____ dans les environs.

17. Où que nous _____ (passer) nos vacances, nous aurons
    beaucoup de plaisir ensemble.

**B. Remplacez les infinitifs entre parenthèses par la forme convenable de
l'indicatif ou du subjonctif, ou bien gardez l'infinitif où il faut.**

1. Nous cherchons une maison qui _____ (être)

   climatisée et qui _____ (avoir) un grand jardin.

2. Claire craint de _____ (rentrer) seule chez elle la nuit.

3. Je vous prêterai cette somme pourvu que vous me

   _____ (promettre) de me _____
   (rembourser) dans un an.

4. Demande l'auto à ton père avant qu'il _____ (aller) se
   coucher.

5. Je sais que vous _____ (plaisanter), mais ce n'est pas le
   moment.

6. Réfléchissez donc avant de _____ (répondre) n'importe
   quoi.

7. Nos parents sont désolés que vous _____ (décider) de
   ne plus venir à nos réunions.

8. Qui que vous _____ (être), vous avez les mêmes droits
   que les autres.

9. Il faut _____ (être) bien naïf pour _____
   (croire) tout ce qu'il raconte.

C. Traduisez en français.

1. It is true that we are sometimes too demanding[1] toward[2] others[3].

   _____

2. (*vous*) Do you know someone who can repair my television right
   away ?

   _____

---

[1]**exigeant** [2]For how to express *toward*, see page 262, §24. [3]**les autres**

3. (*tu*) Madame Lesage is glad that you promised to come to her evening party.

_____

_____

4. (*vous*) I don't find that you are making a great deal of progress.

_____

5. They questioned the suspect until he confessed his crime.

_____

6. (*tu*) I believe that this new novel will interest you, but I do not believe that you can read it in[1] two hours.

_____

_____

7. The boss wants everyone to be at the office at eight o'clock.

_____

8. (*vous*) However busy you may be, give[2] some time[3] to your family.

_____

9. My lawyer wants his oldest daughter to be an[4] architect.

_____

10. (*tu*) It is evident that you are sick and it is important that you go see the doctor.

_____

_____

D. *Traduisez en français.*

1. Are they the only persons who can really save the country ?

_____

2. (*vous*) It is important for you not to say a word about[5] that affair.

_____

---

[1]**en** [2]Use a form of **consacrer**. [3]*some time* **quelques heures** [4]Omit in translation. [5]**sur**

3. Whatever her reasons are, she did not explain them.

_____

4. I'll go to see him next week unless he writes me not[1] to come.

_____

5. I believe that it will soon be necessary to buy a new air conditioner[2].

_____

6. (*tu*) I am giving you this ring so that you will remember me.

_____

7. It is probable that we will not come back before Christmas.

_____

8. I am glad that Michael has arrived but I am sorry that I will not have time[3] to see him.

_____

_____

9. (*vous*) Think[4] before you[5] speak.

_____

10. The children are sorry that they were so nasty[6] this afternoon.

_____

11. His uncle will take him to Paris on the condition that he pass his examination.

_____

_____

---

[1]**de ne pas** [2]**climatiseur** *m* [3]Supply the definite article. [4]Use a form of **réfléchir**. [5]This *you* represents the same subject as in the imperative *think*. [6]**désagréable**

EXERCICES D'ENSEMBLE 12

A. *Voici quelques détails sur le chansonnier-poète Georges Brassens, dont l'interview ouvre le Chapitre 12. Remplacez les tirets par l'équivalent français des mots entre parenthèses.*

1. Georges Brassens est né _____ (*on October 22, 1921*) _____ (*in Sète*), _____ (*a little town*) située au bord de la Méditerranée.

2. Il y fait toujours bon, même _____ (*in winter*).

3. Son père était _____ (*a mason*).

4. Sa mère était née _____ (*at Naples*), _____ (*in Italy*).

5. Tous aimaient _____ (*music*) dans sa famille et chantaient _____ (*night and day*).

6. Il était _____ (*a Catholic*) comme ses parents mais il est vite devenu _____ (*an agnostic*).

7. _____ (*Sunday*) était un jour de fête pour lui comme les autres jours de la semaine.

8. Venu _____ (*to Paris*) en 1939, il a habité longtemps une petite chambre _____ (*on Florimont Street*).

9. Il ne dormait que cinq heures _____ (*per night*) et il pouvait travailler douze heures _____ (*per day*).

10. Il aimait sa famille, naturellement, les amis, _____ (*good wine*), _____ (*cats*), _____ (*birds*).

11. C'était _____ (*an individualist*) qui voulait _____ (*freedom*) avant tout pour le bonheur de tous.

B. *Remplacez les tirets des phrases dans les devoirs B, C et D par l'article défini ou indéfini où un article est nécessaire. Expliquez oralement votre choix.*

1. Depuis quand apprends-tu _____ chimie ?

2. Veux-tu aller _____ voiture ou _____ moto ?

3. _____ dimanche est un jour de fête.

4. Je te verrai _____ mardi, _____ 2 février.

5. Fait-il très froid en _____ hiver ?

6. Bien que je préfère _____ français, je dois apprendre _____ allemand.

7. Tout le monde cherche _____ bonheur.

8. Mme Lebeau, avocate à Bordeaux, fera un voyage en _____ Afrique du Nord.

9. En _____ absence de ses parents, Simone a reçu plusieurs amis.

10. J'ai vu _____ Mme Delaunay dans la rue ce matin.

C.

1. Aimez-vous mieux _____ chats ou _____ chiens ?

2. Parlez-vous _____ espagnol ou _____ portugais ?

3. _____ vie n'est pas toujours agréable, mais elle est toujours supportable.

4. Camus, _____ célèbre romancier, est mort dans un accident d'auto.

5. Christophe, _____ étudiant en _____ médecine depuis le mois d'octobre, passera ses vacances à _____ Québec.

6. Connaissez-vous _____ Lieutenant Beauchamp ?

7. Ma femme a _____ rendez-vous avec _____ Docteur Perrot à cinq heures.

8. _____ Pologne et _____ Roumanie sont dans l'est de _____ Europe.

9. Nous avons marché le long de _____ rue de Seine.

10. Comment dit-on « non » en _____ russe ?

D.

1. —Quand serez-vous de retour, _____ docteur ?

2. Nous avons passé trois jours à _____ Montréal et deux jours à _____ Nouvelle-Orléans.

3. Il faut voir _____ Boulevard des Capucines et _____ Avenue Matignon après six heures du soir.

4. Mlle Mandel est _____ psychiatre; elle a étudié pendant cinq ans

   à _____ Vienne.

5. Trouvez-vous que M. Cumin est _____ bon professeur ?

6. _____ enfants peuvent être très gentils quand ils le veulent.

7. Marc va toujours au cinéma _____ samedi.

8. C'est aujourd'hui _____ 30 octobre.

9. Florence a commencé _____ école _____ automne dernier.

E. *Remplacez les mots entre parenthèses par l'équivalent français. Faites attention à l'emploi de l'article et des prépositions.*

1. Venez-vous _____ (*from*) Danemark ou _____ (*from*) Suède ?

2. Nous avons passé quatre jours _____ (*in*) Baton Rouge.

3. Je suis _____ (*in*) Lyon pour le week-end mais je vais _____ (*to*) Marseille demain.

4. Nous avons trouvé ce collier dans une bijouterie _____ (*in*) rue de la Paix.

5. Il est défendu de faire plus de cent vingt kilomètres _____ (*per*) heure sur cette route.

6. Vous verrez la statue _____ (*in the*) place de la Sorbonne.

7. Combien gagnez-vous _____ (*per*) heure ?

8. Combien d'heures _____ (*per*) jour travaillez-vous ?

9. L'essence coûte dix francs _____ (*per*) litre.

10. Avez-vous voyagé _____ (*by*) autobus, _____ (*by*) train ou

    _____ (*by*) avion ?

EXERCICES D'ENSEMBLE 13

A. *Félix est allé voir un opéra avec Francine. Il raconte ce qui s'est passé. Remplacez les expressions entre parenthèses par leur équivalent français.*

1. J'avais demandé à Francine de m'accompagner à l'opéra et elle avait

   accepté _____ (*with pleasure*).

2. Nous avons passé _____ (*long hours*) à étudier le livret.

3. Elle _____ (*had a headache*), mais nous sommes partis quand même.

4. Nous avons trouvé nos places _____ (*without difficulty*).

5. La salle était complètement remplie _____ (*with¹ spectators*).

6. Nous avons rarement entendu _____ (*music*) aussi mélodieuse.

7. La cantatrice portait _____ (*beautiful costumes of velvet and of silk*).

8. Je crois que le ténor _____ (*had a sore throat*).

9. Le chef d'orchestre dirigeait avec _____ . (*elegance*).

10. Le chœur était composé _____ (*of young people*).

11. Nous avons aimé surtout le ballet exécuté par

    _____ (*some excellent dancers²*).

12. A l'entracte nous sommes allés au foyer, car Francine

    _____ (*was thirsty*) et nous avons bu

    _____ (*some champagne*).

13. Il y avait aussi _____ (*some coca cola*) et

    _____ (*some fruit juices*), mais elle a préféré

    _____ (*a glass of champagne*).

----

¹Not « avec »   ²**danseuses**

14. Il y avait _____ (*a lot of people*[1]) au bar et j'y ai

reconnu _____ (*some old acquaintances*[2]).

15. Je regrette de ne pas avoir _____ (*more time*) pour

aller à l'opéra, mais j'ai _____ (*a great deal of work*).

16. Je suis pourtant entouré _____ (*by people*[3]) qui apprécient la musique.

17. En tout cas, ce soir-là tout était parfait et nous sommes partis

_____ (*with regret*).

B. Remplacez les tirets par de ou par l'article partitif dans les phrases où il faut avoir l'un ou l'autre.

1. Invitez _____ gens amusants à dîner.

2. Ce ne sont pas _____ Japonais, ce sont _____ Chinois.

3. Il faut apprendre le plus tôt possible à se débrouiller sans _____ argent.

4. Si vous voulez faire plaisir à votre femme, achetez-lui un manteau _____ fourrure.

5. Vous avez _____ courage pour parler si franchement.

6. A l'université on ne veut pas _____ professeurs sans _____ doctorat.

7. Il y a bien _____ gens qui aimeraient avoir sa place.

8. Nous avons passé _____ longues heures à Notre-Dame.

9. Il y a beaucoup _____ choses intéressantes à voir quand on voyage.

10. Nous manquons _____ sucre.

11. Je connais _____ jeunes gens qui sont vraiment formidables.

12. Certains auteurs écrivent avec _____ facilité, mais moi, j'écris avec _____ peine.

13. Allez donc dans ce café; on y sert _____ bon vin.

---

[1]**monde** [2]**connaissances** [3]**gens**

C. *Traduisez en français.*

1. One sees a lot of men without hats.

_____

2. There are some valuable pictures in that house.

_____

3. (*vous*) I learned with regret that you will no longer be with us.

_____

4. There are elegant[1] hotels in all the large cities.

_____

5. (*tu*) If you need money, you have only to tell me[2].

_____

_____

6. The majority of the pilots are young.

_____

7. There are still some poor areas where there are no schools.

_____

8. (*vous*) If you have neither pencil nor paper, you can return home.

_____

9. These aren't amateurs; they are true artists.

_____

10. I have just bought a beautiful leather suitcase for my trip.

_____

11. There is enough room in the car for everyone.

_____

---

[1]First write the sentence with **élégant** following its noun; then write it with **élégant** preceding its noun.   [2]French often says *tell me it*.

Exercices d'Ensemble 14

A. *Répondez aux phrases suivantes en vous servant du nom donné après la question et en employant la forme passive.*

> Exemple: Qui a annoncé la nouvelle ? M. Lemaître.
> **La nouvelle a été annoncée par M. Lemaître.**

1. Qui chantera l'hymne national ? Mme Robin, de l'Opéra.

_____

2. Qui vend ces terrains ? Mon frère.

_____

3. Qui a blessé cet homme ? Le patron du café.

_____

4. Qui a attaqué cette ville ? Un group de rebelles.

_____

5. Qui invitera les étudiants après la cérémonie ? Le doyen[1].

_____

6. Qui avait repeint cet appartement ? Le propriétaire lui-même.

_____

7. Qui explorait alors ces territoires ? Les Français.

_____

8. Qui a mené Lucie à la gare ? Henri.

_____

9. Qui a recommandé ce remède ? Le docteur Cler.

_____

10. Qui a écrit cette lettre ? Mon avocat.

_____

_____

[1]dean

B. Un dîner chez les Pauvert, raconté par un invité. Mettez les phrases à la forme passive.

1. Les Pauvert m'ont invité à dîner jeudi dernier.

   _____

2. Des artistes bien connus avaient décoré leur nouvel appartement.

   _____

3. D'abord on nous a servi un excellent sherry.

   _____

4. Monsieur Pauvert avait interdit cigares[1] et cigarettes.

   _____

5. La maîtresse de maison a placé les convives.

   _____

6. Maître Ballard a mis à profit l'occasion pour parler de sa campagne politique.

   _____

   _____

7. Des sourires ont accueilli ses proclamations.

   _____

8. Madame Pauvert avait mis un superbe bouquet de fleurs exotiques sur la table.

   _____

9. La maîtresse de maison avait préparé elle-même le faisan[2] à la royale.

   _____

10. La cuisinière avait cueilli des asperges délicieuses dans le jardin.

    _____

11. Le meilleur pâtissier de la ville avait fait le soufflé au cognac.

    _____

12. Deux garçons en smoking servaient les plats.

    _____

---

[1]In an enumeration of two or more nouns, the nouns are sometimes used without any article. [2]*pheasant*

13. Des vins fins accompagnaient tous les plats.

_____

14. Après le dîner le célèbre acteur Joubert a lu des poèmes.

_____

15. Ensuite des jeunes gens ont joué quelques morceaux de musique.

_____

16. Les invités évoqueront souvent cette belle soirée.

_____

**C. _Les phrases suivantes indiquent que le sujet accomplit une action._
Changez-les de sorte que le sujet fasse accomplir cette action.**

1. Nos voisins peindront leur maison en rouge vif.

_____

2. Suzanne a cueilli les plus belles fleurs pour son salon.

_____

3. Jacques lavait sa voiture quand elle était vraiment sale.

_____

4. Denise a fait une très jolie robe pour le mariage.

_____

5. Je traduirai cette lettre.

_____

6. Vous pouvez ouvrir le coffre-fort.[1]

_____

7. Il faudra tondre la pelouse aujourd'hui.

_____

8. Nous enverrons le colis par exprès.

_____

---

[1]*safe*

D. Le chef du personnel d'un magasin interroge un employé qui ne lui donne pas satisfaction. Remplacez les expressions anglaises entre parenthèses par leurs équivalents français.

1. Je m'excuse _____ (*for[1] having made you wait*).

2. Je _____ (*had you come*) dans mon bureau pour parler de votre travail.

3. Vous n'êtes pas sérieux, vous _____ (*always make your co-workers[2] laugh*).

4. Ils vous écoutent et vous _____ (*make them[3] make*) des erreurs.

5. Vous ne faites pas vos propres comptes, vous

   _____ (*have them done*) par Marie Laforêt.

6. Des clients se sont plaints; je veux _____ (*to have you read*) leurs lettres.

7. Je dois _____ (*have you write*) une lettre d'excuse à chacun.

8. J'espère que je _____ (*am making you understand*) qu'il faut changer vos façons de faire.

9. Sinon, je serai obligé de _____ (*have you discharged[4]*) par le directeur.

10. Voilà. Je voudrais _____ (*to have you think[5] it over*). Bonne journée quand même.

---

[1]**de** [2]**collègues** [3]The direct object of the sentence is **des erreurs**. Therefore, what kind of an object will *them* be in French ? [4]*discharge* **renvoyer** [5]*think it over* **réfléchir**

EXERCICES D'ENSEMBLE 15

A. Un agent d'assurances, Monsieur Boyer, vient voir Monsieur Roussel, qui veut mettre ses affaires en ordre. Remplacez les expressions entre parenthèses par la forme convenable du verbe devoir.

1. M. BOYER : Il _____ (*must be*) trois heures. Excusez-moi d'être en retard.

2. M. ROUSSEL : Cela ne fait rien. D'ailleurs, ma femme n'est pas rentrée.

   Elle _____ (*must have*) être retenue à son club.

3. M. BOYER : Nous pourrons discuter, mais vous _____ (*will have to*) lui faire signer les papiers.

4. M. ROUSSEL : Je _____ (*must*) dire que

   j'_____ (*should have*) m'occuper de ces affaires plus tôt.

5. M. BOYER : Vous _____ (*should*) aussi augmenter votre assurance sur la vie.

6. M. BOYER : Et êtes-vous assuré pour le voyage que vous

   _____ (*are to*) faire au Canada ?

7. M. BOYER : Voilà. Vous ne _____ (*should*) avoir aucune difficulté pour la signature de votre femme.

8. M. ROUSSEL : Elle _____ (*should have*) être rentrée à cette heure.

9. M. ROUSSEL : Voulez-vous un chèque pour ce que je vous

   _____ (*owe*) ?

10. M. BOYER : Non, mais vous _____ (*should*) l'envoyer à la compagnie avant la fin du mois.

11. M. ROUSSEL : Ce _____ (*must*) être bien intéressant d'être agent d'assurances.

12. M. BOYER : Oui, assez, mais j'_____ (*should have*) faire mes études de droit.

B. Remplacez par la forme convenable de devoir les mots anglais entre parenthèses.

1. Nous _____ (*had to*) prendre l'autocar pour aller à Paris hier.

2. Même si cela vous ennuie, vous _____ (*must*) leur faire cette visite.

3. Les acteurs _____ (*must have been*) furieux chaque fois qu'ils lisaient les critiques de M. Lafont.

4. Georges _____ (*has to*) finir cette affaire avant de partir.

5. Maurice est seul; nous _____ (*should have*) l'inviter pour dimanche.

6. Je _____ (*am to*) passer mon examen aujourd'hui.

7. Madame Gervaise est toute pâle, elle _____ (*must*) être malade.

8. François _____ (*must have*) perdre sa montre, il n'en porte plus.

9. Les Gaspard _____ (*were to*) arriver ce matin; je me demande pourquoi ils ne sont pas là.

10. Vous _____ (*should*) acheter une nouvelle voiture.

11. Le gardien _____ (*had to*) nous ouvrir la porte chaque fois que nous arrivions tard dans la nuit.

C. Traduisez en français les phrases suivantes, en employant dans chaque phrase une forme du verbe devoir.

1. (*vous*) You *should* always *knock* before entering a room[1].

_____

2. Mrs. Henriot was always very elegant; her husband *must have spent* a lot of money on[2] her.

_____

3. The visitors *must* not *touch* the paintings.

_____

_____

[1]**pièce** [2]**pour**

4. We *had to hand in* our papers[1] yesterday morning.

_____

5. Hubert *was to write* me every day, but I have received only one letter from him.

_____

6. George doesn't have any money; he *must have spent* it last week.

_____

7. Our neighbors have a new boat; they *must be* rich.

_____

8. My friends are late; they *should have taken* a taxi.

_____

9. We *are to eat dinner* at grandmother's today.

_____

10. When I was young, I *used to have to get up* at six in[2] the morning.

_____

_____

[1]Not « papier »   [2]**du**

EXERCICES D'ENSEMBLE 16

A. *Une actrice connue vient jouer une comédie dans votre ville. Le rédacteur du journal lui demande une interview et envoie un jeune rédacteur qui fait de son mieux. Remplacez les tirets par la préposition convenable si une préposition est nécessaire. Quelques tirets doivent être remplacés par une préposition et l'article défini.*

1. Où avez-vous appris _____ devenir actrice ?

2. Auriez-vous préféré _____ jouer une tragédie ?

3. Quand avez-vous commencé _____ faire du théâtre ?

4. Avez-vous peur _____ entrer en scène ?

5. Vous est-il arrivé de rire _____ vos camarades sur la scène ?

6. Aimez-vous _____ changer souvent _____ rôle ?

7. Est-il difficile _____ prendre une nouvelle personnalité avec chaque nouvelle pièce ?

8. Avez-vous réussi _____ obtenir les rôles que vous désirez ?

9. Vous habituez-vous _____ passer d'une ville à l'autre ?

10. Avez-vous essayé _____ faire du cinéma ?

11. Est-ce que vous regrettez _____ avoir choisi cette carrière ?

12. Conseilleriez-vous _____ des jeunes gens _____ entreprendre une carrière dans le théâtre ?

13. Vous intéressez-vous _____ d'autres choses ?

14. Vous occupez-vous _____ œuvres de charité ?

15. Dans quel pays préférez-vous _____ vivre ?

16. Pourquoi avez-vous cessé _____ sortir avec le fils du sénateur Lemaître ?

17. Pensez-vous _____ épouser Alain Duval, votre partenaire dans cette comédie ?

18. Comptez-vous _____ revenir cette année ?

19. J'espère _____ ne pas vous avoir posé des questions indiscrètes. Bonne soirée.

Dans les trois devoirs suivants, remplacez les tirets par la préposition convenable si une préposition est nécessaire. Quelques tirets doivent être remplacés par une préposition et l'article défini, ou par l'article défini tout seul.

B.

1. Écoutez-moi _____ vous fâcher.

2. Le Grand Bazar importe beaucoup de beaux objets _____ Canada.

3. Laure espère _____ être nommée vice-présidente de la compagnie cette année.

4. Jules est trop âgé _____ conduire un camion[1].

5. Chacun de nos enfants joue _____ la guitare.

6. Il faut que je téléphone _____ fleuriste _____ envoyer des roses à

   Madame Darmoy _____ la remercier _____ son dîner.

7. _____ Belgique on parle deux langues : le français et le flamand.

8. Nous ne savons pas qui a essayé _____ pénétrer chez nous pendant notre absence.

9. Je ne peux pas _____ régler cette affaire avant de partir.

10. Le patron a dit _____ Thomas _____ ne plus être en retard s'il veut _____ garder sa place.

11. Je pense _____ ma tante Julie. N'oublie pas _____ 'inviter pour Pâques cette année.

C.

1. Gilbert a décidé _____ abandonner sa profession et _____ apprendre la mécanique.

2. Il est impossible _____ travailler avec tout ce bruit.

3. Philippe sera en retard. Son sous-sol[2] est plein d'eau et il doit

   _____ attendre _____ le plombier.

4. Des millions de gens dans le monde voudraient _____ vivre

   _____ États-Unis.

5. Monsieur Laroche a des ennuis parce qu'il refuse _____ payer une partie de ses impôts.

---

[1]*truck* [2]*basement*

6. Tu as vu comme ce petit ressemble _____ son père ?

7. Il faut de la patience _____ élever les enfants.

8. Le soleil brille presque toute l'année _____ Afrique du Nord.

9. C'est malheureux mais Paul ne s'intéresse _____ rien.

10. Presque tout le monde écoute _____ la radio en conduisant.

11. Les clients de Maître Gagnon ne veulent pas _____ suivre ses conseils. C'est difficile _____ comprendre.

D.

1. Ne sois pas si timide, invite Simone ou Monique _____ danser, elles seraient ravies.

2. Christiane est assez grande _____ sortir avec qui elle veut.

3. Roger s'est marié _____ Phyllis il y a un an et ils ont déjà un beau bébé.

4. On peut s'étonner _____ voir le nombre de gens qui fréquentent toujours des restaurants aussi chers.

5. _____ Texas il y a des ranches immenses et de vastes gisements de pétrole.

6. Le petit Gervais est revenu _____ Égypte enchanté par son voyage.

7. Demande _____ ton frère _____ t'aider.

8. Ce week-end nous aiderons les voisins _____ déménager.

9. Cet élève est ennuyeux, il demande toujours _____ sortir.

10. Ne manquez pas d'aller au carnaval si vous vous trouvez _____ Nouvelle-Orléans au Mardi gras.

11. Nous préférons _____ prendre nos vacances en juin ou en septembre.

EXERCICES D'ENSEMBLE 17

A. *Un professeur de province venu passer quelque temps à Paris parle de son dernier jour dans la capitale. Remplacez le mot ou l'expression en anglais par son équivalent français.*

1. J'étais à Paris _____ (*for*) deux semaines et c'était mon dernier jour.

2. _____ (*After*) un très bon déjeuner place de la Sorbonne, j'ai quitté mes amis _____ (*except*) Bernard, qui m'a accompagné.

3. _____ (*Because*) c'était mon dernier jour à Paris, je voulais aller voir mon libraire.

4. _____ (*As*) il pleuvait, c'était un bon jour pour cela.

5. Il était _____ (*about*) trois heures de l'après-midi.

6. _____ (*I went across*) la place pour entrer dans la librairie, qui est _____ (*on*) l'autre côté.

7. _____ (*Since*) mon enfance je m'intéresse aux livres.

8. _____ (*Because*) de ma profession, je me tiens au courant de ce qui se publie chaque mois.

9. _____ (*For*) quarante ans le libraire habite avec sa famille _____ (*above*) sa boutique.

10. _____ (*As*) libraire on ne trouve pas son pareil.

11. Il y avait des ouvrages _____ (*on*) tout ce qu'on peut imaginer.

12. Dans un coin sur des rayons, _____ (*about fifty*) de livres étaient couverts de poussière.

13. Le libraire m'a expliqué qu'il s'agissait d'un lot de livres _____ (*up to*) alors invendables.

14. _____ (*In spite of*) la difficulté il venait de penser à un système ingénieux pour s'en débarrasser.

15. Il m'a aussi montré quelques livres qui étaient, _____ (*according to*) lui, très anciens.

16. _____ (*As*) le temps passait, d'assez nombreux acheteurs entraient et sortaient, des étudiants surtout,

_____ (*for*) la librairie est au Quartier latin.

17. Je suis parti juste _____ (*before*) il ferme son magasin.

18. Il ne pleuvait plus et _____ (*I went down*) le boulevard Saint-Michel.

19. Je me suis promené _____ (*along*) des quais où les bouquinistes[1] ont encore des occasions intéressantes.

B. *Remplacez les mots anglais entre parenthèses par l'équivalent français.*

1. Nous ne pourrons pas finir votre livre _____ (*until*) demain.

2. Nous ne pourrons pas finir votre livre _____ (*until*) vous partiez.

3. La femme de ménage a nettoyé la maison hier _____ (*but*) avec cette pluie tout est sale de nouveau.

4. La femme de ménage a tout nettoyé _____ (*but*) la chambre des garçons.

5. Rentrez _____ (*before it rains*).

6. Rentrez _____ (*before midnight*).

7. _____ (*As a doctor*) Georges n'est pas très compétent.

8. _____ (*As it is snowing*), restons à la maison.

9. Je vous verrai _____ (*after*) le concert.

10. Je vous verrai _____ (*after*) vous aurez fini votre travail.

C. *Remplacez les mots anglais entre parenthèses par l'équivalent français.*

1. J'ai perdu la partie _____ (*because*) je n'ai pas assez réfléchi.

2. J'ai perdu la partie _____ (*because*) du bruit autour de nous.

3. Gérard restera en France _____ (*until*) la fin du mois.

[1]book vendors (usually of used books)

4. Gérard restera en France _____ (until) il ait fini ses recherches.

5. Joseph a travaillé _____ (for) il le fallait.

6. Joseph a travaillé _____ (for) sa famille.

7. Frédéric est installé chez nous _____ (since = because) ses frères sont revenus.

8. Frédéric est installé chez nous _____ (since) hier soir.

9. Frédéric est installé chez nous _____ (since) il a eu son accident.

D. Dans les devoirs D et E, sur les trois prépositions proposées, rayez celles qui ne conviennent pas au sens de la phrase.

1. *Malgré / Sauf / Suivant* les risques, les contrebandiers traversent toujours la frontière.

2. Le jeune homme *aux / avec des / des* cheveux longs vient toujours s'asseoir à la terrasse à dix heures.

3. Le Concorde vole de Londres à New York *dans / en / envers* deux heures.

4. De plus en plus, les gens veulent habiter *au-dessus de / hors de / le long de* la ville.

5. J'aime tout dans ce roman *après / sauf / selon* le dernier chapitre.

6. Où peut-on être mieux que *autour de / avec / chez* soi ?

7. Solange s'habille toujours *à la / de / sans* façon extravagante.

8. Dans ce pays, cinq habitants *dans / hors de / sur* six ne savent ni lire ni écrire.

9. Pourquoi est-ce que le bateau se dirige *dans / envers / vers* cette île ?

E.

1. Jeannot a dû faire un mauvais rêve et il est tombé *au-dessus de / dans le / du* lit.

2. Un drôle de bruit m'a réveillé à trois heures *dans le / du / le* matin.

3. Je ne pourrai jamais être à l'aéroport *avec / dans / en* deux heures.

4. Tu ne vas pas t'arrêter *avant / derrière / devant* chaque vitrine ?

5. Essaie de ne pas tousser *depuis / devant / pendant* le concert.

6. Prenez donc l'avion *au lieu de / avec / vers* l'autobus.

7. Il faut faire son chemin avec courage et *avec / sans / vers des* illusions.

8. Votre attitude *envers / sur / vers* vos collègues me semble irréprochable.

Verbs

The Organization of the French Verb

To be able to use the French verb adequately, you must know the forms of the present, imperfect, future and compound past of the indicative, the conditional, and the present and past subjunctive of each type of regular verb and of the common irregular verbs. To have a complete picture of the verb, you should also know the other compound tenses, the simple past, and the imperfect subjunctive of these verbs.

Regular verbs may be classified as follows :

1. **-er** verbs
2. **-ir** verbs which insert **-iss-** in the plural of the present, throughout the imperfect, and in the present subjunctive
3. **-ir** verbs which do not insert **-iss-** anywhere
4. **-re** verbs

In addition to these, you should know the forms of verbs in **-cevoir**, such as **recevoir**, verbs in **-aindre** and **-eindre**, such as **craindre** and **peindre**, verbs with past participles in **-ert**, such as **ouvrir**, and the following frequently used irregular verbs :

aller	**être**	**rire**
avoir	**faire**	**savoir**
boire	**falloir**	**suivre**
courir	**lire**	**tenir**
croire	**mettre**	**valoir**
devoir	**mourir**	**venir**
dire	**pouvoir**	**vivre**
écrire	**prendre**	**voir**
envoyer		**vouloir**

Once you know the forms of an irregular verb such as **prendre**, you can also handle its compounds, such as **apprendre** and **comprendre**.

Regular verbs are formed on the verb stem which is found by taking the infinitive ending from the infinitive :

INFINITIVE	STEM
1. **donn**-er	**donn-**
2. **fin**-ir	**fin-**
3. **dorm**-ir	**dorm-**
4. **perd**-re	**perd-**

333

Both types of **-ir** verbs have peculiarities.

Verbs of the type of **finir** insert an **-iss-** between the stem and the ending in the present participle, the plural forms of the present indicative, throughout the imperfect indicative, and in the present subjunctive.

Verbs of the type of **dormir** drop the last consonant of the stem before adding the endings in the singular of the present indicative.

Irregular verbs are formed on several stems.

In order to get a complete picture of the verb and thus facilitate learning it, it is helpful to know the five principal parts of the verb and also to know which tenses are formed from each of these principal parts.

Below are the five principal parts of the regular verbs and of some of the irregular verbs. The stems are in boldface type.

INFINITIVE	PRESENT PARTICIPLE	PAST PARTICIPLE	PRESENT (*SINGULAR*)	SIMPLE PAST (*SINGULAR*)
donner	**donn**ant	**donn**é	je **donn**e	je **donn**ai
finir	**finiss**ant	**fin**i	je **fin**is	je **fin**is
dormir	**dorm**ant	**dorm**i	je **dor**s	je **dorm**is
perdre	**perd**ant	**perd**u	je **perd**s	je **perd**is
recevoir	**recev**ant	**reç**u	je **reç**ois	je **reç**us
craindre	**craign**ant	**crain**t	je **crain**s	je **craign**is
ouvrir	**ouvr**ant	**ouver**t	j'**ouvr**e	j'**ouvr**is
boire	**buv**ant	**b**u	je **boi**s	je **b**us
écrire	**écriv**ant	**écri**t	j'**écri**s	j'**écriv**is
faire	**fais**ant	**fai**t	je **fai**s	je **f**is
venir	**ven**ant	**ven**u	je **vien**s	je **vin**s

There follows a list of the five principal parts of the verb along with the tenses derived from each principal part :

INFINITIVE	PRESENT PARTICIPLE	PAST PARTICIPLE	PRESENT	SIMPLE PAST
future	plural of	compound	singular of	simple past
conditional	present	past	present	imperfect
	imperfect	pluperfect		subjunctive
	indicative	indicative		
	present	future		
	subjunctive	perfect		
		past		
		conditional		
		past anterior		
		« passé		
		surcomposé »		
		past		
		subjunctive		
		pluperfect		
		subjunctive		

Here is the conjugation of the verb **boire** with the tenses arranged under the principal part from which each is derived.

INFINITIVE	PRESENT PARTICIPLE	PAST PARTICIPLE	PRESENT INDICATIVE	SIMPLE PAST
boire	**buvant**	**bu**	je **bois**	je **bus**
			tu bois	tu bus
	PLURAL OF	COMPOUND	il boit	il but
	PRESENT	PAST		nous bûmes
FUTURE	INDICATIVE	INDICATIVE		vous bûtes
je boirai	nous buvons	j'ai bu, etc.		ils burent
tu boiras	vous buvez			
il boira	ils boivent			
nous boirons		PLUPERFECT		IMPERFECT
vous boirez		INDICATIVE		SUBJUNCTIVE
ils boiront	IMPERFECT	j'avais bu, etc.		que je busse
	INDICATIVE			que tu busses
CONDITIONAL	je buvais	FUTURE PERFECT		qu'il bût
je boirais	tu buvais	j'aurai bu, etc.		que nous bussions
tu boirais	il buvait			que vous bussiez
il boirait	nous buvions	PAST CONDITIONAL		qu'ils bussent
nous boirions	vous buviez	j'aurais bu, etc.		
vous boiriez	ils buvaient			
ils boiraient		PAST ANTERIOR		
	PRESENT	j'eus bu, etc.		
	SUBJUNCTIVE			
	que je boive	PASSÉ SURCOMPOSÉ		
	que tu boives	j'ai eu bu, etc.		
	qu'il boive			
	que nous buvions	PAST SUBJUNCTIVE		
	que vous buviez	que j'aie bu, etc		
	qu'ils boivent			
		PLUPERFECT		
		SUBJUNCTIVE		
		que j'eusse bu, etc.		

The regular and the common irregular verbs are conjugated by tenses on pages 336–353. This is practical for easy reference, but the verbs will be easier to learn if you rearrange them by stems as shown in the above conjugation of the verb **boire**.

At the end of each lesson are two verbs to be reviewed. If your instructor directs you to do so, learn to write each tense under the proper principal part as above. To find the forms you do not know, consult pages 318–335.

The conjugation of the verb

INFINITIVE AND PARTICIPLES	INDICATIVE			
	PRESENT	IMPERFECT	SIMPLE PAST	FUTURE
1. -er *verbs* **parler** *(speak)* parlant parlé	parle parles parle parlons parlez parlent	parlais parlais parlait parlions parliez parlaient	parlai parlas parla parlâmes parlâtes parlèrent	parlerai parleras parlera parlerons parlerez parleront
	COMPOUND PAST	PLUPERFECT	PAST ANTERIOR	FUTURE PERFECT
	ai parlé as parlé a parlé avons parlé avez parlé ont parlé	avais parlé avais parlé avait parlé avions parlé aviez parlé avaient parlé	eus parlé eus parlé eut parlé eûmes parlé eûtes parlé eurent parlé	aurai parlé auras parlé aura parlé aurons parlé aurez parlé auront parlé
	PRESENT	IMPERFECT	SIMPLE PAST	FUTURE
2. -ir *verbs* **finir** *(finish)* finissant fini	finis finis finit finissons finissez finissent	finissais finissais finissait finissions finissiez finissaient	finis finis finit finîmes finîtes finirent	finirai finiras finira finirons finirez finiront
	COMPOUND PAST	PLUPERFECT	PAST ANTERIOR	FUTURE PERFECT
	ai fini as fini a fini avons fini avez fini ont fini	avais fini avais fini avait fini avions fini aviez fini avaient fini	eus fini eus fini eut fini eûmes fini eûtes fini eurent fini	aurai fini auras fini aura fini aurons fini aurez fini auront fini
	PRESENT	IMPERFECT	SIMPLE PAST	FUTURE
3. -re *verbs* **perdre** *(lose)* perdant perdu	perds perds perd perdons perdez perdent	perdais perdais perdait perdions perdiez perdaient	perdis perdis perdit perdîmes perdîtes perdirent	perdrai perdras perdra perdrons perdrez perdront
	COMPOUND PAST	PLUPERFECT	PAST ANTERIOR	FUTURE PERFECT
	ai perdu as perdu a perdu avons perdu avez perdu ont perdu	avais perdu avais perdu avait perdu avions perdu aviez perdu avaient perdu	eus perdu eus perdu eut perdu eûmes perdu eûtes perdu eurent perdu	aurai perdu auras perdu aura perdu aurons perdu aurez perdu auront perdu

La conjugaison du verbe

CONDITIONAL	IMPERATIVE	SUBJUNCTIVE	

PRESENT CONDITIONAL		**PRESENT**	**IMPERFECT**
parlerais		parle	parlasse
parlerais	parle	parles	parlasses
parlerait		parle	parlât
parlerions	parlons	parlions	parlassions
parleriez	parlez	parliez	parlassiez
parleraient		parlent	parlassent

PAST CONDITIONAL		**PAST**	**PLUPERFECT**
aurais parlé		aie parlé	eusse parlé
aurais parlé		aies parlé	eusses parlé
aurait parlé		ait parlé	eût parlé
aurions parlé		ayons parlé	eussions parlé
auriez parlé		ayez parlé	eussiez parlé
auraient parlé		aient parlé	eussent parlé

PRESENT CONDITIONAL		**PRESENT**	**IMPERFECT**
finirais		finisse	finisse
finirais	finis	finisses	finisses
finirait		finisse	finît
finirions	finissons	finissions	finissions
finiriez	finissez	finissiez	finissiez
finiraient		finissent	finissent

PAST CONDITIONAL		**PAST**	**PLUPERFECT**
aurais fini		aie fini	eusse fini
aurais fini		aies fini	eusses fini
aurait fini		ait fini	eût fini
aurions fini		ayons fini	eussions fini
auriez fini		ayez fini	eussiez fini
auraient fini		aient fini	eussent fini

PRESENT CONDITIONAL		**PRESENT**	**IMPERFECT**
perdrais		perde	perdisse
perdrais	perds	perdes	perdisses
perdrait		perde	perdît
perdrions	perdons	perdions	perdissions
perdriez	perdez	perdiez	perdissiez
perdraient		perdent	perdissent

PAST CONDITIONAL		**PAST**	**PLUPERFECT**
aurais perdu		aie perdu	eusse perdu
aurais perdu		aies perdu	eusses perdu
aurait perdu		ait perdu	eût perdu
aurions perdu		ayons perdu	eussions perdu
auriez perdu		ayez perdu	eussiez perdu
auraient perdu		aient perdu	eussent perdu

The conjugation of the verb

INFINITIVE AND PARTICIPLES	INDICATIVE			
	PRESENT	**IMPERFECT**	**SIMPLE PAST**	**FUTURE**
4. 2d *class* **-ir** *verbs* **dormir** (*sleep*) dormant dormi	dors dors dort dormons dormez dorment	dormais dormais dormait dormions dormiez dormaient	dormis dormis dormit dormîmes dormîtes dormirent	dormirai dormiras dormira dormirons dormirez dormiront
	COMPOUND PAST	**PLUPERFECT**	**PAST ANTERIOR**	**FUTURE PERFECT**
	ai dormi as dormi a dormi avons dormi avez dormi ont dormi	avais dormi avais dormi avait dormi avions dormi aviez dormi avaient dormi	eus dormi eus dormi eut dormi eûmes dormi eûtes dormi eurent dormi	aurai dormi auras dormi aura dormi aurons dormi aurez dormi auront dormi
	PRESENT	**IMPERFECT**	**SIMPLE PAST**	**FUTURE**
5. -oir *verbs* **recevoir** (*receive*) recevant reçu	reçois reçois reçoit recevons recevez reçoivent	recevais recevais recevait recevions receviez recevaient	reçus reçus reçut reçûmes reçûtes reçurent	recevrai recevras recevra recevrons recevrez recevront
	COMPOUND PAST	**PLUPERFECT**	**PAST ANTERIOR**	**FUTURE PERFECT**
	ai reçu as reçu a reçu avons reçu avez reçu ont reçu	avais reçu avais reçu avait reçu avions reçu aviez reçu avaient reçu	eus reçu eus reçu eut reçu eûmes reçu eûtes reçu eurent reçu	aurai reçu auras reçu aura reçu aurons reçu aurez reçu auront reçu
	PRESENT	**IMPERFECT**	**SIMPLE PAST**	**FUTURE**
6. *Intransitive verb of motion* **entrer** (*enter*) entrant entré	entre entres entre entrons entrez entrent	entrais entrais entrait entrions entriez entraient	entrai entras entra entrâmes entrâtes entrèrent	entrerai entreras entrera entrerons entrerez entreront
	COMPOUND PAST	**PLUPERFECT**	**PAST ANTERIOR**	**FUTURE PERFECT**
	suis entré(e) es entré(e) est entré(e) sommes entré(e)s êtes entré(e)(s) sont entré(e)s	étais entré(e) étais entré(e) était entré(e) étions entré(e)s étiez entré(e)(s) étaient entré(e)s	fus entré(e) fus entré(e) fut entré(e) fûmes entré(e)s fûtes entré(e)(s) furent entré(e)s	serai entré(e) seras entré(e) sera entré(e) serons entré(e)s serez entré(e)(s) seront entré(e)s

La conjugaison du verbe

CONDITIONAL	IMPERATIVE	SUBJUNCTIVE	

PRESENT CONDITIONAL		PRESENT	IMPERFECT
dormirais		dorme	dormisse
dormirais	dors	dormes	dormisses
dormirait		dorme	dormît
dormirions	dormons	dormions	dormissions
dormiriez	dormez	dormiez	dormissiez
dormiraient		dorment	dormissent

PAST CONDITIONAL		PAST		PLUPERFECT	
aurais dormi		aie dormi		eusse dormi	
aurais dormi		aies dormi		eusses dormi	
aurait dormi		ait dormi		eût dormi	
aurions dormi		ayons dormi		eussions dormi	
auriez dormi		ayez dormi		eussiez dormi	
auraient dormi		aient dormi		eussent dormi	

PRESENT CONDITIONAL		PRESENT	IMPERFECT
recevrais		reçoive	reçusse
recevrais	reçois	reçoives	reçusses
recevrait		reçoive	reçût
recevrions	recevons	recevions	reçussions
recevriez	recevez	receviez	reçussiez
recevraient		reçoivent	reçussent

PAST CONDITIONAL		PAST		PLUPERFECT	
aurais reçu		aie reçu		eusse reçu	
aurais reçu		aies reçu		eusses reçu	
aurait reçu		ait reçu		eût reçu	
aurions reçu		ayons reçu		eussions reçu	
auriez reçu		ayez reçu		eussiez reçu	
auraient reçu		aient reçu		eussent reçu	

PRESENT CONDITIONAL		PRESENT	IMPERFECT
entrerais		entre	entrasse
entrerais	entre	entres	entrasses
entrerait		entre	entrât
entrerions	entrons	entrions	entrassions
entreriez	entrez	entriez	entrassiez
entreraient		entrent	entrassent

PAST CONDITIONAL		PAST		PLUPERFECT	
serais entré(e)		sois entré(e)		fusse entré(e)	
serais entré(e)		sois entré(e)		fusses entré(e)	
serait entré(e)		soit entré(e)		fût entré(e)	
serions entré(e)s		soyons entré(e)s		fussions entré(e)s	
seriez entré(e)(s)		soyez entré(e)(s)		fussiez entré(e)(s)	
seraient entré(e)s		soient entré(e)s		fussent entré(e)s	

The conjugation of the verb

INFINITIVE AND PARTICIPLES	INDICATIVE			

	PRESENT	IMPERFECT	SIMPLE PAST	FUTURE
7. *Reflexive* *verb*	me lave	me lavais	me lavai	me laverai
	te laves	te lavais	te lavas	te laveras
	se lave	se lavait	se lava	se lavera
se laver	nous lavons	nous lavions	nous lavâmes	nous laverons
(*wash*	vous lavez	vous laviez	vous lavâtes	vous laverez
oneself)	se lavent	se lavaient	se lavèrent	se laveront
se lavant				
lavé	COMPOUND PAST	PLUPERFECT	PAST ANTERIOR	FUTURE PERFECT
	me suis lavé(e)	m'étais lavé(e)	me fus lavé(e)	me serai lavé(e)
	t'es lavé(e)	t'étais lavé(e)	te fus lavé(e)	te seras lavé(e)
	s'est lavé(e)	s'était lavé(e)	se fut lavé(e)	se sera lavé(e)
	nous	nous	nous	nous
	sommes lavé(e)s	étions lavé(e)s	fûmes lavé(e)s	serons lavé(e)s
	vous êtes lavé(e)(s)	vous étiez lavé(e)(s)	vous fûtes lavé(e)(s)	vous serez lavé(e)(s
	se sont lavé(e)s	s'étaient lavé(e)s	se furent lavé(e)s	se seront lavé(e)s

	PRESENT	IMPERFECT	SIMPLE PAST	FUTURE
8. *Auxiliary* *verb*	ai	avais	eus	aurai
	as	avais	eus	auras
	a	avait	eut	aura
avoir	avons	avions	eûmes	aurons
(*have*)	avez	aviez	eûtes	aurez
ayant	ont	avaient	eurent	auront
eu				
	COMPOUND PAST	PLUPERFECT	PAST ANTERIOR	FUTURE PERFECT
	ai eu	avais eu	eus eu	aurai eu
	as eu	avais eu	eus eu	auras eu
	a eu	avait eu	eut eu	aura eu
	avons eu	avions eu	eûmes eu	aurons eu
	avez eu	aviez eu	eûtes eu	aurez eu
	ont eu	avaient eu	eurent eu	auront eu

	PRESENT	IMPERFECT	SIMPLE PAST	FUTURE
9. *Auxiliary* *verb*	suis	étais	fus	serai
	es	étais	fus	seras
	est	était	fut	sera
être	sommes	étions	fûmes	serons
(*be*)	êtes	étiez	fûtes	serez
étant	sont	étaient	furent	seront
été				
	COMPOUND PAST	PLUPERFECT	PAST ANTERIOR	FUTURE PERFECT
	ai été	avais été	eus été	aurai été
	as été	avais été	eus été	auras été
	a été	avait été	eut été	aura été
	avons été	avions été	eûmes été	aurons été
	avez été	aviez été	eûtes été	aurez été
	ont été	avaient été	eurent été	auront été

La conjugaison du verbe

CONDITIONAL	IMPERATIVE	SUBJUNCTIVE	

PRESENT CONDITIONAL		PRESENT	IMPERFECT
me laverais		me lave	me lavasse
te laverais	lave-toi	te laves	te lavasses
se laverait		se lave	se lavât
nous laverions	lavons-nous	nous lavions	nous lavassions
vous laveriez	lavez-vous	vous laviez	vous lavassiez
se laveraient		se lavent	se lavassent

PAST CONDITIONAL		PAST	PLUPERFECT
me serais lavé(e)		me sois lavé(e)	me fusse lavé(e)
te serais lavé(e)		te sois lavé(e)	te fusses lavé(e)
se serait lavé(e)		se soit lavé(e)	se fût lavé(e)
nous		nous	nous
serions lavé(e)s		soyons lavé(e)s	fussions lavé(e)s
vous seriez lavé(e)(s)		vous soyez lavé(e)(s)	vous fussiez lavé(e)(s)
se seraient lavé(e)s		se soient lavé(e)s	se fussent lavé(e)s

PRESENT CONDITIONAL		PRESENT	IMPERFECT
aurais		aie	eusse
aurais	aie	aies	eusses
aurait		ait	eût
aurions	ayons	ayons	eussions
auriez	ayez	ayez	eussiez
auraient		aient	eussent

PAST CONDITIONAL		PAST	PLUPERFECT
aurais eu		aie eu	eusse eu
aurais eu		aies eu	eusses eu
aurait eu		ait eu	eût eu
aurions eu		ayons eu	eussions eu
auriez eu		ayez eu	eussiez eu
auraient eu		aient eu	eussent eu

PRESENT CONDITIONAL		PRESENT	IMPERFECT
serais		sois	fusse
serais	sois	sois	fusses
serait		soit	fût
serions	soyons	soyons	fussions
seriez	soyez	soyez	fussiez
seraient		soient	fussent

PAST CONDITIONAL		PAST	PLUPERFECT
aurais été		aie été	eusse été
aurais été		aies été	eusses été
aurait été		ait été	eût été
aurions été		ayons été	eussions été
auriez été		ayez été	eussiez été
auraient été		aient été	eussent été

The conjugation of the verb

INFINITIVE AND PARTICIPLES	INDICATIVE			
	PRESENT	IMPERFECT	SIMPLE PAST	COMPOUND PAST
10. **acquérir** (*acquire*) acquérant acquis	acquiers acquiers acquiert acquérons acquérez acquièrent	acquérais acquérais acquérait acquérions acquériez acquéraient	acquis acquis acquit acquîmes acquîtes acquirent	ai acquis as acquis a acquis avons acquis avez acquis ont acquis
11. **aller** (*go*) allant allé	vais vas va allons allez vont	allais allais allait allions alliez allaient	allai allas alla allâmes allâtes allèrent	suis allé(e) es allé(e) est allé(e) sommes allé(e)s êtes allé(e)(s) sont allé(e)s
12. **asseoir*** (*seat*) asseyant assis	assieds assieds assied asseyons asseyez asseyent	asseyais asseyais asseyait asseyions asseyiez asseyaient	assis assis assit assîmes assîtes assirent	me suis assis(e)* t'es assis(e) s'est assis(e) nous sommes assis(es) vous êtes assis(e)(s) se sont assis(es)
assoyant	assois assois assoit assoyons assoyez assoient	assoyais assoyais assoyait assoyions assoyiez assoyaient		
13. **battre** (*beat*) battant battu	bats bats bat battons battez battent	battais battais battait battions battiez battaient	battis battis battit battîmes battîtes battirent	ai battu as battu a battu avons battu avez battu ont battu
14. **boire** (*drink*) buvant bu	bois bois boit buvons buvez boivent	buvais buvais buvait buvions buviez buvaient	bus bus but bûmes bûtes burent	ai bu as bu a bu avons bu avez bu ont bu

* This verb is usually used in its reflexive form **s'asseoir** (*to sit*). For this reason, the reflexive forms of the compound past and imperative are given.
Certain tenses of this verb have two forms.

La conjugaison du verbe

	CONDITIONAL	IMPERATIVE	SUBJUNCTIVE	
FUTURE			PRESENT	IMPERFECT
acquerrai	acquerrais		acquière	acquisse
acquerras	acquerrais	acquiers	acquières	acquisses
acquerra	acquerrait		acquière	acquît
acquerrons	acquerrions	acquérons	acquérions	acquissions
acquerrez	acquerriez	acquérez	acquériez	acquissiez
acquerront	acquerraient		acquièrent	acquissent
irai	irais		aille	allasse
iras	irais	va	ailles	allasses
ira	irait		aille	allât
irons	irions	allons	allions	allassions
irez	iriez	allez	alliez	allassiez
iront	iraient		aillent	allassent
assiérai	assiérais		asseye	assisse
assiéras	assiérais	assieds-toi*	asseyes	assisses
assiéra	assiérait		asseye	assît
assiérons	assiérions	asseyons-nous	asseyions	assissions
assiérez	assiériez	asseyez-vous	asseyiez	assissiez
assiéront	assiéraient		asseyent	assissent
assoirai	assoirais		assoie	
assoiras	assoirais	assois-toi	assoies	
assoira	assoirait		assoie	
assoirons	assoirions	assoyons-nous	assoyions	
assoirez	assoiriez	assoyez-vous	assoyiez	
assoiront	assoiraient		assoient	
battrai	battrais		batte	battisse
battras	battrais	bats	battes	battisses
battra	battrait		batte	battît
battrons	battrions	battons	battions	battissions
battrez	battriez	battez	battiez	battissiez
battront	battraient		battent	battissent
boirai	boirais		boive	busse
boiras	boirais	bois	boives	busses
boira	boirait		boive	bût
boirons	boirions	buvons	buvions	bussions
boirez	boiriez	buvez	buviez	bussiez
boiront	boiraient		boivent	bussent

* This verb is usually used in its reflexive form **s'asseoir** (*to sit*). For this reason, the reflexive forms of the compound past and imperative are given.

The conjugation of the verb

INFINITIVE AND PARTICIPLES	INDICATIVE			
	PRESENT	IMPERFECT	SIMPLE PAST	COMPOUND PAST
15. conduire (*lead*) conduisant conduit	conduis conduis conduit conduisons conduisez conduisent	conduisais conduisais conduisait conduisions conduisiez conduisaient	conduisis conduisis conduisit conduisîmes conduisîtes conduisirent	ai conduit as conduit a conduit avons conduit avez conduit ont conduit
16. connaître (*be acquainted*) connaissant connu	connais connais connaît connaissons connaissez connaissent	connaissais connaissais connaissait connaissions connaissiez connaissaient	connus connus connut connûmes connûtes connurent	ai connu as connu a connu avons connu avez connu ont connu
17. courir (*run*) courant couru	cours cours court courons courez courent	courais courais courait courions couriez couraient	courus courus courut courûmes courûtes coururent	ai couru as couru a couru avons couru avez couru ont couru
18. craindre (*fear*) craignant craint	crains crains craint craignons craignez craignent	craignais craignais craignait craignions craigniez craignaient	craignis craignis craignit craignîmes craignîtes craignirent	ai craint as craint a craint avons craint avez craint ont craint
19. croire (*believe*) croyant cru	crois crois croit croyons croyez croient	croyais croyais croyait croyions croyiez croyaient	crus crus crut crûmes crûtes crurent	ai cru as cru a cru avons cru avez cru ont cru
20. devoir (*owe, have to*) devant dû, due*	dois dois doit devons devez doivent	devais devais devait devions deviez devaient	dus dus dut dûmes dûtes durent	ai dû as dû a dû avons dû avez dû ont dû

* The masculine singular form of the past participle is written with the circumflex accent to distinguish it from the word **du**. All other forms are written without the accent (**dû, due, dus, dues**).

La conjugaison du verbe

	CONDITIONAL	IMPERATIVE	SUBJUNCTIVE	
FUTURE			**PRESENT**	**IMPERFECT**
conduirai	conduirais		conduise	conduisisse
conduiras	conduirais	conduis	conduises	conduisisses
conduira	conduirait		conduise	conduisît
conduirons	conduirions	conduisons	conduisions	conduisissions
conduirez	conduiriez	conduisez	conduisiez	conduisissiez
conduiront	conduiraient		conduisent	conduisissent
connaîtrai	connaîtrais		connaisse	connusse
connaîtras	connaîtrais	connais	connaisses	connusses
connaîtra	connaîtrait		connaisse	connût
connaîtrons	connaîtrions	connaissons	connaissions	connussions
connaîtrez	connaîtriez	connaissez	connaissiez	connussiez
connaîtront	connaîtraient		connaissent	connussent
courrai	courrais		coure	courusse
courras	courrais	cours	coures	courusses
courra	courrait		coure	courût
courrons	courrions	courons	courions	courussions
courrez	courriez	courez	couriez	courussiez
courront	courraient		courent	courussent
craindrai	craindrais		craigne	craignisse
craindras	craindrais	crains	craignes	craignisses
craindra	craindrait		craigne	craignît
craindrons	craindrions	craignons	craignions	craignissions
craindrez	craindriez	craignez	craigniez	craignissiez
craindront	craindraient		craignent	craignissent
croirai	croirais		croie	crusse
croiras	croirais	crois	croies	crusses
croira	croirait		croie	crût
croirons	croirions	croyons	croyions	crussions
croirez	croiriez	croyez	croyiez	crussiez
croiront	croiraient		croient	crussent
devrai	devrais		doive	dusse
devras	devrais	dois	doives	dusses
devra	devrait		doive	dût
devrons	devrions	devons	devions	dussions
devrez	devriez	devez	deviez	dussiez
devront	devraient		doivent	dussent

The conjugation of the verb

INFINITIVE AND PARTICIPLES	INDICATIVE			
	PRESENT	IMPERFECT	SIMPLE PAST	COMPOUND PAST
21. **dire** (*say, tell*) disant dit	dis dis dit disons dites disent	disais disais disait disions disiez disaient	dis dis dit dîmes dîtes dirent	ai dit as dit a dit avons dit avez dit ont dit
22. **écrire** (*write*) écrivant écrit	écris écris écrit écrivons écrivez écrivent	écrivais écrivais écrivait écrivions écriviez écrivaient	écrivis écrivis écrivit écrivîmes écrivîtes écrivirent	ai écrit as écrit a écrit avons écrit avez écrit ont écrit
23. **envoyer** (*send*) envoyant envoyé	envoie envoies envoie envoyons envoyez envoient	envoyais envoyais envoyait envoyions envoyiez envoyaient	envoyai envoyas envoya envoyâmes envoyâtes envoyèrent	ai envoyé as envoyé a envoyé avons envoyé avez envoyé ont envoyé
24. **faire** (*do, make*) faisant* fait	fais fais fait faisons faites font	faisais* faisais faisait faisions faisiez faisaient	fis fis fit fîmes fîtes firent	ai fait as fait a fait avons fait avez fait ont fait
25. **falloir**** (*be necessary*) fallu	il faut	il fallait	il fallut	il a fallu
26. **fuir** (*flee*) fuyant fui	fuis fuis fuit fuyons fuyez fuient	fuyais fuyais fuyait fuyions fuyiez fuyaient	fuis fuis fuit fuîmes fuîtes fuirent	ai fui as fui a fui avons fui avez fui ont fui
27. **lire** (*read*) lisant lu	lis lis lit lisons lisez lisent	lisais lisais lisait lisions lisiez lisaient	lus lus lut lûmes lûtes lurent	ai lu as lu a lu avons lu avez lu ont lu

* The ai of the stem of these forms is pronounced like mute **e** [ə].
** Used in third person singular only.

La conjugaison du verbe

	CONDITIONAL	IMPERATIVE	SUBJUNCTIVE	
FUTURE			PRESENT	IMPERFECT
dirai	dirais		dise	disse
diras	dirais	dis	dises	disses
dira	dirait		dise	dît
dirons	dirions	disons	disions	dissions
direz	diriez	dites	disiez	dissiez
diront	diraient		disent	dissent
écrirai	écrirais		écrive	écrivisse
écriras	écrirais	écris	écrives	écrivisses
écrira	écrirait		écrive	écrivît
écrirons	écririons	écrivons	écrivions	écrivissions
écrirez	écririez	écrivez	écriviez	écrivissiez
écriront	écriraient		écrivent	écrivissent
enverrai	enverrais		envoie	envoyasse
enverras	enverrais	envoie	envoies	envoyasses
enverra	enverrait		envoie	envoyât
enverrons	enverrions	envoyons	envoyions	envoyassions
enverrez	enverriez	envoyez	envoyiez	envoyassiez
enverront	enverraient		envoient	envoyassent
ferai	ferais		fasse	fisse
feras	ferais	fais	fasses	fisses
fera	ferait		fasse	fît
ferons	ferions	faisons	fassions	fissions
ferez	feriez	faites	fassiez	fissiez
feront	feraient		fassent	fissent
il faudra	il faudrait		il faille	il fallût
fuirai	fuirais		fuie	fuisse
fuiras	fuirais	fuis	fuies	fuisses
fuira	fuirait		fuie	fuît
fuirons	fuirions	fuyons	fuyions	fuissions
fuirez	fuiriez	fuyez	fuyiez	fuissiez
fuiront	fuiraient		fuient	fuissent
lirai	lirais		lise	lusse
liras	lirais	lis	lises	lusses
lira	lirait		lise	lût
lirons	lirions	lisons	lisions	lussions
lirez	liriez	lisez	lisiez	lussiez
liront	liraient		lisent	lussent

The conjugation of the verb

INFINITIVE AND PARTICIPLES	INDICATIVE			
	PRESENT	IMPERFECT	SIMPLE PAST	COMPOUND PAST
28. mettre (*put*) mettant mis	mets mets met mettons mettez mettent	mettais mettais mettait mettions mettiez mettaient	mis mis mit mîmes mîtes mirent	ai mis as mis a mis avons mis avez mis ont mis
29. mourir (*die*) mourant mort	meurs meurs meurt mourons mourez meurent	mourais mourais mourait mourions mouriez mouraient	mourus mourus mourut mourûmes mourûtes moururent	suis mort(e) es mort(e) est mort(e) sommes mort(e)s êtes mort(e)(s) sont mort(e)s
30. naître (*be born*) naissant né	nais nais naît naissons naissez naissent	naissais naissais naissait naissions naissiez naissaient	naquis naquis naquit naquîmes naquîtes naquirent	suis né(e) es né(e) est né(e) sommes né(e)s êtes né(e)(s) sont né(e)s
31. ouvrir (*open*) ouvrant ouvert	ouvre ouvres ouvre ouvrons ouvrez ouvrent	ouvrais ouvrais ouvrait ouvrions ouvriez ouvraient	ouvris ouvris ouvrit ouvrîmes ouvrîtes ouvrirent	ai ouvert as ouvert a ouvert avons ouvert avez ouvert ont ouvert
32. peindre (*paint*) peignant peint	peins peins peint peignons peignez peignent	peignais peignais peignait peignions peigniez peignaient	peignis peignis peignit peignîmes peignîtes peignirent	ai peint as peint a peint avons peint avez peint ont peint
33. plaire (*please*) plaisant plu	plais plais plaît plaisons plaisez plaisent	plaisais plaisais plaisait plaisions plaisiez plaisaient	plus plus plut plûmes plûtes plurent	ai plu as plu a plu avons plu avez plu ont plu
34. pleuvoir* (*rain*) pleuvant plu	il pleut	il pleuvait	il plut	il a plu

* Used only in third person singular.

La conjugaison du verbe

	CONDITIONAL	IMPERATIVE	SUBJUNCTIVE	
FUTURE			PRESENT	IMPERFECT
mettrai	mettrais		mette	misse
mettras	mettrais	mets	mettes	misses
mettra	mettrait		mette	mît
mettrons	mettrions	mettons	mettions	missions
mettrez	mettriez	mettez	mettiez	missiez
mettront	mettraient		mettent	missent
mourrai	mourrais		meure	mourusse
mourras	mourrais	meurs	meures	mourusses
mourra	mourrait		meure	mourût
mourrons	mourrions	mourons	mourions	mourussions
mourrez	mourriez	mourez	mouriez	mourussiez
mourront	mourraient		meurent	mourussent
naîtrai	naîtrais		naisse	naquisse
naîtras	naîtrais	nais	naisses	naquisses
naîtra	naîtrait		naisse	naquît
naîtrons	naîtrions	naissons	naissions	naquissions
naîtrez	naîtriez	naissez	naissiez	naquissiez
naîtront	naîtraient		naissent	naquissent
ouvrirai	ouvrirais		ouvre	ouvrisse
ouvriras	ouvrirais	ouvre	ouvres	ouvrisses
ouvrira	ouvrirait		ouvre	ouvrît
ouvrirons	ouvririons	ouvrons	ouvrions	ouvrissions
ouvrirez	ouvririez	ouvrez	ouvriez	ouvrissiez
ouvriront	ouvriraient		ouvrent	ouvrissent
peindrai	peindrais		peigne	peignisse
peindras	peindrais	peins	peignes	peignisses
peindra	peindrait		peigne	peignît
peindrons	peindrions	peignons	peignions	peignissions
peindrez	peindriez	peignez	peigniez	peignissiez
peindront	peindraient		peignent	peignissent
plairai	plairais		plaise	plusse
plairas	plairais	plais	plaises	plusses
plaira	plairait		plaise	plût
plairons	plairions	plaisons	plaisions	plussions
plairez	plairiez	plaisez	plaisiez	plussiez
plairont	plairaient		plaisent	plussent
il pleuvra	il pleuvrait		il pleuve	il plût

The conjugation of the verb

INFINITIVE AND PARTICIPLES	INDICATIVE			
	PRESENT	IMPERFECT	SIMPLE PAST	COMPOUND PAST
35. **pouvoir** (*be able*) pouvant pu	peux, puis peux peut pouvons pouvez peuvent	pouvais pouvais pouvait pouvions pouviez pouvaient	pus pus put pûmes pûtes purent	ai pu as pu a pu avons pu avez pu ont pu
36. **prendre** (*take*) prenant pris	prends prends prend prenons prenez prennent	prenais prenais prenait prenions preniez prenaient	pris pris prit prîmes prîtes prirent	ai pris as pris a pris avons pris avez pris ont pris
37. **rire** (*laugh*) riant ri	ris ris rit rions riez rient	riais riais riait riions riiez riaient	ris ris rit rîmes rîtes rirent	ai ri as ri a ri avons ri avez ri ont ri
38. **savoir** (*know*) sachant su	sais sais sait savons savez savent	savais savais savait savions saviez savaient	sus sus sut sûmes sûtes surent	ai su as su a su avons su avez su ont su
39. **suivre** (*follow*) suivant suivi	suis suis suit suivons suivez suivent	suivais suivais suivait suivions suiviez suivaient	suivis suivis suivit suivîmes suivîtes suivirent	ai suivi as suivi a suivi avons suivi avez suivi ont suivi
40. **tenir** (*hold, keep*) tenant tenu	tiens tiens tient tenons tenez tiennent	tenais tenais tenait tenions teniez tenaient	tins tins tint tînmes tîntes tinrent	ai tenu as tenu a tenu avons tenu avez tenu ont tenu

La conjugaison du verbe

	CONDITIONAL	IMPERATIVE	SUBJUNCTIVE	
FUTURE			PRESENT	IMPERFECT
pourrai	pourrais		puisse	pusse
pourras	pourrais		puisses	pusses
pourra	pourrait		puisse	pût
pourrons	pourrions		puissions	pussions
pourrez	pourriez		puissiez	pussiez
pourront	pourraient		puissent	pussent
prendrai	prendrais		prenne	prisse
prendras	prendrais	prends	prennes	prisses
prendra	prendrait		prenne	prît
prendrons	prendrions	prenons	prenions	prissions
prendrez	prendriez	prenez	preniez	prissiez
prendront	prendraient		prennent	prissent
rirai	rirais		rie	risse
riras	rirais	ris	ries	risses
rira	rirait		rie	rît
rirons	ririons	rions	riions	rissions
rirez	ririez	riez	riiez	rissiez
riront	riraient		rient	rissent
saurai	saurais		sache	susse
sauras	saurais	sache	saches	susses
saura	saurait		sache	sût
saurons	saurions	sachons	sachions	sussions
saurez	sauriez	sachez	sachiez	sussiez
sauront	sauraient		sachent	sussent
suivrai	suivrais		suive	suivisse
suivras	suivrais	suis	suives	suivisses
suivra	suivrait		suive	suivît
suivrons	suivrions	suivons	suivions	suivissions
suivrez	suivriez	suivez	suiviez	suivissiez
suivront	suivraient		suivent	suivissent
tiendrai	tiendrais		tienne	tinsse
tiendras	tiendrais	tiens	tiennes	tinsses
tiendra	tiendrait		tienne	tînt
tiendrons	tiendrions	tenons	tenions	tinssions
tiendrez	tiendriez	tenez	teniez	tinssiez
tiendront	tiendraient		tiennent	tinssent

The conjugation of the verb

INFINITIVE AND PARTICIPLES	INDICATIVE			
	PRESENT	IMPERFECT	SIMPLE PAST	COMPOUND PAST
41. **vaincre** (*conquer*) vainquant vaincu	vaincs vaincs vainc vainquons vainquez vainquent	vainquais vainquais vainquait vainquions vainquiez vainquaient	vainquis vainquis vainquit vainquîmes vainquîtes vainquirent	ai vanicu as vaincu a vaincu avons vaincu avez vaincu ont vaincu
42. **valoir** (*be worth*) valant valu	vaux vaux vaut valons valez valent	valais valais valait valions valiez valaient	valus valus valut valûmes valûtes valurent	ai valu as valu a valu avons valu avez valu ont valu
43. **venir** (*come*) venant venu	viens viens vient venons venez viennent	venais venais venait venions veniez venaient	vins vins vint vînmes vîntes vinrent	suis venu(e) es venu(e) est venu(e) sommes venu(e)s êtes venu(e)(s) sont venu(e)s
44. **vivre** (*live*) vivant vécu	vis vis vit vivons vivez vivent	vivais vivais vivait vivions viviez vivaient	vécus vécus vécut vécûmes vécûtes vécurent	ai vécu as vécu a vécu avons vécu avez vécu ont vécu
45. **voir** (*see*) voyant vu	vois vois voit voyons voyez voient	voyais voyais voyait voyions voyiez voyaient	vis vis vit vîmes vîtes virent	ai vu as vu a vu avons vu avez vu ont vu
46. **vouloir** (*wish, want*) voulant voulu	veux veux veut voulons voulez veulent	voulais voulais voulait voulions vouliez voulaient	voulus voulus voulut voulûmes voulûtes voulurent	ai voulu as voulu a voulu avons voulu avez voulu ont voulu

La conjugaison du verbe

FUTURE	CONDITIONAL	IMPERATIVE	SUBJUNCTIVE PRESENT	IMPERFECT
vaincrai	vaincrais		vainque	vainquisse
vaincras	vaincrais	vaincs	vainques	vainquisses
vaincra	vaincrait		vainque	vainquît
vaincrons	vaincrions	vainquons	vainquions	vainquissions
vaincrez	vaincriez	vainquez	vainquiez	vainquissiez
vaincront	vaincraient		vainquent	vainquissent
vaudrai	vaudrais		vaille	valusse
vaudras	vaudrais	vaux	vailles	valusses
vaudra	vaudrait		vaille	valût
vaudrons	vaudrions	valons	valions	valussions
vaudrez	vaudriez	valez	valiez	valussiez
vaudront	vaudraient		vaillent	valussent
viendrai	viendrais		vienne	vinsse
viendras	viendrais	viens	viennes	vinsses
viendra	viendrait		vienne	vînt
viendrons	viendrions	venons	venions	vinssions
viendrez	viendriez	venez	veniez	vinssiez
viendront	viendraient		viennent	vinssent
vivrai	vivrais		vive	vécusse
vivras	vivrais	vis	vives	vécusses
vivra	vivrait		vive	vécût
vivrons	vivrions	vivons	vivions	vécussions
vivrez	vivriez	vivez	viviez	vécussiez
vivront	vivraient		vivent	vécussent
verrai	verrais		voie	visse
verras	verrais	vois	voies	visses
verra	verrait		voie	vît
verrons	verrions	voyons	voyions	vissions
verrez	verriez	voyez	voyiez	vissiez
verront	verraient		voient	vissent
voudrai	voudrais		veuille	voulusse
voudras	voudrais	veuille	veuilles	voulusses
voudra	voudrait		veuille	voulût
voudrons	voudrions		voulions	voulussions
voudrez	voudriez	veuillez	vouliez	voulussiez
voudront	voudraient		veuillent	voulussent

Verbs with Spelling Changes

A. Verbs in -cer

Since **c** is pronounced like **s** only before **e** and **i** and like **k** before **a**, **o**, and **u**, verbs whose infinitives end in **-cer** change **c** to **ç** when the **c** is followed by **a**, **o**, or **u**, in order to preserve the *s* sound of the **c**. Changes are made then in the tenses below and in the imperfect subjunctive.

EXAMPLE: **effacer.**

PRESENT PARTICIPLE	PRESENT INDICATIVE	IMPERFECT INDICATIVE	SIMPLE PAST
effaçant	j'efface	j'effaçais	j'effaçai
	tu effaces	tu effaçais	tu effaças
	il efface	il effaçait	il effaça
	nous effaçons	nous effacions	nous effaçâmes
	vous effacez	vous effaciez	vous effaçâtes
	ils effacent	ils effaçaient	ils effacèrent

B. Verbs in -ger

Since **g** is pronounced like *g* in *get* before **a**, **o**, and **u**, and like *s* in *pleasure* before **e** and **i**, verbs whose infinitives end in **-ger** insert **e** between **g** and the next vowel whenever that vowel is not **e** or **i**. Changes are made then, in the tenses below and in the imperfect subjunctive.

EXAMPLE: **changer.**

PRESENT PARTICIPLE	PRESENT INDICATIVE	IMPERFECT INDICATIVE	SIMPLE PAST
changeant	je change	je changeais	je changeai
	tu changes	tu changeais	tu changeas
	il change	il changeait	il changea
	nous changeons	nous changions	nous changeâmes
	vous changez	vous changiez	vous changeâtes
	ils changent	ils changeaient	ils changèrent

C. Verbs in -yer

Verbs in **-yer** (**-ayer**, **-oyer**, **-uyer**) change **y** to **i** before a mute **e** in the following syllable. This change occurs throughout the present except for the **nous** and **vous** forms and throughout the entire future and conditional.

EXAMPLE: **nettoyer.**

PRESENT INDICATIVE	PRESENT SUBJUNCTIVE	FUTURE	CONDITIONAL
je nettoie	que je nettoie	je nettoierai	je nettoierais
tu nettoies	que tu nettoies	tu nettoieras	tu nettoierais
il nettoie	qu'il nettoie	il nettoiera	il nettoierait
nous nettoyons	que nous nettoyions	nous nettoierons	nous nettoierions
vous nettoyez	que vous nettoyiez	vous nettoierez	vous nettoieriez
ils nettoient	qu'ils nettoient	ils nettoieront	ils nettoieraient

D. Verbs in -e- + { a single consonant } + -er

Many verbs, such as **mener, lever,** and **acheter,** whose stems end in unaccented e plus a single consonant, place a grave accent (`) over this e whenever the following syllable also has a mute e. This indicates that the pronunciation of the e [ə] of the stem becomes è [ɛ]. The grave accent is found throughout the singular and in the third person plural of the present indicative and subjunctive and throughout the entire future and conditional of all these verbs.

EXAMPLE: **mener.**

PRESENT INDICATIVE	PRESENT SUBJUNCTIVE	FUTURE	CONDITIONAL
je mène	que je mène	je mènerai	je mènerais
tu mènes	que tu mènes	tu mèneras	tu mènerais
il mène	qu'il mène	il mènera	il mènerait
nous menons	que nous menions	nous mènerons	nous mènerions
vous menez	que vous meniez	vous mènerez	vous mèneriez
ils mènent	qu'ils mènent	ils mèneront	ils mèneraient

E. Verbs in -é- + { a single consonant } + -er

Verbs whose stems end in é followed by a single consonant change this é to è throughout the singular and in the third person plural of the present indicative and present subjunctive, that is, in those forms in which the following syllable has a mute e. In the future and conditional the é is retained in writing, but this é is usually pronounced è because a vowel tends to open in a closed syllable[1].

---

[1]The fact that the mute e of the infinitive drops out in pronunciation closes the preceding syllable, thus tending to open the e; e.g., j'espérerai [ʒ ɛ spe rre]; il espérerait [ilɛ spe rre]; tu céderas [tysɛ dra].

EXAMPLE: **espérer**

PRESENT INDICATIVE	PRESENT SUBJUNCTIVE	FUTURE	CONDITIONAL
j'espère	que j'espère	j'espérerai	j'espérerais
tu espères	que tu espères	tu espéreras	tu espérerais
il espère	qu'il espère	il espérera	il espérerait
nous espérons	que nous espérions	nous espérerons	nous espérerions
vous espérez	que vous espériez	vous espérerez	vous espéreriez
ils espèrent	qu'ils espèrent	ils espéreront	ils espéreraient

F. Verbs in -eler and some in -eter

Verbs in **-eler** and a few verbs in **-eter** double the l or t when the next syllable contains a mute **e**. This change takes place in the singular and third person plural of the present indicative and of the present subjunctive and throughout the future and conditional.

EXAMPLE: **appeler.**

PRESENT INDICATIVE	PRESENT SUBJUNCTIVE	FUTURE	CONDITIONAL
j'appelle	que j'appelle	j'appellerai	j'appellerais
tu appelles	que tu appelles	tu appelleras	tu appellerais
il appelle	qu'il appelle	il appellera	il appellerait
nous appelons	que nous appelions	nous appellerons	nous appellerions
vous appelez	que vous appeliez	vous appellerez	vous appelleriez
ils appellent	qu'ils appellent	ils appelleront	ils appelleraient

French-English Vocabulary

Abbreviations

adj.	adjective	*irr. sp.*	irregular spelling	*pers.*	person
adv.	adverb	*lit.*	literally	*prep.*	preposition
cond.	conditional	*m.*	masculine	*pres.*	present
conj.	conjugated	*n.*	noun	*pron.*	pronoun
conjunc.	conjunction	*obj.*	object	*rel.*	relative
f.	feminine	*p.*	page	*sing.*	singular
fut.	future	*part.*	participle	*s.p.*	simple past
indic.	indicative	*pl.*	plural	*subj.*	subjunctive
inf.	infinitive	*p.p.*	past participle	*v.*	verb
interr.	interrogative				

* = aspirate *h*   (2) = -**ir** verbs that do not insert -**iss**-; all other -**ir** verbs insert -**iss**.

Verbs whose principal parts are given are irregular, and their conjugations may be found on pages 318–335. The use of the principal parts is explained on pages 315–317. Verbs followed by (*conj. like...*) are irregular and follow the pattern of the verb indicated.

Verbs followed by (*irr. sp.* **A** to **F**) undergo a spelling change in certain forms. The letter refers to the appropriate type of change explained on pages 354–356.

This vocabulary contains all words used in the text and in the Exercise Manual except words that have the same form in English and French and words whose French spelling is so near to the English that they are easily recognizable.

Adverbs ending in **-*ment*** are omitted when the corresponding adjective is included and when the English adverb ends in -*ly*.

A

à at; with; in; by; **à peu près** about; **à votre accent** from (by) your accent; **c'est à lui** it is up to him.

a (*pres. of* **avoir**) has; **il y a** there is, there are; **il y a un an** a year ago

abandonner abandon; **s'abandonner** give way (to)

abattre (*conj. like* **battre**) tear down

abondamment abundantly

abord : d'abord at first; from the very beginning; **tout d'abord** first of all

aboyer (*irr. sp.* **C**) bark

abri *m.* shelter; **se mettre à l'abri** take shelter

abrupt steep

absolu absolute

Académie *f.* Academy; **Académie française** the French Academy, founded in 1635, is made up of 40 prominent personalities, mainly writers; **Académie Goncourt** a group of writers which each year awards a prize for works that depart from traditional patterns

accablé overwhelmed; weary

accablement *m.* despondency; deep or intense boredom

accent *m.* accent; **à votre accent** from (by) your accent

accompagner accompany

accomplir accomplish; **accomplir un mouvement** make a movement

accomplissement *m.* accomplishment

accord *m.* agreement; **être d'accord** agree; **se mettre d'accord** come to an agreement

accueillir receive, welcome

accusé *m.* defendant

achat *m.* purchase

acheter (*irr. sp.* **D**) buy

Acropole *m.* Acropolis, famous temple overlooking Athens

acteur *m.* actor

actif (*f.* **active**) active

actrice *f.* actress

actuel (*f.* **actuelle**) present-day

addition *f.* check (in a restaurant)

adieu *m.* goodbye; **faire ses adieux** say goodbye

admettre (*conj. like* **mettre**) admit

adresser (**s'**) (**à** + *n.*) go to; ask at; apply

aéroport *m.* airport

affaiblir weaken

affaire *f.* affair; thing; deal; business; **les affaires** business; one's things; **tirer quelqu'un d'affaire** get someone out of trouble

affectueusement affectionately

affiche *f.* poster; bulletin

affirmativement affirmatively

affirmer affirm

affolement *m.* panic

affreux (*f.* **affreuse**) horrible

afin de in order to; **afin que** in order that

Irregular verbs are conjugated on pp. 318–335.

Afrique *f.* Africa; **Afrique du Nord** North Africa

agacer (*irr. sp.* **A**) provoke

âgé old

agence *f.* agency

agent *m.* policeman; **agent de change** stockbroker; **agent d'assurances** insurance agent; **agent de voyage** travel agent

aggloméré *m.* conglomerate

agir act; **s'agir de** be a question of, be about

agitation *f.* movement

agiter wave

agneau *m.* lamb

agnostique agnostic, nonbeliever

agrandir enlarge

agréable pleasant, agreeable

agrément *m.*; **voyage d'agrément** pleasure trip

aider (+ *person* + **à** + *inf.*) help

aïeul *m.* (*pl.* **aïeux**) ancestor

aile *f.* wing

aille (*pres. subj. of* **aller**) go

ailleurs elsewhere; **d'ailleurs** besides; **nulle part ailleurs** nowhere else

aimer (+ *inf.*) like; love

ainsi thus; so; as; **pour ainsi dire** so to speak

air *m.* air; appearance; look; **air libre** open air; **avoir l'air** (+ *adj.*) look; seem; **avoir l'air de** (+ *inf.*) seem to; **d'un air** with a look; **en plein air** in the open

aise *f.* ease; **être à l'aise** be comfortable; **mal à l'aise** ill at ease

ait (*pres. subj. of* **avoir**) has; have

ajouter add

alcool [alkɔl] *m.* alcohol

algèbre *m.* algebra

Alger Algiers, a city on the coast of North Africa, capital of Algeria

Algérie *f.* Algeria

allée *f.* land; alley

Allemagne *f.* Germany

allemand German

aller (**allant**, **allé**, **je vais**, **j'allai**) (+ *inf.*) go; **aller voir** go and see, visit; **ça va de soi** that goes without saying; **cette**

robe vous va bien this dress fits you well, this dress looks very becoming on you; **quelque chose ne va pas** there's something wrong; **s'en aller** go away, leave; start on one's way
allergie *f.* allergy
allié *m.* ally
allô hello (in answering the telephone)
allonger (s') (*irr. sp.* **B**) stretch out
allons bon there now
allumer light; turn on the lights
alors then; **alors que** when; whereas
Alpes *f. pl.* Alps
alpiniste *m./f.* mountain climber
âme *f.* soul
amener (*irr. sp.* **D**) bring; take
amer (*f.* **amère**) bitter
américain American
Amérique *f.* America; **Amérique du Sud** *f.* South America
amertume *f.* bitterness
ami *m.* friend
amie *f.* friend; **bonne amie** girlfriend
amitié *f.* friendship; **faites-lui mes amitiés** give him/her my best regards
amollir (s') soften
amorcer (*irr. sp.* **A**) initiate
amour *m. in sing., f. in pl.* love
amoureusement lovingly
amoureux *m. s. or pl.* people in love
amoureux (*f.* **amoureuse**) in love
ampleur *f.* magnitude
amusant entertaining; amusing
amuser entertain; **s'amuser** (**à** + *inf.*) have fun; have a good time; amuse oneself
amuseur *m.* entertainer
an *m.* year
analogue similar
ancêtre *m./f.* ancestor
ancien (*f.* **ancienne**) old; former
âne *m.* donkey, ass
anéantir (s') be destroyed
anglais English
Angleterre *f.* England
angoissant anguished, distressed

Verbs with spelling changes are explained on pp. 336–338.

angoissé in a state of anxiety
animé animated, lively; **dessin animé** cartoon; **s'animer** become alive, come to life
année *f.* year
anniversaire *m.* anniversary; birthday
annonce *f.* announcement
annoncer (*irr. sp.* **A**) announce; say; herald
anxiété *f.* anxiety, worry
anxieux (*f.* **anxieuse**) anxious, worried
apercevoir (*conj. like* **recevoir**) (+*n.*) notice; catch sight of; **s'apercevoir (de** + *n.*; **que** + *clause*) notice, realize
apéritif *m.* slightly alcoholic drink taken before a meal
apparaître (*conj. like* **connaître**) appear (physically)
appareil *m.* apparatus; machine; **appareil de photo** camera
appartement *m.* apartment
appartenir (*conj. like* **tenir**) belong
appeler (*irr. sp.* **F**) call; **s'appeler** be called, be named
appétissant appetizing
applaudir applaud
appliquer (s') apply oneself; work hard at
apporter bring
apprécier appreciate
appréhender seize
apprendre (*conj. like* **prendre**) (*thing* + **à** + *person*; **à** + *inf.*) learn; teach; **apprendre par cœur** memorize, learn by heart
apprêter (s') get ready
approcher (**de** + *n.*) approach; **s'approcher** (**de** + *n.*) approach
approfondir delve into
approuver approve
appuyer (*irr. sp.* **C**) lean; support; **s'appuyer** lean
après after; afterwards; **d'après** according to; after
après-midi *m./f.* afternoon
arabe arabic
arbre *m.* tree; **arbre fruitier** fruit tree
Arc de Triomphe *m.* Arch of Triumph
ardemment ardently
ardeur *f.* enthusiasm, ardor

...lver; **papier d'argent**

Armée du Salut Salva-
ti...
armoire *f.* ...pboard; large piece of furniture used as a wardrobe
arracher snatch, grab
arrangé set
arranger (*irr. sp.* **B**) fix; arrange; **s'arranger** come out all right; manage
arrêt *m.* stop; stoppage; **sans arrêt** without stopping, ceaselessly
arrêter (**de** + *inf.*) stop; arrest; fix; **s'arrêter** (**de** + *inf.*) stop
arrière : en arrière behind
arrivé : les nouveaux arrivés the people who have just arrived
arrivée *f.* arrival
arriver arrive, reach; happen; **en arriver à** reach such a point
arroser water
art *m.* art; **beaux-arts** fine arts
ascenseur *m.* elevator
asile *m.* mental institution
asperge *f.* asparagus
aspirateur *m.* vacuum cleaner
asseoir (**asseyant, assis, j'assieds, j'assis**) sit; seat; **s'asseoir** sit down
assez enough; rather
assiette *f.* plate
assis (*p.p. and s.p. of* **asseoir**) seated; sitting
assister (**à** + *n.*) attend, be present at
assombri darkened
assurance *f.* insurance; **assurance sur la vie** life insurance; **bureau d'assurances** *m.* insurance office
assurer guarantee; insure; **s'assurer** make sure, assure oneself
astiquer polish
atomique atomic, nuclear
attacher (**s'**) attach; become fond of; **s'attacher aux pas** follow closely
attaquer attack

Irregular verbs are conjugated on pp. 318–335.

atteindre (*conj. like* **peindre**) reach; affect; damage
attendre (+ *n.*) wait; wait for; expect; **s'attendre** (**à** + *n.*) expect
attente *f.* wait
attentif (*f.* **attentive**) attentive
attention *f.* attention; **faire attention à** watch out for; pay attention to; **faire bien attention** pay special attention to; be very careful about; **faites attention** look out
atténué subdued
atterrir land
attirer attract; **s'attirer** attract to oneself
attraper catch
au to the; **au revoir** goodbye
aube *f.* dawn
aubergiste *m./f.* innkeeper
aucun any; **ne... aucun** no; none
audacieux (*f.* **audacieuse**) audacious; bold
au-dehors outside
au-delà beyond
au-dessus above
augmentation *f.* raise
augmenter increase; raise
auparavant formerly
auprès near; **auprès de** at the side of, near; compared with
aurai, aurais (*fut. and cond. of* **avoir**) will have; would have
aussi also; (at beginning of sentence) so, therefore
aussitôt at once, immediately; **aussitôt que** as soon as
autant as much; **d'autant plus que** all the more because
auteur *m.* author
auto *f.* car, auto; **parc à autos** *m.* parking lot
autobus *m.* (city) bus
autocar *m.* (interurban) bus
automne *m.* autumn, fall
autoportrait *m.* self-portrait
autoriser authorize
autoritaire dominating, bossy
autoroute *f.* freeway
autour around
autre other

autrefois formerly
autrement differently; otherwise
Autriche *f.* Austria
auxiliaire auxiliary
avance : à l'avance in advance; **d'avance**
in advance
avancé advanced
avancer (*irr. sp.* **A**) advance, move forward; **s'avancer** advance; approach
avant before; ahead; formerly;
avant-dernier next to the last;
avant-hier the day before yesterday;
avant tout above all
avare *m.* miser
avec with
avenir *m.* future
aventure *f.* adventure
aventurer (**s'**) venture
aventureux adventurous, rash
avertir warn, inform
avertissement *m.* notice, indication
aveugle (*adj.*) blind; (*n.*) blind person
aveuglément blindly
aviateur *m.* flier
avion *m.* airplane
avis *m.* opinion; **changer d'avis** change
one's mind; **être de l'avis de** be of the
opinion that
avocat *m.* lawyer
avoir (**ayant, eu, j'ai, j'eus**) (**à** + *inf.*)
have; **avoir beau faire quelque
chose** do something in vain; **avoir
de la chance** be lucky; **ce qu'il y a**
the trouble is; **il y a** there is, there
are; ago
avouer confess; admit
ayant (*pres. part. of* **avoir**) having
azur blue; **Côte d'Azur** *f.* French Riviera

B

baccalauréat *m.* baccalaureat (state
examination given to secondary
school students)

Verbs with spelling changes are explained on
pp. 336–338.

bagage *m.* baggage; **faire les bagages**
pack
bagarre *f.* brawl
bague *f.* ring
baigné suffused
bain *m.* bath
baissé lowered
baisser lower; **se baisser** bend over
bal *m.* dance
balancer (*irr. sp.* **A**) swing
balayer (*irr. sp.* **C**) sweep away, push
away
ballon *m.* ball
ballot *m.* bundle
Balzac, Honoré de (1799–1850) French
realistic novelist, author of *La
Comédie humaine*
bande *f.* strip; tape (for tape recorder);
platebande de fleurs flower bed;
bande dessinée comic strip
banlieue *f.* suburbs
banque *f.* bank; **billet de banque** *m.*
banknote
banquier *m.* banker
baptisé baptized
barbe *f.* beard
barrer cross out; cut off
barrière *f.* fence
bas (*f.* **basse**) low; **en bas** downstairs;
tout bas in a whisper
basé based
bassine *f.* pan
Bastille *f.* a square in Paris, formerly the
site of the state prison that was
taken and destroyed by the people on
July 14, 1789
bataille *f.* battle
bateau *m.* boat; **bateau à moteur** motorboat; **bateau à voiles** sailboat; **faire du
bateau** take a boat ride; go boating;
traversée en bateau *f.* boat trip
bâtiment *m.* building
bâtir build
bâton *m.* stick; cane
Baton Rouge capital of Louisiana
battre (**battant, battu, je bats, je battis**)
beat; **se battre** fight
bavard talkative
bavarder talk; chat

store

,ound **bel**; *f.* **belle**)

,ome; **avoir beau faire**
do something in vain;
.e weather is good; **un**
.ie fine day; a certain day

beaucou, ch, many, a great deal, a great many, a lot

beaux-parents *m. pl.* parents-in-law

bébé *m.* baby

bec *m.* beak, bill (of a bird)

Bédouin *m.* Bedouin, nomadic Arab

belette *f.* weasel

Belge *m./f.* Belgian

Belgique *f.* Belgium

belle (*f. of* **beau**) beautiful; **à la belle étoile** in the open; **de belle taille** huge; **la belle saison** the summer months

belle-fille *f.* daughter-in-law

belle-mère *f.* mother-in-law

berger *m.* shepherd; **l'étoile du Berger** Venus

besoin *m.* need; **avoir besoin** (**de** + *n*; **de** + *inf.*) need; **être dans le besoin** be poverty-stricken

bêta *m.* blockhead

bête *f.* beast; animal

bêtement stupidly

bêtise *f.* foolish action; **faire des bêtises** do something foolish

beurre *m.* butter

bibelots *m. pl.* curios

bibliothèque *f.* library

bicyclette *f.* bicycle

bien well; well-off; comfortable; good; indeed; really; very; very much; right; **bien en face** straight in the eye; **bien que** although; **bien se porter** be well; **faire du bien** do good; **ou bien** or else; **qu'on est bien** how comfortable we are; **vouloir bien** be willing; **vous comprenez bien** you must understand

bien-aimé beloved

bien-être *m.* ease, well-being

Irregular verbs are conjugated on pp. 318–335.

bienfaiteur *m.* benefactor

bienheureux blessed; blissful; fortunate

bientôt soon

bienveillance *f.* kindness, benevolence

bienvenue *f.* welcome

bière *f.* beer

bifteck *m.* steak

bigot narrow-minded, devout

bijou *m.* jewel

bijouterie *f.* jewelry store

bijoutier *m.* jeweler

bilingue bilingual

billet *m.* ticket; **billet de banque** banknote

bistrot *m.* small café or restaurant (patronized principally by the working class)

bizarre odd, strange, outlandish; strangely

blanc (*f.* **blanche**) white

blé *m.* wheat

blessé *m.* wounded man

blesser wound

bleu blue

boire (**buvant, bu, je bois, je bus**) drink

bois *m.* wood

boîte *f.* box

bon (*f.* **bonne**) good; fit; **allons bon** there now; **bon marché** cheap; **il fait bon** it is cozy; it is comfortably warm; the weather is good; **il serait bon** it would be advisable

bonbon *m.* candy

bondir jump

bonheur *m.* happiness; **faire le bonheur** make one happy

bonhomme *m.* man; fellow; **bonhomme de neige** snowman

bonjour good morning, hello

bonne *f.* maid

bonnet *m.* cap

bord *m.* edge

bordé (**de**) lined (with)

Bordeaux city in southwestern France near the Atlantic

borne *f.* limit

borner limit

bosquet *m.* grove; thicket

bouche *f.* mouth

boucher : se boucher les oreilles stop one's ears
bouclé curled
bouger (*irr. sp.* **B**) move
bougie *f.* candle
boulanger *m.* baker; **chez le boulanger** at the bakery
boule *f.* ball
boulette *f.* pellet
bourgeois middle-class
bourse *f.* stock exchange
bout *m.* end; tip
bouteille *f.* bottle
boxe *f.* boxing
Brahma *m.* Hindu god
brahmin *m.* priest of Brahma
bras *m.* arm
brave worthy; fine
Brésil *m.* Brazil
Bretagne *f.* Brittany, province in western France
breton from Brittany
brève (*f. of* **bref**) short
brillant brilliant; bright
briller shine
broder embroider
brosser brush
bruit *m.* noise; rumor
brûlant burning; passionate; scorching
brûler burn
brume *f.* haze; mist
brun brown; dusky
brune *f.* brunette
brusque blunt; brusk, abrupt
brusquement suddenly; bruskly
brutalement brutally
bruyant noisy
bu, bus (*p.p. and s.p. of* **boire**) drunk; drank
buffet *m.* sideboard
bureau *m.* desk; office; **bureau d'assurances** insurance office; **bureau de tabac** tobacco shop
buste *m.* bust; torso
but *m.* aim

Verbs with spelling changes are explained on pp. 336–338.

buvant (*pres. part. of* **boire**) drinking
buvons we drink; let's drink

C

ça that; it; **çà et là** here and there
cabane *f.* hut
cabinet *m.* doctor's office
cacher hide
cacheter (*irr. sp.* **F**) seal
cadeau *m.* gift; **faire un cadeau** give a present
café *m.* coffee; café, coffee house, tavern
cahier *m.* notebook
caillou *m.* stone
calcul *m.* calculation
calculer calculate; estimate
calme *m.* peace, calm; (*adj.*) calm
calmement calmly
camarade *m./f.* friend; pal; **camarade de classe** classmate; **camarade d'études** school friend
camion *m.* truck
camp *m.* camp; team
campagne *f.* country; countryside, landscape; **maison de campagne** *f.* country home
campement *m.* camping site
camper camp
Camus, Albert (1913-1960) well-known philosopher, novelist, and playwright, winner of the Nobel Prize for Literature
canapé *m.* sofa
Cannes town on the French Riviera
cantatrice *f.* professional singer
capable capable, able; **capable de tout** capable of anything
capitaine *m.* captain
car for
caractère *m.* character (attributes or features that distinguish a person)
cardiologue *m./f.* heart specialist
caresser caress, fondle
carnaval *m.* carnival
carnet *m.* small notebook
carré square
carrefour *m.* crossing; crossroad
carrière *f.* career

carte *f.* card; map; **carte d'identité** identification card; **carte postale** postcard;
carte de visite visiting card
cas *m.* case; **en tout cas** in any case;
faire grand cas de attach much importance to
casser break; **se casser** break
Caucase *m.* the Caucasus, a mountain-
ous area in southern Russia
cause *f.* cause; **à cause de** because of
causer talk; chat; cause
cave *f.* cellar
ce (*adj.*) this; that; (*pron.*) this; that; it;
he; she; they
céder (*irr. sp.* E) yield
cela that
célèbre famous
célibataire *m.* bachelor
celui (*f.* **celle**) this one, that one; the
one; **celui-ci** this one, that one; the
latter
cendrier *m.* ashtray
censure *f.* censorship
cent hundred
centaine *f.* about a hundred; **des
centaines** hundreds
centenaire hundred years old
centre *m.* center; **centre commercial**
shopping center
cependant however
cerise *f.* cherry
certain some; certain
certainement certainly
certes certainly
cesse : sans cesse constantly, ceaselessly
cesser (**de** + *inf.*) stop, cease
cet this; that
cette (*f. of* **ce**) this; that
chagrin *m.* sorrow; chagrin
chaise *f.* chair
chalet *m.* cottage
chaleur *f.* heat
chambre *f.* bedroom; **robe de chambre** *f.*
gown
chameau *m.* camel

champignon *m.* mushroom
Champs-Élysées avenue in Paris leading
from the Place de la Concorde to the
Place Charles de Gaulle
chance *f.* luck; **avoir de la chance** be
lucky
change *m.* exchange; **agent de change** *m.*
stockbroker
changement *m.* change
changer (*irr. sp.* **B**) change; **changer
d'avis** change one's mind; **changer de
rôle** change roles
chanson *f.* song
chansonnier *m.* writer and performer of
popular and satirical songs
chant *m.* song
chantant melodious
chanter sing
chanteur *m.* singer
chanteuse *f.* singer
chapeau *m.* hat
chaque each
chargé loaded; overloaded; **chargé de**
filled with
charger (**se**) (**de** + *inf.*) take care
charité *f.* charity; **œuvres de charité** *f.*
pl. charitable works
charmant charming
Chartres town southwest of Paris, famous for its Gothic cathedral
chasse *f.* hunt, hunting; **aller à la chasse**
go hunting
chasser hunt; throw out; chase away;
blow around
chat *m.* cat; **chat de gouttière** alley cat;
chat perché children's game of tag
château *m.* castle
Chateaubriand, René de (1769-1848)
early 19th-century Romantic writer
chaud hot; warm; **j'ai chaud** I am warm;
il fait chaud it is warm; it is hot
chauffeur *m.* driver; chauffeur
chaussé shod, wearing shoes
chaussette *f.* sock
chaussure *f.* shoe; *pl.* footwear; shoes
chauve bald
chef *m.* head, leader; chief; **chef
d'orchestre** conductor; **chef d'œuvre**
masterpiece

Irregular verbs are conjugated on pp. 318–335.

chemin *m.* road; path; way; **chemin faisant** on one's way
cheminée *f.* fireplace
chemise *f.* shirt
chêne *m.* oak
chèque *m.* check
cher (*f.* **chère**) dear; expensive
chercher (+ *n.*) look for; meet; go and get; pick up; (**à** + *inf.*) try to, seek to; **envoyer chercher** send for
chérie *f.* dear
cheval *m.* (*pl.* **chevaux**) horse; **faire du cheval** go horseback riding
chevelure *f.* head of hair
cheveux *m. pl.* hair
chez at; with; in; at the house of; in the case of; **allez chez vous** go home; **chez le directeur** in the director's office; **chez nous** at our house; in our country; **chez qui** at whose home
chien *m.* dog; **chien-loup** *m.* German shepherd
chiffre *m.* figure
chimie *f.* chemistry
Chine *f.* China
chinois Chinese
choc *m.* shock
chœur *m.* choir
choisir choose
choix *m.* choice
chômage *m.* unemployment
Chopin, Frédéric (1810-1849) 19th-century Romantic composer
chose *f.* thing; **pas grand-chose** not much, not very much
chouette *f.* owl
Cid *m.* *Le Cid*, a well-known play by Pierre Corneille (1636)
ci-dessus above
ciel *m.* sky
cinéma *m.* movie; movie theatre; movies; **faire du cinéma** be in the movies
cinq five
cinquante fifty
cinquième fifth

Verbs with spelling changes are explained on pp. 336–338.

circuler drive
cirer wax; shine
cirque *m.* circus
cité *f.* city
citer quote; mention
citron *m.* lemon
clair clear, light; obvious; **clair de lune** *m.* moonlight; **nous y verrons plus clair** we'll see better
clairvoyante *f.* seer
classe *f.* class; classroom; **camarade de classe** classmate; **faire une classe** teach
classique classical
clé *f.* key; **fermer à clé** lock
client *m.* client; customer; patron
climatiser air-condition
clinique *f.* private hospital
cloche *f.* bell
clochette *f.* small bell
clos (*p.p.* of **clore**) shut
clou *f.* nail
clown *m.* [klun] clown
cochon *m.* pig, hog
cœur *m.* heart; **apprendre par cœur** memorize; **au cœur de** in the middle of; **avoir mal au cœur** be nauseated
coffre *m.* safe; **coffre-fort** *m.* safe
cognac *m.* brandy
cogner (**se**) bump into
coiffeur *m.* hairdresser; barber
coiffure *f.* hairdo
coin *m.* corner
colère *f.* anger; **en colère** angry; **faire une colère** throw a tantrum; **se mettre en colère** get angry
colis *m.* package
collaborer collaborate
collation *f.* light meal; snack
colle *f.* glue
collé pressed; stuck; failed; **collé au corps** pressed against the body
collectionner collect
collectionneur *m.* collector
collégien *m.* secondary school student
coller (+ *person*) (*colloquial*) fail (someone in a test or a course)
collier *m.* necklace; **monter en collier** make into a necklace

colline *f.* hill
colon *m.* colonist
colonne *f.* column
colosse *m.* colossus, a huge figure
combien how much; how many; **tous les combien** how often
combiner plan; draw up; figure out; combine
comédie *f.* comedy; play
comédien *m.* actor; comedian
commander order; require
comme as; like; as well as; since; **comme si** as if; **comme d'habitude** as usual; **comme il faut** properly
commencement *m.* beginning
commencer (*irr. sp.* **A**) begin
comment how; what; What !; What do you mean ?; **comment trouvez-vous** what do you think of
commerce *m.* business
commettre (*conj. like* **mettre**) commit
commissaire *m.* police commissioner
commission *f.* errand; **faire des commissions** go shopping
commode convenient
commun common
communauté *f.* community
compagnie *f.* company; firm
compagnon *m.* companion
complètement completely
complice *m./f.* accomplice
compliqué complicated
complot *m.* plot; conspiracy
comportement *m.* behavior; attitude
comporter require; include; comprise; **se comporter** behave
composé compound; **passé composé** compound past
composition *f.* composition; theme
comprendre (*conj. like* **prendre**) understand; comprise
comprenez (*from* **comprendre**) you understand; **vous comprenez bien** you must understand
compromettre (*conj. like* **mettre**) jeopardize
comptable *m./f.* bookkeeper, accountant

Irregular verbs are conjugated on pp. 318–335.

compte *m.* account; **faire ses comptes** do one's accounts; **se rendre compte** (**de** + *n.*) realize
compter count (+ *inf.*) expect; intend; include; **sans compter que** besides the fact that
comptoir *m.* counter
concevoir conceive
concierge *m./f.* janitor; superintendent; caretaker
concilier reconcile; unite
conclure (*irr. v.*) conclude; **l'affaire sera conclue** the deal will be closed
Concorde *m.* supersonic Anglo-French plane
concours *m.* competitive examination
condamnable seriously questionable
condamner condemn
condition *f.* condition; social level; **à condition que** provided that
conduire (**conduisant, conduit, je conduis, je conduisis**) drive; take; **se conduire** behave
conduite *f.* behavior
conférence *f.* lecture; **en conférence** in conference, at a meeting
conférencier *m.* speaker, lecturer
confiance *f.* trust; faith
confier à trust (someone with)
confiture *f.* jam
conflit *m.* conflict
confort *m.* comfort
conjonction *f.* conjunction
connaissance *f.* acquaintance; knowledge; **faire connaissance avec** get acquainted with, meet; **faire la connaissance de** get acquainted with, meet
connaître (**connaissant, connu, je connais, je connus**) know, be acquainted with
connu well-known, famous
consciencieux (*f.* **consciencieuse**) conscientious
conscient conscious, fully aware of
conseil *m.* piece of advice; *pl.* advice; **tenir conseil** have a meeting
conseiller *n.m.* counselor; (*v*) (**à** + *person* + **de** + *inf.*) to advise

conservateur *m.* curator
consolant consoling
consommer accomplish
conspiration *f.* conspiracy
constamment constantly
construction *f.* construction work
construire (*conj. like* **conduire**) build
conte *m.* short story
contempler view; observe
contenir (*conj. like* **tenir**) contain
contenter satisfy; **se contenter de** be satisfied with
contestataire *m./f.* protester
contestation *f.* protest
conteur *m.* storyteller
continuellement continually; incessantly
continuer (à + *inf.*) continue; keep on
contraire *m.* contrary; **au contraire** on the contrary
contrebandier *m.* smuggler
contribuer contribute
convaincre (*conj. like* **vaincre**) convince
convaincu (*p.p. of* **convaincre**) convinced
convenable proper, fitting
convenir (*conj. like* **venir**) agree; be proper; be suiting; **convenir de** accept; **quelque chose convient** something is proper, something is suitable
convenu agreed; OK; agreed upon
convertir convert
convive *m./f.* guest
convoquer summon
copain *m.* pal, chum, close friend
copie *f.* paper (to hand in); (school) exercise
copier copy
copieux (*f.* **copieuse**) copious, plentiful
coq *m.* rooster
coquille *f.* shell
corde *f.* chord
corps *m.* body
correctement correctly
corriger (*irr. sp.* **B**) correct

Verbs with spelling changes are explained on pp. 336–338.

cortège *m.* procession
cosmique cosmic, vast
costume *m.* suit
côte *f.* coast; **côte à côte** side by side; **Côte d'Azur** French Riviera
côté *m.* side; **à côté de** near, beside, alongside of; in addition to; in the direction of; nearby; on the side of; **du côté de** toward; near; **mettre de côté** save; **tout à côté** right near
cou *m.* neck
couchant *m.* sunset
couché stretched out
coucher put to bed; spend the night; **se coucher** go to bed; *n. m.* bedtime; **coucher de soleil** *m.* sunset
couler flow
couleur *f.* color
couloir *m.* corridor
coup *m.* blow; "coup"; **coup d'œil** glance; **coup de poing** punch; **coup de tonnerre** thunderclap; **tout à coup** all of a sudden; **tout d'un coup** all of a sudden
coupable guilty; *n. m./f.* the guilty one
couper cut; cut down
cour *f.* yard; courtyard; court; **faire la cour** woo; court
courageux (*f.* **courageuse**) brave
courant running; **au courant** informed; **dans le courant de** during; **tenir au courant** keep informed
courber lean
courir (**courant, couru, je cours, je courus**) run; **courir des dangers** run some risks
couronne *f.* crown
courrier *m.* mail
cours *m.* course; **au cours de** during; **cours de vacances** summer courses; **faire ses cours** teach
course *f.* errand; race; trip; **faire des courses** go shopping, do errands
court short
courtisan *m.* courtier
couteau *m.* knife
coûter cost; **coûter cher** be expensive
coûteux (*f.* **coûteuse**) expensive
couturière *f.* seamstress

couvert (*p.p. of* **couvrir**) covered; *n.m.* cover; silverware; **enlever le couvert** clear the table; (*adj.*) covered
couverture *f.* blanket
couvrir (**se**) become covered
craie *f.* chalk
craignais (*imperfect of* **craindre**) feared
craindre (**craignant, craint, je crains, je craignis**) fear
crainte *f.* fear
crâne *m.* skull; head
crayon *m.* pencil
créancier *m.* creditor
créateur *m.* creator
créer create
crème *f.* cream
crêpe *f.* pancake
crépuscule *m.* twilight
creuser dig
creux (*f.* **creuse**) hollow
crevette *f.* shrimp
cri *m.* cry; screaming; **pousser un cri** utter a cry
criant : criant de vérité extremely realistic
crier yell; cry out
critique *f.* criticism; review
critiquer criticize
crochet *m.* hook
croire (**croyant, cru, je crois, je crus**) believe; **croire bon** deem fit
croisade *f.* crusade
croisé crossed; **mots croisés** *m. pl.* crossword puzzle
croiser cross
croisière *f.* cruise
croissant *m.* crescent-shaped French pastry
croix *f.* cross
croyant *m.* believer
cru harsh
cru, crus (*p.p. and s.p. of* **croire**) believed
cueillir pick
cuir *m.* leather
cuire (**cuisant, cuit, je cuis, je cuisis**) cook

Irregular verbs are conjugated on pp. 318–335.

cuisine *f.* cooking; kitchen
cuisinière *f.* cook
cultivé educated
cultiver cultivate
curé *m.* priest
curieux (*f.* **curieuse**) curious; odd; strange; inquisitive; eager; *n. pl.* curious people

D

d'abord at first; **tout d'abord** first of all
d'ailleurs besides
dame *f.* lady; **dame !** (*interjection*) why, of course
Danemark *m.* Denmark
dans in, on
dansant : soirée dansante evening party where people dance
danse *f.* dancing; **leçon de danse** *f.* dancing lesson
danser dance
danseuse *f.* dancer
dater date
d'avance in advance
de of; from; by; in; out of; with
débarrasser (**se**) (**de** + *n.*) get rid of
débattre (**se**) resist, struggle
déborder overflow
debout standing; **puisque vous êtes debout** since you are up
débrouiller (**se**) get along; figure a way out
début *m.* beginning
décapotable *f.* convertible (car)
décence *f.* decency
déception *f.* disappointment
décerner award
décès *m.* death
déchirer tear up
décider (**de** + *inf.*) decide; **se décider** (**à** + *inf.*) make up one's mind
décisif (*f.* **décisive**) decisive
décision *f.* decision; **prendre une décision** make a decision, make up one's mind
décor *m.* setting
décorer decorate
décorateur *m.* interior decorator

découper cut; cut out
décourager (*irr. sp.* **B**) discourage
découverte *f.* discovery
découvrir (*conj. like* **ouvrir**) discover
décrire (*conj. like* **écrire**) describe
déçu disappointed
défaut *m.* defect; shortcoming
défendre defend; (**à** + *pron.* + **de** + *inf.*) forbid
défilé *m.* march; procession; parade
définir define
définitivement definitely
défunt *m.* deceased person
dehors outside
déjà already
déjeuner have breakfast; have lunch; *n. m.* noon meal (main meal in France); **petit déjeuner** breakfast
délicatesse *f.* consideration
délicieux (*f.* **délicieuse**) delightful
délivrance *f.* emancipation
délivrer free
Delphes Delphi, Greek city famous for its oracles
demain tomorrow; **à partir de demain** from tomorrow on
demande *f.* demand
demander ask; (**à** + *person* + **de** + *inf.*) ask someone to; (**à** + *inf.*) ask to; **se demander** wonder
démarche *f.* step; **faire une démarche** take a step
déménager (*irr. sp.* **B**) move
demeurer remain
demi half; **demi-heure** *f.* half an hour; **demi-obscurité** *f.* semidarkness; shadowy light
demoiselle *f.* young lady; maiden
démission *f.* resignation
démolir demolish
dent *f.* tooth
dentelle *f.* lace
d'entre of
départ *m.* departure
dépasser go beyond; go around

Verbs with spelling changes are explained on pp. 336–338.

dépêcher (**se**) (**de** + *inf.*) hurry
déplacer (**se**) (*irr. sp.* **A**) go around; shift
déplaire (*conj. like* **plaire**) displease
déposer (**se**) be found; settle
dépourvu without
dépression *f.* hollow; fall
déprimant depressing
depuis since; from; for; **depuis peu** recently, since not very long ago
déranger (*irr. sp.* **B**) disturb, bother
dernier (*f.* **dernière**) last; latter
déroulement *m.* development
dérouler (**se**) unfold; develop; take place
derrière behind; **la porte de derrière** the back door
dès from; **dès l'aube** from early dawn; **dès que** as soon as; **dès que possible** as soon as possible
désagréable unpleasant
désastre *m.* disaster
désastreux (*f.* **désastreuse**) disastrous
descendre come down; go down; descend; **descendre à un hôtel** go to a hotel
désert deserted
désespéré desperate
désespérer (**se**) despair
désintéresser (**se**) lose interest
désirer (+ *inf.*) wish, desire
désolé sorry
désoler grieve, distress
désordonné disordered; wild
désordre *m.* disorder; **en désordre** in a mess
désormais from now on
dessin *m.* drawing; **dessin animé** cartoon
dessiné : **bande dessinée** *f.* comic strip
dessus upstairs; on it; **prendre le dessus** prevail
détourner turn away from
détruire (*conj. like* **conduire**) destroy
dette *f.* debt
deux two; **à deux** the two of us; together; **tous deux** both; **vous deux** both of you
devant before
devenir (*conj. like* **venir**) become
deviner guess

dévisager (*irr. sp.* **B**) stare at
devoir (*pp.* 216–221) (**devant, dû, je dois, je dus**) have to, must, ought to; should; probably + *verb*; *n. m.* duty, exercise, homework; **devoir connaître** be able to, know
dévorer devour
devrais (*cond. of* **devoir**) should, ought to
diable *m.* devil
diamant *m.* diamond
diapositive *f.* (photographic) slide
dictionnaire *m.* dictionary
Dieu *m.* God
difficile difficult
diffuser broadcast
Dijon city in eastern France between Paris and Lyons
dimanche *m.* Sunday
diminuer diminish
diner dine, have dinner
dire (**disant, dit, je dis, je dis**) (à + *person* + **de** + *inf.*) say; tell; **c'est-à-dire** that is to say; **en dire trop** say too much; **on dirait** one would say; it seems; **pour ainsi dire** so to speak; **vouloir dire** mean
directeur *m.* director; manager
dirigeant *m.* leader
diriger (*irr. sp.* **B**) direct; conduct; **se diriger** go
disant (*pres. part. of* **dire**) saying
discours *m.* speech
discuter discuss; argue about; talk something over
disparaître (*conj. like* **connaître**) disappear
dispenser give out, distribute
disposé arranged
disposer have available
disque *m.* (phonograph) record
dissimuler hide
distingué distinguished
distraction *f.* type of amusement; pastime

distraitement absentmindedly
dit (*pres. and p.p. of* **dire**) say; said; so-called
divers various, different
divertir amuse
divertissement *m.* pastime
dizaine *f.* about ten
docteur *m.* doctor
doigt *m.* finger
doit (*pres. of* **devoir**) must; has to; is to; probably does
domaine *m.* estate; grounds
domestique *m./f.* servant
dominer reign over; overlook
dommage too bad
dompteur *m.* trainer
don *m.* gift
donc then; thus; therefore; now; **allez donc voir** be sure and see; **entrez donc** do come in; **pensez donc** think of it; **qui donc** who is that ?; whom do you mean ?
donné : étant donné taking into account
donner give; **donner raison** justify one's action, prove that one is right; **donner sur** look out upon
doré gilded; golden
dormir (2) sleep
dos *m.* back
dossier *m.* file
Dostoïevski, Féodor (1821-1881); 19th-century Russian novelist
douane *f.* customs
doucement gently; softly
douceur *f.* softness
doué gifted
douleur *f.* pain; suffering; sorrow
douloureux (*f.* **douloureuse**) painful
doute *m.* doubt; **sans doute** probably
douteux (*f.* **douteuse**) doubtful
doux (*f.* **douce**) mild, soft
douzaine *f.* dozen
doyen *m.* dean; oldest member
dramaturge *m./f.* dramatist
drame *m.* drama
drapeau *m.* flag
dresser raise; **dresser les oreilles** prick up one's years; **se dresser** straighten oneself up; get up

---

Irregular verbs are conjugated on pp. 318–335.

drogue *f.* drug
droit *m.* study of law; justice; law; (*adj.*) right; straight; **tout droit** erect; straight ahead
droite *f.* right; **à ma droite** to my right
drôle funny; odd
drôlement in a peculiar manner
du of the; some
dû, due (*p.p. of* **devoir**) had to, etc.; due to
Dumas, Alexandre (1802-1870) 19th-century novelist and dramatist, author of *Les Trois mousquetaires*
dur hard; **dur d'oreille** hard of hearing
durer last

E

eau *f.* water; **eau de vie** brandy; **troubler l'eau** make the water murky
écart : à l'écart aside
échange *m.* exchange
échanger (*irr. sp.* **B**) exchange
échapper (**à** + *n.*) escape, avoid; **s'échapper** (**de** + *n.*) escape
écharpe *f.* scarf
échecs *m. pl.* chess
échelle *f.* ladder
éclabousser splash
éclairage *m.* light; lighting
éclaircir explain, clarify
éclairer light; throw a light
éclat *m.* gleam; brightness
éclater burst; break out; flash; **éclater de rire** burst out laughing
école *f.* school
économies *f. pl.* savings; **faire des économies** save
économiser save
écouler (**s'**) elapse, pass
écouter (+ *n.*) listen; listen to
écrasé crushed; overwhelmed
écrire (**écrivant, écrit, j'écris, j'écrivis**) write; **machine à écrire** *f.* typewriter
écrits *m. pl.* writings

Verbs with spelling changes are explained on pp. 336–338.

écrit : par écrit in writing
écrivain *m.* writer
édifice *m.* building; framework, structure
éducation *f.* education; bringing up; **éducation poussée** college education
effacer (*irr. sp.* **A**) erase; obliterate; draw in; **s'effacer** vanish
effet *m.* effect; **en effet** in fact; **exercer un effet** have an effect; **faire cet effet** have this effect; **par l'effet de** because of
effort *m.* effort
effrayer (*irr. sp.* **C**) scare, frighten; **s'effrayer** (**de**) become frightened (at)
effroyable frightful
égal equal; **cela m'était égal** it did not make any difference to me
également also
égaler equal
égard : à tous les égards in all respects
égarer (**s'**) wander; lose one's way
église *f.* church
égoïste selfish
égratignure *f.* scratch
élancer (**s'**) (*irr. sp.* **A**) dart forth
élargir (**s'**) widen
électricien *m.* electrician
électricité *f.* electricity; **panne d'électricité** power failure
élève *m./f.* pupil
élevé high; brought up; **bien élevé** well-mannered; **mal élevé** ill-mannered, ill-bred
élever raise; **s'élever** rise, get up
élire (*conj. like* **lire**) elect
éloigner keep away; **s'éloigner** go off, go away
élu (*p.p. of* **élire**) elected
émaner emanate; proceed
emballer wrap up
embarrassé embarrassed
embêter annoy
emboîter : emboîter le pas fall into step
embouteillage *m.* traffic jam
embrasser kiss; hug
emerger (*irr. sp.* **B**) emerge
émigré *m.* migrant
émigrer emigrate

éminent prominent

emmener (*irr. sp.* **D**) take away; take along

émouvant touching; stirring

emparer (**s'**) (**de** + *n.*) seize

empêcher (*n.* + **de** + *inf.*) hinder, prevent; **il n'empêche pas** that doesn't prevent

empereur *m.* emperor

empiéter encroach

. **emplir** fill

emploi *m.* use; job

employé *m.* clerk; employee; **petit employé** minor office clerk

employer (*irr. sp.* **C**) use

empoigner seize, grab

emporter take away (a thing); take along (a thing); **l'emporter** prevail

emprunter borrow

ému moved

en in; to; as; while; by; **en dehors** outside; **en vis-à-vis** opposite each other

encercler encircle

enchanté delighted

enchanteur *m.* enchanter; magician

encore again; still; yet; **encore un mot** one more word

encourageant encouraging

encre *f.* ink

encrier *m.* inkwell

endommager damage

endormi asleep; sleeping

endormir (**s'**) (2) fall asleep

endroit *m.* place

endurci hardened; confirmed

énergie *f.* energy; power

enfance *f.* childhood

enfant *m./f.* child

enfantin childish; **école enfantine** *f.* kindergarten

enfermer fence in

enfin finally, at last; in short, anyway; well

enfuir (**s'**) (*conj. like* **fuir**) flee; run

engagé engaged, involved

engagement *m.* involvement

engager (*irr. sp.* **B**) hire; start; encourage

enivrant intoxicating

enjoué sprightly, lively

enlever (*irr. sp.* **D**) take away; take off; **enlever le couvert** clear the table

ennui *m.* boredom; trouble; **quel ennui** what a shame, what a nuisance

ennuyer (*irr. sp.* **C**) bore; bother; **s'ennuyer** get bored; be lonesome; be bored

ennuyeux (*f.* **ennuyeuse**) annoying; boring

énorme enormous

énormément very much; considerably

enrégistrer record; register; check (baggage)

enrégistreur *m.* tape recorder

enseigner (*thing* + **à** + *person*; *person* + **à** + *inf.*) teach

ensemble together; whole; **exercices d'ensemble** summing-up exercises, review exercises

ensuite then

ensuivre (**s'**) (*conj. like* **suivre**) result from

entassé packed

entasser stack up

entendre hear; mean; **entendre dire que** hear that; **entendre parler de** hear of; **s'entendre** be heard; get along

entendu agreed

entente *f.* understanding; agreement; harmony

enterrement *m.* burial

entier (*f.* **entière**) entire; whole; **tout entier** completely

entièrement entirely

entouré surrounded

entourer (**de** + *n.*) surround; cover over

entracte *m.* intermission

entraîneur *m.* trainer

entre between; **d'entre** of

entr'ouvert half open

entrée *f.* entrance; beginning

entreprendre (*conj. like* **prendre**) undertake

entrer (**dans** + *n.*) enter; penetrate

entrevoir (*conj. like* **voir**) imagine

envahir invade; come over

envahissement *m.* encroachment, invasion

Irregular verbs are conjugated on pp. 318–335.

enveloppe *f.* envelope
envelopper wrap; wrap up
envers toward
envie *f.* wish, desire; **avoir envie de**
   feel like
envier envy
environ about, approximately
environs *m. pl.* surroundings; surrounding territory; vicinity
envisager (*irr. sp.* **B**) consider
envoi *m.* parcel
envoler (**s'**) fly away
envoyer (**envoyant, envoyé, j'envoie,**
   j'envoyai) send; **envoyer chercher**
   send for
épais (*f.* **épaisse**) thick
épaisseur *f.* depth
épargner spare
épatant wonderful; stunning
épaule *f.* shoulder; **hausser les épaules**
   shrug one's shoulders
éperdu in a panic
épidémie *f.* epidemic
épigraphe *f.* epigraph, quotation at the
   beginning of a book
épinard *m.* spinach
époque *f.* time; period
épouser (+ *person*) marry
épouvantable appalling, frightful
éprouver feel; experience
épuisant exhausting
épuisé exhausted
épuiser (**s'**) wear oneself out
errer wander
erreur *f.* mistake; **faire erreur** make a
   mistake
érudit *m.* scholar; learned person
escale *f.* port of call; **faire escale** stop at
   (a port)
escroc *m.* swindler
espace *m.* space
espacé spaced
Espagne *f.* Spain
espagnol Spanish
espèce *f.* kind; race
espérance hope; expectation

espérer (*irr. sp.* **E**) (+ *inf.*) hope; expect
espion *m.* spy
espoir *m.* hope
esprit *m.* spirit; wit; mind
essai *m.* essay
essayer (*irr. sp.* **C**) (**de** + *inf.*) try; try on
essayiste *m.* essayist
essence *f.* essence; gasoline
essuyer (*irr. sp.* **C**) wipe
estimer think, consider
établir establish
étage *m.* floor; **le premier étage** the
   second floor
étaler display
étang *m.* pond
étant (*pres. part. of* **être**) being
étape *f.* step
état *m.* state; shape; **examen d'état** state
   examination
États-Unis *m. pl.* United States
été (*v.*) (*p.p. of* **être**) been
été *n.m.* summer
éteindre (*conj. like* **peindre**) turn off;
   s'éteindre come to an end; die out
étendre (**s'**) stretch out
étendue *f.* expanse
étoffe *f.* fabric, material, cloth
étoile *f.* star; **à la belle étoile** in the
   open; **l'étoile du Berger** Venus
étonnant astonishing; remarkable; surprising, amazing
étonné surprised
étonnement *m.* surprise
étonner astonish; surprise; **s'étonner** be
   surprised
étouffant oppressive
étouffé stifled
étouffer choke, smother
étrange strange
étranger *m.* (*f.* **étrangère**) foreigner;
   strange person; stranger; **à l'étranger**
   abroad; (*adj.*) foreign; strange
étrangeté *f.* strangeness
étrangler strangle
être (**étant, été, je suis, je fus**) be; **être à**
   l'aise be comfortable; **ne pas être en**
   reste be equal to the situation; **vous**
   n'en seriez pas là you wouldn't be in
   such a fix; *n. m.* being

Verbs with spelling changes are explained on
pp. 336–338.

étroit narrow; close

étude *f.* study; **camarade d'étude** school friend

étudiant *m.* (college) student

eu, eus (*p.p. and s.p. of* **avoir**) had

européen (*f.* **européenne**) European

eux *m.* them

évader (**s'**) escape

évanouir (**s'**) faint

éveiller awaken; arouse

événement *m.* event

évidemment obviously

évident obvious

éviter (**de** + *inf.*) avoid

évocateur suggestive; meaningful, inspiring

évoluer develop; evolve; change

évoquer evoke, bring up

exact true; correct

exactement exactly

examen *m.* examination; **examen d'état** state examination; **passer un examen** take an examination

examiner examine

exaucer grant; fulfill

excepté except

excès *m.* excess; **excès de vitesse** speeding; **faire des excès** "go overboard"

excuser (**s'**) apologize

exécuter (**s'**) take place

exemple *m.* example; **par exemple** for exemple; what do you know (*exclamation*); **servir d'exemple** serve as an example

exempt free

exercer (*irr. sp.* **A**) : **exercer un effet** have an effect

exercice *m.* exercise; **exercices d'ensemble** summing-up exercises; review exercises

exigeant demanding

exiger (*irr. sp.* **B**) require; call for; demand

existence *f.* existence; life

existentialiste existentialist; referring to the philosophy of existentialism

exotisme *m.* exoticism; being from another and strange land

expérience *f.* experience; experiment

explication *f.* explanation

expliquer explain; **s'expliquer** be explained

exposer exhibit

exposition *f.* fair

exprès on purpose; **par exprès** special delivery

exprimer express

extraire extract

extrêmement extremely

F

fabriquer make; manufacture

fabuliste *m./f.* writer of fables

face *f.* face; **bien en face** straight in the eye; **de face** face to face; **d'en face** on the opposite side (of the street); **face à** facing; **face à face** facing each other; **faire face à** face up to; accept

fâché angry; sorry

fâcher (**se**) (**contre** + *person*) get angry

fâcheux (*f.* **fâcheuse**) unfortunate, annoying

facilement easily

façon *f.* manner; way; **de la même façon** in the same way; **façons de faire** ways of doing things

facteur *m.* mail carrier

faculté *f.* college or school of a university, including buildings and teaching staff

faible weak

faim *f.* hunger; **avoir faim** be hungry

faire (**faisant, fait, je fais, je fis**) (+ *inf.*) do; make; carry out; have (done)*

faire des provisions buy groceries

faisan *m.* pheasant

faisant : **chemin faisant** on one's way

fait *m.* fact

falloir (**fallu, il faut, il fallut**) (+ *inf.*) must; be necessary; **comme il faut**

Irregular verbs are conjugated on pp. 318–335.

*Expressions beginning with faire are defined under the other significant word(s) of the expression.

properly; **il faut** it takes; one must; **il me faut** I need

familial (*adj.*) family

familier (*f.* **familière**) familiar; intimate

famille *f.* family; **famille nombreuse** large family

faner (**se**) wilt

fantaisiste whimsical; fanciful

fantastique *m.* the fantastic, the fanciful; the fantastic quality

farce *f.* farce; **faire des farces** play tricks; play jokes

farine *f.* flour

fasciner fascinate

fasse (*pres. subj. of* **faire**) make; do

fatigant tiring; tiresome

fatiguer tire

faudra : il me faudra I will need

faut (*pres. of* **falloir**) must, has to; **il faut** one must; it takes; **comme il faut** properly; **il me faut** I need

faute *f.* mistake; **sans faute** without fail

fauteuil *m.* armchair

fauve tawny; wild

faux (*f.* **fausse**) false

faveur *f.* favor

favori (*f.* **favorite**) favorite

favoriser favor

féliciter congratulate

femme *f.* woman; wife; **femme de ménage** cleaning woman

fenêtre *f.* window

fente *f.* crack, slit

ferai, ferais (*fut. and cond. of* **faire**) will make, will do; would make, would do

ferme *f.* farm; (*adj.*) firm; **tenir ferme** hold fast

fermement firmly

fermer close; **fermer à clé** lock

fermier *m.* farmer

féroce ferocious

fervent *n. m.* enthusiastic fan

fête *f.* holiday; festivity; celebration; birthday; party

Verbs with spelling changes are explained on pp. 336–338.

feu *m.* fire; **en feu** on fire; **feu rouge** red light; traffic light

feuille *f.* leaf; sheet

feuillet *m.* leaf

ficelle *f.* string; piece of string

fidèle faithful

fidélité *f.* loyalty

fier (**se**) trust; have confidence in

fier (*f.* **fière**) proud

figure *f.* face

fil *m.* wire

filer speed

fille *f.* daughter; girl; **jeune fille** *f.* girl

fillette *f.* young girl; little girl

fils *m.* son

fin *n. f.* end; (*adj.*): **vin fin** vintage wine

finalement finally

finesse *f.* subtlety; finesse; fineness

finir finish; **finir mal** end up badly; **finir par** end up by; **il n'en finit pas** he never stops

fixer fix; retain

flairer sniff

flamand Flemish

flambé bright-colored

flanc *m.* side

flatter satisfy

flatteur (*f.* **flatteuse**) flattering; *n. m.* flatterer

Flaubert, Gustave (1821–1885) well-known 19th-century French novelist, author of *Madame Bovary*

flèche *f.* arrow

fleur *f.* flower; **fleur d'eau** water flower

fleuriste *m./f.* florist

flottant windblown

foie *m.* liver

foire *f.* fair

fois *f.* time; **à la fois** at the same time; **une fois pour toutes** once and for all; **maintes fois** many times

fol (*before vowel sound*) crazy

folie *f.* folly; joke

folle (*f. of* **fou**) crazy, reckless

follement wildly; ardently

foncé dark

fonctionnaire *m./f.* government employee

fond *m.* bottom; background; end; **au**

fond deep down inside; indeed; essentially; in the depths of
fonder found
fondre melt
fontaine *f.* fountain
football *m.* football; ball; soccer
force *f.* strength; force; **de toutes ses forces** with all his/her strength
forêt *f.* forest
formation *f.* development
formidable marvelous
fort (*adj.*) loud; strong; (intellectually) good; (*adv.*) hard; very
fou (*before vowel sound* **fol**, *f.* **folle**) crazy; reckless
fouet *m.* whip
fouille *f.* search; **faire des fouilles** dig, excavate
fouine *f.* marten, weasel
foule *f.* crowd
fouler sprain
fourchette *f.* fork
fournir furnish; provide
fourrure *f.* fur
foyer *m.* fireplace; lobby (in a theater)
fraîcheur *f.* freshness
frais (*f.* **fraîche**) fresh; cool
fraise *f.* strawberry
framboise *f.* raspberry
franc (*f.* **franche**) frank
Français *m.* Frenchman; **Française** *f.* Frenchwoman
français French
franchement frankly
frappant striking
frapper strike; knock
fraternité *f.* fraternity; brotherhood
frémir quiver; shudder; **il en frémit** it made him shudder
fréquemment frequently
fréquenté visited; **peu fréquenté** not very often visited
fréquenter frequent, go to regularly
frère *m.* brother
frigidaire *m.* refrigerator
frissonner shiver

froid *m.* cold; **avoir froid** be cold; **il fait froid** it is cold
froidement coldly; cooly
front *m.* forehead
fugitif (*f.* **fugitive**) fleeting
fuir (**fuyant, fui, je fuis, je fuis**) flee; avoid
fumer smoke
furieux (*f.* **furieuse**) furious
furtivement furtively
fus, fut (*s.p. of* **être**) was
fusil *m.* gun; rifle
fusse, fût (*imperfect subj. of* **être**) was
fuyant (*pres. part. of* **fuir**) fleeing

G

gâcher spoil
gagner win; gain; earn
gai cheerful
gaillard *m.* a vigorous, strapping fellow
galerie *f.* gallery; **Galeries Lafayette** a well-known chain of French department stores
Gange *m.* the Ganges, sacred river of India
gant *m.* glove
garagiste *m./f.* auto mechanic; garage owner
garçon *m.* boy; waiter
garde *m.* watchman; guard; **être de garde** be on duty
garder keep; watch
gardien *m.* watchman
gare *f.* station; railroad station
gare à lui ! he'd better look out
Garonne *f.* river in southwestern France
gâteau *m.* cake
gâter spoil
gauche *f.* left
gazon *m.* lawn
gelée *f.* jelly
gêné embarrassed
gêner disturb; bother; embarrass
génie *m.* genius
genou *m.* knee
genre *m.* type
gens *m. pl.* people; **braves gens** fine people; **les gens de dessus** the people

---

Irregular verbs are conjugated on pp. 318–335.

who live above; **jeunes gens** young men; young people

gentil (*f.* **gentille**) nice

gentiment in a friendly, nice way

geste *m.* gesture

gifle *f.* slap

gifler slap

gisement *m.* mineral field

glace *f.* mirror; ice; ice cream

glacial icy

glissement *m.* sliding; sliding noise; swishing

glisser slip

gloire *f.* glory; **valoir la gloire** bring glory

glorieux (*f.* **glorieuse**) glorious

Goncourt, Edmond (1822–1896) **et Jules** (1830–1870) 19th-century naturalist writers

gonfler swell

gorge *f.* throat

gorgée *f.* spoonful (*lit.* throatful)

goût *m.* taste

goûter taste

gouverner govern

gracieux (*f.* **gracieuse**) graceful; gracious

grammaire *f.* grammar

grand great; large; main; **il est grand temps** it is high time

grand-chose much; **votre idée ne vaut pas grand-chose** your idea isn't worth much

grand-mère *f.* grandmother

grand-père *m.* grandfather

grands-parents *m. pl.* grandparents

grandir grow

grange *f.* barn

gras (*f.* **grasse**) fat

gratter scratch

Grèce *f.* Greece

grenier *m.* attic

grève *f.* strike; beach

gréviste *m./f.* striker

grille *f.* iron gate

grillé toasted

gris gray

Verbs with spelling changes are explained on pp. 336–338.

griser intoxicate

gronder scold; grumble; rumble

gros (*f.* **grosse**) big; fat; important

grossir get fat

grotte *f.* grotto; cave

guère scarcely, hardly

guéri cured; healed

guéridon *m.* small, round table

guérison *m.* recovery; cure

guerre *f.* war; **faire la guerre** wage war

guitare *f.* guitar

gymnastique *f.* exercise; **faire de la gymnastique** exercise

H

*indicates an aspirate *h*

habileté *f.* cleverness; ability

habiller dress; **s'habiller** dress oneself

habiter (+ *place*; **à** + *place*) live; inhabit

habitude *f.* habit; **comme d'habitude** as usual

habituel usual

habituer (**s'**) (**à** + *inf.*) get used to

*haine *f.* hate

haleine *f.* breath

*haletant breathless, panting

*hameau *m.* hamlet

*hanté haunted

hardi bold

*haricots verts *m. pl.* green beans

harmonica *m.* mouth organ

harmonieux (*f.* **harmonieuse**) harmonious

*hasard *m.* hazard; chance; **au hasard** at random

*hâte *f.* haste; **avoir hâte** be in a hurry

*hausser raise; **hausser les épaules** shrug one's shoulders

*haut high; **à haute voix** aloud

*hauteur *f.* height; level

*Haye, La *f.* The Hague, capital of the Netherlands

*hélas alas

héritier *m.* heir

*héros *m.* hero

hésiter hesitate

heure *f.* hour; o'clock; time; **à l'heure** on time; **de bonne heure** early; **tout à**

l'heure in a little while; a little while ago
heureux (*f.* **heureuse**) happy
*__heurter__ (**se**) (**à** + *n.*) run up against
hier yesterday; **avant-hier** the day before yesterday
histoire *f.* story; history; trouble; **faire des histoires** complicate things; **quelle histoire !** what a fuss !
hiver *m.* winter
*__hocher__ nod; **hocher la tête** nod one's head
homme *m.* man; **homme politique** politician
*__Hongrois__ *m.* Hungarian
honneur *m.* honor; **faire honneur** honor
*__honteusement__ in embarrassment
*__honteux__ (*f.* **honteuse**) ashamed
hors outside; **hors de lui** beside himself
hôte *m.* guest; host
hôtel *m.* hotel; **hôtel de ville** city hall
huiler oil
huître *f.* oyster
humain human
humble *m.* humble person, meek person
humeur *f.* humor; mood; **de mauvaise humeur** in a bad mood
hurler howl
hypocondriaque a person who is overconcerned about his or her health
hypocrite (*adj.*) hypocritical
hypothèse *f.* hypothesis

I

ici here
idée *f.* idea
identité *f.* identification; **carte d'identité** *f.* identification card
ignorer not to know; be unaware of
île *f.* island
illusoire illusory
illustre illustrious
illustré illustrated
îlot *m.* small island; small block

image *f.* picture
imbécile *m./f.* fool
immédiatement immediately
immobile motionless
imparfait *m.* imperfect (tense)
impatienter (**s'**) become impatient
imperméable *m.* raincoat
impertinent bad
importe : n'importe quoi anything
importer matter; be important
impôt *m.* tax
imprévu unforeseen
imprimer print
inaltérable unchangeable
inattendu unexpected
incapable unable
incendie *m.* fire
incendier set fire
incertain uncertain
incertitude *f.* uncertainty
incliné sloping
incliner bend
inconnu *m.* stranger; (*adj.*) unknown
incroyable unbelievable
inculpé *m.* accused one
indécis irresolute, indecisive
indemne untouched, unharmed
Inde *f.* India
indien (*f.* **indienne**) Indian
indiquer indicate; show
indiscutable indisputable
individu *m.* person; individual (often with an unfavorable connotation)
inébranlable unshakable
inépuisable inexhaustible
inestimable priceless
inexplicable unexplainable
inextricable inextricable, difficult to solve
infesté tormented
infiniment infinitely
infirmier (*f.* **infirmière**) nurse
influent influential
influer influence
informé informed
informer (**s'**) (**sur** + *n.*) inquire for information; get information about
ingénieur *m.* engineer
ingénieux clever

Irregular verbs are conjugated on pp. 318–335.

ingrat *m.* ungrateful man; (*adj.*) dull;
   thankless
injuste unjust
innombrable innumerable
inoffensif (*f.* **inoffensive**) harmless
inondation *f.* flood
inonder flood
inquiet (*f.* **inquiète**) uneasy, worried
inquiétant alarming
inquiéter (**s'**) (*irr. sp.* **E**) worry
inquiétude *f.* uneasiness; worry
inscrire (*conj. like* **écrire**) inscribe
insignifiant insignificant
insister (**sur** + *thing;* **pour** + *inf.;* **pour**
   que + *subj.*) insist
inspecteur *m.* detective
installer (**s'**) get settled
instant *m.* instant; moment; **à l'instant**
   même où at the very moment when
instantanément suddenly; instantly
institutrice *f.* woman teacher
instruire (**s'**) learn
insuffisant insufficient
insupportable unbearable
intention *f.* intention; **avoir l'intention**
   de intend to
interdire (*conj. like* **dire**) forbid
intéressé self-seeking
intéresser interest; **s'intéresser** (**à** + *n.*)
   be interested in
intérêt *m.* interest
intérieur *m.* inside
intime intimate; **journal intime** *m.*
   diary
intoxiqué *m.* addict
introduire (*conj. like* **conduire**) introduce (something into); insert
intrus *m.* intruder, trespasser
inutile useless
invendable unsaleable
inverse inverted
inversé inverted; upside down
invité *m.* guest
inviter (**à** + *inf.*) invite; entice
involontaire involuntary

Verbs with spelling changes are explained on
pp. 336–338.

invoquer invoke
irai, irais (*fut. and cond. of* **aller**) will go;
   would go
ironique ironical
Isle-Adam a town near Paris
isoler isolate
issue *f.* exit; **sans issue** impassable
italien (*f.* **italienne**) Italian
italique *m.* italics
itinéraire *m.* itinerary

J

jadis [ʒ adis] formerly
jaloux (*f.* **jalouse**) jealous
jamais ever; never; **à jamais** forever;
   ne... jamais never
jambe *f.* leg
jambon *m.* ham
Japon *m.* Japan
japonais Japanese
jardin *m.* garden; park; **jardin**
   zoologique zoo
jardinage *m.* gardening
jardinier *m.* gardener
jaunâtre yellowish
jaune yellow
Jeannot Johnnie
jet *m.* flow
jeter (*irr. sp.* **F**) throw; **jeter les yeux**
   glance; **jeter le trouble** disrupt; **se**
   jeter throw oneself; empty
jeu *m.* game; play; **jeu de cartes** deck
   of cards; **jeu de mots** play on words,
   pun; **jeu vidéo** video game
jeudi *m.* Thursday
jeune young; **jeune fille** *f.* girl; **jeunes**
   gens *m.* young men; young people
jeunesse *f.* youth
joie *f.* joy
joindre (*conj. like* **craindre**) join
joli pretty
joliment nicely
jongleur *m.* juggler
joue *f.* cheek
jouer (**de** + *instrument;* **à** + *game*) play;
   jouer de make use of; turn on; **jouer**
   un tour play a trick
jouet *m.* toy

joueur *m.* player
jouir enjoy
jour *m.* day; **au jour le jour** day by day; from one day to the other; **un beau jour** one fine day; a certain day; **dans les beaux jours** during the summer months; **de nos jours** in our day; in our time
journal *m.* newspaper; magazine; **journal intime** diary; **journal de sport** sports magazine
journaliste *m./f.* journalist
journée *f.* day; **bonne journée** have a good day
jovial fun-loving
joyeusement joyfully
joyeux (*f.* **joyeuse**) joyful
juge *m./f.* judge
juger (*irr. sp.* **B**) deem; judge; examine; scan; **juger bon** deem advisable
jugement *m.* judgment
juin *m.* June
jumelles *f. pl.* twin sisters; field glasses
jurer swear
jus *m.* juice
justifier justifier
jusqu'à up to; as far as; to the point of
jusqu'à ce que (+ *subj.*) until
juste just; exact
justice *f.* justice; **palais de justice** *m.* courthouse

K

kilo *m.* kilogram (2.2 pounds)
kilomètre *m.* kilometer (approximately 5/8 of a mile); **faire cent kilomètres** go a hundred kilometers
kiosque *m.* newspaper stand

L

là there; here; **çà et là** here and there
là-bas over there
là-haut up there
lac *m.* lake

---

lâcher let go
laideur *f.* ugliness
laine *f.* wool
laisser (+ *inf.*) let; leave
lait *m.* milk
laitier *m.* milk dealer; milkman
lamentable woeful
lampe *f.* lamp; **lampe à pied** floor lamp
lancer (*irr. sp.* **A**) throw
langage *m.* manner of speech
langue *f.* tongue; language
lapin *m.* rabbit
large *m.* open sea; (*adj.*) wide
largement widely
lasser (**se**) get tired
lauréat *m.* prizewinner
Lausanne town situated on Lake Geneva in the French part of Switzerland
laver wash; **se laver** wash oneself
le, la, les (*definite article*) the; (*personal pron.*) him; her; it; them
leçon *f.* lesson; **leçon de danse** dance lesson
lecteur *m.* reader
lecture *f.* reading
léger (*f.* **légère**) light; slight
léguer bequeath; leave
lendemain *m.* next day; **le lendemain matin** the next morning
lent slow
lequel (*f.* **laquelle**) (*inter.*) which; which one; (*rel.*) whom; which
lettre *f.* letter; **faire une lettre** write a letter; **homme (femme) de lettres** writer
leur (*pron.*) them; to them; (*adj.*) their; **le leur,** *etc.* theirs
lever : lever du soleil *m.* sunrise
lever (*irr. sp.* **D**) raise; lift; **se lever** get up
lèvre *f.* lip
lézard *m.* lizard
libérer free, liberate
liberté *f.* freedom
libertin *m.* libertine; nonconformist
libraire *m.* bookseller
libre free; open
Libye *f.* Libya, country in North Africa

lier link; tie; **se lier avec** form a friendship with
lieu *m.* place; spot; **s'il y a lieu** if necessary; **au lieu de** instead; **avoir lieu**
take place
ligne *f.* line; continuity; outline; manner; **pilote de ligne** *m.* commercial
pilot
limbes *f. p.* limbo
linge *m.* dirty clothes; linen; laundry
lire (lisant, lu, je lis, je lus) read
lisant (*pres. part.* of **lire**) reading
lisse smooth
lit *m.* bed
litre *m.* liter (about 1.06 quarts)
livre *m.* book; *f.* pound
livrer (se) à have recourse to
livret *m.* libretto, text (of an opera)
loger (*irr. sp.* **B**) lodge, live
loi *f.* law
loin far; **de loin** by far
lointain distant
Loire *f.* river in central and western
France
loisir *m.* leisure time
Londres *m.* London
long (*f.* **longue**) long; **le long de** along
longer (*irr. sp.* **B**) go along the edge of
longtemps a long time
longuement at length
lot *m.* : **un lot de livres** a batch of books
louable praiseworthy
louer rent; reserve (a seat); hire
Louisiane *f.* Louisiana
loup *m.* wolf
lourd heavy
Louvre *m.* famous museum in Paris
lu, lus (*p.p. and s.p. of* **lire**) read
luisant shiny
lui him, to him; to her; it, to it; **bien à**
lui typical, characteristic
lumière *f.* light; **mettre en lumière**
throw light upon
lumineux (*f.* **lumineuse**) bright
lundi *m.* Monday

lune *f.* moon; **clair de lune** *m.* moonlight; **lune de miel** honeymoon
lutte *f.* struggle; wrestling
luxe *m.* luxury
lycée *m.* French secondary school, somewhat equivalent to American high
school and junior college combined
lycéen *m.* high school student
Lyon Lyons, second largest city of
France, located on the Rhône
lyrique lyrical
lyrisme *m.* lyricism

M

machine *f.* machine; **machine à écrire**
typewriter; **taper à la machine** type
madrigal *m.* a short love poem
magasin *m.* store
magnétophone *m.* tape recorder
magnifique magnificent
maigre very thin, skinny; low (salary);
poor
maigrir get thin
main *f.* hand; **porter la main à** put one's
hand on
maintenant now
maintes : maintes fois many times
maire *m.* mayor
mairie *f.* city hall; town hall
mais but; **mais non** why, no; **mais oui**
certainly; why, yes
maïs *m.* corn
maison *f.* house; home; **maison de**
campagne country home
maître *m.* teacher;, master; leader; title
given to lawyers and to country resi-
dents of a certain stature
maîtresse *f.* teacher; **maîtresse de**
maison lady of the house
maîtriser control; master
majestueux (*f.* **majestueuse**) majestic
majorité *f.* majority
mal *m.* evil; sickness; (*adv.*) badly; not
well; **avoir mal** be sore; ache; **avoir**
mal au cœur feel nauseated; **avoir**
mal à la tête have a headache; **avoir**
un terrible mal de tête have a terrible
headache; **finir mal** end up badly;

Verbs with spelling changes are explained on
pp. 336–338.

mal à l'aise ill at ease; **mal élevé**
ill-bred; **se faire mal** hurt oneself; **se
sentir mal** feel sick; **se trouver mal**
faint; feel sick
malade *m./f.* patient; sick person; (*adj.*)
sick; **tomber malade** get sick
maladie *f.* sickness
malaise *m.* uneasiness; discomfort
malchance *f.* bad luck
malédiction *f.* curse
malgré in spite of; **malgré lui** in spite of
himself
malheur *m.* misfortune
malheureux (*f.* **malheureuse**) unhappy
malin smart
manche *f.* sleeve; **la Manche** the English
Channel
manger (*irr. sp.* **B**) eat; **salle à manger** *f.*
dining room
manie *f.* mania
manière *f.* manner, way
manifestation *f.* demonstration
manifeste obvious
Manitoba *m.* province in Western Canada
mannequin *m.* model; mannikin
manquer (pp. 114, 143) miss; lack; **elle
manqua de savon** she was short
of soap
mansarde *f.* attic, garret
manteau *m.* overcoat
manuscrit *m.* manuscript
marchand *m.* merchant; storekeeper
marche *f.* walking; progress; **faire de la
marche** take walks
marché *m.* market; **bon marché** cheap
mardi *m.* Tuesday; **le Mardi gras** the last
Tuesday before Lent
marée *f.* tide; flood
mari *m.* husband
mariage *m.* wedding; marriage
marier (*person* + **à** + *person*) marry; **se
marier** (**avec** + *person*) marry; get
married
Maroc *m.* Morocco
marquer mark; measure; indicate
marquise title given to the wife of a
marquis

Irregular verbs are conjugated on pp. 318–335.

mars *m.* March
Marseille *f.* Marseilles, large port city in
France on the Mediterranean
marteau *m.* hammer
masse *f.* juggler's club
massif (*f.* **massive**) massive; large and
heavy
match *m.* game
maternel (*f.* **maternelle**) : **l'école
maternelle** *f.* kindergarten
matin *m.* morning; **de bon matin** early
Matisse (1869–1954) famous French
post-Impressionist painter
maudit cursed; damned
mauvais bad
me me, to me
mécanique *f.* mechanics
mécanicien *m.* mechanic
méchant mean, vicious; bad; naughty
mécontent displeased, dissatisfied
médecin *m.* doctor
méfiance *f.* distrust
méfier (**se**) (**de** + *n.*) mistrust; distrust
mégaphone *m.* loudspeaker
meilleur better; best; **meilleur marché**
cheaper; **de meilleure heure** earlier
mélancolie *f.* melancholy
mélancolique melancholy
mélange *m.* mixture
mélanger (*irr. sp.* **B**) mix
mêlé mixed; involved in
mêler mix; **se mêler** be mixed; be
blended; make oneself a part; mingle
mélomane *m./f.* music lover
même self; same; even; itself; mere;
very; **quand même** even so, just the
same; **tout de même** all the same;
exactly as, just as
mémoire *f.* memory
mémoires *m. pl.* memoirs
menace *f.* threat
menacer (*irr. sp.* **A**) (**de** + *inf.*) threaten
ménage *m.* household; housework;
femme de ménage *f.* cleaning woman
mener (*irr. sp.* **D**) lead, take (a person)
mensonge *m.* lie
mentir lie
menu small, tiny
menuisier *m.* carpenter

mer *f.* sea; **revenir de la mer** come back from the seaside

mercredi *m.* Wednesday

mère *f.* mother; old Mrs. (used in the country); **mère de famille** mother (of a family)

mériter deserve

merveilleux *m.* marvelous quality

merveilleux (*f.* **merveilleuse**) marvelous

messieurs (*pl. of* **monsieur**) gentlemen

mesure *f.* measure; **à mesure que** as; **au fur et à mesure** gradually

mesurer measure; look over

méthodique methodical

métier *m.* trade; type of work

mètre *m.* meter (39.37 inches)

métro (*abbreviation for* **métropolitain**) *m.* subway

mettre (**mettant, mis, je mets, je mis**) put, put on; turn on; **mettre à la poste** mail; **mettre en lumière** throw light on; **mettre en œuvre** apply; illustrate; **mettre la table** set the table; **mettre à profit** take advantage; **se mettre** become; **se mettre à** begin; **se mettre à l'abri** take shelter; **se mettre à table** sit down at the table; **se mettre au lit** go to bed; **se mettre au travail** set oneself to work; **se mettre d'accord** agree; **se mettre en colère** get angry; **se mettre en quête** set out in search of

meuble *m.* (piece of) furniture

meubler furnish

Mexique *m.* Mexico

mi-corps : à mi-corps halfway into

midi *m.* noon

miel *m.* honey; **lune de miel** *f.* honeymoon

mieux better; best; **faire de son mieux** do one's best

mignon (*f.* **mignonne**) cute

milieu *m.* middle; **milieu mondain** high society

militaire *m.* soldier; (*adj.*) **militaire** military

militant militant

mille thousand

millier *m.* thousand

mine *f.* looks, appearance

ministre *m.* minister

minute *f.* minute; **une minute** just a minute

minutie *f.* attention to minute detail

miraculeux (*f.* **miraculeuse**) miraculous

mirage *m.* delusion

miroir *m.* mirror

mis (*p.p. and s.p. of* **mettre**) put

misérable *m./f.* scoundrel; unfortunate person

mode *f.* fashion; style

modéré moderate; subdued

modifier modify

mœurs *f. pl.* mores; customs

moi me, to me; self; I

moindre least; slightest

moins less; **de moins en moins** less and less; **du moins** at least; **à moins que** (+ *subj.*) unless

moisson *f.* harvest

moitié *f.* half

Molière (1622–1673) French dramatist, writer of comedies

molle (*f. of* **mou**) soft; weak

mollet *m.* calf of the leg

moment *m.* moment; time; **ce n'est pas le moment** it isn't the proper time; **d'un moment à l'autre** from one minute to the next; at any time

monarque *m.* monarch

mondain fashionable; **milieu mondain** *m.* high society

monde *m.* world; people; **tout le monde** everybody; **trop de monde** too many people

monsieur *m.* (*pl.* **messieurs**) sir, Mr.; gentleman

monstrueux (*f.* **monstrueuse**) monstrous

mont *m.* small mountain

Mont Blanc *m.* highest peak of the French Alps

montagne *f.* mountain

montée *f.* rise

monter go up; go up to; rise; climb; bring up; **monter en collier** make

---

Verbs with spelling changes are explained on pp. 336–338.

into a necklace; **monter dans une chambre** go up to a room; **monter dans un train** get on a train; **monter sur** get on

montre *f.* watch

Montréal largest city in French Canada (Québec)

montrer show; **se montrer** appear

moquer (se) (de + *n.*) make fun of; not care about

morale *f.* moral; lesson

moralité *f.* morality

morceau *m.* piece

mordre bite

mort (*p.p. of* **mourir**) died; dead

mort *f.* death

mortel (*f.* **mortelle**) mortal

Moscou *m.* Moscow

mot *m.* word; **encore un mot** one more word; **jeu de mots** *m.* play on words; pun; **mots croisés** crossword puzzle; **mot de passe** password

moteur *m.* motor; **bateau à moteur** *m.* motorboat

moto *f.* motorcycle; **en moto** on a motorcycle

motocyclette *f.* motorcycle

mou (*before vowel sound* **mol**; *f.* **molle**) weak; soft

moucher (se) blow one's nose

mouchoir *m.* handkerchief

mouillé wet

mouiller wet, moisten; **se mouiller** get wet

mourir (mourant, mort, je meurs, je mourus) die

moustique *m.* mosquito

mouton *m.* sheep

mouvement *m.* movement; **rentrer en mouvement** be on the move again

moyen *m.* means; way

muet (*f.* **muette**) silent

mur *m.* wall

mûr ripe

mûre *f.* mulberry

musée *m.* museum

musicalité *f.* musical quality

musicien *m.* musician

musique *f.* music; **faire de la musique** play music

mystère *m.* mystery

mystérieux (*f.* **mystérieuse**) mysterious

N

nager (*irr. sp.* **B**) swim

naïf (*f.* **naïve**) naive

naissance *f.* birth

naître (naissant, né, je nais, je naquis) be born

nappe *f.* : **nappe d'eau** sheet of water

narrateur *m.* (**narratrice** *f.*) narrator

natif (*f.* **native**) native

Nations unies *f. pl.* United Nations

nationalité *f.* nationality

natte *f.* braid of hair; pigtail

naturellement naturally

navire *m.* ship

né (*p.p. of* **naître**) born

néanmoins nevertheless

négatif *m.* negative

négligemment absent-mindedly

négliger (*irr. sp.* **B**) neglect

neige *f.* snow; **bonhomme de neige** *m.* snowman

neiger (*irr. sp.* **B**) snow

nerf *m.* nerve

nerveusement nervously

nerveux (*f.* **nerveuse**) nervous

netteté *f.* sharpness; clearness

nettoyage *m.* cleaning; **faire un grand nettoyage** do a thorough cleaning

nettoyer (*irr. sp.* **C**) clean

neuf nine

neuf (*f.* **neuve**) new; **à neuf** anew

neutre neutral; impersonal

neuve (*f. of* **neuf**) new

neveu *m.* nephew

nez *m.* nose

ni neither; **ni... ni** neither... nor

Nice resort town on the French Riviera

noblesse *f.* nobility; nobleness

Noël *m.* Christmas

noir *m.* dark; darkness; night; (*adj.*) black

Irregular verbs are conjugated on pp. 318–335.

nom *m.* name
nombre *m.* number
nombreux (*f.* **nombreuse**) many; numerous; **famille nombreuse** *f.* large family
nommer call; appoint
nord *m.* north
normand pertaining to Normandy
Normandie *f.* Normandy, a province in northwestern France
Norvège *f.* Norway
nos (*pl. of* **notre**) our
nostalgie *f.* nostalgia; longing
notaire *m.* notary
notamment especially
note *f.* check; bill; grade; note
noter note; notice; put down, list
notre (*possessive adj.*) our
nôtre (*possessive pron.*) ours
Notre-Dame famous Gothic cathedral in Paris
nourrir feed; give substance to
nourrissant nourishing
nourriture *f.* food
nouveau (*before vowel sound* **nouvel**; *f.* **nouvelle**) new; **à nouveau** again; **de nouveau** again, once more; **les nouveaux arrivés** *m. pl.* the people who have just arrived
nouvel, nouvelle (*m. and f. of* **nouveau**) new
nouvelle *f.* piece of news; novelette; **les nouvelles** *f. pl.* news; **nous avons de ses nouvelles** we've heard from him/her
Nouvelle-Orléans *f.* New Orleans
nu bare
nuage *m.* cloud
nuit *f.* night; **table de nuit** *f.* nightstand; **tombée de la nuit** *f.* nightfall
nul (*pron.*) no one; (*adj.*) **nul** (*f.* **nulle**) : **nulle part ailleurs** nowhere else
numéro *m.* number
nuque *f.* nape (of the neck)

Verbs with spelling changes are explained on pp. 336–338.

O

obéir (**à** + *n.*) obey
obéissant obedient
objet *m.* object
obligatoire compulsory
obliger (*irr. sp.* **B**) force; oblige
obscur difficult to understand
observation *f.* remark; observation
observer watch; observe
obstruer obstruct
occasion *f.* opportunity; bargain
occupé busy
occuper (**s'**) (**de** + *n.*) take care of; turn one's attention to; take charge of; busy oneself with
odeur *f.* odor, smell
œil *m. sing.* (*m. pl.* **yeux**) eye; **coup d'œil** *m.* glance
œillet *m.* carnation
œuf *m.* egg; **œufs au plat** fried eggs
œuvre *f.* work; **mettre en œuvre** make use of; **œuvres de charité** charitable works
offenser offend
officier *m.* officer
offre *f.* offer
offrir (*conj. like* **ouvrir**) offer
oiseau *m.* bird; **oiseau de mer** sea bird
olivier *m.* olive tree
ombre *f.* shade; shadow
on (*indefinite pron.*) one; we; you; they; people
oncle *m.* uncle
ondulation *f.* ripple; wave
ongle *m.* nail
opéra *m.* opera; opera house
opérer operate; work
opinion *f.* opinion, view
opposé opposite
opposer (**s'**) come face to face
or *m.* gold
or (*conjunc.*) it so happens
orage *m.* storm
oralement orally
orangé (*adj.*) orange-colored
oranger *m.* orange tree
orchestre *m.* orchestra; **chef d'orchestre** *m.* conductor
ordinaire : **d'ordinaire** usually

ordinateur *m.* computer
ordonner (**à** + *person* + **de** + *inf.*) order
ordre *m.* order; **à vos ordres** at your orders
oreille *f.* ear; **dur d'oreille** hard of hearing
organiser organize; plan; utilize
orgueil *m.* pride
originaire native
original original; odd, strange, eccentric
Orléans French city on Loire between Paris and Tours
oser (+ *inf.*) dare
ou or
où where; in which; when; **au moment où** at the time when; **où que** wherever
oubli *m.* oblivion
oublier (**de** + *inf.*) forget
ouf ! phew ! (with a sigh of relief)
oui yes; **mais oui** certainly; why, yes
ours [urs] *m.* bear
outil *m.* tool
outre besides, in addition to
outre-tombe beyond the grave
ouvert open; exposed to; aware
ouverture *f.* opening
ouvrage *m.* work
ouvrier *m.* (*f.* **ouvrière**) worker
ouvrir (**ouvrant, ouvert, j'ouvre, j'ouvris**) open; **s'ouvrir** lay open one's heart; get open

P

paie, paient (**payer**) pay
paille *f.* straw
pain *m.* bread; **pain grillé** toast
paix *f.* peace
palais *m.* palate; palace; **palais de justice** courthouse
pâle pale
pamplemousse *m.* grapefruit
pancarte *f.* sign
panier *m.* basket

Irregular verbs are conjugated on pp. 318–335.

panne *f.* breakdown; **panne d'électricité** power failure; **tomber en panne** have a (mechanical) breakdown
papier *m.* paper; **papier à lettre** stationery; writing paper; **papier d'alu** or **d'argent** aluminum foil
Pâques *f. pl.* Easter
paquet *m.* package; pack
par through; by; with; for; per; **par ce temps** in such weather; **par jour** per day, each day
paraître (*conj. like* **connaître**) look, seem; appear
parallèlement parallel
parc *m.* park; **parc à autos** parking lot
parcourir (*conj. like* **courir**) travel; go through
parcours *m.* trip
pardonner (**à** + *person* + **de** + *inf.*) pardon; forgive
pareil (*f.* **pareille**) same, identical; such a; **il n'a pas son pareil** there is no one like him
pareillement similarly
parent *m.* parent; relative
parfaitement perfectly
parfois sometimes
parfum *m.* perfume
parler (**à** + *person*; **de** + *n.*) speak; talk
parmi among
paroi *f.* wall
parole *f.* (spoken) word
part *f.* part; **à part** except; **de ma part** for me, in my behalf; **nulle part** nowhere; **nulle part ailleurs** nowhere else
partager (*irr. sp.* **B**) share
partenaire *m./f.* partner
parti *m.* party; **prendre le parti de** side with
participe *m.* participle
participer participate, take part
particulier (*f.* **particulière**) particular; peculiar; **rien de particulier** nothing particular
particulièrement particularly
partie *f.* part; **faire partie de** belong to, be a part of
partir (2) leave; go away; depart; **lui parti**

once he had left (*lit.* he having left); **à partir de demain** from tomorrow on

partout everywhere

paru, parus (*p.p. and s.p. of* **paraître**) seemed, looked, appeared

pas *m.* step; footstep; gait; **avancer d'un pas** take one step forward; **pas à pas** step by step; **s'attacher aux pas** follow closely; **faire quelques pas, faire un pas** take a step

passage *m.* passage; passing

passant *m.* passer-by

passé *m.* past; **passé composé** compound past; (*adj.*) past

passe-partout *m.* master key

passer pass; pass by; give; spend (time); advance; be shown; go down; **j'ai passé par là** I've gone through that; **passer** (**à** + *inf.*) spend time; **passer un examen** take an examination; **se passer** happen; take place; be done; **il se passe quelque chose** something is happening; **se passer de** do without

passif (*f.* **passive**) passive

passionnant fascinating

passionné ardent

pasteur *m.* minister (in church)

Pasteur, Louis (1822–1895) French scientist

pâtisserie *f.* pastry

pâtissier *m.* owner of a pastry shop

patron *m.* (*f.* **patronne**) boss; owner

patte *f.* paw; foot

pauvre *m.* poor man; (*adj.*) poor

payer (*irr. sp.* **C**) pay; pay for

pays *m.* country

paysage *m.* countryside; landscape

paysan *m.* (*f.* **paysanne**) peasant; farmer

peau *f.* skin

pêche *f.* fishing

peindre (**peignant, peint, je peins, je peignis**) paint; portray

peine *f.* trouble; difficulty; pain; grief; **à peine** slightly, scarcely; not very; **cela me fait de la peine** I am sorry;

it saddens me; **valoir la peine** be worthwhile

peiner hurt

peint (*p.p. of* **peindre**) painted

peintre *m.* painter

peinture *f.* painting; portrayal

pelouse *f.* lawn

penché : la tête penchée his head cocked

pencher lean

pendant during; **pendant que** while

pendule *f.* clock

pénétrer fill; enter

penser (**à** + *n.*) think; think of; believe; (+ *inf.*) intend; (**à** + *inf.*) consider; (**de** + *n.*) have an opinion of

pension *f.* boarding house; boarding school

pensionnaire *m./f.* boarder

pente *f.* slope

perché perched; **chat perché** *m.* children's game of tag

perçois (*pres. of* **percevoir**) perceive

perdre lose

père *m.* father

période *f.* period; **faire une période militaire** do a short tour of military duty

périodiquement periodically

perle *f.* perle

permettre (*conj. like* **mettre**) (**à** + *person* + **de** + *inf.*) permit, allow

permis *m.* license; **permis de conduire** driver's license

Pérou *m.* Peru

perpendiculairement perpendicularly

perpétuer perpetuate

perron *m.* porch

personnage *m.* character (in a literary work)

personne *f.* person

personne no one, nobody; **ne... personne** no one, nobody

personnellement personally

perspective *f.* prospect

peser (*irr. sp.* **D**) weigh; **peser lourd** be heavy; be important

peste *f.* plague

petit *m.* baby; little boy; (*adj.*) small, little; **petit déjeuner** *m.* breakfast;

Verbs with spelling changes are explained on pp. 336–338.

petit employé *m.* minor office clerk;
un petit cognac a small glass of
brandy; **petits pois** *m. pl.* peas
petit-fils *m.* grandson
pétrole *m.* oil
peu little; **à peu près** about, approximately; **depuis peu** recently, since
not very long ago; **un peu** a little, a
bit; **peu fréquenté** not very often
visited; **quelque peu** somewhat
peuple *m.* people; masses
peupler inhabit; throng; settle in, popu-
late
peur *f.* fear; **avoir peur** be afraid; **de peur**
for fear; **faire peur** scare
peut, peuvent, peux (**pouvoir**) can
pharmacien *m.* druggist, pharmacist
philosophie *f.* philosophy; **faire sa
philosophie** study philosophy, carry
on one's studies in philosophy
philosophique philosophical
photo *f.* photograph; snapshot
photographier photograph
phrase *f.* sentence
physique physical
Picasso, Pablo (1881–1973) famous
Spanish painter and sculptor, founder
of cubism
pièce *f.* play; room; coin; **pièce
d'identité** identification card
pied *m.* foot; **à pied** on foot; **lampe à
pied** *f.* floor lamp
piège *m.* trap
pierre *f.* stone
Pierre Peter; **Pierre le Grand** (1672–
1725) 18th-century czar of Russia
Pierrot (*diminutive of* **Pierre**) little Peter
pilote *m.* pilot; **pilote de ligne** commercial air pilot
pilule *f.* pill
pionnier *m.* pioneer
pire (*comparative of* **mauvais**) worse
pis worse; worst; **tant pis** so much the
worse
pisciculture *f.* pisciculture (fish raising)
piscine *f.* swimming pool

Pise Pisa, town in central Italy famous
for its Leaning Tower
piste *f.* trail; slope (ski)
pistolet *m.* pistol
place *f.* seat; public square; place (space);
spot; job; **sur place** on the spot
placer (*irr. sp.* **A**) place; find a home for;
se placer take place
plage *f.* beach
plaindre (*conj. like* **craindre**) pity; feel
sorry for; **se plaindre** (**de** + *n.*) complain
plaire (**plaisant, plu, je plais, je plus**) (**à** +
person) please
plaisanter joke
plaisir *m.* pleasure; **faire plaisir à** please,
give pleasure to
plaît (*pres. of* **plaire**) pleases; **s'il vous
plaît** please; **si ça vous plaît** if you
wish
plan *m.* plan; map (of a city)
planter plant
plat *m.* dish; **œufs au plat** *m. pl.* fried
eggs; (*adj.*) flat
plein full; **en plein air** in the open; **en
pleine poitrine** right in the chest
pleinement fully
pleurer cry
pleut (*pres. of* **pleuvoir**) it is raining;
it rains
pleuvoir (**pleuvant, plu, il pleut, il plut**)
rain
plombier *m.* plumber
plonger (*irr. sp.* **B**) plunge
plu, plut (*p.p. and s.p. of* **pleuvoir**)
rained
plu, plus (*p.p. and s.p. of* **plaire**) pleased
pluie *f.* rain
plupart *f.* majority
pluriel *m.* plural
plus more; most; **de plus** moreover; **de
plus en plus** more and more; **ne...
plus** no more; no longer; **non plus**
either; neither; not... either; **qui plus
est** what's more
plusieurs several
plutôt rather
poche *f.* pocket
poids *m.* weight; responsibility

Irregular verbs are conjugated on pp. 318–335.

poignant gripping
poing *m.* fist; **coup de poing** *m.* punch
point *m.* point; period; **point de vue** point of view; **être sur le point de** be about to; *(adv.)* **ne... point** not at all
pointu sharp
poire *f.* pear
pois *m.* pea; **petits pois** *m. pl.* peas
poisson *m.* fish
poitrine *f.* chest; **en pleine poitrine** right in the chest, in the middle of the chest
poli polite
policier *m.* policeman; **roman policier** *m.* detective story
politique *f.* politics
polluer pollute
Pologne *f.* Poland
polonais Polish
pomme *f.* apple; **pomme de terre** potato
pommier *m.* apple tree
Pompéi Pompeii
pompeux *(f.* **pompeuse)** pompous
pompier *m.* fireman
pont *m.* bridge
populaire popular; well liked by the masses
population *f.* people
port *m.* seaport; port
porte *f.* door; doorway; **porte de derrière** back door; **prendre la porte** get out
portefeuille *m.* billfold
porte-monnaie *m.* change purse
porte-plume *m.* pen
porter carry; bear; lift; raise; wear; **porter la main à** put one's hand on; **se porter bien** be well
porto *m.* port wine
portrait *m.* picture, portrait
portugais Portuguese
posé resting
poser put; pose; put down; rest; **poser une question** ask a question; **un problème se pose** a problem presents itself
posséder *(irr. sp.* **E)** possess

Verbs with spelling changes are explained on pp. 336–338.

possible possible; **dès que possible** as soon as possible
poste *m.* position, job
poste *f.* post office; **mettre à la poste** mail
pouce *m.* thumb
poudre *f.* powder
poule *f.* hen
poulet *m.* chicken
poupée *f.* doll
pour for; in order to; **pour que** in order that
pourquoi why
pourrai, pourrais *(fut. and cond.* of **pouvoir)** will be able to; would be able to
poursuivre *(conj. like* **suivre)** continue; pursue
pourtant however; yet
pourvu que provided that
poussé : éducation poussée *f.* college education
pousser push; grow; incite; **pousser un cri** utter a cry
poussière *f.* dust
pouvoir **(pouvant, pu, je peux, je pus)** *(+ inf.)* can, be able to; may; **il se peut** it is possible; **puis-je** can I; may I; **sauve qui peut !** look out ! run for your life !
pouvoir *m.* power
pratiquant practicing
pratiquer practice
pré *m.* meadow
précédent preceding; **le jour précédent** the day before
précéder *(irr. sp.* **E)** precede
précieux *(f.* **précieuse)** precious
précipitamment precipitately, hurriedly
précipité hasty
précipiter (se) rush
prédilection *f.* preference
prédire *(conj. like* **dire)** predict
préféré favorite
préférence *f.* preference; **de préférence** preferably
premier *(f.* **première)** first; prime
prendre **(prenant, pris, je prends, je pris)** *(+ thing +* **à** *[from] + person)* take;

have; catch; **comment s'y prendre** how to go about it; **prendre une décision** make a decision; **prendre le dessus** prevail; **prendre le parti de** side with; **prendre la porte** leave the room; get out; **prendre rendez-vous** make an appointment; **prendre au sérieux** take seriously; **prendre sa source** (of river) begin; **prendre ses responsabilités** assume some responsibility; **prendre un verre** have a drink

prénom *m.* first name

près (**de** + *n.*) near; **à peu près** about, approximately

présent *m.* gift; (*adj.*) present

présenter (*person* + **à** + *person*) introduce

presque almost

presser press; weigh; rush; **il a pressé des mains sur nos épaules** he placed his hands on our shoulders; **le temps presse** time is getting short; **se presser** crowd; hasten

prêt (**à** + *inf.*) ready

prétendre claim

prêter lend

preuve *f.* proof

prévenir (*conj. like* **venir**) warn; inform; let someone know; call (the doctor)

prévoir (*conj. like* **voir** *except in fut. and cond.*) foresee; plan

prier (*person* + **de** + *inf.*) pray; ask; beg; **je vous prie** please

printemps *m.* spring

pris (*p.p. and s.p. of* **prendre**) taken; took

prisonnier *m.* prisoner

priver (**de** + *n.*) deprive

prix *m.* price; prize

problème *m.* problem; **poser un problème** present a problem

procédé *m.* process; method, procedure

prochain next

proche near; close to

procurer give

producteur *m.* producer

produire (*conj. like* **conduire**) produce; create; **se produire** happen

produit *m.* product

professeur *m.* professor; teacher

profil *m.* profile; side; **de profil** in profile

profit *m.* profit; **mettre à profit** take advantage; **tirer profit de** profit from

profiter (**de** + *n.*) take advantage of

profond deep

profondeur *f.* depth

programmeur, programmateur *m.* programmer

progrès *m.* progress

progresser progress, advance

projections *f. pl.* slides

projet *m.* plan; project

prolonger (**se**) (*irr. sp.* **B**) last

promenade *f.* walk; **faire une promenade** take a walk

promener (**se**) (*irr. sp.* **D**) take a walk

promeneur *m.* stroller

promesse *f.* promise

promettre (*conj. like* **mettre**) (**à** + *person* + **de** + *inf.*) promise

promis (*p.p. and s.p. of* **promettre**) promised

promotion *f.* graduation

pronom *m.* pronoun

prononcer (*irr. sp.* **A**) pronounce

prophétesse *f.* seer

propos *m.* remark; **à propos de** concerning

proposer propose; suggest

proposition *f.* proposition; proposal

propre own; clean

propriétaire *m./f.* owner; landlord, landlady

protestataire *m./f.* protester

protestation *f.* protest

prouver prove

Provence *f.* region of southern France

province *f.* : **de province** from the provinces

provisoire temporary

provisions *f.* groceries

provoquer challenge; set into motion; cause

prudence *f.* prudence, care

prudent cautious; prudent

Irregular verbs are conjugated on pp. 318–335.

psychologique psychological
pu, pus (*p.p. and s.p. of* **pouvoir**) could, was able
public *m.* audience; people
publier publish
puis then
puis, puisse (*pres. indic. and pres. subj. of* **pouvoir**) can, am able; may
puissance *f.* power
puissant powerful; all-powerful, over-whelming
puits *m.* well
pull-over *m.* sweater
pûmes (*1st pers. pl. s.p. of* **pouvoir**) could
punir punish
pur pure
pus (*s.p. of* **pouvoir**) could
Pyrénées *f. pl.* Pyrenees

Q

quai *m.* wharf; quay; bank
quand when; **quand même** just the same, even so
quant : quant à as for
quarante forty
quart *m.* quarter
quartier *m.* district
quatorze fourteen
que that; which; what; whom; how; when; than; **que (vous ayez ou non)** whether (you have or not); **qu'on est bien !** how comfortable one is !
le Québec *m.* province in eastern Canada; **Québec** capital of the province
quel (*f.* **quelle**) which; what; **quel que soit** whatever is
quelconque some sort of
quelque some; **en quelque sorte** some-how; **quelque peu** somewhat
quelque chose something
quelqu'un someone
quereller (se) (*irr. sp.* **F**) quarrel

Verbs with spelling changes are explained on pp. 336–338.

question *f.* question; **poser une question** ask a question
questionner question; inquire
quête *f.* quest
qui who; whom; that; which; **à qui le dites-vous !** you're telling me ! **à qui que ce soit** to whomever; **qui que ce soit** whoever he is
quiconque whoever
quinze fifteen
quitter (+ *n.*)leave; **ne pas quitter quelqu'un des yeux** not to take one's eyes off someone
quoi what; **de quoi** the money; the wherewithall; **n'importe quoi** any-thing, anything whatever; **quoi que** whatever; **quoi qu'il en soit** how-ever that may be, however the case may be
quoique although
quotidiennement daily

R

rabais *m.* discount
Racine (1639–1699) famous French writer of tragedies
raccommoder mend
raconter tell
radiateur *m.* radiator
rage *f.* rabies; fury
raide steep
raison *f.* reason; **à plus forte raison** all the more reason; **avoir raison de** overcome; **donner raison** justify, prove to be right
raisonnable reasonable
raisonner (se) reason with oneself; try to be reasonable
ramener (*irr. sp.* **D**) bring back
rang *m.* row; **au premier rang** of the first rank; **en rang** in a row
rangé dutiful; of regular habits
ranger (*irr. sp.* **B**) put in order; arrange; put away
ranimer (se) regain consciousness, come to
râper grate
rapide fast

rappeler (*irr. sp.* **F**) remind; call back **se rappeler** (+ *n.*) remember
rapport *m.* report
rapporter bring back; relate; **se rapporter** refer, be based on
rapprocher (**se**) draw near
raser shave; **se raser** shave oneself
rasoir *m.* razor
rassurant reassuring
rassurer reassure
rater miss; fail
ratine *f.* woolen cloth
rattacher à associate with
ravi delighted
ravissant delightful, ravishing
rayon *m.* ray; shelf
réagir react
réaliser (**se**) happen
rebelle *m./f.* rebel
récemment recently
récepteur *m.* (radio or TV) set
recette *f.* recipe
recevoir (**recevant, reçu, je reçois, je reçu**) receive; entertain
recherche *f.* research; hunt; **à la recherche de** in search of
rechercher search for
récit *m.* story
réclame *f.* advertisement
réclamer ask for
récolter harvest
recommencer (*irr. sp.* **A**) do over; begin again; resume; make a fresh start
récompenser reward
réconfortant comforting
reconnaître (*conj. like* **connaître**) recognize
reconsidérer reconsider; take another long look at
recouvert de covered with
reçu, reçus (*p.p. and s.p. of* **recevoir**) received
recul *m.* recoil, withdrawal, drawing back; **prendre du recul** withdraw
rédacteur *m.* editor
redécouvrir discover again

redemander ask again
redescendre go down again; lower again
redevenir become again
rédiger (*irr. sp.* **B**) write; compose
redire (*conj. like* **dire**) repeat
redonner give again
redouter fear
réduction *f.* : **réduction de prix** discount
réduire (*conj. like* **conduire**) reduce
réduit small
refaire (*conj. like* **faire**) do again; write again
refermer close up
réfléchir think; reflect
refléter (**se**) (*irr. sp.* **E**) be reflected
réflexion *f.* reflection; **faire des réflexions** think about, reflect on
réfugié *m.* refugee; (*adj.*) alone; withdrawn
réfugier (**se**) take refuge
refuser (**de** + *inf.*) refuse
regagner regain
régaler (**se**) **de** feast on
regard *m.* look; glance; observation; **jeter un regard** glance
regarder (+ *n.*) look; look at
régime *m.* regime; diet; **régime de faveur** privileged status
règlement *m.* rule
régler (*irr. sp.* **E**) settle
régner (*irr. sp.* **E**) reign; exist
regret *m.* regret; grief; **comme à regret** as if he regretted it
régulier (*f.* **régulière**) regular
rejeter (*irr. sp.* **F**) reject
rejoindre (*conj. like* **craindre**) meet again; join
relatif (*f.* **relative**) relative
religieux (*f.* **religieuse**) religious
relique *f.* relic
relire (*conj. like* **lire**) read again
relu, relus (*p.p. and s.p. of* **relire**) read again
remarier (**se**) marry again
remarquable remarkable
remarque *f.* remark
remarquer notice
rembourser pay back
remède *m.* remedy; medicine

Irregular verbs are conjugated on pp. 318–335.

remercier (*person* + **de** *or* **pour** + *thing;* *person* + **de** + *inf.*) thank

remettre (*conj. like* **mettre**) put back on again; hand in; turn in; put back; postpone; **remettre de l'ordre** put things back; **remettre en mémoire** remind; **se remettre** go back

remis (*p.p. and s.p. of* **remettre**) put back on; handed in; postponed

remonter go up; go up again; raise again; **remonter la rue** go up the street

remplacer (*irr. sp.* **A**) replace

remplir fill; fill up; fill out; fulfill

renard *m.* fox

rencontre *f.* meeting

rencontrer meet (by chance)

rendez-vous *m.* date; appointment

rendre return (something); (+ *adj.*) make; **rendre service** do a favor; **se rendre** go; **se rendre compte** realize; **rendre visite** visit; **se rendre malade** make oneself sick

rêne *f.* rein

renommé famous

renoncement *m.* renouncing

renoncer (*irr. sp.* **A**) give up; renounce

renouveler (*irr. sp.* **F**) change; be renovated

renseignement *m.* information

renseigner give information; **se renseigner** ask for information; get information, inform oneself

rentrer return; come back home; go back home; come back in

renverser overthrow; tip over

renvoyer (*conj. like* **envoyer**) dismiss

répandre spread; **se répandre** spread out

répandu common

réparation *f.* repair

réparer repair, fix

repartir start on one's way again

repas *m.* meal

repeindre (*conj. like* **peindre**) paint again

répondre (**à** + *n.*) answer, reply to

reposer (**se**) rest

repousser push aside; push back

reprendre (*conj. like* **prendre**) resume; take again; regain; continue

représentation *f.* show; performance

représenter (**se**) imagine

repris (*p.p. and s.p. of* **reprendre**) resumed; regained; continued

reproche *m.* reproach

reproduire reproduce

république *f.* republic

réputé famous; well known

réserver reserve; make a reservation

résidu *m.* remnant

résister (**à** + *n.*) resist

résoudre solve

respectueux (*f.* **respectueuse**) respectful

respirer breathe; take a breath; feel relieved

responsabilité *f.* responsibility; **prendre ses responsabilités** assume some responsibility

ressembler (**à** + *n.*) look like, resemble

ressortir (*conj. like* **sortir**) take out

ressource *f.* resource

reste *m.* remainder; **ne pas être en reste** be equal to the situation; not be backward

rester remain; stay; stand; **il me reste à** I'll have to; **il me reste une inquiétude** I still have a worry; **il ne me reste rien** I have nothing left; **rester une demi-heure à bavarder** spend a half-hour talking

résultat *m.* result

résumer sum up

retard *m.* delay; **avoir du retard, être en retard** be late

retarder delay

retenir (*conj. like* **tenir**) reserve; hire in advance; detain

retirer (**se**) withdraw; **se retirer** withdraw

retour *m.* return; **à ton retour** when you return; **être de retour** be back

retourner return, go back; turn again; turn around; **se retourner** turn around; look back; **s'en retourner** go back

retraite *f.* retreat; retirement; **prendre sa retraite** retire

---

Verbs with spelling changes are explained on pp. 336–338.

retraverser cross again
retrouver find; discover; find once more; join; recover
réunion *f.* meeting
réussi successful
réussir (à + *n.*; à + *inf.*) succeed
réussite *f.* success
revanche *f.* revenge; **en revanche** on the other hand
rêve *m.* dream; **faire un rêve** have a dream
réveil *m.* waking up; alarm clock; **au réveil** on awakening
réveiller awaken; **se réveiller** wake up
révéler (*irr. sp.* E) reveal; discover; **se révéler** prove to be
revenant *m.* ghost
revendeur *m.* seller of used books
revendication *f.* demand
revenir (*conj. like* **venir**) return; come back
revenu *m.* income
rêver (de + *n.*; de + *inf.*) dream
rêverie *f.* daydream
rêveur *m.* dreamer
reviendrai, reviendrais (*fut. and cond. of* **revenir**) will, would come back
revivre (*conj. like* **vivre**) live again; relive; come back to life
revoir (*conj. like* **voir**) see again; **se revoir** meet again; **au revoir** goodbye
révoltant revolting
revue *f.* magazine; review
rez-de-chaussée *m.* ground floor, first floor
Rhin *m.* Rhine
Rhône *m.* Rhone, a river whose source is in Switzerland and which flows through France and empties into the Mediterranean near Marseilles
rhume *m.* cold
ri, ris, rit (*p.p., pres., s.p. of* **rire**) laughed; laughs; laughed
riche rich
richesse *f.* wealth
ridé wrinkled

rideau *m.* curtain
rien nothing; **cela ne fait rien** it doesn't matter; **ne... rien** nothing; **servir à rien** be useless
rigolo very funny
rire (**riant, ri, je ris, je ris**) (de + *n.*) laugh; **éclater de rire** burst out laughing; **rire de quelqu'un** make fun of someone
risée *f.* ripple; light squall
rivière *f.* river; stream; tributary
robe *f.* dress; **robe de chambre** gown
roc *m.* rock
roche *f.* rock
rocher *m.* rock
rocheux (*f.* **rocheuse**) rocky
rôder prowl about
rôle *m.* role; part
roman *m.* novel; **roman policier** detective story; (*adj.*) Romance
romancier *m.* (*f.* **romancière**) novelist
rompre break
rond *m.* circle; **tourner en rond** run around in circles; go round and round; (*adj.*) round
ronronner purr
rose in good condition
rosée *f.* dew
rosier *m.* rosebush
rôti *m.* roast beef; roast; (*adj.*) roasted
rôtir roast
rouet *m.* spinning wheel
rouge red; **feu rouge** *m.* red light; traffic light
rougeole *f.* measles
roulant : table roulante *f.* table with wheels
rouleau *m.* roll
rouler drive; go; roll; move
Roumanie *f.* Romania
route *f.* way; road; **en route** on the way; **se tromper de route** take the wrong road
roux (*f.* **rousse**) (referring to the hair) red, reddish
royal : à la royale gourmet way to prepare some dishes (especially venison)
rude hard, harsh, severe
rue *f.* street
ruiner (**se**) ruin oneself

Irregular verbs are conjugated on pp. 318–335.

ruisseau *m.* brook
rusé sly; tricky
russe Russian

S

sa (*f. of* **son**) his; her; its
sable *m.* sand
sac *m.* bag; handbag; knapsack
saccadé jerky
sachant (*pres. part. of* **savoir**) knowing
sache, sachiez (*pres. subj. of* **savoir**) know
sacré sacred; damned
sacrifier (**se**) sacrifice oneself
sage wise; (speaking of behavior) good, well behaved
sagesse *f.* wisdom
saigner bleed
sain healthy
sais, sait (*pres. of* **savoir**) know
saisir seize
saison *f.* season; **la belle saison** the summer months
sale dirty; (*fig.*) lousy
salé salted
sali soiled, dirty
salir soil
salle *f.* room (for meetings); **salle à manger** dining room; **salle de séjour** living room
salon *m.* drawing room; living room
saluer greet; say hello
salut *m.* salute; salvation
samedi *m.* Saturday
sans without; **sans compter que** besides the fact; **sans doute** probably
santé *f.* health
satisfaire (*conj. like* **faire**) satisfy
sauf except; but
saule *m.* willow tree
saurai, saurais (*fut. and cond. of* **savoir**) will know; would know
sauvage wild
sauver save; **sauve qui peut !** look out !,

Verbs with spelling changes are explained on pp. 336–338.

run for your life !; **se sauver** escape, flee
sauvetage *m.* rescue
savane *f.* savannah, prairie
savant *m.* scientist; (*adj.*) learned; trained; **Les Femmes savantes** (*The Learned Women*), a play by Molière (1672)
savoir (**sachant, su, je sais, je sus**) know; (+ *inf.*) know how to; **savoir bien** know very well
savon *m.* soap
savourer enjoy
savoureux (*f.* **savoureuse**) tasty
scène *f.* scene; stage
scie *f.* saw
science *f.* science; **homme de science** scientist
scolaire of the school
sec (*f.* **sèche**) dry
sécheresse *f.* drought, dry spell
secondaire secondary
secouer shake off
secrétaire *m./f.* secretary
secrètement secretly
séduisant extremely attractive
seigneur *m.* lord
sein *m.* breast
Seine *f.* French river that crosses Paris
séjour *m.* stay, sojourn; **salle de séjour** *f.* living room
sel *m.* salt
selon according to
semaine *f.* week
semblable similar; (*n. m./f.*) fellow being
sembler (+ *inf.*) seem
sens [sãs] *m.* way; direct; meaning; **dans un sens** in a way
sensibilité *f.* sensitiveness
sensible sensitive
sensiblement more or less; perceptibly; noticeably
sentier *m.* path
sentiment *m.* feeling; sensation
sentir (2) feel; smell; **se sentir** feel; **se sentir mal** feel sick
séparer separate
serai, serais (*fut. and cond. of* **être**) will be; would be

serein serene; satisfied
série *f.* collection
sérieux (*f.* **sérieuse**) serious; **au sérieux**
  seriously
serpent *m.* snake
serré crowded
serrer shake; press; **serrer les dents**
  clench one's teeth
serrure *f.* lock
serviable obliging, willing to help
service *m.* service; silverware; **rendre**
  service do a favor
serviette *f.* towel; briefcase
servir (2) serve; **ne servir à rien** be useless; **servir de** use as; **servir**
  d'exemple serve as an example; **se**
  servir de use; make use of
serviteur *m.* servant
seul alone; lonely; only; solely; single;
  être seul à be the only one to
seulement only
sévère strict
sévèrement in a stern manner
si so; yes; **si riches qu'ils soient** however
  rich they are
siècle *m.* century
siège *m.* seat
sien (*f.* **sienne**) his; hers; its
sieste *f.* siesta
siffler whistle
signal *m.* (*pl.* **signaux**) signal
signaler point out
signe *m.* sign; **faire signe** signal
signification *f.* signification, meaning
signifier mean
silencieusement silently
silencieux (*f.* **silencieuse**) silent
simple : simple soldat *m.* private
simplement simply
singe *m.* monkey
singulier *m.* singular; (*adj.*) (*f.*
  singulière) singular; strange
sinon otherwise
sirène *f.* siren; factory whistle
sitôt que as soon as
ski *m.* ski; **faire du ski** go skiing

Irregular verbs are conjugated on pp. 318–335.

sobre sober
société *f.* society; firm, company
sœur *f.* sister
soi oneself; **en soi** in itself; **ça va de soi**
  it goes without saying
soif *f.* thirst; **il a soif** he is thirsty
soigné : bien soigné well kept
soigner take care of, care for; treat (a
  patient)
soigneusement carefully
soin *m.* task; care; worry
soir *m.* evening
soirée *f.* evening party; **soirée dansante**
  evening party where people dance
soit... soit either... or
soixante sixty
soldat *m.* soldier
soleil *m.* sun; **coucher de soleil** *m.* sunset; **lever de soleil** *m.* sunrise
solidarité *f.* solidarity
sombre dark; **il fait sombre** it is dark
somme *f.* sum (of money); amount
sommeil *m.* sleep; **avoir sommeil** be
  sleepy
sommet *m.* peak; top
son, sa, ses his; her; its; one's
songer (*irr. sp.* **B**) think
songeur (*f.* **songeuse**) pensive, dreamy
sonner ring
sonnerie *f.* ring; doorbell; ringing
Sorbonne *f.* building that formerly
  housed the *Faculté des Lettres et des*
  Sciences of the University of Paris
sort *m.* fate
sorte *f.* sort; **de sorte que** so that, in
  such a way that; **en quelque sorte**
  somehow
sortie *f.* exit; **à la sortie de l'école** after
  school
sortilège *m.* magic spell; charm
sortir (2) leave, go out
sot (*f.* **sotte**) foolish; silly; (*n.*) dumb
  person; fool
sottement foolishly; sheepishly
sou *m.* penny, cent
souci *m.* worry; care; **se faire du souci**
  worry
soucieux (*f.* **soucieuse**) eager
soucoupe *f.* saucer

soudain *(adj.)* sudden; *(adv.)* suddenly
souffle *m.* breath
soufflé *m.* : **soufflé au cognac** a gourmet dessert, a soufflé with cognac (brandy)
souffrance *f.* suffering
souffrir *(conj. like* **ouvrir***)* suffer
souhaiter wish
soulagement *m.* relief
soulever raise
soulier *m.* shoe
souligner underline
soupçon *m.* suspicion
soupe *f.* soup
souper *m.* supper; evening meal
soupirer sign
souple supple, pliant
source *f.* source; **prendre sa source** (of a river) begin
sourcil *m.* eyebrow
sourd deaf
souriant smiling
sourire *(conj. like* **rire***)* (à + *n.*) smile; *n. m.* smile
souris *f.* mouse
sous-sol *m.* basement
soutenir *(conj. like* **tenir***)* support; insist
souterrain *m.* underground passage, cavern; *(adj.)* underground
souvenir (se) *(conj. like* **venir***)* (de + *n.*; de + *inf.*) remember; *n. m.* souvenir; memory; remembrance; recollection; keepsake
souvent often
spectacle *m.* show; sight
spectateur *m.* spectator
splendide marvelous
spontané spontaneous
sport *m.* sport; **faire des sports** participate in sports; **journal de sport** *m.* sports magazine
sportif *(f.* **sportive***)* sports loving; inclined toward sports; athletic
squelette *m.* skeleton

stage *m.* : **faire un stage** spend a period for work or study
station *f.* station; **station d'hiver** winter resort
stationner park
statistique *f.* statistics
stéréotypé stereotyped
stoïquement stoically
stopper stop
stratagème *m.* deception, ruse, trick
strictement strictly
stupéfaction *f.* amazement
stupéfait amazed
stylo *m.* fountain pen
su, sus *(p.p. and s.p. of* **savoir***)* known; knew; learned, found out
subit sudden
subjonctif *m.* subjunctive
subordonné subordinate
subtil subtle
subtilement subtly
succéder (à) take the place of; inherit from
succomber succumb; die
sucre *m.* sugar
sud *m.* south
Suède *f.* Sweden
suédois Swedish
suffire (**suffisant, suffi, je suffis, je suffis**) suffice; be enough
suffisamment enough
suggérer *(irr. sp.* E*)* suggest
suis *(pres. of* **être***)* I am; *(pres. of* **suivre***)* I, you follow
Suisse *f.* Switzerland
suite *f.* continuation; aftermath, consequence; **à la suite** as a result; **à sa suite** after them, following them; **tout de suite** right now, right away, immediately; in succession
suivant *(adj.)* following; next; *(prep.)* according to
suivi successful; popular
suivre (**suivant, suivi, je suis, je suivis**) follow; **suivre un cours** take a course
sujet *m.* subject; **au sujet de** about, concerning
superficie *f.* surface
superflu superfluous

Verbs with spelling changes are explained on pp. 336–338.

supermarché *m.* supermarket
supportable bearable
supporter put up with, stand for
supprimer suppress
sur on; out of
sûr sure; firm
surabondance *f.* overabundance
sûrement surely
sûreté *f.* confidence
surgir appear suddenly
surnaturel (*f.* **surnaturelle**) supernatural
surprendre (*conj. like* **prendre**) surprise
surprenant surprising
surprise *f.* surprise, astonishment
surtout especially; above all; mostly
surveillant *m.* guard
surveiller watch over; keep an eye on
survenir (*conj. like* **venir**) appear
survoler fly over
sus (*s.p. of* **savoir**) knew; learned
suspendre (*conj. like* **prendre**) suspend
suspens *m.* suspense; **en suspens** hanging
symbole *m.* symbol
sympathique nice, understanding

T

tabac *m.* tobacco; **bureau de tabac** *m.* tobacco shop
table *f.* table; **mettre la table** set the table; **se mettre à table** sit down at the table; **table de nuit** night stand; **table roulante** table with wheels
tableau *m.* picture; painting; **tableau noir** blackboard
tache *f.* spot; **une tache de soleil** a bit of sun
tâche *f.* task; duty
tâcher try
Tahiti French island in the South Pacific
taille *f.* height; **de belle taille** huge
tailler cut
tailleur *m.* tailor
taire (**se**) be quiet, keep still

tambour *m.* drum
tandis que while, whereas
tant so much; **tant pis** so much the worse; **tant que** as long as
tante *f.* aunt
taper type, typewrite; **taper à la machine** type
tapis *m.* rug
taquiner tease
tard late; **au plus tard** at the latest
tarder (**à** + *inf.*) be late; delay, put off
tari dried up
tasse *f.* cup
taudis *m.* slum; hovel, shack
tel (*f.* **telle**) such, such a
téléphoner (**à** + *person*) telephone
téléspectateur *m.* television viewer
télévision *f.* television; television set
tellement so; so much
témérité recklessness
témoignage *m.* testimony
témoigner show; witness
témoin *m.* witness
temps *m.* time; weather; tense; **de temps en temps** from time to time; **en même temps** at the same time; **il est grand temps** it is high time; **le temps presse** time is getting short; **par ce temps** in this weather; **le temps de** long enough to
tenace tenacious
tendance *f.* tendency
tendre (*v.*) hold out; extend; give; stretch; **tendre la main** hold out one's hand; (*adj.*) tender
tendresse *f.* tenderness
ténèbres *f. pl.* obscurity
tenez (*interjection*) look here !
tenir (**tenant, tenu, je tiens, je tins**) hold; keep; **tenir à** insist on; be eager to; care; **tenir au courant** keep informed; **tenir conseil** have a meeting; **tenir de** inherit from; **tenir ferme** hold fast; **se tenir** be; stand
tentative *f.* attempt
tenter try; tempt
terminer finish
terrain *m.* ground; land; tract of land; field

Irregular verbs are conjugated on pp. 318–335.

terrasse *f.* terrace; outdoor part of a
  French café
terre *f.* earth; land; **pomme de terre** *f.*
  potato
terreur *f.* terror
terriblement terribly
testament *m.* will
tête *f.* head; **en tête** at the beginning;
  hocher la tête nod one's head
thé *m.* tea
théorie *f.* theory
thèse *f.* thesis; dissertation
tiens (*interjection*) look here !
tige *f.* stem
tigre *m.* tiger
timbre *m.* stamp
timidité *f.* timidity
tirelire *f.* piggy bank
tirer take out; pull; shoot; pull the trig-
  ger; acquire; (**sur** + *person*) shoot at;
  tirer profit profit by; **tirer quelqu'un
  d'affaire** get someone out of trouble
tiret *m.* dash
tiroir *m.* drawer
toile *f.* linen; canvas, painting; **toile
  cirée** oilcloth
toit *m.* roof
tombée *f.* fall (of night, etc.); **tombée de
  la nuit** nightfall
tomber fall; **tomber en panne** have a
  (mechanical) breakdown; **tomber
  malade** get sick
ton *m.* tone
tondre mow
tonnerre *m.* thunder; **coup de tonnerre**
  m. thunderclap
tort *m.* wrong; **avoir tort** be wrong
tôt early; soon
totalement completely
touchant concerning
toucher touch
toujours always; still; continually
Toulon seaport in southern France
tour *m.* stroll; trip; trick; turn; **à son
  tour** in turn; **faire le tour du monde**

Verbs with spelling changes are explained on
pp. 336–338.

take a trip around the world; **jouer
  un tour** play a trick; *f.* tower
Touraine *f.* French province southwest
  of Paris
touriste *m./f.* tourist; (*adj.*) tourist; for
  tourists
tourmenter torment; bother
tourner turn; **tourner à** become; **tourner
  en rond** turn around in circles
tournoyer (*irr. sp.* **C**) circle around
Tours French city southwest of Paris in
  Loire valley
tousser cough
tout (*m. pl.* **tous**) (*adj.*) all, every; whole;
  tout le monde everyone; **tous les
  samedis** every Saturday
tout (*pron.*) everything; **avant tout** above
  all; **capable de tout** capable of anything; **en tout cas** in any case; **une
  fois pour toutes** once and for all; **pas
  du tout** not in the least, not at all;
  tous deux both
tout (*adv.*) very, quite; **tout à côté** right
  near; **tout à coup** all of a sudden; **tout
  à fait** quite, completely; **tout à
  l'heure** in a little while; a little while
  ago; **tout bas** in a whisper; **tout
  d'abord** first of all; **tout droit** erect;
  straight ahead; **tout de même** all the
  same; exactly as, just as; **tout de
  suite** immediately, right now; **tout
  en lisant** while reading
tracasser (**se**) worry
trace *f.* footprint
tracer (*irr. sp.* **A**) lay out
tract *m.* leaflet
traduction *f.* translation
traduire (*conj. like* **conduire**) translate
trahison *f.* treason
train *m.* train; **en train de** in the act of
traînant languid, slow
traîneau *m.* sleigh
traîner lie about
traité *m.* treaty
traiter treat; **traiter de** call
traître *m.* traitor
trajet *m.* trip
tranquille quiet, calm; **nous avons été
  tranquilles** we were in peace

tranquillement calmly

tranquillisant (*n.*) tranquilizer; (*adj.*) tranquilizing

tranquillité *f.* calm

transatlantique *m.* ocean liner

transmettre (*conj. like* **mettre**) transmit

transport *m.* transportation

transporter carry

travail *m.* work; job; **se mettre au travail** set to work

travailleur (*f.* **travailleuse**) hardworking; industrious; *n.m.* worker

travers : à travers across; through; **en travers** across

traversée *f.* crossing; **traversée en bateau** boat trip

traverser cross

treize thirteen

tremblant shivering

trembler shake; tremble

tremper wet; soak; dunk

trente thirty

très very

trésor *m.* treasure

trésorier *m.* treasurer; cashier

trêve *f.* truce; solace

trimestre *m.* trimester; (school) quarter

trinquer clink glasses; toast

triste sad

tristesse *f.* sadness

trois three

tromper deceive; **se tromper de route** take the wrong road

trompette *f.* trumpet

trop too much; **trop tard** too late

trottoir *m.* sidewalk

trou *m.* hole

troublant upsetting, troubling

trouble *m.* trouble; **jeter le trouble** perturb

troubler trouble; move; **troubler l'eau** make the water murky; **troubler** (**se**) become upset; become embarrassed

troupe *f.* flock

trouver find; **comment trouvez-vous** what do you think of; **se trouver** be

found, be located; lie; find oneself; **se trouver mal** faint; **se trouver mieux** feel better

tuer kill

tumulte *m.* uproar

Tunisie *f.* Tunisia

turc *m.* Turk

tus (*s.p. of* **taire**) was silent, kept still

tutoyer (*irr. sp.* **C**) use the **tu** form in speaking to someone

type *m.* fellow; guy; person

U

un a, an; one

universel (*f.* **universelle**) universal; versatile

usé worn out

user (**s'**) wear oneself out

usine *f.* factory

utile useful

utiliser use

utilité *f.* usefulness; purpose

V

va (*pres. of* **aller**) goes; **ça va de soi** it goes without saying

vacances *f. pl.* vacation; **cours de vacances** *m.* summer courses; **en vacances** on vacation

vaccin *m.* vaccine

vache *f.* cow

vaciller stagger

vague *f.* wave

vaguement vaguely

vaille (*pres. subj. of* **valoir**) be worth

vainement in vain

vaisselle *f.* dishes; **faire la vaisselle** do the dishes

valeur *f.* value

valide valid, good

valise *f.* suitcase; **faire une valise** pack a suitcase

vallée *f.* valley

valoir (**valant, valu, je vaux, je valus**) be worth; **valoir la gloire** bring glory; **il vaut mieux** it is better; **valoir la peine** be worth the trouble; **votre**

Irregular verbs are conjugated on pp. 318–335.

idée ne vaut pas grand-chose your idea isn't worth much

vanter (se) boast

vapeur *f.* steam

Vatican *m.* Vatican, papal headquarters in Rome

vaut (*pres. of* **valoir**) is worth

veau *m.* calf; veal

vécu, vécus (*pp. and sp. of* **vivre**) lived

veille *f.* watch

veiller watch; **veiller sur quelqu'un** watch over someone

vélo *m.* bicycle

velours *m.* velvet

vendeur *m.* (*f.* **vendeuse**) salesperson

vendre sell

vendredi *m.* Friday

venir (**venant, venu, je viens, je vins**) come; **faire venir** send for; **venez me voir** come and see me; **venir de** have just (**il vient d'arriver** he has just arrived); **il en vint à conclure** he finally concluded; **venir en voyage avec** accompany someone on a trip

Venise *f.* Venice

vent *m.* wind

vente *f.* sale; **en vente** on sale

ventre *m.* belly; abdomen; stomach; **le ventre plein** on a full stomach

ventru potbellied

verdure *f.* grass; green meadows; greenery

verglas *m.* ice

véritable real

véritablement really; truly

vérité *f.* truth; resemblance; **criant de vérité** extremely realistic; **en vérité** in fact

Verlaine, Paul (1844–1896) French symbolist poet

verni varnished; shiny

vernir varnish

verrai, verrais (*fut. and cond. of* **voir**) will see; would see

verre *m.* glass; **prendre un verre** have a drink

verrons : nous y verrons plus clair we'll see better

vers toward; around, about

vers *n. m.* verse; **faire des vers** write poetry

verser pay (a sum of money)

vert green

vertu *f.* virtue

vestiaire *m.* cloakroom

veston *m.* suitcoat; jacket

vêtu dressed

veuf *m.* widower

veut (*pres. of* **vouloir**) wants, wishes

vexer vex; hurt

viande *f.* meat

victorieux (*f.* **victorieuse**) victorious

vide empty

vider empty

vie *f.* life; **assurance sur la vie** life insurance; **eau de vie** brandy

vieillard *m.* old man; *m. pl.* old people

vieillir grow old

Vienne *f.* Vienna

viens, vient, viennent (*pres. of* **venir**) comes; come

vieux (*before vowel sound* **vieil**; *f.* **vieille**) old

vif (*f.* **vive**) alert; quick

vilain ugly; bad

villa *f.* country home; summer house

ville *f.* city; town; **en ville** downtown; **hôtel de ville** *m.* city hall

vin *m.* wine; **vin fin** vintage wine

vingt twenty

vingtaine *f.* about twenty

violent violent; very strong

violet purple

violon *m.* violin; **faire du violon** play the violin

virtuose *m./f.* virtuoso

visage *m.* face

viser aim at

vision *f.* vision; point of view

visite *f.* visit; **rendre visite à** visit (a person)

visiter visit (a place)

visiteur *m.* visitor

Verbs with spelling changes are explained on pp. 336–338.

vit (*s.p. of* **voir**) saw; (*pres. of* **vivre**) lives
vite quick; quickly, fast
vitesse *f.* speed; **excès de vitesse** *m.* speeding
vitre *f.* window pane
vitrine *f.* store window; show window
vivant living; merry; alive; *n.m.* living person
vivre (**vivant, vécu, je vis, je vécus**) live
vœu *m.* wish
voici here is, here are; **et voici que** and now; **voici que** then
voie *f.* way; direction; lane
voie (*1st person pres. subj. of* **voir**) see
voilà there is, there are; here it is; **les voilà** here they come
voile *m.* veil; *f.* sail
voiler hide
voir (**voyant, vu, je vois, je vis**) see; notice; **aller voir** go and see; visit; **faire voir** show; **venez me voir** come and see me
voisin *m.* neighbor; (*adj.*) near
voisinage *m.* vicinity
voiture *f.* car
voix *f.* voice; **à haute voix** aloud; **à trois voix** between three people
vol *m.* flight; theft
volant flying; *n. m.* steering wheel
voler fly; rob
volet *m.* shutter
voleur *m.* thief
volontairement willingly; voluntarily
volonté *f.* will
volontiers willingly; with pleasure
Voltaire (1694–1778) 18th-century writer of philosophical novels, essays, poems, and plays
vont (*pres. of* **aller**) go
vos (*pl. of* **votre**) your

votre (*pl.* **vos**) your
vôtre (*pron.*) yours
voudrai, voudrais (*fut. and cond. of* **vouloir**) will want; would like
vouloir (**voulant, voulu, je veux, je voulus**) want; wish; desire; **que voulez-vous** what do you expect; **voulez-vous** will you please; **vouloir bien** be willing; **vouloir dire** mean
vous you; **vous deux** both of you
voyage *m.* trip; **voyage d'agrément** pleasure trip; **faire un voyage** take a trip; **agent de voyage** *m.* travel agent; **venir en voyage avec quelqu'un** accompany someone on a trip
voyager (*irr. sp.* **B**) travel
voyageur *m.* traveler; passenger
voyant (*pres. part. of* **voir**) seeing; (*adj.*) clairvoyant
voyante *f.* clairvoyant, seer
voyons (**voir**) we see; (*interjection*) come now; look here; let's see
voyou *m.* hoodlum
vrai true; real
vraiment really; truly
vu (*p.p. of* **voir**) seen
vue *f.* view; sight; **en vue** prominent

Y

y there; in it
yeux (*m. pl. of* **œil**) eyes; **jeter les yeux** glance; **quitter quelqu'un des yeux** take one's eyes off someone

Z

zoologique zoological; **jardin zoologique** zoo
zut shucks, heck

Irregular verbs are conjugated on pp. 318–335.

English-French Vocabulary

Abbreviations

adj.	adjective	*irr. sp.*	irregular spelling	*pers.*	person
adv.	adverb	*m.*	masculine	*prep.*	preposition
cond.	conditional	*n.*	noun	*pres.*	present
conj.	conjugated	*obj.*	object	*pron.*	pronoun
conjunc.	conjunction	*p.*	page	*rel.*	relative
f.	feminine	*part.*	participle	*sing.*	singular
fut.	future	*pl.*	plural	*s.p.*	simple past
inf.	infinitive	*p.p.*	past participle	*subj.*	subjunctive
interr.	interrogative			*v.*	verb

*aspirate *h*   (2) -**ir** verbs that do not insert -**iss**-; all other -**ir** verbs insert -**iss**-.

Page references immediately following the English word refer to explanations of the word in question.

Verbs whose principal parts are given are irregular, and their conjugations may be found on pages 336–353. The use of principal parts is explained on pages 333–335. Verbs followed by (*conj. like...*) are irregular and follow the pattern of the verb indicated.

Verbs followed by (*irr. sp.* **A** to **F**) undergo a spelling change in certain forms. The letter refers to the appropriate type of change explained on pages 336–338.

A

a un, une
able capable; **be able** pouvoir (pouvant, pu, je peux, je pus) (+ *inf.*)
about (p. 255) de; sur; environ; à peu près; vers; au sujet de; à propos de; **about fifty** une cinquantaine (de); **about that** à ce sujet; **be about to** être sur le point de; **talk about** parler de; **tell about** parler de
above (pp. 255–56) sur; au-desus de
abroad à l'etranger; **from abroad** de l'étranger
absence absence *f.*; **in the absence** en l'absence
absent absent

absolutely absolument
accent accent *m.*
accept accepter
accident accident *m.*
according to (p. 256) selon, suivant, d'après
accused (*n.*) accusé *m.*
accustomed : get accustomed to s'habituer (à + *inf.*)
ache (*v.*) faire mal; **I have a headache** j'ai mal à la tête
acquaintance connaissance *f*; relation *f.*
across (p. 256) à travers; de l'autre côté de; **run across** traverser en courant; **travel across** traverser

act agir
action action *f.*
actress actrice *f.*
actually (pp. 10–11) vraiment, réellement; en fait, à vrai dire
address adresse *f.*
admire admirer
admit admettre (*conj. like* mettre)
adopt adopter
adore adorer
adventure aventure *f.*
advice (p. 11) conseil *m.*; **a piece of advice** un conseil *m.*
advise conseiller (à + *person* + de + *inf.*); **advise against** déconseiller
affair affaire *f.*
afraid : be afraid avoir peur, craindre; **became afraid** *compound past of* avoir peur, prendre peur
Africa Afrique *f.*
after (pp. 241, 250, 256) après; d'après; **after hearing** après avoir entendu
afternoon après-midi *m./f.*
again (pp. 11–12) encore, encore une fois, de nouveau, à nouveau; re- + *verb*
against contre; **advise against** déconseiller
age âge *m.*; **old age** vieillesse *f.*, vieux jours *m. pl.*
agnostic agnostique
ago il y a; **a little while ago** tout à l'heure; **a month ago** il y a un mois
agree (p. 12) s'accorder; consentir (à + *inf.*); être d'accord
agreed d'accord, c'est entendu, entendu
aim but *m.*
air air *m.*; **in the air** en l'air
air conditioner climatiseur *m.*
airplane avion *m.*
airport aéroport *m.*
alarm clock réveil *m.*
Albert Albert
Alexander Alexandre
all tout (*f.* toute, *m. pl.* tous); **all the same** quand même; **all the while**

(p. 111) tout en; **come out all right** finir bien; **not at all** pas du tout
allow laisser (*person* + *inf.*); permettre (à + *person* + de + *inf.*); **I was allowed** j'ai pu
almost presque
alone seul; **leave me alone** laissez-moi tranquille
along (pp. 256–57) le long de; **get along** se débrouiller; **go along the road** suivre le chemin
already déjà
although bien que, quoique (+ *subj.*)
always toujours
amateur amateur *m.*
ambassador ambassadeur *m.*
ambitious ambitieux (*f.* ambitieuse)
America Amérique *f.*
American Américain *m.*; **South American** Sud-Américain *m.*
amuse amuser; **amuse oneself** s'amuser (à + *inf.*)
amusing amusant
Andrew André
anger colère *f.*
angry fâché, en colère, vexé; **get angry** se mettre en colère; se fâcher
animal animal *m.*
anniversary anniversaire *m.*; **wedding anniversary** anniversaire de mariage
announcement annonce *f.*
announcer speaker *m.*
annoying ennuyeux (*f.* ennuyeuse)
another encore un(e)
answer (*v.*) répondre (à + *n.*); (*n.*) réponse *f.*
any du, de la, des; quelque; (*obj. pron.*) en; **any at all** pas du tout; **in any case** en tout cas; **not any** pas de, ne... aucun; **not any more** ne... plus
anyone quelqu'un; **not... anyone** ne... personne
anything quelque chose; **not... anything** ne... rien
apartment appartement *m.*
approach approcher (de + *n.*); s'approcher (de + *n.*)
April avril *m.*
Arabic (*n.*) arabe *m.*
architect architecte *m./f.*

Irregular verbs are conjugated on pp. 318–335.

ardent ardent

are sont; se trouvent; **are to** doivent; **there are** il y a

area région *f.*

aren't you ? isn't it ? n'est-ce pas ?

arm bras *m.*

armchair fauteuil *m.*

army armée *f.*

around : get around se déplacer (*irr. sp.* **A**)

arrest arrêter

arrive arriver

art art *m.*

artist artiste *m./f.*

as (pp. 21, 250–51) comme; **as... a** en; **as... as** aussi... que; **as for** quant à; **as long as** tant que; **as soon as** dès que

ashamed : be ashamed avoir honte

ask demander (*thing* + à + *person*; à + *person* + de + *inf.*); **ask a question** poser une question; **ask for something** demander quelque chose; **ask of someone** demander à quelqu'un; **he asked my pardon** il m'a demandé pardon

asleep : be asleep dormir (2)

aspirin aspirine *f.*

assistant assistant *m.*

astronaut astronaute *m./f.*

at (pp. 228–29, 257–58) à; chez; **at length** longuement; **at once** tout de suite; **not at all** pas du tout

Athens Athènes

attend (p. 86) aller à; assister à

attention attention *f.*

attentively attentivement

attitude attitude *f.*

attract attirer

aunt tante *f.*

author auteur *m.*

automatically automatiquement

awaken réveiller; se réveiller

away : go away s'en aller, partir (2); **right away** tout de suite

---

Verbs with spelling changes are explained on pp. 336–338.

B

baby bébé *m.*

back (*n.*) dos *m.*

back : come back revenir; **come back home** rentrer; **go back** retourner

bad (*n.*) mauvais *m.*; (*adj.*) mauvais

ball danse *f.*; bal *m.*

ball (point) pen stylo à bille *m.* bic *m.*

bank banque *f.*

barber coiffeur *m.*

bare nu

bark aboyer (*irr. sp.* **C**)

bathe se baigner

be être (étant, été, je suis, je fus); **be able** pouvoir (pouvant, pu, je peux, je pus); **be asleep** dormir (2); **be better** aller mieux; être mieux; valoir mieux; **be bored** s'ennuyer (*irr. sp.* **C**); **be careful !** attention !; **be mistaken** se tromper; **be warm** avoir chaud; **be well** aller bien; **be willing** vouloir bien

beach plage *f.*

beautiful beau (*before vowel sound* bel; *f.* belle)

beauty beauté *f.*

because (p. 251) parce que; **because of** à cause de

become (pp. 26–27, 75) devenir (*conj. like* venir); **become afraid** prendre peur; **become frightened** s'effrayer; **become interested in** s'intéresser à; **it became cold** il a fait froid

bed lit *m.*; **go to bed** se coucher

bedtime : at bedtime avant de se coucher, à l'heure de se coucher

before (pp. 241, 251, 258) (*time*) avant (+ *n. or pron.*), avant de (+ *inf.*), avant que (+ *subj.*); (*place*) devant

begin commencer (à + *inf.*) (*irr. sp.* **A**); se mettre (à + *inf.*)

beginning commencement *m.*

believe croire (croyant, cru, je crois, je crus) (+ *inf.*; + *person*; à + *thing*; en + *person* [with the sense of *to have faith in*])

belong appartenir (*conj. like* tenir)

best (*adj.*) meilleur; (*adv.*) mieux

better (pp. 27–28) (*adj.*) meilleur; (*adv.*)

mieux; **be better** valoir mieux, être mieux; (*referring to health*) aller mieux

between entre

big grand

billfold portefeuille *m.*

bird oiseau *m.*

bit : a bit un peu

blame blâmer

blanket couverture *f.*

blue bleu

boat bateau *m.;* **sailboat** bateau à voiles

book livre *m.;* **telephone book** annuaire *m.*

bored ennuyé; **be bored** s'ennuyer (*irr. sp.* **C**)

boring ennuyeux (*f.* ennuyeuse)

born : be born naître (naissant, né, je nais, je naquis); **he was born** il est né

boss patron *m.*

both les deux, tous les deux; **both of you** vous deux

bother déranger (*irr. sp.* **B**); ennuyer (*irr. sp.* **C**)

boy garçon *m.*

brave courageux (*f.* courageuse)

Brazil Brésil *m.*

break casser; se casser; **break down** être en panne

bridge (*over river*) pont *m.;* (*game*) bridge *m.*

briefcase serviette *f.*

brilliantly brillamment

bring (p. 28) (*a thing*) apporter; (*a person*) amener (*irr. sp.* **D**)

brother frère *m.;* **brother-in-law** beau-frère *m.;* **oldest brother** aîné *m.,* frère aîné

brush brosser

Brussels Bruxelles

build construire (*conj. like* conduire)

building immeuble *m.;* bâtiment *m.;* édifice *m.*

bus (*within city*) autobus *m.;* (*between cities*) autocar *m.*

Irregular verbs are conjugated on pp. 318–335.

business affaire *f.;* les affaires *f. pl.;* **businessman** homme d'affaires *m.;* **talk business** parler affaires, parler des affaires

busy (p. 112) occupé; **be busy** être en train de; **he was busy writing** il était occupé à écrire, il était en train d'écrire

but (p. 252) (*conjunc.*) mais; (*prep.*) sauf, excepté

buy acheter (*irr. sp.* **D**)

by par; de; en; **by falling** en tombant; **by plane** par avion, en avion; **by the time** quand; **go by** passer

C

café café *m.*

call appeler (*irr. sp.* **F**); téléphoner (à + *person*)

can (pp. 28–29) pouvoir (pouvant, pu, je peux, je pus); (*know how*) savoir (sachant, su, je sais, je sus)

Canada Canada *m.*

candidate candidat *m.*

capable capable

car voiture *f.,* auto *f.,* automobile *f.*

care soin *m.;* prudence *f.*

careful : be careful ! attention !

carefully attentivement

careless négligent

carnation œillet *m.*

carol : Christmas carol cantique de Noël *m.*

carpenter menuisier *m.*

case cas *m.;* **in any case** en tout cas; **in case of** en cas de

cash (*a check*) toucher (un chèque)

cat chat *m.*

catastrophe catastrophe *f.*

catch attraper; **catch sight of** apercevoir (*conj. like* recevoir)

Catholic catholique

caught pris

celebrate célébrer

center : shopping center centre commercial *m.*

certain certain

chair chaise *f.*

champagne champagne *m.*
change (pp. 41–42) (*v.*) (*irr. sp.* **B**) changer; **change one's mind** changer d'avis; (*n.*) changement *m.*; (*small*) **change** monnaie *f.*
character (p. 42) personnage (*in a literary work*) *m.*; (*n.*) caractère *m.*
charge prendre (prenant, pris, je prends, je pris)
charm charme *m.*
charming charmant
chat bavarder
chauffeur chauffeur *m.*
cheap bon marché
check chèque *m.*
chess échecs *m. pl.*
child enfant *m./f.*
Chinese chinois
Christmas Noël *m.*; **Christmas carol** cantique de Noël *m.*
church église *f.*
cider cidre *m.*
cigarette cigarette *f.*
city ville *f.*; **city hall** hôtel de ville *m.*, mairie *f.*
claim prétendre
class classe *f.*; **conversation class** classe de conversation *f.*
classmate camarade de classe *m./f.*
cleaner teinturier *m.*; **to the cleaner's** à la teinturerie, chez le teinturier
cleaning woman femme de ménage *f.*
clear évident
clear the table débarrasser la table
climate climat *m.*
clock : alarm clock réveil *m.*
close (*v.*) fermer; (*adj.*) proche; **a close friend** un ami intime *m.*
clothes habits *m. pl.*, vêtements *m. pl.*
club club *m.*, cercle *m.*
coat (*overcoat*) manteau *m.*; (*suitcoat*) veste *m.*
Coca-Cola Coca-Cola *m.*
coffee café *m.*

Verbs with spelling changes are explained on pp. 336–338.

cold (*n.*) rhume *m.*; (*adj.*) froid; **it became cold** il a fait froid; **it was cold** il faisait froid
colleague collègue *m./f.*
collection collection *f.*
colonel colonel *m.*
come venir (venant, venu, je viens, je vins); **come back** revenir (*conj. like* venir); **come back home** rentrer; **come and see me** venez me voir; **come in** entrer; **come to dinner** venir dîner; **come out all right** finir bien; s'arranger
comfortable confortable
company compagnie *f.*; maison *f.*; société *f.*
completely complètement
computer ordinateur *m.*
concern : concern oneself with s'occuper (de + *n.*)
concerning (p. 255) au sujet de; sur; **concerning them** à leur sujet
concert concert *m.*
condemn condamner
condition condition *f.*; **on the condition that** à (la) condition que (+ *subj.*)
conditioner : air conditioner climatiseur *m.*
confess avouer
considerable considérable
construct construire (construisant, construit, je construis, je construisis)
contest concours *m.*
continue continuer (à + *inf.*); **continue on our way** continuer notre route
convention congrès *m.*
conversation conversation *f.*; **conversation class** classe de conversation *f.*
convince convaincre (*conj. like* vaincre)
cook faire la cuisine
cookie biscuit *m.*
copy copier; **copy again** recopier
correct (*v.*) corriger (*irr. sp.* **B**); (*adj.*) exact
corridor corridor *m.*; couloir *m.*
Corsica Corse *f.*
cost (*n.*) prix *m.*; (*v.*) coûter
costume costume *m.*
count compter (+ *inf.*)

country pays *m.*; (*opposite of city*) campagne *f.*
courage courage *m.*
course cours *m.*; **take a course** suivre un cours; **course** (*of action*) démarche *f.*; **drop a course** abandonner un cours, laisser tomber un cours
cousin cousin *m.*; cousine *f.*
co-worker collègue *m./f.*
cream crème *f.*; **ice cream** glace *f.*
create créer
crime crime *m.*
criminal criminel *m.*
criticize critiquer
cross traverser
crossword puzzle mots croisés *m. pl.*
crowd foule *f.*
cry pleurer
cultured cultivé
curious curieux (*f.* curieuse)
curtain rideau *m.*
cut couper; **cut down** couper
cute mignon (*f.* mignonne)

D
dance danse *f.*, bal *m.*
dancer danseur *m.*, danseuse *f.*
danger danger *m.*
dangerous dangereux (*f.* dangereuse)
dark brun; sombre
date rendez-vous *m.*
daughter fille *f.*
dawn aube *f.*
day (p. 43) jour *m.*; journée *f.*; **the day after tomorrow** après-demain; **the next day** le lendemain, le jour suivant, le jour après
daylight jour *m.*
dead mort
deal : a great deal beaucoup
December décembre *m.*
decide décider (de + *inf.*), se décider (à + *inf.*)
decision décision *f.*; **make a decision** prendre une décision

decorator : interior decorator décorateur *m.*, décoratrice *f.*
deep profond
deep-seated profond
defend défendre
defendant inculpé *m.*
delegate délégué *m.*, déléguée *f.*
delighted enchanté, ravi
demanding exigeant
democracy démocratie *f.*
Denmark Danemark *m.*
dentist dentiste *m./f.*
departure départ *m.*
describe décrire (*conj. like* écrire)
desk bureau *m.*
destiny destinée *f.*
detective inspecteur *m.*; **detective story** roman policier *m.*
diamond diamant *m.*
dictionary dictionnaire *m.*
die mourir (mourant, mort, je meurs, je mourus)
difference différence *f.*
different différent
difficult difficile
difficulty difficulté *f.*
dinner (*n.*) dîner *m.*; **come to dinner** venir dîner; **have dinner, eat dinner** dîner
directly directement
director directeur *m.*, directrice *f.*
discharge remercier, renvoyer
discuss discuter
discussion discussion *f.*
dishes vaisselle *f. sing.*; **wash the dishes** faire la vaisselle
disillusion désillusion *f.*
distance distance *f.*; **in the distance** au loin
distribute distribuer
do faire (faisant, fait, je fais, je fis); **do without** se passer de; **do wrong** faire du tort
doctor docteur *m.*; médecin *m.*
doctorate doctorat *m.*
dog chien *m.*
dollar dollar *m.*
door porte *f.*
dormitory dortoir *m.*, résidence *f.*

doubt douter (de + *n.*)
doubtful douteux (*f.* douteuse)
down (p. 258) en bas; **cut down** couper;
  go down descendre; **slow down**
  ralentir
drawer tiroir *m.*
dream rêver (de + *n.*; de + *inf.*)
dress (*n.*) robe *f.*; (*v.*) **get dressed**
  s'habiller
drink boire (buvant, bu, je bois, je bus)
drive conduire (conduisant, conduit, je
  conduis, je conduisis)
drop (*a course*) abandonner, laisser
  tomber
duck canard *m.*
duty devoir *m.*

E

each chacun; **each other** se... l'un l'autre
ear oreille *f.*
earlier plus tôt; de meilleure heure
early (p. 57) tôt, de bonne heure; en
  avance
earn gagner
ease facilité *f.*
easily facilement
Easter Pâques *m.*
easy facile; **easy-going** indulgent
eat manger (*irr. sp.* **B**); **eat dinner** dîner
egg œuf *m.*
Egypt Égypte *f.*
eight huit
either non plus
elbow coude *m.*
election élection *f.*
elegance élégance *f.*
elegant élégant
else : something else autre chose
elsewhere ailleurs, autre part
emergency urgence *f.*
encourage encourager (*irr. sp.* **B**)
end (pp. 57–58) fin *f.*; bout *m.*
energetically énergiquement
engineer ingénieur *m.*
England Angleterre *f.*

Verbs with spelling changes are explained on
pp. 336–338.

English (*n.*) Anglais *m.*; (*adj.*) anglais
enough assez
enter entrer (dans + *n.*)
entertain amuser, distraire
entertaining amusant
erase effacer (*irr. sp.* **A**)
error erreur *f.*, faute *f.*
escape (p. 58) échapper (à + *n.*);
  s'échapper (de + *n.*)
especially surtout
Europe Europe *f.*
even même; **even though** bien que,
  quoique; tout en (+ *pres. part*)
evening (pp. 43, 145) soir *m.*, soirée *f.*;
  evening party soirée *f.*; **last evening**
  hier soir
event événement *m.*
ever jamais
every (p. 59) chaque; tous les; **every
  other year** tous les deux ans
everyone (p. 59) tout le monde
everything (pp. 59, 138) tout; n'importe
  quoi; **everything that** tout ce qui,
  tout ce que
everywhere partout
evident évident
examination examen *m.*
excellent excellent
except (p. 258) sauf, à part, excepté
exchange (p. 42) échanger (*irr. sp.* **B**)
exercise devoir *m.*, exercice *m.*
exist exister; régner
exotic exotique
expect (pp. 71–72) attendre (+ *n.*);
  s'attendre (à + *n.*); compter (+ *n.*);
  what do you expect que voulez-vous
expensive cher (*f.* chère); **be expensive**
  coûter cher
experience expérience *f.*
explain expliquer
explosion explosion *f.*
exterior extérieur *m.*
extraordinary extraordinaire
eye œil *m.*, *pl.* yeux

F

face figure *f.*
factory usine *f.*

fail (pp. 72–73) manquer (de + *inf.*);
échouer (à un examen); coller
(quelqu'un)
fair exposition *f.*
fall tomber; **fall out** tomber de
family famille *f.*
famous célèbre, connu
fantastic fantastique
far loin
farmer fermier *m.*
fast rapide; vite
fate sort *m.*
father père *m.*
father-in-law beau-père *m.*
faucet robinet *m.*
favorite préféré
February février *m.*
feel (pp. 73–74) sentir; se sentir; **feel
well** se sentir bien; **how do you feel ?**
comment allez-vous ?
few peu; **a few** quelques
field champ *m.*; domaine *m.*
fifty cinquante
fight se battre (battant, battu, je bats, je
battis)
fill remplir (de + *n.*)
film film *m.*
finally enfin, finalement
find trouver; **find again** retrouver; **find
out** découvrir (*conj. like* ouvrir),
apprendre (*conj. like* prendre)
fine excellent; beau (*before vowel sound*
bel, *f.* belle); **those fine people** ces
braves gens *m. pl.*
finger doigt *m.*
finish finir
fire incendie *m.*
first premier (*f.* première); **on the first
floor** au rez-de-chaussée
fish poisson *m.*
five cinq
fix réparer
floor plancher *m.*; étage *m.*; **on the first
floor** au rez-de-chaussée
Florida Floride *f.*
florist fleuriste *m./f.*
flower fleur *f.*

fluently couramment
follow suivre (suivant, suivi, je suis, je
suivis)
foolish stupide
foot pied *m.*; **on foot** à pied
football ballon *m.*; football *m.*; **football
game** un match de football, une
partie de football
for (pp. 252, 259) (*conjunc.*) car; (*prep.*)
pour; pendant; depuis; il y a... que,
voilà... que
forbid défendre (à + *person* + de + *inf.*)
foreign étranger (*f.* étrangère)
forget oublier (de + *inf.*)
former ancien (*f.* ancienne); **the former**
celui-là
formerly autrefois
fortune fortune *f.*
forty quarante
fountain pen stylo *m.*
four quatre
France France *f.*
Frances Françoise *f.*
Francis François *m.*
frankly franchement
Frederick Frédéric
free libre
freedom liberté *f.*
French français; **French class** classe de
français *f.*
Friday vendredi *m.*
friend ami *m.*, amie *f.*; **a close friend** un
ami intime
frightened effrayé; **become frightened**
s'effrayer (*irr. sp.* **C**)
from de; **keep from** empêcher (+ *person*
+ de + *inf.*)
front : in front of devant
fruit fruit *m.*; **fruit juice** jus de fruit *m.*
full plein
fun : make fun of se moquer (de + *n.*)
funny amusant
fur fourrure *f.*
furious furieux (*f.* furieuse)

G

gain gagner; **gain ground** avancer (*irr.
sp.* **A**)

Irregular verbs are conjugated on pp. 318–335.

game match *m.*, partie *f.*; **a football game** une partie de football, un match de football
garden jardin *m.*
general général *m.*
generous généreux (*f.* généreuse)
gentleman monsieur *m.*
George Georges
German (*adj.*) allemand
Germany Allemagne *f.*
get (pp. 74–75) chercher; recevoir; prendre; faire; avoir; obtenir; atteindre; **get along** se débrouiller; **get angry** se fâcher; **get around** se déplacer; **get dressed** s'habiller; **get into** entrer dans; **get married** se marier; **get out of** sortir de; **get pale** pâlir; **get somewhere** arriver; **get tired** se fatiguer; **get up** se lever (*irr. sp.* **D**) **get used to** s'habituer; **it got warm** il a fait chaud
gift cadeau *m.*; **give a gift** faire un cadeau
girl jeune fille *f.*
give donner; consacrer; **give a lecture** faire une conférence
glad content, heureux (*f.* heureuse)
glance regard *m.*
glass verre *m.*; **champagne glass** verre de champagne
go (pp. 85–86, 262) aller (allant, allé, je vais, j'allai); **go and see** aller voir; **go away** partir (2), s'en aller; **go back** retourner; **go by** passer; **go down** descendre; **go for a walk** aller se promener; **go out** sortir (2); **go to bed** se coucher; **go through** passer par; **go up** monter; remonter
going : easy-going indulgent
golf golf *m.*
good (*n.*) bon *m.*; bien *m.*; (*adj.*) bon; (*well behaved*) sage; **good looks** beauté *f.*; **have a good time** s'amuser
goodbye au revoir
grandchild petit-fils *m.*, petite-fille *f.*; petits-enfants *m./f. pl.*

Verbs with spelling changes are explained on pp. 336–338.

grandfather grand-père *m.*
grandmother grand-mère *f.*
grandparents grands-parents *m. pl.*
grapefruit pamplemousse *m.*
grave grave
great grand; **a great deal** beaucoup; **a great many** beaucoup
Greece Grèce *f.*
green vert
ground : gain ground avancer (*irr. sp.* **A**)
group groupe *m.*

H

hair cheveux *m. pl.*
hairdresser coiffeur *m.*, coiffeuse *f.*
half (*n.*) moitié *f.*; (*adj.*) demi; **a half hour** une demi-heure
hall : city hall hôtel de ville *m.*, mairie *f.*
hand main *f.*; **shake hands** se serrer la main
hand in remettre (*conj. like* mettre); donner
happen (pp. 86–88) se passer; arriver; se trouver; **it happened to me** cela m'est arrivé
happiness bonheur *m.*
happy heureux (*f.* heureuse), content; **Happy New Year** Bonne Année, une Bonne Nouvelle Année
hard (*adj*) dur; difficile; (*adv.*) dur
hateful méchant
have avoir (ayant, eu, j'ai, j'eus); (pp. 206–07, 216–20) (*causative*) faire (+ *inf.*); **have dinner** dîner; **have a good time** s'amuser, bien s'amuser; **have lunch** déjeuner; **have to** devoir, falloir, être obligé de
head tête *f.*
headache mal de tête *m.*; **have a headache** avoir mal à la tête
hear (p. 88) entendre; **hear of** entendre parler de; **hear that** entendre dire que
heartily de bon cœur
heaven ciel *m.*
heavy lourd
Helen Hélène
hell enfer *m.*

help (*v.*) aider (*person* + à + *inf.*); (*n.*) aide
   f.
her (*direct obj.*) la; (*indirect obj.*) lui;
   (*with prep.*) elle; (*adj.*) son, sa, ses
here ici; **here is, here are** voici
hero *héros *m.*
hesitate hésiter
high élevé; *haut
hill colline *f.*
him (*direct obj.*) le; (*indirect obj.*) lui;
   (*with prep.*) lui
hire engager (*irr. sp.* **B**)
his (*adj.*) son, sa, ses; (*pron.*) le sien, la
   sienne, etc.
history histoire *f.*
hold tenir (tenant, tenu, je tiens, je tins);
   avoir lieu
home maison *f.*; **at home** chez soi; chez
   nous; **be home** être chez soi; **come
   back home** rentrer; **return home**
   rentrer
homework devoir *m.*
honor honneur *m.*
hope espérer (+ *inf.*) (*irr. sp.* **E**); **hope for**
   espérer (+ *n.*)
horrified scandalisé
horseback : go horseback riding faire du
   cheval, faire une promenade à cheval
hostile hostile
hotel hôtel *m.*
hour heure *f.*; **a half hour** une
   demi-heure
house maison *f.*; **at your house** chez
   vous
housework ménage *m.*
how comment; **how often** tous les
   combien; **know how to do something**
   (p. 100) savoir faire quelque chose
however cependant, pourtant; si (+ *adj.*);
   however rich he is (may be) si riche
   qu'il soit; **however that may be** quoi
   qu'il en soit
humble humble
hundred (*n.*) centaine *f.*; (*adj.*) cent
hurry se dépêcher (de + *inf.*)

hurt (*v.*) avoir mal; faire mal (à + *person*)
   (*adj.*) vexé; **hurt oneself** se faire mal
husband mari *m.*
hypothesis hypothèse *f.*

I

I je; moi
ice glace *f.*; **ice cream** glace *f.*; **ice water**
   eau glacée
idea idée *f.*
if si
illness maladie *f.*
illustrated illustré
imagine imaginer
immediate immédiat
immediately immédiatement
import importer
important important
impression impression *f.*
in (pp. 228–31, 259–60) dans; en; à; de;
   eight in the evening huit heures du
   soir; **in that manner** de cette façon;
   in the theater au théâtre; **in two
   hours** dans deux heures; en deux
   heures
in spite of (p. 261) malgré
indifference indifférence *f.*
individualist individualiste *m./f.*
information information *f.*;
   renseignements *m. pl.*
initiative initiative *f.*
inquire se renseigner
inspect inspecter
instead of (p. 261) au lieu de
insult insulte *f.*
intelligence intelligence *f.*
intelligent intelligent
intend (pp. 98–99) avoir l'intention de;
   compter (+ *inf.*); penser (+ *inf.*)
interest (*v.*) intéresser; s'intéresser (à +
   n.); (*n.*) intérêt *m.*; **take an interest in**
   s'intéresser (à + *n.*)
interested : become interested in
   s'intéresser (à + *n.*)
interesting intéressant
interior intérieur *m.*; **interior decorator**
   décorateur *m.*, décoratrice *f.*
interrupt interrompre

Irregular verbs are conjugated on pp. 318–335.

intervene intervenir (*conj. like* venir)
into dans; en
introduce (p. 99) présenter
invitation invitation *f.*
invite inviter (à + *inf.*)
Ireland Irlande *f.*
Irene Irène
is est
isn't it ? n'est-ce pas ?
it (*subject*) il; elle; ce; ça; (*direct obj.*)
   le, la
Italian (*n.*) Italien *m.*; (*adj.*) italien (*f.*
   italienne)
Italy Italie *f.*

J

Jack Jacques
Japan Japon *m.*
Japanese japonais
Jean Jeanne
job (p. 181) place *f.*; travail *m.*; position
   f.; situation *f.*
Johnnie Jeannot
joke plaisanterie *f.*
joy joie *f.*
judge juge *m.*
juice jus *m.*; **fruit juice** jus de fruit
Julia Julie
July juillet *m.*
June juin *m.*
just juste; **I have just done something** je
   viens de faire quelque chose; **just
   now** tout à l'heure

K

keep garder; **keep from** empêcher;
   s'empêcher (*n.* + de + *inf.*)
key clé *f.*
kilometer kilomètre *m.* (5/8 of a mile)
kind aimable
kindness bonté *f.*
king roi *m.*
knife couteau *m.*

Verbs with spelling changes are explained on
pp. 336–338.

knock frapper; **there was a knock** (p. 99)
   on a frappé
know (pp. 99–100) (*something*) savoir
   (sachant, su, je sais, je sus); (*be acquainted with someone or something*) connaître (connaissant, connu,
   je connais, je connus); **know how to**
   savoir (+ *inf.*)

L

laboratory laboratoire *m.*
lack (p. 114) manquer (de + *n.*)
ladder échelle *f.*
lady dame *f.*; femme *f.*
lake lac *m.*
lamp lampe *f.*
language langue *f.*
large grand; gros (*f.* grosse)
last dernier (*f.* dernière); **last evening**
   hier soir; **last night** (pp. 114–15) cette
   nuit; la nuit dernière
late (p. 115) (*not early*) tard; (*not on
   time*) en retard
Latin Quarter quartier Latin *m.*
latter : the latter celui-ci; ce dernier
laugh (*v.*) rire (riant, ri, je ris, je ris) (de +
   n.); **laugh at** rire de, se moquer de; (*n.*)
   rire *m.*
Laura Laure
Lawrence Laurent
lawyer avocat *m.*
lazy paresseux (*f.* paresseuse)
learn apprendre (*conj. like* prendre)
leather cuir *m.*
leave (pp. 115–17) (*something somewhere*) laisser; (*a place*) quitter; partir
   (de + *n.*) (2); sortir (de + *n.*) (2); **leave
   me alone** laissez-moi tranquille
lecture conférence *f.*
leg jambe *f.*; (*of an animal*) patte *f.*
lend prêter
length longueur *f.*; **at length**
   longuement
lesson leçon *f.*
letter lettre *f.*
library bibliothèque *f.*
lie mentir (2)
lieutenant lieutenant *m.*

life vie *f.*
light lumière *f.*
like (*v.*) aimer; vouloir; (*prep.*) comme
lip lèvre *f.*
Lisbon Lisbonne
listen écouter; **listen to** écouter (+ *n.*)
little (*adj.*) petit; (*adv.*) (p. 131) peu;
un peu
live (p. 131) habiter (+ *n.* or : à + *n.*, or :
dans + *n.*); vivre (vivant, vécu, je vis,
je vécus)
living room salle de séjour *f.*; salon *m.*
lock fermer à clé
London Londres *m.*
long (p. 132) long (*f.* longue); **a long time**
longtemps; **as long as** tant que; **how**
long depuis quand, depuis combien
de temps; combien de temps, pendant combien de temps
longer (time) plus longtemps; **no...**
longer ne... plus
look regarder; **look after** s'occuper (de +
n.); **look out on** donner sur; **look at**
regarder (+ *n.*); **look for** chercher (+
n.); **look well on someone** aller bien
à quelqu'un
looking : good looking joli; beau
looks : good looks beauté *f.*
lose perdre
lot : a lot beaucoup
loud fort
Louvre Louvre *m.*
love aimer
luck chance *f.*
Lucy Lucie
lunch déjeuner *m.*; **have lunch** déjeuner
Lyons Lyon

M

machine machine *f.*
magazine revue *f.*; magazine *m.*
mail mettre à la poste
main principal
majority plupart *f.*; majorité *f.*

make faire (faisant, fait, je fais, je fis);
make + *adj.* (p. 133) rendre (+ *adj.*);
make fun of se moquer de; **make a**
decision prendre une décision; **make**
a trip faire un voyage
man homme *m.*; **businessman** homme
d'affaires; **old man** viel homme *m.*,
vieillard *m.*; homme âgé *m.*; (*adj.*
used as n.) vieux *m.*; **young man**
jeune homme, (*pl.*) jeunes gens
manage to s'arranger pour
manager gérant *m.*
many beaucoup; **a great many**
beaucoup; énormément, des tas de;
many times bien des fois
March mars *m.*
Margaret Marguerite
Mark Marc
marriage mariage *m.*
married marié; **get married** se marier
marry (p. 142) épouser; se marier avec;
marier (quelqu'un à quelqu'un)
Martha Marthe
marvelous superbe; merveilleux
(*f.* merveilleuse)
mason maçon *m.*
master maître *m.*
mathematics mathématiques *f. pl.*
matter : what is the matter with me ce
que j'ai
mayor maire *m.*
me me, moi
meager maigre
meal repas *m.*
mean vouloir dire; signifier
meet (p. 100) (*by appointment*)
retrouver; (*by chance*) rencontrer;
(*make the acquaintance of*) faire la
connaissance de, connaître
meeting réunion *f.*
mention mentionner
Mexico Mexique *m.*
Michael Michel
midnight minuit *m.*
military militaire
milk lait *m.*
milliner modiste *f.*
mind esprit *m.*; **change one's mind**
changer d'avis

Irregular verbs are conjugated on pp. 318–335.

mine le mien, la mienne, etc.; à moi
minister (of the gospel) pasteur *m.*
minute minute *f.*
miss (p. 142–43) manquer; regretter
mission mission *f.*
mistake faute *f.*; erreur *f.*
mistaken : be mistaken se tromper
model mannequin *m.*
modern moderne
money argent *m.*
monster monstre *m.*
month mois *m.*
moon lune *f.*
more (pp. 143–44) plus; **more and more**
de plus en plus; **the more... the more**
plus... plus; **no longer** ne... plus; **not
any more** ne... plus
morning (p. 43) matin *m.*; matinée *f.*;
the next morning le lendemain
matin, le matin suivant; **yesterday
morning** hier matin
most plus; le plus
mother mère *f.*
mother-in-law belle-mère *f.*
motorcycle motocyclette *f.*, moto *f.*; **on
a motorcycle** en moto
mountain montagne *f.*
mouth bouche *f.*
move bouger (*irr. sp.* **B**); remuer; (*change
dwellings*) déménager (*irr. sp.* **B**)
movie cinéma *m.*; film *m.*; **movies**
cinéma *m.*
much beaucoup; **so much** tellement;
tant; **very much** (p. 244) beaucoup
museum musée *m.*
music musique *f.*
musical musicien (*f.* musicienne)
must (pp. 216–20) devoir (devant, dû, je
dois, je dus) (+ *inf.*); falloir (fallu, il
faut, il fallut) (+ *inf.*); être obligé (de +
inf.)
my mon, ma, mes

—————
Verbs with spelling changes are explained on
pp. 336–338.

N

name (*v.*) appeler
Naples Naples
nasty désagréable
native natal; **native language** langue
maternelle *f.*
natural naturel (*f.* naturelle)
nature nature *f.*
near près de, à côté de
necessary nécessaire; **it is necessary** il
faut
necklace collier *m.*
need (*v.*) avoir besoin de; (*n.*) besoin *m.*
neighbor voisin *m.*; (*biblical sense*)
prochain *m.*
neither... nor ni... ni... ne
nervous nerveux (*f.* nerveuse)
never jamais; ne... jamais
new nouveau (*before vowel sound*
nouvel; *f.* nouvelle); neuf
news nouvelles *f. pl.*; informations *f. pl.*
piece of news nouvelle *f.*
newscast informations *f. pl.*
newspaper journal *m.*
next (pp. 144–45) prochain; suivant; **the
next day** le lendemain, le jour
suivant, le jour après; **the next morning** le lendemain matin, le matin
suivant
nice (*of person*) gentil; (*of things*) joli;
beau; **he is nice to us** il est gentil
avec nous; **it is nice of him** c'est
gentil de sa part
niece nièce *f.*
night nuit *f.*; **night and day** jour et nuit
nine neuf
no (*adj.*) aucun; ne... aucun; **no longer**
ne... plus; **no more** ne... plus; (*adv.*)
non
no one personne; ne... personne
noise bruit *m.*
noon midi *m.*
not ne... pas; **not any** pas de
nothing rien; ne... rien
notice (pp. 162–63) remarquer; voir;
s'apercevoir (*conj. like* recevoir)
novel roman *m.*
now maintenant; **just now** tout à
l'heure; **right now** immédiatement,

tout de suite; **up to now** jusqu'à
présent
number nombre *m.*; (*street, telephone*)
numéro *m.*
numerous nombreux (*f.* nombreuse);
beaucoup de
nylon nylon *m.*

O

obey obéir (à + *person*)
obliged obligé (de + *inf.*)
observe observer
obviously évidemment
o'clock heure *f.*
of de; **both of you** vous deux
office bureau *m.*; (*doctor's*) cabinet *m.*
often souvent; **how often** tous les
combien
old vieux (*before vowel sound* vieil; *f.*
vieille); âgé; **I was four years old**
j'avais quatre ans; **old age** vieillesse
f.; vieux jours *m. pl.*; **old man** vieil
homme *m.*, vieillard *m.*; homme âgé
m.; (*adj. used as n.*) vieux *m.*
oldest : oldest brother aîné, frère aîné;
oldest daughter aînée, fille aînée
Oliver Olivier
on sur; dans; de; en; pour; à; **on the
condition** à (la) condition; **on foot** à
pied; **on a motorcycle** en moto; **on
Saturdays** le samedi; **on the telephone** au téléphone; **on the way** en
route; **try on** essayer (*irr. sp.* **C**)
once une fois; **at once** de suite; tout de
suite
one un; on; **the one** celui qui; **no one**
ne... personne
only seulement, ne... que
open (*v.*) ouvrir (ouvrant, ouvert,
j'ouvre, j'ouvris); (*adj.*) ouvert
opera opéra *m.*
operation opération *f.*
opinion opinion *f.*; avis *m.*
opportunity (p. 163) occasion *f.*;
possibilité *f.*
optimistic optimiste

Irregular verbs are conjugated on pp. 318–335.

or ou
orange orange *f.*
order (*v.*) ordonner; (*meal*) commander;
(*prep.*) **in order to** pour
other autre; **each other** se; l'un l'autre;
every other year tous les deux ans;
others (*pron.*) les autres
ought to (pp. 218–19) devrais, devrait,
etc. (*cond. form of verb* devoir)
out (pp. 261–62) dehors; **fall out** tomber
de; **go out** sortir (2); **one out of three**
un sur trois; **out of** hors de; **out of
money** sans argent
overtake rattraper
owe devoir

P

pack one's suitcase faire sa valise
package colis *m.*
page page *f.*
paint peindre (peignant, peint, je peins,
je peignis)
painter *m.* peintre
painting tableau *m.*; peinture *f.*
pale pâle
paper (pp. 163–64) papier *m.*; copie *f.*;
composition *f.*; (*newspaper*) journal *m.*
parade défilé *m.*
pardon pardon *m.*; **he asked my pardon**
il m'a demandé pardon
parent parent *m.*
part partie *f.*; (*in a play*) rôle *m.*
partner associé *m.*
party soirée *f.*
pass passer; **pass an examination** réussir
à un examen
passport passeport *m.*
past passé *m.*
patient *m.* patient; (*adj.*) patient
pay (*v.*) payer (*irr. sp.* **A**); (*n.*) salaire *m.*;
paie *f.*
peace paix *f.*; **in peace** en paix; **Peace
Street** rue de la Paix
peaceful tranquille, calme, paisible
pen plume *f.*; **fountain pen** stylo *m.*
pencil crayon *m.*
people (pp. 164–65) gens *m. pl.*; on;
personnes *f. pl.*; (*nation*) peuple *m.*;

those fine people ces bravs gens; **young people** jeunes gens *m. pl.*
per par; à; de; le; la
percent pourcent *m.*
perfume parfum *m.*
perhaps peut-être
permit permettre (*conj. like* mettre) (à + *person* + de + *inf.*)
permission permission *f.*
person personne *f.*
personal personnel (*f.* personnelle)
piano piano *m.*; **play the piano** jouer du piano
pick up ramasser; cueillir
picture tableau *m.*; peinture *f.*
picturesque pittoresque
piece (pp. 179–80) morceau *m.*; bout *m.*; (*of advice*) conseil *m.*; (*of paper*) feuille *f.*
pilot pilote *m.*
place (pp. 180–81) endroit *m.*; lieu *m.*; place *f.*; espace *m.*; **at their place** chez eux
plain : in plain daylight en plein jour
plan (*n.*) projet *m.*; (*v.*) projeter (*irr. sp.* **D**)
plane avion *m.*
plant plante *f.*
play (*v.*) jouer (de + *instrument*; à + *game*); (*n.*) pièce *f.*
pleasant agréable
please plaire (plaisant, plu, je plais, je plus) (à + *person*); faire plaisir à; s'il vous plaît
pleasure plaisir *m.*
pocket poche *f.*
poetry poésie *f.*
point point *m.*
poker poker *m.*
Poland Pologne *f.*
police police *f.*
policeman agent *m.*, agent de police *m.*, policier *m.*
polite poli
politics politique *f. sing.*

Verbs with spelling changes are explained on pp. 336–338.

pool (**swimming**) piscine *f.*
poor pauvre
popular populaire
portrait portrait *m.*; photo *f.*
Portugal Portugal *m.*
Portuguese portugais
position place *f.*; position *f.*; situation *f.*
possible possible
postcard carte postale *f.*
powerful puissant
practice pratique *f.*
preach prêcher
prefer préférer (*irr. sp.* **E**); aimer mieux
prepare préparer
present (*time*) présent *m.*; (*gift*) cadeau *m.*
president président *m.*
pressed together serré(e)s
pretty joli
prevent empêcher
prince prince *m.*
prison prison *f.*
prize prix *m.*
probable probable
probably probablement
problem problème *m.*
prodigy prodige *m.*
product produit *m.*
professor professeur *m.*
program programme *m.*
progress progrès *m.*; **make progress** faire des progrès
promise promettre (*conj. like* mettre) (à + *person* + de + *inf.*)
proper convenable
Protestant protestant *m.*, protestante *f.*
proud fier (*f.* fière)
prove prouver
provided that pourvu que (+ *subj.*)
public public, publique *f.*
publish publier
publisher éditeur *m.*
punish punir
pupil élève *m./f.*
purple mauve
purse sac *m.*
put mettre (mettant, mis, je mets, je mis); **put away** ranger (*irr. sp.* **B**); **put down** baisser; **put on** mettre

puzzle : crossword puzzle les mots croisés *m. pl.*
Pyrenees Pyrénées *f. pl.*

Q

quality qualité *f.*
question (*v.*) questionner; interroger (*irr. sp.* **B**); (*n.*) question *f.*; **ask a question** poser une question
quickly vite
quiet tranquille, calme

R

radio radio *f.*
rain (*v.*) pleuvoir (pleuvant, plu, il pleut, il plut); (*n.*) la pluie *f.*
raise (*v.*) lever (*irr. sp.* **D**); (*n.*) augmentation *f.*
rapidly vite; rapidement
rare rare
rather (pp. 181–82) plutôt; plutôt que de; assez; aimer mieux; au lieu de
read lire (lisant, lu, je lis, je lus)
real vrai
realize se rendre compte
really vraiment
reason (p. 182) raison *f.*; **the reason for** la raison de; **the reason that** la raison pour laquelle
reassure rassurer
reassured rassuré
receive recevoir (recevant, reçu, je reçois, je reçus)
recently récemment
reception réception *f.*
recognize reconnaître (*conj. like* connaître)
recommend recommander
recommendation recommandation *f.*
record disque *m.*
red rouge
redhead roux *m.*; rousse *f.*
refrigerator réfrigérateur *m.*
refuse refuser (de + *inf.*)

Irregular verbs are conjugated on pp. 318–335.

regret (*v.*) regretter; (*n.*) regret *m.*
relate raconter
relative parent *m.*
religion religion *f.*
remain rester
remarkable remarquable
remember se souvenir (*conj. like* venir) (de + *n.*; de + *inf.*); se rappeler (*irr. sp.* **F.**) (+ *n.*)
repair réparer
repent se repentir (2)
reply (*v.*) répondre (à + *n.*); (*n.*) réponse *f.*
report compte rendu *m.*; (*v.*) rendre compte, faire un rapport
require exiger (*irr. sp.* **B**)
resemble ressembler (à + *n.*)
reserve réserver, louer
resignation démission *f.*
resist résister (à + *n.*)
rest se reposer
restaurant restaurant *m.*
restful reposant
result résultat *m.*
résumé résumé *m.*
retire prendre (sa) retraite
retirement retraite *f.*
return (*v.*) (pp. 193–94) (*come back*) revenir (*conj. like* venir); (*go back*) retourner; (*go back home*) rentrer; (*give back*) rendre; (*n.*) retour *m.*
reward récompenser
Rhone Rhône *m.*
rich riche
ridiculous ridicule
riding : go horseback riding faire du cheval, faire une promenade à cheval
right bon; juste; **right away** tout de suite; **right now** immédiatement, tout de suite; en ce moment; **be right** avoir raison; **on the right** à droite
ring (*v.*) sonner; (*n.*) bague *f.*
river fleuve *m.*; rivière *f.*
Riviera Côte d'Azur *f.*
road route *f.*; chemin *m.*; **go along the road** suivre la route (le chemin)
roast rôti *m.*
roasted rôti
room (p. 194) (*in general*) pièce *f.*; (*bedroom*) chambre *f.*; (*room for*

meetings) salle *f*.; (*living room*) salle de séjour *f*.; salon *m*.; (*space*) place *f*.
rose rose *f*.
row rang *m*.
rub frotter
rule règle *f*.
rummage around fouiller
run courir (courant, couru, je cours, je courus); **run across** traverser en courant
rush se précipiter
Russia Russie *f*.
Russian (*language*) russe *m*.

S

sad triste
sailboat bateau à voiles *m*.
salesman vendeur *m*.; représentant *m*.
same même; **all the same** quand même
sample échantillon *m*.
sandwich sandwich *m*.
satisfied content; satisfait
Saturday samedi *m*.
save (pp. 194–95) sauver; économiser; faire des économies; garder; mettre de côté
say dire (disant, dit, je dis, je dis) (à + *person* + de + *inf*.)
scarcely à peine
scarf écharpe *f*.
school école *f*.; **to, in, at school** à l'école
scientific scientifique
scientist savant *m*.
season saison *f*.
secretary secrétaire *m*./*f*.
see voir (voyant, vu, je vois, je vis) **see again** revoir (*conj. like* voir); **come and see me** venez me voir
seem sembler (+ *inf*.); paraître (*conj. like* connaître) (+ *inf*.); avoir l'air (+ *adj*.; de + *inf*.)
sell vendre
senator sénateur
send envoyer (envoyant, envoyé, j'envoie, j'envoyai)

Verbs with spelling changes are explained on pp. 336–338.

sentence phrase *f*.
separate séparer
serious sérieux (*f*. sérieuse)
servant serviteur *m*.; domestique *m*./*f*.
serve servir (2)
service service *m*.
set (*v*.) (*the sun*) se coucher; (*n*.) (*television*) télévision *f*.
seven sept
several plusieurs
shake secouer; serrer; **shake hands** se serrer la main
sharp : at one o'clock sharp à une heure précise
shave (**oneself**) se raser
sheet drap *m*.
shirt chemise *f*.
shopping center centre commercial *m*.
short court, bref (*f*. brève); **short story** conte *m*.
shortcoming défaut *m*.
should (pp. 218–19) devrais, devrait, etc. (*cond. form of verb* devoir)
shoulder épaule *f*.
show montrer
shrug hausser; **shrug one's shoulders** hausser les épaules
shut fermer; (*adj*) **shut up** enfermé
sick malade
sight vue *f*.; **catch sight of** apercevoir (*conj. like* recevoir) (+ *n*.)
sign signer
silk soie *f*.
silly bête; sot (*f*. sotte)
silver (*n*.) argent *m*.; (*adj*.) d'argent
silverware argenterie *f*.
since (pp. 47–48, 252–53) puisque; comme; depuis que; depuis
single seul
sister sœur *f*.; **sister-in-law** belle-sœur *f*.
sit, sit down (pp. 195–96) s'asseoir (s'asseyant, assis, je m'assieds, je m'assis) (*imperative*) asseyez-vous
sitting assis
situate situer; **be situated** se trouver
situation situation *f*.
six six
sixteen seize
skin peau *f*.

sleep dormir (2)
sleepy : be sleepy avoir sommeil
slide projection *f.*; diapositive *f.*
slight léger (*f.* légère)
slightest moindre
slow down ralentir
small petit
smile (*n.*) sourire *m.*; (*v.*) sourire (souriant, souri, je souris, je souris)
smoke (*v.*) fumer; (*n.*) fumée *f.*
snapshot photo *f.*; photographie *f.*
snow (*v.*) neiger (*irr. sp.* **B**) (*n.*) neige *f.*
so si; tant; tellement; le; **so much** tant, tellement; **so that** pour que
soap savon *m.*
sofa sofa *m.*; canapé *m.*
soft doux (*f.* douce)
solve résoudre; (*p.p.*) résolu
soldier soldat *m.*; militaire *m.*
somber sombre
some (*adj.*) du, de la, de l', des; quelque; (*pron.*) quelques-uns; en
someone quelqu'un
something quelque chose; **something else** autre chose
sometimes quelquefois, parfois
somewhere quelque part
son fils *m.*
soon (pp. 210–11) tôt; bientôt; **as soon as** dès que
sooner plus tôt
sore douloureux (*f.* douloureuse); **I have a sore throat** j'ai mal à la gorge
sorrow chagrin *m.*; **to my great sorrow** à mon vif regret
sorry désolé; **be sorry** regretter; **I'm sorry** pardon
sort sorte *f.*
soundly profondément
south sud *m.*
South American Sud-Américain *m.*
Spain Espagne *f.*
Spanish espagnol
speak parler
special particulier (*f.* particulière); spécial

specialist spécialiste *m.*
spectator spectateur *m.*
spend (p. 211) (*money*) dépenser; (*time*) passer
spite; in spite of (p. 261) malgré
sport sport *m.*
spring printemps *m.*
spy espion *m.*
square place *f.*
stamp timbre *m.*
stand se tenir, se tenir debout; (*bear*) supporter
state état *m.*
station gare *f.*
stay rester
step (*course of action*) démarche *f.*
still encore; toujours
stocking bas *m.*
stop (pp. 211–12) cesser (de + *inf.*); arrêter (+ *n.*; de + *inf.*); s'arrêter (de + *inf.*) **without stopping** sans arrêt
store magasin *m.*
storm orage *m.*
story histoire *f.*; **detective story** roman policier *m.*; **short story** conte *m.*
strange étrange; curieux (*f.* curieuse)
stranger étranger *m.*
street rue *f.*; **on the street** dans la rue
stretch étendre; **stretched out** tendu; étendu
strict sévère
strong fort
stubborn entêté, têtu
student (*college*) étudiant *m.*, étudiante *f.*; (*grade and high school*) élève *m./f.*
study (*v.*) travailler; étudier; (*n.*) étude *f.*
stupid stupide
style style *m.*
succeed réussir (à + *inf.*)
success succès *m.*
such (p. 212) tel (*f.* telle); aussi; comme ça; pareil (*f.* pareille)
suddenly soudain; tout à coup; tout d'un coup
suffer souffrir (*conj. like* ouvrir)
sugar sucre *m.*
suit costume *m.*
suitcase valise *f.*; **pack one's suitcase** faire sa valise

---

Irregular verbs are conjugated on pp. 318–335.

sum somme *f.*; somme d'argent *f.*
summer été *m.*
sun soleil *m.*; **it is sunny** il fait du soleil, il y a du soleil; **the sun set** le soleil s'est couché
Sunday dimanche *m.*
sunlight soleil *m.*
sure ! bien sûr !
surprise étonner
surprised étonné
surprising étonnant
Susan Suzanne
suspect suspect *m.*
Sweden Suède *f.*
swim nager (*irr. sp.* **B**)
swimming pool piscine *f.*

T
table table *f.*; **clear the table** débarrasser la table
tail queue *f.*
take (pp. 221–23) prendre (prenant, pris, je prends, je pris); mener (*irr. sp.* **D**); emmener (*irr. sp.* **D**); amener (*irr. sp.* **D**); apporter; (= *subscribe to*) s'abonner à, être abonné à; **take a course** suivre un cours; **take an interest in** s'intéresser (à + *n.*); **take a trip** faire un voyage; **take a walk** se promener (*irr. sp.* **D**), faire une promenade
talent talent *m.*
talk (*v.*) parler; (*n.*) causerie *f.*; **give a talk** faire une causerie; **talk business** parler affaires, parler des affaires
taxi taxi *m.*
tea thé *m.*
teach (pp. 223–24) enseigner; apprendre (*conj. like* prendre)
teacher professeur *m.*; maître *m.*
team équipe *f.*
teenagers les jeunes, les adolescents, les « teenagers », les moins de vingt ans

Verbs with spelling changes are explained on pp. 336–338.

telephone (*v.*) téléphoner (à + *person*); (*n.*) téléphone *m.*; **telephone book** annuaire *m.*; **telephone number** numéro de téléphone *m.*
television télévision *f.*; la télé, la TV; **television set** télévision *f.*
tell dire (disant, dit, je dis, je dis) (à + *person* + de + *inf.*); raconter; **tell about** parler de
ten dix
tender tendre
terrible terrible
than que; (*before numerals*) de
thank remercier (de *or* pour + *thing*; de + *inf.*)
that (*conjunc.*) que; **so that** pour que; (*demonstrative*) ce, cet, cette, ces; celui, etc., cela; (*rel.*) qui; que
the le, la, l', les
theatre théâtre *m.*; **in the theatre** au théâtre
their leur
then ensuite, puis; alors
theory théorie *f.*
there y; là; **from there** en; de là; **there is, there are** il y a; voilà
these ces
they ils; on; eux
thief voleur *m.*
thing chose *f.*
think penser (à + *n.*); croire (croyant, cru, je crois, je crus); **think (something) over** réfléchir
third troisième
thirsty : I am thirsty j'ai soif
thirty trente
this ce, cet, cette
though bien que, quoique; **even though** quoique; bien que; tout en (+ *pres. part.*)
thought pensée (*f.*)
three trois
throat gorge *f.*; **I have a sore throat** j'ai mal à la gorge
through par; **go through** passer par; parcourir (*conj. like* écrire)
Thursday jeudi *m.*
tie cravate *f.*
tied up attaché

time (pp. 224–25) temps *m.*; fois *f.*; heure
 f.; époque *f.*; moment *m.*; **by the time**
 quand; **for a long time** longtemps;
 from time to time de temps en
 temps; **have a good time** s'amuser,
 bien s'amuser; **in time** à temps;
 many times bien des fois; **more time**
 plus de temps; **on time** à l'heure
tired fatigué
title titre *m.*
to à; chez; dans; en
today aujourd'hui
together ensemble; **pressed together**
 serré(e)s
tomorrow demain; **the day after tomorrow** après-demain
tonight ce soir
too trop
tool outil *m.*
top sommet *m.*
tourist touriste *m./f.*
tournament tournoi *m.*
toward (p. 262) vers; envers
town ville *f.*
toy jouet *m.*
traffic (*adj.*) de la circulation
train train *m.*; **by train** en train, par le
 train
translate traduire (*conj. like* conduire)
travel (*v.*) voyager (*irr. sp.* **B**) (p. 230)
 travel across traverser; (*n.*) voyage *m.*
traveller voyageur *m.*
tray plateau *m.*
trip voyage *m.*; **take a trip** faire un voyage
troop troupe *f.*
trouble histoire *f.*; ennuis *m. pl.*;
 difficultés *f. pl.*
true vrai
truly vraiment
truth vérité *f.*
try essayer (*irr. sp.* **C**) (de + *inf.*);
 chercher (à + *inf.*); **try on** essayer
turn around se retourner
twelve douze
twenty vingt

twice deux fois
twist tordre
two deux
type taper à la machine, écrire à la machine

U

ugly vilain
unbearable insupportable
under (pp. 262–63) sous; au-dessous de
understand comprendre (*conj. like*
 prendre)
undeveloped sous-développé
uneasiness malaise *m.*
unfortunately malheureusement
United States États-Unis *m. pl.*
university université *f.*
unless à moins que (+ *subj.*)
until (p. 253) (*conjunc.*) jusqu'à ce que (+
 subj.); (*prep.*) jusqu'à
up (p. 263) dessus; sur; en haut; **go up**
 remonter; monter; **up to now** jusqu'à
 présent
use se servir (de + *n.*); employer (*irr. sp.*
 C); **used to** (pp. 79–80) *a form of the
 imperfect tense*
used : get used to s'habituer à
useful utile
useless inutile

V

vacation vacances *f. pl.*
valuable précieux (*f.* précieuse); de prix;
 de valeur
vase vase *m.*
velvet velours *m.*
very très; **very much** (p. 244) beaucoup
 beaucoup; énormément, un tas de,
 des tas de
vicious méchant
village village *m.*
violin violon *m.*
visit (pp. 244–45) (*a place*) visiter; (*a
 person*) aller voir; rendre visite à;
 faire une visite à
visitor visiteur *m.*
voice voix *f.*

Irregular verbs are conjugated on pp. 318–335.

W

wait attendre; **wait for** attendre (+ n.)
waiter garçon m.
wake up réveiller; se réveiller
walk (v.) marcher; se promener (irr. sp. D); (n.) promenade f.; **go for a walk, take a walk** aller se promener, faire une promenade, se promener (irr. sp. D)
want vouloir (voulant, voulu, je veux, je voulus) (+ inf.)
war guerre f.; **World War** guerre mondiale f.
warm chaud; **be warm** avoir chaud
wash laver; **wash and dress** faire sa toilette; **wash the dishes** faire la vaisselle
waste perdre; gaspiller
watch (v.) regarder, observer; surveiller; (n.) montre f.
water eau f.; **ice water** eau glacée
way route f.; manière f.; façon f.; **continue on our way** continuer notre route; **in that way** de cette façon; **on the way** en route
wear porter
weather temps m.; **the weather is good** il fait beau
wedding mariage m.; **wedding anniversary** anniversaire de mariage m.
week semaine f.
weekend week-end m.
well bien; **well known** connu, célèbre; bien connu
what (interr.) qu'est-ce qui; que, qu'est-ce que; quoi; quel, quelle; comment; (relative) ce qui; ce que
whatever quoi que; quel que (f. quelle que)
when (p. 140) quand; où
where où
whereas tandis que
wherever où que (+ subj.)
whether si

Verbs with spelling changes are explained on pp. 336–338.

which (interr.) quel, quelle; lequel, laquelle; (rel.) qui; que; lequel; quoi
while (pp. 110–11, 245) (at the same time) pendant que; (whereas) tandis que; **a little while ago** tout à l'heure; **all the while** tout en (+ pres. part.)
white blanc (f. blanche)
who (interr.) qui; (rel.) qui; que
whoever qui que; quel que; **whoever it is (may be)** qui que ce soit; quel qu'il soit
whole tout (m. pl. tous)
whom (interr.) qui; (rel.) que
why pourquoi
wife femme f.
willing : be willing vouloir bien
win gagner; remporter
window fenêtre f.; vitre f.
windowpane vitre f.
wine vin m.
winner gagnant m.
winter hiver m.
Wisconsin Wisconsin m.
wish (pp. 149–50, 245–46) vouloir (voulant, voulu, je veux, je voulus) (+ inf.); désirer (+ inf.); souhaiter
with (pp. 263–64) avec; sur; de; chez
without sans; **do without** se passer de
woman femme f.; **cleaning woman** femme de ménage f.
wonder se demander
wonderful merveilleux (f. merveilleuse)
won't ne pas vouloir (+ inf.)
wood bois m.
word mot m.; (spoken word) parole f.; **word processor** machine à traitement de texte
work (v.) travailler; (n.) travail m.; **out of work** sans travail
workman ouvrier m.
World War guerre mondiale f.
worried inquiet (f. inquiète)
worry inquiéter; s'inquiéter (irr. sp. E)
would (pp. 54–55, 79–80, 266) vouloir; as auxiliary verb; (in cond.) cond. of main verb; (= used to) imperfect of main verb
write écrire (écrivant, écrit, j'écris, j'écrivis)

writer écrivain *m.*
wrong faux (*f.* fausse); **be wrong** avoir
tort; **do wrong** faire du tort

Y

yawn bâiller
year (p. 267) an *m.*; année *f.*; **Happy New
Year** Bonne Année, Bonne Nouvelle
Année; **I was ten years old** j'avais dix
ans; **twice a year** deux fois par an;
every year tous les ans; **youthful
years** années de jeunesse *f. pl.*

yes (pp. 267–68) oui; si
yesterday hier; **yesterday evening** hier
soir; **yesterday morning** hier matin
you tu; vous; **both of you** vous deux
young jeune; **young men** (p. 268) jeunes
gens *m. pl.*
your votre, vos
yours le vôtre, la vôtre, etc.
yourself vous-même
youthful jeune; **youthful years** années
de jeunesse *f. pl.*

Irregular verbs are conjugated on pp. 318–335.

Index